1989

CONTEMPORARY LEARNING THEORIES:
Instrumental Conditioning Theory and the Impact of Biological Constraints on Learning

CONTEMPORARY LEARNING THEORIES:
Instrumental Conditioning Theory and the Impact of Biological Constraints on Learning

Edited by
STEPHEN B. KLEIN
Fort Hays State University
ROBERT R. MOWRER
Angelo State University

LEA LAWRENCE ERLBAUM ASSOCIATES, PUBLISHERS
1989 Hillsdale, New Jersey   Hove and London

Lawrence Erlbaum Associates, Inc., Publishers
365 Broadway
Hillsdale, New Jersey 07642

Library of Congress Cataloging in Publication Data

Contemporary learning theories: instrumental conditioning theory and the impact of biological constraints on learning/edited by Stephen B. Klein, Robert R. Mowrer.
  p.   cm.
Includes bibliographies and indexes.
ISBN 0-8058-0319-X (set). — ISBN 0-8058-0318-1
  1. Operant Conditioning. 2. Learning—Physiological aspects.
3. Learning in animals. 4. Psychology, comparative. I. Klein, Stephen B.
II. Mowrer, Robert R., 1956–
BF319.5.06C66 1989
156'.31526—dc19   88-38937
                                                                      CIP

Printed in the United States of America
10 9 8 7 6 5 4 3 2 1

Dedicated to Marie
and
Gail, Chelsea, and Shawna

Contents

CONTEMPORARY LEARNING THEORIES:
Pavlovian Conditioning and the Status of Traditional Learning Theory

Contents

Preface

Theoretical interpretations of the learning process have concerned experimental psychologists for well over 100 years and have been a dominant force in psychology in general. Many of the initial theories, such as those of Hull and Tolman, attempted to capture the entire essence of learned behavior—the age of global theories of learning. In the past 10 to 15 years, theoretical concepts of the way in which human and non-human organisms learn or acquire information have undergone a dramatic metamorphosis. This change has involved moving from the broad, all-encompassing theories of Hull, Tolman, Guthrie and Thorndike to more specific, focused theories.

Most learning texts available to upper level students reviewing various theories of learning cover the traditional theories in detail, while only casually addressing more contemporary theories. Detailed treatment of these modern theories is available but can be found only by searching through a variety of sources (i.e., book chapters, review articles or a series of research articles). Feeling that there is a definite need to put all of these ideas into a single easily accessible medium, we contacted many noted modern learning theorists who graciously agreed to provide a discussion of their most recent research and theorizing. The result is a two-volume text dealing with the most up-to-date conceptualizations of the learning process. The first volume describes the ideas of sixteen psychologists on Pavlovian conditioning and modifications of traditional learning theory. This companion second volume presents the views of seventeen psychologists on instrumental conditioning and biological constraints on learning.

The material in this two volume text is appropriate for several different audiences. It could be used in an upper division learning theories course, a graduate learning theories class, or as reference text for researchers. We hope that the ideas of these noted psychologists will be as enlightening and stimulating to you as it has been to us.

Stephen B. Klein
Robert R. Mowrer

Contributors

JAMES ALLISON, Indiana University
LINDA PHILLIPS BRETT, Syntex Laboratories, Inc.
RUSSELL M. CHURCH, Brown University
ANASTASIA DROUNGAS, Dalhousie University
JOHN GARCIA, University of California, Los Angeles
STEPHEN E. GLICKMAN, University of California, Berkeley
STEPHEN B. KLEIN, Fort Hays State University
VINCENT M. LoLORDO, Dalhousie University
GARY A. LUCAS, Indiana University
STEVEN F. MAIER, University of Colorado
ROBERT R. MOWRER, Angelo State University
ANTHONY L. RILEY, American University
KENNETH W. RUSINIAK, Eastern Michigan University
BERNARD B. SCHIFF, University of Toronto
WILLIAM TIMBERLAKE, Indiana University
FRANCO VACCARINO, University of Toronto
CORA LEE WETHERINGTON, University of North Carolina—Charlotte

I INTRODUCTION

1

A Contrast Between Traditional and Contemporary Learning Theory

Robert R. Mowrer
Angelo State University
Stephen B. Klein
Fort Hays State University

I. INTRODUCTION

The chapters in this text discuss the process of learning and the modern theories designed to explain this process. In particular, this volume focuses on instrumental learning and the biological constraints on learning. Learning is defined as "a relatively permanent change in the ability to exhibit a behavior; this change occurs as the result of successful or unsuccessful experience" (Klein, 1987, p. 2). Investigations of the learning process have occupied psychologists for over 100 years and remains a central research topic to this day. Many different views of learning have been proposed by a group of psychologists known as behaviorists and this chapter briefly examines the early or traditional conceptualizations of the learning process. These early theories were intended to explain all aspects of the learning process and may be referred to as "global" theories of learning. While this approach provided substantial information about learning, the more contemporary learning theorists investigate and describe more specific aspects of the learning process. After a brief description of traditional learning theories, we look at the reasons why many contemporary learning theories focus on specific learning principles rather than attempting to explain all aspects of learning. The remaining 8 chapters present the ideas and research of a number of noted contemporary learning theorists regarding instrumental conditioning and biological constraints.

II. EARLY CONCEPTS OF LEARNING

At the crux of learning theory is the school of psychology known as *Behaviorism*, which emphasizes the role of experience in controlling behavior. According to

1

this position, all organisms possess innate motives which drive instinctive behavior, but the more important determinants of behavior are those that are learned.
These acquired or learned drives come to motivate behavior and are learned
through the organisms interaction with the environment. The primary goal of the
behaviorist (and learning theorist) is to determine the rules or laws governing
this learning and use these laws to predict, control, and understand behavior.
Although a number of ideas have impacted on the behavioral view, the concept
of a reflex has been especially important.

Descartes and the role of reflexes.   According to the 17th-century philosopher,
Rene Descartes (1662/1972), all human and nonhuman behavior is a reflexive
response to environmental events. An external stimulus excites a given sense,
then sends this excitation to the brain, which in turn conveys this excitation to
the muscle, resulting in behavior. This reflexive system is purely mechanical in
that the behavior is an automatic response to the environment. The reflex concept was particularly important in the early investigations of classical or Pavlovian conditioning, which is detailed in the companion volume "Contemporary
Learning Theories: Pavlovian Conditioning and the Status of Traditional Learning Theory."

The Role of the British Associationists.   Locke (1690) argued that all ideas are
developed through experience and that the neonate begins with an absence of any
ideas (tabula rosa) and that ideas are imprinted on this blank slate as a result of
experience. According to Locke, the slate is imprinted with associations or links
between events. He suggested that events that are contiguous become associated
and the activation of one event will automatically activate its associate. Likewise,
David Hume (1739) posited that causal associations could also be formed as a
result of experience. A causal association is formed when it is believed that one
event causes the occurrence of another event. The concept of an association is
central to the learning process and was especially so for the work of Edward Thorndike (1898).

III. A BRIEF REVIEW OF TRADITIONAL LEARNING
THEORY

Thorndike's Role.   Thorndike's studies established that an animal's behavior could
change as a result of experience. In his classic puzzle box experiments with cats,
Thorndike noticed that if he placed a hungry cat in the box with food located
outside, the cat would engage in a variety of behaviors in its attempt to obtain
the food. The cat eventually happened onto a response which resulted in its escape from the box and access to the food (pulling a string or pressing a pedal).
With each successive trial, the time to escape decreased.

　　Thorndike reasoned that the animal formed an association between the stimulus (box) and response (string pull or pedal push). This S–R association devel-

oped because the hungry cat was rewarded with food following the response, resulting in a satisfying state of affairs. The association's strength increased with each successive trial. Thorndike labeled this strengthening of an S–R bond by pleasant events the "law of effect." Thorndike further proposed that learning was a trial and error process. His cat simply changed behaviors until it discovered an effective one. Reward then functioned to strengthen the correct response. This point, that reward (or reinforcement) was essential for learning, resulted in Thorndike becoming the first "reinforcement" theorist. In contrast, two other influential learning theorists, Edwin Guthrie and John Watson (whose work was very similar to Thorndike's) appealed only to the contiguity between events such as a stimulus and response to explain the learning process, relegating reinforcement to only a secondary role.

The Influence of Watson and Guthrie. John Watson regarded all learning as classical conditioning. He believed that all organisms are born with certain S–R connections of reflexes. In addition, any new S–R connection was learned through the process of classical conditioning described by Pavlov (1927) or Bekhterev (1913).

Two important learning principles described by Watson were frequency and recency. Frequency refers to the notion that the more frequently a certain response is made to a stimulus, the more likely that response will occur again in the presence of that stimulus. The recency principle states that the more recently a given response was made to a stimulus, the more likely that response will occur again when the stimulus is presented. Why does one response occur over others? Unlike Thorndike, who believed that the response which was followed by reward would be strengthened, Watson felt that the response that resulted in the greatest change in the stimulus situation would gain strength. For example, in the puzzle box problem, pulling the string allowed the cat to escape. This response changed the stimulus situation such that the cat was no longer in the presence of the stimulus (box). It was this repeated change in stimuli following a response that stamps in the S–R bond in accord with the rules of frequency and recency. How does reward function in Watson's theory? According to Watson, reward has no function and as long as a response occurred in a specific context, an association would develop regardless of whether or not reward occurred. Further, Watson felt that all behavior, even complex behavior, could be explained by stamping in a series of S–R bonds.

Edwin Guthrie's position on the learning process was very similar to that described above for Watson. Like Watson, Guthrie rejected Thorndike's law of effect and felt that contiguity between a stimulus and response was sufficient to establish an S–R association. He felt that anytime a response occurs in the presence of some stimulus they automatically become associated. Unlike Watson (or Thorndike), Guthrie believed that the S–R association was at full strength following a single pairing. That is, the formation of an S–R bond was all or none, and there was no gradual strengthening or stamping in of an association through repetition. To explain the apparent gradual strengthening of an S–R bond, Guthrie appealed to three principles. First, while numerous stimuli may be present in a given situation, only a portion of these are being attended to by the organism and thus available for association. Since the particular stimuli attended to will vary from trial to trial, for a particular stimulus to produce a response it must be attended to on the previous and subsequent trials. Thus, the change in behavior from trial to trial reflects an attentional process not a learning process. Second, any number of different stimuli can become associated with a certain response. Over trials, as more and more stimuli become associated with the response, the likelihood of making a response on later trials increases. This increase is not due to a strengthening of the S–R bond but rather to an increase in the number of stimuli available to elicit the response. Finally, a complex behavior consists of many separate responses. For responding to be effective, each behavior must become associated with the stimulus. This process occurs gradually over trials and results in the apparent strengthening of the association.

What then is the role of reinforcement? Guthrie, like Watson, claimed that the response that changes the stimulus situation is the one which gets associated. According to Guthrie, reinforcement changes the stimulus situation (internal or external) and ensures that the response immediately preceding it enters into the S–R association. This change in stimulus context also prevents new responses from being associated with the original stimulus.

While Thorndike is considered the first reinforcement theorist, a second reinforcement theory was developed by Clark Hull. Hull's reinforcement theory stands in contrast to Watson's and Guthrie's contiguity version of learning theory.

Hull-Spence Learning Theory.   From the 1930s to the early 1960s the most elegant and dominant theory of learning was that developed by Clark Hull and later modified by Kenneth Spence. This theory is detailed in the companion volume in this set, so we only engage in a cursory examination here.

The critical component of this theory was the concept of DRIVE (Woodworth, 1918). A drive is defined as an intense internal force which motivates behavior. According to Hull (1943), this intense internal arousal, drive or D, automatically motivates behavior and further, could be either unconditioned or acquired.

All organisms are motivated to maintain biological homeostasis. When a given biological system is "out of balance," the organism is automatically motivated to adjust in order to restore the biological system to normal. For example, in the absence of food, an organism will utilize stored energy to maintain normal functioning. If this absence persists, behavior will be activated to resolve the deficiency (i.e., seek food sources). In addition to maintaining homeostasis, organisms are also motivated to avoid intense environmental events such as shock or loud noise. That is, these events activate the internal drive state and the organism behaves appropriately. All organisms behave in order to reduce this internal drive or tension.

Hull suggested that through classical conditioning, previously neutral environmental events can acquire the ability to produce internal drive states resulting in conditioned drives. What determines the behavior elicited by various drive states? For Hull, while drive is a general state of tension, each instrumental action depends on the environment. When a given response results in a reduction of drive, the stimuli present become associated with that response; thus, the likelihood of that response occurring again increases when in the presence of the stimuli. The strength of this association was termed habit strength and increased each time the response resulted in drive reduction. Unsuccessful behavior causes the drive to persist and behavior may be suppressed temporarily by a process referred to as reactive inhibition (similar to fatigue). Reactive inhibition eventually decreases and an animal again will engage in behavior intended to reduce the drive state. When behavior continues to be unable to reduce the drive, a more permanent suppression of responding may occur due to conditioned inhibition.

Hull initially felt that the intensity of the reinforcer influenced habit strength: the greater the reinforcement (larger reduction in drive), the stronger the habit strength. Studies by Crespi (1942) and others indicated that reinforcer magnitude had a significant effect on an animal's motivation; these experiments led Hull to add the notion of reward magnitude or K to his theory. The specific role of K or incentive was detailed by Kenneth Spence. Briefly, when an animal traversed a maze or alley and was met with reward in the goal box, environmental stimuli in that goal box became associated with reward and elicited anticipatory goal responses on the next trial. These anticipatory goal responses are accompanied by internal stimulus changes which motivate instrumental behavior. This mechanism essentially moves back through the maze or alley until even stimuli present in the start box will elicit the anticipatory goal response and stimuli, thus motivating behavior. For Spence, the larger the reward, the stronger the anticipatory goal mechanism and the higher the incentive motivation of K. While Hull's reinforcement theory had wide application, it failed to explain a number of learning phenomena. Many of these phenomena evolved out of the work of Edward Tolman.

Tolman's Expectancy Theory.   Tolman introduced to learning theory the concept of an expectancy. This notion was in wide contrast to the mechanistic views of behavior briefly described above. Indeed, for Tolman, behavior was not considered an automatic response to the environment but reflected direction and purpose. According to Tolman, an organism's behavior is goal-directed in that they are motivated to approach or avoid a specific situation depending on whether that situation is rewarding or aversive. In addition, organisms are capable of understanding the structure of the environment and behaving appropriately. Importantly, it was not necessary that the organism be aware of the purpose or direction of behavior only that they behave *as if* they were aware.

For Tolman, behavior is not only goal-oriented, but specific outcomes are expected to follow specific behaviors. How does the organism know which behavior to exhibit? Tolman suggested the certain events in the environment convey information about where goals are located and the organism behaves appropriately only after learning the environmental signs leading to reward or away from punishment. As organisms explore their environment, a mental representation or cognitive map develops. This map guides exploration through the environment to obtain reward or avoid punishment.

Like Guthrie and Watson, Tolman did not feel that reward was necessary for learning to occur. The best example of this idea may be seen in his famous place learning studies, which also provided a great deal of trouble for the Hull-Spence theory of learning. The simplest design for such a study involved two groups of rats, one which was allowed to explore a maze without reinforcement and a second which recieved no treatment. Tolman found that when reinforcement was introduced, speed to traverse the maze was equivalent on the first trial but substantially faster on subsequent trials for animals first allowed to explore the maze. For Tolman, animals who had explored the maze learned something (perhaps a cognitive map of the maze), but this learning was not translated into behavior until reinforcement was introduced.

Skinner and Operant Conditioning.   Skinner (1938) asserted that the goal of behaviorism was to identify the environmental events that control behavior and avoid postulating internal, unobservable mechanisms as explanatory tools. In Skinner's view, the most interesting aspect of behavior is the relationship between a response and the consequence of that response, a relationship known as a reinforcement contingency. The environment determines the contingency and the organism must discover this contingency to obtain reinforcement. He found that behavior varies greatly depending on the "schedule of reinforcement" and has spent considerable time arguing that all behavior can be explained by appealing to these various schedules.

IV.   CONTEMPORARY LEARNING THEORY: THE CONTRAST

Each theory mentioned above purports to explain all aspects of the learning process and how it is translated into behavior; Thorndike with reinforcement and S–R bonds, Guthrie and Watson with the contiguous relationship between stimuli and responses, Hull with habit strength, drive, and incentive, Tolman with expectancies and cognitive maps, and Skinner with schedules of reinforcement. Given the diversity of these theories, each with significant advantages and disadvantages, it has been argued that the fundamental or global nature of learning may never be completely explained by a single theory (Bolles, 1979). This skepticism has led more contemporary researchers to focus on specific aspects of learned behavior, recognizing perhaps that different mechanisms (and thus different explanations) are responsible for different behaviors. This is not to say that a single theory may never eventually evolve which encompasses all learning, just that at the present many researchers focus on a more limited range of behavior.

A number of incidents or difficulties have led researchers away from global theories. For example, much of the traditional learning theories have dealt with either classical, instrumental conditioning or a combination. There are several forms of learning that have defied explanation by these early theories including concept formation, problem solving, language, insight, covariation of events, and other more cognitive forms of learning. How are these learning situations a problem for early learning theories?

A concept is defined as a symbol that represents a group of objects with common properties (Klein, 1987). How does an organism learn or form a concept? Hull (1920) attempted to explain this aspect of learning by appealing to discrimination learning. When the subject makes a response as to whether a certain object is an example of a concept, it is given feedback. This feedback constitutes reinforcement (correct) and increases habit strength; in contrast negative feedback (incorrect) weakens habit strength to irrelevant stimulus attributes. While it has been shown that concept formation certainly has an associative component, subsequent research has demonstrated the necessity of including a cognitive component to fully explain this phenomenon (Brooks, 1978; Bruner, Goodnow, & Austin, 1956; Levine, 1966).

Problem solving was another area which caused problems for traditional learning theory. Thorndike (1898) assumed that both animals and humans solved problems through a process of trial and error. He did not assume that his cats "knew" how to escape from the box but rather emitted a large number of responses and those that led to escape were reinforced and thus increased in strength. More recent evidence suggests that animals do not randomly emit responses which are then strengthened or weakened based on their consequences but rather that animals consider the problem, rejecting improbable responses until developing insight as to the correct solution (Epstein, 1981)

The importance of biological constraints on learning was not appreciated until the classic work of John Garcia (Garcia & Koelling, 1966) and his work on taste aversion learning. Simply, Garcia paired one of two CSs (flavor or light/noise) with one of two USs (illness or shock) in a 2×2 factorial design. The results were not in accord with those expected by traditional learning theory. There was little or no association between the light + noise CS and the illness US nor between flavor CSs and shock USs. Conversely, a strong association was found when light + noise was paired with shock as well as when flavor was paired with illness. These data indicate that animals come into a situation prepared to associate some CSs with some USs and are not prepared to associate other CSs with some USs (see Seligman, 1970, for a complete discussion of this notion). This preparedness is apparently dependent on an animal's biological character (Wilcoxon, Dragoin, & Kral, 1971).

Another situation in which the biology of the animal has an effect on learning is termed "animal misbehavior" (Breland & Breland, 1961, 1966). The Brelands trained a number of animals (pigs, raccoons, chickens) to perform a variety of operant responses. These behaviors included hitting a ball (chicken), depositing coins into a piggy bank (pig and raccoon), playing hockey (two turkeys), tap dancing (hen), and many others. At first, the animals were exceptionally proficient at these tasks but their performance quickly deteriorated as training continued regardless of reinforcement. For example, rather than placing the coins in the bank, the pig began to root at the coins while the raccoon rubbed them together. Further, a chicken taught to run the bases after hitting the ball, chased the ball rather than run the bases. The Brelands attributed this behavior to what they called instinctive drift. These instinctive behaviors, strengthened by reinforcement, eventually dominated the operant behavior. Again, an animal's biological character must be taken into account by any theory of learning.

Another important event involving the biological aspects of learning involves the incredibly rapid advances in neurophysiology, neurochemistry, and neuroanatomy. Individuals such as Eric Kandel, Larry Squire, James McGaugh and a number of others have made fantastic advances into our understanding of the neural mechanisms underlying learning. Richard Thompson and his colleagues have even developed a neurological model of classical conditioning in the cerebellum based on the Rescorla-Wagner model of learning (1972). Thus, there is a greater focus on the neural mechanisms of learning by contemporary learning theorists.

Other examples of the biological influence on the learning process which cannot be accounted for by previous learning theories include electrical stimulation of the brain (ESB) by Olds and Milner (1954), schedule-induced polydipsia (Falk, 1961, 1967), schedule-induced wheel running (Staddon & Ayres, 1975), imprinting (Lorenz, 1952), timing behavior (Church, this volume), song learning in birds (Nottebaum, 1980), and many others too numerous to mention. Thus, the fact that biological character influences learning has led to ever increasing specific theories of learning.

An Overview of the Chapters to Follow.   The following chapters represent a discussion of the current research and theory in instrumental learning and biological influences on learning by some of the most prominent psychologists working today. We begin with Chapter 2 provided by James Allison who examines the nature of reinforcement by looking at such concepts as learning vs. performance, response deprivation, and related issues. Chapter 3, written by Russell Church, discusses timing behavior in nonhuman animals and is followed by Chapter 4, authored by Steven Maier, who discusses the history and current status of learned helplessness. Chapter 5 by Franco Vaccarino, Bernard Schiff, and Stephen Glickman describes a biological view of reinforcement dealing with such topics as the function of reinforcement and neural substrates of reward.

We begin the second section on biological constraints with Chapter 6 by Vincent LoLordo and Anastasia Droungas who review the general process view of biological constraints on learning. Following this is Chapter 7 provided by John Garcia, Linda Brett, and Kenneth Rusiniak, which covers an evolutionary approach to limitations on learning. Chapter 8 by Anthony Riley and Cora Lee Wetherington discusses schedule-induced polydipsia and its relation to alcoholism and other drug related behavior. The volume ends with Chapter 9 authored by William Timberlake and Gary Lucas who provide us with a behavior systems approach to learning including a discussion of the evolutionary aspects of behavior systems.

The companion volume in this set discusses Pavlovian conditioning and modifications of traditional learning theory beginning with Chapter 2 by Paula Durlach which reviews the Rescorla-Wagner model (1972) of conditioning and is followed by a comparison of associative and comparator models of Pavlovian conditioning. The third chapter, authored by Ralph Miller and Louis Matzel provides evidence in support of the comparator models of learning processes. Andy Baker and Pierre Mercier provide Chapter 4 in which they discuss attentional processes in Pavlovian conditioning in relation to retrospective processing and cognitive representations. This focus on attention continues with Chapter 5 by Geoffrey Hall and Robert Honey concerning perceptual and associative points of view. Chapter 6 by Allan Wagner and Susan Brandon represents their most recent model of Pavlovian conditioning (AESOP). Ending the section on Pavlovian conditioning is Chapter 7 provided by Arthur Tomie, William Brooks, and Barbara Zito, which concerns sign-tracking or autoshaping. The second section on the current status of traditional learning theory begins with Chapter 8 by Donald Levis who argues for a two-factor theory of avoidance behavior and its relation to psychopathology. The final chapter in this volume, Chapter 9 by Anthony Dickinson, discusses the current status of expectancy theory.

REFERENCES

Bechterev, V. M. (1913). *La psychologie objective*. Paris: Librairie Felix Alcan.

Bolles, R. C. (1979). *Learning theory* (2nd ed.). New York: Holt, Rinehart & Winston.

Breland, K., & Breland, M. (1961). The misbehavior of organisms. *American Psychologist, 16,* 681–684.

Breland, K., & Breland, M. (1966). *Animal behavior*. New York: Macmillan.

Brooks, L. R. (1978). Nonanalytic concept formation and memory for instances. In E. Rosch & B. B. Lloyd (Eds.), *Cognition and categorization*. Hillsdale, NJ: Lawrence Erlbaum Associates.

Bruner, J. S., Goodnow, J. J., & Austin, G. A. (1956). *A study of thinking*. New York: Wiley.

Crespi, L. P. (1942). Quantitative variation of incentive and performance in the white rat. *American Journal of Psychology, 55,* 467–517.

Descartes, R. (1662/1972). *Treatise on man* (Translated by T. S. Hall). Cambridge, MA: Harvard University Press.

Epstein, R. (1981). On pigeons and people: A preliminary look at the Columban Simulation Project. *The Behavior Analyst, 4,* 43–55.

Falk, J. L. (1961). Production of polydipsia in normal rats by an intermittent food schedule. *Science*, *133*, 195–196.

Falk, J. L. (1967). Control of schedule-induced polydipsia: Type, size and spacing of meals. *Journal of the Experimental Analysis of Behavior*, *10*, 199–206.

Garcia, J., & Koelling, R. A. (1966). Relation of cue to consequence in avoidance learning. *Psychonomic Science*, *4*, 123–124.

Hull, C. L. (1920). Quantitative aspects of the evolution of concepts: An experimental study. *Psychological Monographs*, *28*, Whole no. 123.

Hume, D. (1739). *A treatise of human nature: Being an attempt to introduce the experimental method of reasoning into moral subjects*. London: J. Noon.

Klein, S. B. (1987). *Learning*. New York: McGraw Hill.

Levine, M. (1966). Hypothesis behavior by humans during discrimination learning. *Journal of Experimental Psychology*, *71*, 331–338.

Locke, J. (1690). *An essay concerning human understanding*. London: Basset.

Lorenz, K. (1952). The past twelve years in the comparative study of behavior. In C. H. Schiller (Ed.), *Instinctive behavior*. New York: International Universities Press.

Nottebaum, F. (1980). Brain pathways for vocal learning in birds: A review of the first 10 years. In J. M. Sprague & A. N. Epstein (Eds.), *Progress in psychology and physiological psychology*. New York: Academic.

Olds, J., & Milner, P. (1954). Positive reinforcement produced by electrical stimulation of septal area and other regions of the rat brain. *Journal of Comparative and Physiological Psychology*, *47*, 419–427.

Pavlov, I. P. (1927). *Conditioned reflexes*. Oxford: Oxford University Press.

Rescorla, R. A., & Wagner, A. R. (1972). A Theory of Pavlovian conditioning: Variations in the effectiveness of reinforcement and non-reinforcement. In A. H. Black & W. F. Prokasy (Eds.), *Classical Conditioning II*. New York: Appleton-Century-Crofts.

Skinner, B. F. (1938). *The behavior of organisms: An experimental analysis*. New York: Appleton-Century-Crofts.

Staddon, J. E. R., & Ayres, S. L. (1975). Sequential and temporal properties of behavior induced by a schedule of periodic food delivery. *Behavior*, *54*, 26–49.

Thorndike, E. L. (1898). Animal intelligence: An experimental study of the associative processes in animals. *Psychological Review Monograph Supplement*, *2*, 1–109.

Wilcoxon, H. C., Dragoin, W. B., & Kral, P. A. (1971). Illness-induced aversions in rat and quail: Relative salience of visual and gustatory cues. *Science*, *7*, 489–493.

Woodworth, R. S. (1918). *Dynamic psychology*. New York: Columbia University Press.

II THEORIES OF INSTRUMENTAL CONDITIONING

2 The Nature of Reinforcement

James Allison
Indiana University

In the context of instrumental conditioning, "reinforcement" and its cognates mean several different things. Used to describe a *procedure*, they typically mean the scheduled consequence of an instrumental response, and nothing more. For example, an investigator may refer to the continuous reinforcement of the instrumental response by means of food, when nothing more is meant than that the animal received food each time it pressed a lever. Thus, "reinforcement" and its cognates are usually redundant when used to specify procedure. An example is the second word in the phase "food reinforcer"—unless it refers to an agent that strengthens food, such as glue applied to a food pellet as a pellet-hardening agent.

In another widespread usage, the term "reinforcement" is used to specify a *manifest effect upon the instrumental response*. Used in that mode, the term typically means nothing more than an increase in the rate of the instrumental response, relative to some baseline rate. "Response rate" may be defined broadly enough to encompass a wide variety of paradigms, procedures, and hardware. Thus, in the context of a lever box the term might refer to an increase in the number of lever presses per second. In the context of behavior at the choice point of a simple T-maze, it might refer to an increase in the number of left turns per opportunity. Often it refers to an increase in speed, such as the speed of the cat's escape from a puzzle box—escapes/sec, or 1/latency of escape. An increase in speed may refer to an increase in velocity, feet/sec, as in the speed of the rat's traversal of a straight runway to a goal box baited with food. Time-based response requirements can also be encompassed. For example, a schedule might define the instrumental requirement in terms of some minimum time between successive pecks at a key: The food hopper will open if, and only if, the next peck occurs at least *t* sec after the last peck. The reinforcement effect might then take the form of an increased proportion of relatively long interresponse times.

A third mode is deliberately *interpretive*. For example, certain immediate consequences of the response may be thought to strengthen the instrumental response (Skinner, 1938), or its connection with the situation (Thorndike, 1911), in a manner more than metaphorical. There are thought to be strengthening agents, or reinforcers, such as food for the hungry animal; and there are thought to be instrumental behaviors, such as pressing a lever, that somehow gain strength from the intermediate application of such agents. The manifest reinforcement effect is thought to be caused by the reinforcement procedure. Thus, the rate of the instrumental response supposedly rose above the baseline rate *because* the response was followed closely by its scheduled consequence.

This chapter reviews some theoretical and empirical developments that have raised fundamental questions about instrumental conditioning. As some of these questions concern the "reinforcement" terminology, other terms are suggested as possible replacements. More important, the chapter shows why many investigators have come to suppose that the Thorndikian view of instrumental behavior, as behavior controlled by its immediate consequences, has become a burdensome oversimplification that perhaps no longer merits a central role in any theoretical account of instrumental performance.

I. PROBABILITY-DIFFERENTIAL THEORY

The trouble started with Premack's explanation of the descriptive reinforcement effect (Premack, 1959, 1965). According to Premack, the reason a particular stimulus consequence of an instrumental response reinforces that response—drives it above some baseline rate—is that the stimulus consequence allows the organism to perform some other response that is more probable than the instrumental response. For example, suppose we keep food away from a laboratory rat for 24 hours. If we then give it free access to food in a chamber equipped with a freely accessible lever, it will probably spend more time eating the free food than pressing the free lever. Because relative time supposedly measured relative probability, eating would then be said to be more probable than pressing the lever. Accordingly, if we tested the same hungry rat under the constraints of a schedule, contingent food would be found to reinforce instrumental pressing of the lever, because—as we have already observed—in the hungry rat, eating is the more probable response. More precisely, instrumental pressing of the lever produces an external consequence, a food pellet, that allows the rat to engage in a contingent behavior, eating, whose probability exceeds that of the instrumental behavior, pressing the lever.

Probability–differential theory was a curious blend of opposites: simple, but often intractable; radical on many points, but reactionary on perhaps the most important point.

On the favorable side of the ledger, it had genuine predictive power. To predict whether one behavior will reinforce another, simply measure their probabilities under what many now call a "paired baseline" condition, with both behaviors freely available in the absence of schedule constraint. Tested later under schedule constraint, the one behavior should reinforce the other if, and only if, it was more probable than the other under the free baseline condition. It did not matter whether the one behavior was relatively pleasant, preferred, a reducer of drive or need, a preventer of counterconditioning, a consummatory response, a drive inducer, a species-specific approach behavior, a source of physiological arousal, or an activator of any particular neural center. All that mattered was its relatively high probability under the conditions laid down for the measurement of baseline probabilities.

On the other hand, the commensurate measurement of behaviors in terms of their common unit, time, was often problematical. For example, consider the simple task of measuring how much time a rat spends drinking from a metal spout. It is easy to register each tongue contact with the spout, an essential step in the measurement of time spent drinking. However, the next essential step does not come so easily. How does one partition the record of intermittent contacts into episodes of drinking and not drinking? The first recorded contact marks the start of a bout of drinking, but when does that bout stop? What interlick interval is characteristic of a pause between bouts, rather than a pause inside the same bout—which pauses are "exterior," and which are "interior"? Each time we turn to another behavior, such as eating, we are confronted anew by a similar set of questions.

Rational theoretical solutions were devised for this important general problem, that of defining a distinct episode in the temporal flow of behavior. One successful solution was the log survivorship function used to identify pauses within bursts, and pauses between bursts of licks (Allison & Castellan, 1970). But such solutions were applied only sporadically (e.g., Gawley, Timberlake, & Lucas, 1986; Machlis, 1977). Certainly they imposed technical requirements that were difficult to meet at that time, a few years before the era of the inexpensive microcomputer. For the most part, investigators contented themselves with convenient but relatively arbitrary rules for defining the beginning and the end of a particular behavioral episode.

Thus, the theory was simple in principle—simply measure time—but difficult to apply with the rigor it truly required. The unit of measurement was deceptively simple, and finally too restrictive. Recent work suggests in addition that in some instances, the amount of time allocated to a particular behavior may be less important to the individual than other measures of the same behavior. Specifically, rats seem to defend total licks and total volumetric intake more closely than they defend the total amount of time spent drinking from the water spout (Allison, Moore, Gawley, Mondloch, & Mondloch, 1986).

The theory was radical in several respects. For example, it denied the transsituationality that had supposedly rescued the law of effect from the charge of circularity (Meehl, 1950). According to the transsituationality property, if a particular kind of consequence reinforces one behavior, that demonstration suffices to indicate that the same kind of consequence can reinforce some other behavior. Probability-differential theory plainly denied the sufficiency of any such demonstration: if eating, for example, reinforces one instrumental behavior, then eating should not reinforce another behavior unless it too happens to be less probable than eating. In the best known example, from the monkey Chicko, the most probable of three different responses—manipulating a horizontal lever—reinforced each of the other two, as if it were a classic transsituational reinforcer. The least probable response—manipulating a spring-loaded plunger—reinforced neither of the other two responses, and seemed to have the status of a classic reinforceable. But the intermediate response—manipulating a door—defied classification, as it reinforced the low-probability response, but did not reinforce the high-probability response (Premack, 1965). Yet, the entire pattern of results, part of which violated transsituationality, was predicted by a theory that purported to be a theory of reinforcement.

The theory also denied the traditional supposition that different reinforcers, such as food and water, exerted their common effects upon an instrumental response through some intrinsic property held in common. A well-known example is the old proposal that many different reinforcers share in common an intrinsic ability to reduce biological need. A more recent proposal from the same mold contends that reinforcers are "biologically significant events." Probability-differential theory allows that a particular behavior may be more or less probable, and therefore more or less effective as a reinforcer; but how can one and the same behavior both be and not be a reducer of biological need; both be and not be a biologically significant event; both activate and fail to activate whatever part of the neural machinery one supposes to be responsible for the manifest reinforcement effect?

On the other hand, the theory failed to break entirely with tradition. *Instrumental behavior was still seen as behavior governed by its immediate consequences.* True, the key principle now had nothing to do with the intrinsic properties of the consequence viewed in isolation; now all turned on the relative probability of two responses. However, attention still focused on the instrumental response and its immediate consequence. For a sense of the theory's reactionary ties to the past, consider how easily Thorndike's law of effect can conform to probability-differential theory: "A response will be more firmly connected to the situation if it is followed by another more probable response," rather than by Thorndike's "satisfying state of affairs."

Perhaps that conventional focus on the response and its consequences gave the theory more influence than it would have had otherwise. But perhaps the same convention made it hard to understand the theory's first failures, and hard to come to terms with them.

The failures in question, as reported by Premack (1965), involved thirsty rats running in an activity wheel and drinking water. Baseline measurements showed drinking to be more probable than running. Similar experiments had managed to reinforce instrumental running with contingent drinking. Accordingly, there seemed to be every reason to expect that the schedule would engender more running than observed in the baseline condition. However, it failed to produce the expected reinforcement effect, despite many within-session instances in which drinking closely followed running.

The search for the source of the failure unearthed a critical feature that had little to do with the probability-differential condition. It also had little to do with the immediate consequence of the instrumental response. This critical feature has since come to be known as the response deprivation condition. A full understanding of this antecedent condition should leave little doubt that reinforcement is largely a performance effect, a phenomenon of motivation as well as learning.

II. RESPONSE DEPRIVATION

Of the schedules that failed to reinforce running, Premack found that they allowed the rat to perform its baseline amount of drinking simply by performing its baseline amount of running. Thus, under schedules of this sort, drinking might frequently follow running in close temporal contiguity, and thereby realize the condition traditionally thought sufficient to produce a manifest reinforcement effect. But by the time the rat had performed its normal amount of running, it would also have performed its normal amount of drinking. It would then run no further, and would thus evince no reinforcement of running.

Of otherwise similar schedules that *had* reinforced running, he found that the baseline amount of instrumental running would have gained access to *less* than the baseline amount of contingent drinking. In the terminology developed later (Allison & Timberlake, 1973), such schedules "deprived the rat of drinking," or "satisfied the response deprivation condition with respect to drinking." In more general terms, a schedule may be said to deprive the individual of one response if, and only if, the individual could not perform the baseline amount of that response except by performing more than the baseline amount of the other response.

Premack responded to this pattern of results by proposing a relatively conservative revision of the probability-differential hypothesis. The revision preserved a major role for his updated version of the local Thorndikian sequence, the instrumental response followed by another more probable response. But now it appeared that two antecedent conditions were necessary for the manifest reinforcement of an instrumental response: the probability-differential condition, and the response deprivation condition. Specifically, the consequent or contingent response must be more probable than the instrumental, and the schedule must deprive the individual of the consequent response.

Others familiar with this pattern of results soon proposed a more radical revision. This extremist proposal left no place for the probability-differential condition. It also left, incidentally, no place for the immediate consequence as the cause of a higher response rate. Its authors proposed simply that a schedule might drive the instrumental response above its baseline rate if, and only if, the schedule deprived the individual of the contingent response (Eisenberger, Karpman, & Trattner, 1967). This proposal has come to be known as the "response deprivation hypothesis."

Given the historical context of the issue, it was natural that the first experimental tests of the response deprivation hypothesis take the form that they did. Here was the pivotal issue of the day: Can we violate the probability–differential condition, but still get a manifest reinforcement effect, if our schedule satisfies the antecedent response deprivation condition? The most dramatic confrontation would come when (a) the two responses had very different baseline probabilities, (b) the high-probability response was instrumental, and (c) the schedule deprived the individual of the low-probability contingent response. In its Premackian phraseology, the effect expected on the response deprivation hypothesis sounded most counterintuitive: reinforcement of a *high*-probability instrumental response by a *low*-probability contingent response.

The first reported test (Eisenberger et al., 1967) employed humans given free access to two manipulatory activities, pressing a lever and turning a knob. Among 12 of the 25 individuals, turning the knob was more probable than pressing the lever. Those 12 went on to the next phase of the experiment, in which the high-probability knob response was treated as instrumental, with the low-probability lever response contingent. The schedule was designed to satisfy the response deprivation condition with respect to the lever response. Thus, if the person were to perform the instrumental knob-turning response at only its baseline level, the person would fall short of the baseline level of the contingent lever-pressing response. The results showed that the schedule produced a significant reinforcement of the high-probability knob-turning response (Eisenberger et al., 1967, Experiment 4).

These important results appeared in a highly visible journal. However, the next tests did not emerge until some years later, in a series of experiments in which rats licked saccharin solutions of different concentrations (Allison & Timberlake, 1973, 1974). Paired baseline measurements showed that the rats spent more time drinking the sweeter of the two solutions. The rats were then tested with schedules that deprived them of the less probable response. In other words, if they were to lick the sweeter solution no longer than they had done in baseline, they would fall short of the total time they had allocated to the other solution in the paired baseline condition. The results revealed a reinforcement of the high-probability response. Another experiment in this series showed that similar schedules produced no such effect if they did not satisfy that antecedent condition, deprivation of the low-probability response. Thus, it appeared that the response deprivation condition might be not only sufficient, but also necessary, for reinforcement of the other response. It was plainly not enough merely to impose some kind of schedule constraint on the animal's performance of the contingent response.

Soon there appeared many other demonstrations of the same kind, in which reinforcement effects occurred despite the violation of the probability-differential condition supposedly necessary to produce those effects. An experiment with rats employed the drinking of sugar water as the high-probability response, and running as the low-probability response (Mazur, 1975). In an experiment with adult humans, pressing a lever served as the high-probability response, and pushing a spring-loaded plunger served as the low-probability response (Klajner, 1975). An experiment with grade-school children used work with coloring books as the high-probability response, and work on mathematical problems as the low-probability response (Konarski, Johnson, Crowell, & Whitman, 1980).

One of the experiments in the saccharin series reported by Allison and Timberlake (1973, 1974) used an unusual "reciprocal" schedule that has since become more common. This schedule required that the rat perform a certain number of licks at each spout for access to the other spout. The experimenters used reciprocal schedules in an effort to gain relatively close control over the response ratios the rats would actually experience during the training sessions under schedule constraint. The reciprocal schedule offered closer control, for example, than might be afforded by a schedule that required a certain number of licks at the instrumental spout for each 10-sec *presentation* of the contingent spout. A comparison of those reciprocal schedules will illustrate some of the fundamental issues that separate the response deprivation approach from the Thorndikian conceptions of reinforcement.

Each of four different schedules imposed an overall response ratio of 10 licks at the sweeter solution per lick at the other solution. One of the four schedules achieved that ratio by requiring 100 licks at the sweeter solution for each access to the other, and 10 licks at the other for renewed access to the sweeter. The other three schedules required 200/20, 300/30, and 400/40. Thus, each schedule used a "molar" response ratio of 10/1, but the "local" requirements used to achieve that ratio varied widely, by a factor as large as 4 (100/10 as compared with 400/40). Note that each of those four schedules imposed the same amount of contingent-response deprivation. The latter quantity is simply the amount by which the animal would fall short of its baseline number of licks at the other solution, should it perform only the baseline number of licks at the sweeter solution. Within limits, the amount of response deprivation depends only on the molar response ratio—10/1 in each of the four schedules. Accordingly, there was no reason to expect from a response deprivation approach that the schedules would result in different levels of instrumental performance (Timberlake & Allison, 1974).

Other considerations lead to other expectations. Suppose the rat were to perform some large total number of instrumental licks—e.g., 1200 licks—under each of the four schedules. Note that the rat would then experience the local instrumental-contingent sequence more frequently as the local requirements diminished. For example, in performing a total of 1200 instrumental licks, the rat would experience the local Thorndikian sequence 12 times under the 100/10 schedule, but only 3 times under the 400/40 schedule. Accordingly, if the manifest reinforcement effect increased with the frequency of the instrumental-contingent sequence, one might expect the 100/10 schedule to result in a higher level of instrumental performance than the 400/40 schedule.

However, the results revealed no significant difference among the four schedules, in agreement with (admittedly weak) predictions based on the molar schedule properties. A localist proponent might contend that the greater frequency was counterbalanced by the smaller magnitude of reward that accompanied the decrease in the local requirements. On that hypothesis, three 40-lick rewards might be expected to have the same manifest reinforcement effect as twelve 10-lick rewards. However, subsequent research has shown that in the free operant setting, the relation between magnitude of reward and instrumental responding may oppose the one assumed by the localist proponent. That is, over a considerable range of reward magnitudes, the total amount of instrumental responding typically *increases* as the magnitude of reward *decreases* (see Allison, Miller, & Wozny, 1979, for primary data and a review of literature showing similar results; for a recent example, see Collier, Johnson, Hill, & Kaufman, 1986).

Another issue that distinguished the probability-differential hypothesis from the response deprivation hypothesis concerned the conditions needed to reverse the manifest reinforcement effect. Reversibility may be defined in the following terms: Under one experimental condition, response A is reinforced when A is instrumental and B is contingent; under another experimental condition with the same two responses, B is reinforced when B is instrumental and A is contingent.

According to the probability-differential hypothesis, the necessary condition for reversibility of the reinforcement effect is reversal of the relative probabilities. In other words, response B must have the higher probability under one condition, and response A must have the higher probability under the other condition. The supporting evidence came chiefly from two experiments. One of the two capitalized on individual differences among children in terms of the probability of eating candy and the probability of playing with a pinball machine (Premack, 1959). The second experiment manipulated the probabilities of drinking and running by manipulating the rats' access to those two activities during the interval before the experimental measurements. Given no prior chance to drink but free access to the activity wheel, drinking was more probable than running, and reinforced instrumental running. Given no prior chance to run but free access to water, running was more probable than drinking, and reinforced instrumental drinking (Premack, 1962).

According to the response deprivation hypothesis, it is not necessary that the probabilities be changed at all: To reinforce A(B) it is sufficient that the schedule deprive the individual of response B(A). The first test of reversibility through changes in the schedule requirements alone was reported by Timberlake and Allison (1974). The results supported the response deprivation hypothesis. Specifically, a schedule that deprived the rats of saccharin-drinking reinforced instrumental running in an activity wheel; and a schedule that deprived the same rats of running reinforced instrumental drinking of saccharin.

There were several subsequent demonstrations of reversibility through variations in the schedule requirements. These included a closely comparable experiment in which rats drank water and ran in an activity wheel (Wozny, 1979). They also included disparate experiments in which humans listened to music and viewed random varicolored lights (Heth & Warren, 1978), pressed a trigger and performed a pursuit rotor task (Podaskoff, 1982), and worked at reading and mathematics (Konarski, Crowell, Johnson, & Whitman, 1982).

Several of these experiments made use of an important measurational advantage afforded by the definition of response deprivation. The probability-differential approach required that the two behaviors be measured in terms of time. In contrast, the response deprivation approach allowed measurement of either behavior in terms of any unit that happened to be convenient—frequency, mL, g, or seconds. The reason for this flexibility was that the response deprivation condition was defined in terms of the amount of each behavior, not probability. For example, a schedule would be said to deprive the rat of drinking if the schedule requirements were such that the baseline number of lever presses would allow the rat to take in fewer mL than the baseline volume. This flexibility proved attractive to those who sought practical applications of reinforcement theory.

III. APPLICATIONS

Like its Premackian predecessor (Danaher, 1974), the response deprivation approach soon caught the attention of psychologists concerned with behavior modification as a problem in applied psychology. It offered great flexibility in the measurement of behavior. It provided a clear specification of the elements needed to design a practical plan for behavior modification, elements consisting of the baseline levels and the schedule requirements. It promised a relatively easy reversibility of reinforcement effects through simple changes in the schedule requirements. It made allowances for both individual differences and direct motivational manipulations. The first kind of allowance took the form of measured individual differences in the baseline levels of the behaviors. The second kind took the form of dependent variations in baseline levels in response to experimental manipulation of the organism or the character of the behavior: Thirsty rats lick a water spout more often than rats less thirsty (''drive''), and a water spout more often than a dry spout (''incentive motivation''). It offered some guidance on the expected size of the behavioral effect that might proceed from any particular schedule (Timberlake & Allison, 1974, p. 156). Its empirical base was relatively secure and broad, as the mounting evidence in support of the analysis came from a variety of laboratory experiments with both humans and nonhuman animals.

Some of the best known field applications came from Konarski's award-winning work with educable mentally retarded students (Konarksi, 1985). In this research, already cited in connection with the reversibility issue, Konarski and his collaborators used classroom settings to compare two approaches, response deprivation and probability-differential, as alternative guides for the modification of educationally relevant classroom behaviors. The behavioral categories included reading, coloring, cursive writing, and arithmetic.

Other work with children used the response deprivation approach in an effort to induce preschoolers to drink more fruit juice. The contingencies were patterned on common parental practice, as in "Drink your milk, then you can watch TV" (Birch, Birch, Marlin, & Kramer, 1982). Schedules that deprived the children of contingent play activities were found to increase instrumental drinking of the fruit juice. There was a secondary result of interest to those concerned with residual effects of contingency training: When the schedule constraints were lifted, ratings revealed a decrease in the children's liking for the previously instrumental fruit juice. The decreased liking for the instrumental behavior may be an example of the overjustification effect: "If I'm rewarded for doing this, I must not like to do it very much" (Deci, 1975). However, it is important to recognize that the latter effect is far from inevitable. It often fails to appear, and its necessary and sufficient antecedent conditions remain unclear (Allison, 1983, pp. 15–16.)

The response deprivation approach has proved useful in clinical settings. Dougher (1983), working with two schizophrenic patients, reported successful application of schedules that made use of such contingent behaviors as coffee drinking. The schedules were designed to increase "positive" behaviors, such as social talk and social interactions, and to decrease "negative" behaviors, such as psychotic talk and excessive coughing.

This approach carries an incidental advantage, fully realized in Dougher's applications. Specifically, it allows one to target an undesirable behavior for a decrease without scheduling painful consequences (e.g., electric shock). The advantage proceeds from a serendipitous but highly consistent result of response deprivation schedules. Typically, schedules that deprive the individual of behavior B have *two* effects: In addition to the expected increase in the other behavior, A, one also sees a suppression of B relative to the baseline level. Thus, the individual typically responds to such a schedule by performing A above its baseline level, and performing B below its baseline level. The suppression of B can be an artifactual result of a session too brief to allow any other result, but it also occurs reliably in settings designed specifically to exclude that artifact. Indeed, the recognition that both effects were genuine and reliable, and the desire to predict both facilitation and suppression, motivated the development of one of the performance models discussed later, the conservation model.

In another clinical application Richard McFall, in collaboration with James Allison, used the response deprivation approach to reduce a patient's skeleto-muscular pain. Apparently psychosomatic, the pain interfered with the performance and acquisition of some highly demanding psychomotor skills crucial to the furtherance of the patient's professional career. Treatment involved the daily paired baseline recording, by the patient, of two measures: time spent in the absence of pain, and time spent in a preferred activity specified by the patient. Given those baseline measures, it was possible to devise a kind of omission training schedule that deprived the patient of the preferred activity. Specifically, the patient earned a certain amount of time for the contingent activity by logging a certain amount of pain-free time. If the patient were to log only the baseline amount of pain-free time, the time allowed for the contingent preferred activity would fall short of the baseline amount. After a few days under schedule constraint, the patient reported a substantial increase in the amount of daily pain-free time. Subsequent reports over several months indicated a continued remission of pain and full recovery of the ability to practice the essential professional skills.

IV. TERMINOLOGICAL AND CONCEPTUAL IMPLICATIONS

Under the response deprivation hypothesis, one should not call the consequence of the instrumental response the "reinforcer." Response deprivation focuses on the prediction of instrumental performance, which means performance of the instrumental response above the baseline level—the manifest reinforcement effect. According to the response deprivation hypothesis, it is not the local Thorndikian response-consequence sequence that produces the reinforcement effect, but rather the schedule constraint in relation to the paired basepoint. Instrumental performance is an adaptive response to the molar constraints the schedule places on specific behaviors. The response to schedule constraint is to be understood in terms of the individual's free performance of the same behaviors in the absence of schedule constraint (Rachlin & Burkhard, 1978; Staddon, 1979; Timberlake & Allison, 1974).

Admittedly, the response-consequence sequence may play a role in the learning of the contingent relationship and the terms of the schedule. But learning is not sufficient for performance. As Blodgett showed nearly 60 years ago, deficient performance in the multiple-unit T-maze may conceal abundant learning of the layout of the maze (Blodgett, 1929). Contemporary investigators have discovered latent learning—hidden learning—in many other guises. For example, a stimulus that seems to have been "overshadowed" may reveal an ability to suppress a response if the "overshadowing" stimulus is extinguished (Matzel, Schachtman, & Miller, 1985). Another contemporary example involves a stimulus subjected to a backward conditioning procedure. Otherwise ineffective, such a stimulus may prove capable of suppressing a response if the stimulus is presented alone as a "reminder" shortly before the test for conditioned suppression (Gordon, McGinnis, & Weaver, 1985). In a third recent example, animals that show little evidence of discrimination learning during the training phase may show unmistakable evidence during experimental extinction (Hearst, 1987). Finally, consider college students who are first told about a contingent relationship betwen two manipulatory responses, then tested with that contingency under nondeprivation schedules. In accordance with the response deprivation hypothesis, such schedules produce no increase in the rate of instrumental responding, no manifest reinforcement effect (Podsakoff, 1982). But it is difficult to believe that the students finish their experimental sessions in a state of ignorance about the contingency of which they have already been told, and which they have just experienced first hand.

An individual may or may not have learned the contingent relationship and the terms of a particular schedule. But it is still only a schedule that can satisfy the response deprivation condition, increase the rate of the instrumental response, and thereby allow us to infer learning. No isolated response consequence, specified independently of the schedule and the basepoint, can do so.

It follows that the search for an omnipotent reinforcer must fail. If we can devise a schedule at all in the free operant setting, we can always devise one that does not deprive the individual of the consequence. In that event the consequence, whatever it might be, should produce no manifest reinforcement effect. Thus, the response deprivation hypothesis denies the existence of an omnipotent response consequence.

It would seem to be erroneous at worst, and incomplete at best, to call any scheduled consequence a reinforcer if, by calling it so, one means to identify it as the source of the increased rate of instrumental responding. If one believes consequence X to be a reinforcer, then its failure to reinforce an instrumental response under a nondeprivation schedule shows that a reinforcer is not sufficient to reinforce a response. If one believes that consequence Y is not a reinforcer, then its ability to reinforce an instrumental response under a deprivation schedule shows that a reinforcer is not necessary to reinforce a response. And if reinforcers are neither necessary nor sufficient to produce a manifest reinforcement effect, then why call any particular consequence a reinforcer? It would seem more reasonable to give up the belief that some kinds of consequence are reinforcers, and others are not.

Thus, the response deprivation hypothesis implies that consequences traditionally thought to be reinforcers are neither necessary nor sufficient for reinforcement. This implication is not unique to the response deprivation hypothesis. It is shared by other models that treat instrumental performance as an adaptive response to molar schedule constraint.

Accordingly, a new terminology seems to be in order. Perhaps the noun *rein-*

forcer could be replaced by either of two relatively neutral nouns, *consequence* or *contingent*. Thus, "The instrumental requirement was 10 lever presses, and the consequence was a 45-mg food pellet (a 10-lick access to the water spout, a 5-s train of electrical stimulation of the brain, etc.)." Alternatively, "The instrumental requirement was 5 pecks, and the contingent was a 3-s access to grain."

As reinforcement often connotes a process or effect attributable to the response consequence, it has also been suggested that we abandon the use of reinforcement when referring to a manifest effect upon response rate. Specifically, increases and decreases relative to the baseline rate might be referred to as *facilitation* and *suppression* effects, terms more neutral than *reinforcement* or *punishment* (Allison, 1976, 1983). Thus, "The schedule deprived the rat of drinking, and had two effects: It facilitated lever pressing, and suppressed drinking."

V.   PERFORMANCE MODELS

The work on response deprivation began as an effort to specify the conditions necessary and sufficient for reinforcement of the instrumental response. It soon spawned more comprehensive models of instrumental performance that transcended the original concern, new models rich in implications for behavioral economics and behavioral ecology (Allison, 1983).

One broad class of models interprets the paired basepoint as a "bliss point" (Allison, 1983)—an interpetation sympathetic to the response deprivation model (Timberlake & Allison, 1974, p. 150). These models assume that the paired basepoint functions as a behavioral ideal that drives performance under schedule constraint (Hanson & Timberlake, 1983; Rachlin & Burkhard, 1978; Staddon, 1979). They differ in detail, but are well illustrated by Staddon's minimum deviation model. This model proposes that the individual's performance under schedule constraint represents the closest approach to the basepoint the schedule allows. Figure 2.1 illustrates its predictions with respect to two behaviors, A and B. The figure includes a paired basepoint in the upper left and a line of schedule constraint sloping upward from the origin.

Suppose response A is instrumental, response B contingent. More specifically, suppose the schedule requires that the animal perform x units of A instrumentally for each opportunity to perform y units of B. Then during a contingency training session, the schedule would permit the animal to migrate from its starting point at the origin to any point in the bivariate space on or below the line of schedule constraint. Accordingly, the slope of the line of schedule constraint is the largest amount of B the schedule allows per unit of A. Thus, under the constraints of that particular schedule, the animal can come no closer to the paired basepoint than some point on the line of schedule constraint.

Suppose the animal attaches some importance—i.e., assigns some weight greater than zero—to the baseline level of each behavior. If we assume equal positive

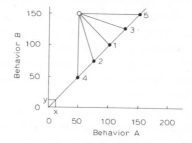

FIG. 2.1.   Behavior B as a function of Behavior A under the paired baseline condition and the constraints of a schedule, with x and y as the schedule requirements; five hypothetical schedule equilibrium points.

weights for the two baseline levels, we can predict the schedule equilibrium point
by dropping a perpendicular from the paired basepoint to the line of schedule
constraint. The perpendicular meets the line of schedule constraint at Point 1,
the predicted schedule equilibrium point. If the animal were to stop short, say
at Point 2 instead of Point 1, it would fail to minimize its distance from the paired
basepoint. The failure becomes apparent when one notes that the distance between Point 2 and the basepoint is the hypotenuse of a right triangle—necessarily
longer than the leg between Point 1 and the basepoint. Similarly, if the animal
were to ascend beyond Point 1, say to Point 3, it would again fail to minimize
its distance from the basepoint.

In constructing a physical representation of the model from hardware, one might
use a magnet for the paired basepoint, and panes of glass for the two axes and
the schedule constraint line. An iron pellet at the origin, beneath the schedule
constraint pane, would represent the animal at the start of a contingency session.
The point at which the pellet came to rest would represent the predicted schedule
equilibrium point. (A "reciprocal" schedule keeps the animal on or near the line
of schedule constraint by requiring completion of the contingent response before
the next access to the instrumental response. The hardware incarnation of a reciprocal schedule would therefore call for two parallel panes enclosing the iron pellet.)

Through the use of weighted distance functions, the model can represent
differential importance of the two baseline levels. Thus, in Fig. 2.1 Point 2 represents an equilibrium point that might be predicted on the assumption that the animal
attaches some importance to the baseline level of each behavior, but more to A
than to B. Thus, Point 2 represents the shortest distance to the paired basepoint
according to some weighted distance function, one that assigns a greater weight
to A's distance from its baseline level than to B's distance from its baseline level.
Point 3 illustrates the reverse, a least-distance equilibrium point reflecting more
weight for the baseline level of B than A. If the animal attached no importance
to the baseline level of B, but some importance to A, the expected equilibrium
would occur at Point 4. In the reverse case, the equilibrium would occur at Point

5. The model can also take into account the contribution of behaviors other than those constrained directly by the schedule (for further details, see Staddon, 1979).

This kind of model generally predicts a concave schedule function. In other words, if we tested the individual with several schedules, and plotted a schedule function by connecting the several empirical schedule equilibrium points, the plot should look concave from the origin. This feature can be seen in Fig. 2.2, a hypothetical schedule function constructed by assuming equal weights for the two measured baselines (food pellets consumed, and lever presses emitted under the paired baseline condition).

Students of economics can easily infuse Fig. 2.2 with economic content (Allison, 1983). For example, consider the slopes of the schedule constraint lines in the figure. Suppose we interpret each slope, food pellets per press, as a ratio analogous to wage rate, dollars per unit of work supplied. Then the schedule function in the figure resembles the backward bending labor supply curve encountered in microeconomics textbooks (Awh, 1976, p. 96; Samuelson, 1976, p. 580). In conformity with that curve, the greatest amount of labor—i.e., the largest number of lever presses—occurs at an intermediate wage rate, rather than the highest or lowest wage rate. Labor supply theory would analyze the situation in Fig. 2.2 in terms of income opportunity lines, rather than schedule constraint lines, that limit the worker's access to two different goods, leisure and income, that function as imperfect substitutes for each other. A typical labor-supply analysis (e.g., Awh, 1976, p. 96; Green, Kagel, & Battalio, 1982) might include indifference contours with respect to income and leisure. Such contours would purport to show how much income the worker is willing to accept in place of leisure, and vice versa. It might also include a bliss point located in the upper left-hand part of the space. That bliss point would represent both much income (much food), and much leisure (few lever presses). The alternative theoretical accounts of the schedule function in the figure include, of course, the psychological model of performance under schedule constraint from which the function was derived. That would be the minimum deviation model, in which the measured paired basepoint has essentially the same function as the bliss point of the economic analysis.

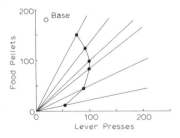

FIG. 2.2.   Food pellets as a function of lever presses under the paired baseline condition and the constraints of six schedules (hypothetical data).

Alternatively, students of economics might interpret the inverse slope of the constraint line, presses per pellet, as the unit behavioral price of the food. In that event, the schedule function exemplifies some fundamental concepts from the economics of consumer demand. Note that the top schedule offers the cheapest food, the bottom schedule the most expensive. Note too that as the price rises from the top schedule to the bottom, there is a steady decrease in the amount of food consumed. The latter relation illustrates the demand law, the fundamental empirical relation of economics: All else equal, as the unit price of the good rises, total consumption of that good declines.

In the economics of consumer demand, total lever presses would correspond to revenue on sales of the food pellets. It is not difficult to demonstrate this correspondence. If P is the unit price of the good (e.g., dollars/bottle), and Q is the total number of units consumed (e.g., total bottles), then the product PQ is revenue on sales (total dollars received from the sale of Q bottles). It follows that if P is the unit price of the food pellet (presses/pellet), and Q is the total number of food pellets consumed, then the product PQ is the total number of lever presses emitted during the contingency session.

Accordingly, the schedule function in Fig. 2.2, viewed as a consumer demand function, illustrates not only the demand law but another empirical relation familiar to economists, one having to do with price elasticity of demand. When price is relatively low, an increase in price (P) may result in such a small drop in consumption (Q) that revenue on sales (PQ) increases. In that event, demand is said to be "inelastic." As the price rises further, the demand function may pass through a region of "unit elasticity," where consumption drops but revenue on sales remains constant. At still higher prices, the next rise in price may occasion such a large drop in consumption that revenue on sales also declines, in which case demand is said to be elastic. The relations in Fig. 2.2 illustrate that relation between price and elasticity: Starting at the lowest prices, rising prices are accompanied by an increase in total lever presses (inelastic demand for food), no change (unit elasticity), and finally by a drop in total lever presses (elastic demand for food). (Students of economics may notice that the consumer demand function in the figure is "uncompensated." However, the Slutsky compensation can be and has been applied to such functions—see Allison, 1983.)

There is much empirical support for the contention that food is an economic good, with a behavioral price defined by the presses/pellet ratio. Some of this support comes from the observed functional relation between price and the amount of food consumed (for reviews of the literature on food and many of the other common laboratory rewards, see Allison, 1979, 1983, and Lea, 1978). It is also pertinent to note that economic goods are conventionally defined in terms of scarcity and exchange: They are relatively scarce in one sense or another, and they are things for which people are willing to pay. Note that each of the schedules in Fig. 2.2 deprives the individual of eating—a precisely defined form of scarcity—and that the typical effect of this antecedent condition would be a larger number of instrumental responses than would occur in the absence of schedule constraint—a precisely defined exchange.

Economic interpretations of the kinds of relations shown in Fig. 2.2 have been gathering force for years (Allison, 1977a, 1977b, 1979, 1981, 1982, 1983; Allison, Miller, & Wozny, 1979; Hursh, 1980, 1984; Lea, 1978; Rachlin, Battalio, Kagel, & Green, 1981; Rachlin, Green, Kagel, & Battalio, 1976). Along with the pertinent psychological models of performance under schedule constraint, they have begun to appear in textbooks on learning (e.g., Domjan & Burkhard, 1986) and as topics for major conferences and symposia. They can hardly fail to appear in the literature on behavioral ecology. The principal connection, destined no doubt for numerous revisions and refinements, can be recognized in a fundamental proposition of optimal foraging theory. According to this proposition, as a result of evolutionary pressures the foraging animal should have behavioral mechanisms that allow it to maximize the ratio E/T: the amount of energy taken in, relative to the amount expended in foraging (Krebs & Davies, 1984; Shettleworth, 1985). Note that the inverse of the foraging ratio closely resembles the unit behavioral price of food: T/E is the amount of energy expended per unit taken in. Accordingly, this fundamental proposition of optimal foraging theory is essentially the same as the proposition that rational economic creatures can behave so as to minimize price. It is instructive to compare the logical bases. Foragers who maximize E/T—and thereby tend to minimize the behavioral price of food—will have the greatest amount of time and energy left over for other biologically important pursuits, chiefly reproduction. Consumers who pay the smallest unit price for any particular commodity will have the greatest amount of money left over for the purchase of other goods and services, and can thereby maximize utility.

Note that none of the pertinent theoretical analyses mentioned above finds it necessary to assume that the item scaled on the ordinate is a reinforcer. Indeed, both the psychological model and the economic model would predict that if the schedule constraint line (the income opportunity line) were projected through the paired base point (the bliss point), then that schedule (the wage rate) would result in no more lever pressing (no more labor) than the individual would perform (would supply) in the absence of schedule constraint.

Although the blisspoint models may give a satisfactory account of many instances of performance under schedule constraint, they cannot account satisfactorily for all conceivable instances. This is no perfunctory disclaimer. In particular, no blisspoint model can apply when the two behaviors constrained by the schedule happen to be perfect mutual substitutes, as assumed by the linear conservation model (Allison, 1976, 1983; Allison et al., 1979; Allison & Moore, 1985).

An essential characteristic of perfect substitutes is that the individual is always willing to trade X units of one for pX units of the other. The exchange constant p that applies to two perfect substitutes might be unity in some cases (e.g., one dime for another), or something other than unity in other cases (e.g., one dime for two nickels). It is easy to show that if the two behaviors constrained by the schedule are perfect substitutes, then performance under schedule constraint will be governed not by a bliss point, but a conservation "stop line."

For example, suppose the paired baseline condition presents the thirsty rat with two adjacent water spouts, identical except for location—one is a little left of the center of the wall, the other a little right. Suppose further that the rat consistently makes more licks at one spout than the other, as shown hypothetically in Fig. 2.3. It is possible that the paired base point in the figure might function as a blisspoint. In other words, if both behaviors were brought under schedule constraint, performance might be drawn toward the paired base point, and the schedule equilibrium point might therefore settle at the smallest possible distance from the base point. If the base point is to function in that capacity, as a kind of behavioral magnet, the rat must attach some unique importance to one or both of the two locations. Thus, licks at one spout would not be interchangeable with licks at the other spout. Spout location would matter.

Alternatively, the location preference revealed by the paired baseline condition may prove inconsequential under challenge by a schedule. Coupled by a reciprocal contingency schedule, licks at either spout may come to function as a perfect substitute for licks at the other spout. Thus, the rat may perform X licks at one spout in place of pX licks at the other. In that event, performance under schedule constraint will not be governed by a unique blisspoint. Many different numerical combinations of licks at one spout, plus licks at the other spout, will prove satisfactory. Accordingly, the rat will climb the line of schedule constraint until it reaches any one of these combinations—including the paired base point, if it happens to be attainable under schedule constraint. Thus, performance under schedule constraint will be drawn toward a stop line, and not toward a unique bliss point. The stop line will pass downward through the paired base point, and its slope will depend on p, the rate of exchange. Each point on the stop line represents an acceptable combination of licks at the two spouts.

Fig. 2.3 illustrates these two theoretical alternatives, the stop line and the blisspoint, and introduces a special test condition that can distinguish between the two.

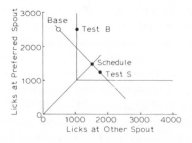

FIG. 2.3.   Licks at the preferred water spout as a function of licks at the other water spout (hypothetical example): Paired base point (Base), schedule equilibrium point (Schedule), and test points illustrating predictions of the blisspoint model (Test B) and the stop line model (Test S).

The line that slopes upward from the origin represents the constraints of a reciprocal contingency schedule. The hypothetical data point on that line signifies schedule equilibrium, the stable level of performance under schedule constraint. The special test comes after the schedule equilibrium point has been measured experimentally. This "contingency-paired" test session begins the same way as a standard contingency session. But when the individual reaches a point halfway on the horizontal axis between the paired base point and the schedule equilibrium point, the condition reverts to the paired baseline condition, with both spouts freely available for the rest of the session. The second pair of coordinates in the figure originate at the point where the condition changes from contingency to paired baseline. After the change, given enough time, the individual can migrate to any part of the behavioral space that lies to the right of the second vertical axis and above the second horizontal.

Point B represents the result to be expected under the special test condition if performance under schedule constraint was governed by the paired basepoint in the functional role of a bliss point. To approach the paired base point as closely as possible, the animal can move no more to the right. Instead, it must move straight up the vertical axis to the baseline number of licks at the preferred spout, neither stopping short of that point nor ascending beyond.

In contrast, test Point S represents one of the possible results to be expected if the two behaviors functioned as perfect substitutes. The stop line drawn through the base point and the schedule equilibrium point comprises combinations equivalent to those two points. Point S is one of those combinations, and one of the subset reachable after the change from the contingency condition to the paired.

Fig. 2.4 summarizes the results of an experiment, like the one outlined above (Allison, Buxton, & Moore, 1987). Five thirsty rats were tested in 60-min sessions with access to two water spouts, one left of center, one right. The reciprocal contingency schedule was designed so as to deprive each individual of licks at the preferred water spout. As expected from the response deprivation hypothesis, the schedule facilitated licking at the other spout, and suppressed licking at the

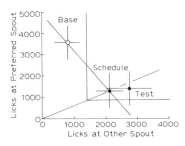

FIG. 2.4.   Licks at the preferred water spout as a function of licks at the other water spout (group means and standard errors for five rats): Paired base point (Base), schedule equilibrium point (Schedule), and test point Test).

preferred spout. The figure shows group means and standard errors with respect to the paired base point, the schedule equilibrium point, and the contingency-paired test point. The paired part of the test session began after a 30-s intermission during which both spouts were closed. When both reopened simultaneously after the brief intermission, the rats typically performed many additional licks at both water spouts, and thereby failed to minimize their distance from the paired base point. The test point did not differ significantly from the schedule equilibrium point. Thus, licks at the two water spouts appear to have functioned as perfect substitutes, with performance under schedule constraint governed by a stop line. The paired base point had no apparent status as a bliss point. The location preference revealed under the paired baseline condition proved inconsequential under schedule constraint.

One would expect the paired basepoint to function more as a bliss point if the two behaviors were not so similar to each other as licking water from two adjacent spouts. For example, suppose one of the two spouts were empty. If the schedule were designed so as to deprive the animal of licks at the water spout, it would probably facilitate licking of the empty spout, and suppress licking of the water spout. In terms of the minimum deviation model, such a result would indicate that the animal assigned some importance to each of the two behaviors constrained by the schedule. Consider those extra instrumental licks at the empty spout, far in excess of the baseline number. If one imagined licks at the empty spout to be no substitute for licks at the water spout, one would expect the rat to respond to the contingency-paired test by climbing straight up the vertical axis to the baseline number of water licks. It should perform no more licks at the empty spout, because any additional empty licks would merely carry the rat still further from the paired base point.

Fig. 2.5 presents the results of such an experiment, group means and standard errors from five rats (Allison, Buxton, & Moore, 1987). When both spouts became available during the contingency-paired session, after the 30-s intermission, the rats performed significantly more empty licks, and significantly fewer water licks, than predicted by the minimum deviation model. Thus, the paired basepoint

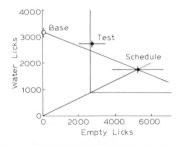

FIG. 2.5.   Licks at the water spout as a function of licks at the empty spout (group means and standard errors for five rats): Paired base point (Base), schedule equilibrium point (Schedule), and test point (Test).

seemed not to function as a bliss point, contrary perhaps to intuition as well as the minimum deviation model. The typical response pattern in the paired part of the test session showed several hundred licks at the water spout, followed by several licks at the empty spout, and finally one or two bouts at each spout. Thus, the original baseline preference for water over empty held up under schedule constraint, unlike the location preference revealed in the water-water experiment. Note that the test point in the figure also contradicts the stop line model: That measured test point was significantly higher than the stop line drawn between the base point and the schedule equilibrium point.

There are several reasonable explanations of the data in Fig. 2.5. One of the more interesting possibilities is that the two behaviors are perfect substitutes, but only when they are coupled by means of a contingency schedule (Allison & Moore, 1985). Thus, their mutual substitutability may have been concealed by the paired part of the contingency-paired test. Another possibility is that performance under schedule constraint is governed by a stop line, but that the stop line is concave with respect to the origin—perhaps because of the contribution of some third substitute behavior, a behavior not constrained by the schedule (Allison, 1981, 1983).

Both of these possibilities can be tested experimentally. One can easily imagine outcomes that might have a major impact upon current theoretical accounts of performance under schedule constraint. In the meantime, the two experiments reported above should prove newsworthy to psychologists and economists who rely upon the notion of a blisspoint. According to those experiments, something that looks like a blisspoint may lose that look under more direct light.

VI. LOCAL ORGANIZATION

Although the concept of reinforcement owes much to Thorndike's law of effect, the theoretical developments discussed above may seem to have little connection with his paradigmatic use of the puzzle box. His experiments exemplified the controlled-amount paradigm, in which each session—often called a ''discrete trial''—ends with the completion of a fixed amount of responding. In that paradigm, rate varies inversely with the latency of completion. In Thorndike's experiments, rate of escape varied inversely with the latency of escape from the puzzle box. Because the *number* of instrumental responses and the *number* of contingent rewards are not free to vary from one session or trial to the next, controlled-amount experiments may have a more tenuous connection with behavioral economics or behavioral ecology than controlled-time experiments, where the amount of responding is free to vary. But the rising importance of such connections should not be allowed to obscure the controlled-amount paradigm as a potential test arena for models of performance under schedule constraint.

The response deprivation approach was developed in the context of the controlled-time paradigm—often called the "free-operant procedure"—where each session has the same fixed duration, but the individual is free to vary the amount of responding from one session to another. However, a few models related to the response deprivation approach have also been developed for the controlled-amount paradigm. The key to this attempt at a unified theoretical analysis is that both paradigms employ the same dependent variable, rate of responding. In the controlled-time paradigm, the individual varies rate by varying the amount of responding. In the controlled-amount paradigm, exemplified by Thorndike's puzzle box experiments and, more profusely, by later experiments with the straight runway, the individual varies rate by varying latency.

The few controlled-amount models focus on patterns of free behavior, in relation to the constraints the contingency puts on those patterns. For a simple example, imagine that in the contingency phase each session or trial will end when the rat has completed one instrumental lever press, and 25 contingent licks at a water spout. Notice that the structure of that contingency would force a particular sequential pattern upon the animal. Specifically, the trial would start with the presentation of the lever alone; when the rat pressed the lever, the lever would retract and the spout shutter would open simultaneously; upon the 25th lick at the spout, the shutter would close and the session would end. Thus, the pattern forced upon the rat is one in which all lever pressing must occur before any lick may occur.

The paired baseline session or trial would require the same amount of each behavior, but would force no particular pattern. Thus, the paired baseline session would start with the *simultaneous* presentation of both lever and spout; the shutter would close at the 25th lick, the lever would retract at the first press, and the baseline session would end when both of those events had transpired, regardless of the order of their occurrence. The manifest "reinforcement" effect—i.e., the facilitation of lever pressing—would show up as a shorter lever-press latency, and thus a higher rate of lever pressing, during the contingency session than the baseline session.

One of the models developed for this paradigm focuses on the *average* rate of responding, and therefore the time at which the individual *completes* each requirement (Allison, 1982). In like manner, the average speed of a car is simply the total distance covered, divided by the total time it took to complete the trip.

According to this "completion" model, a controlled-amount contingency will deprive the individual of the contingent response if, in the baseline session, the individual completed the contingent requirement before the instrumental. To understand that implication, note again that the contingency requires completion of the instrumental requirement first. Thus, completion of the instrumental requirement at its baseline time would delay completion of the contingent requirement to a time after its baseline time. In that event, the contingent response would have a lower average rate in the contingency session than the baseline session. There is, of course, an alternate wording of the antecedent response deprivation condition: Only if the rat were to press the lever sooner than it did in baseline could it complete its 25 licks as soon as it did in baseline.

Allison (1982) reported some preliminary support for this model. The pertinent experiment began by showing that thirsty rats faced with two requirements, 25 licks at a water spout and one press of a lever, displayed a consistent free baseline pattern: They typically began each baseline session by performing all 25 licks, and ended by pressing the lever.

Next came two different contingencies, one of which deprived the rats of licking. When pressing the lever once was the instrumental requirement, with 25 licks contingent, the contingency deprived the rats of licking. In other words, performance of the instrumental lever press at its baseline time would have delayed the 25th lick to a point beyond its baseline time. This contingency facilitated instrumental lever pressing, and suppressed licking. In other words, the rats pressed the lever sooner than they had done in baseline, but made the 25th lick later than they had done in baseline.

When the roles were reversed, the contingency imposed no response deprivation. That is, when licking the spout 25 times was the instrumental requirement, with one press of the lever contingent, the contingency did not deprive the rat of contingent lever-pressing. By completing the 25th lick at or before the baseline time, the rat could press the lever at the baseline time. As expected, this nondeprivation contingency, because it forced no change in the free baseline pattern, failed to facilitate or suppress either response. The results of both contingencies were predicted by a conservation model, but are no doubt consistent with various blisspoint models as well.

Some controlled-amount models focus on more detailed aspects of sequential patterning in the free baseline condition. According to these models, it is not merely the completion times, and thus the average rates, that matter. What truly matters is the time at which each elemental part of the response requirement takes place. Accordingly, the model must deal with the integral of the elemental rates (Allison, 1982). For example, these "integration" models imply that one ought to record in the paired baseline session the time at which the rat completes each one of the 25 required licks, and not merely the 25th. A similar view has led to the suggestion that a controlled-amount contingency deprives the individual of the contingent response if, and only if, in the free behavior pattern the contingent response *began* before completion of the instrumental requirement (Allison & Timberlake, 1975).

None of the controlled-amount models has received a definitive experimental test, or indeed much mention of any kind. The apparent neglect may indicate an absorbing interest in the controlled-time paradigm, with its historic ties to operant conditioning and its newly recognized bearing on behavioral economics and behavioral ecology. However, the paradigmatic feature of the ancestral experiments on "instrumental conditioning" has appeared in guises other than those discussed above. Other models have focused on patterns of free behavior, and have tried to predict schedule effects in terms of schedule constraints on those patterns—constraints that probably incorporate the essential feature of Thorndike's procedure. Accounts of such work have been furnished by Dunham (1977), Gawley (1986), and Gawley, Timberlake, and Lucas (1986).

VII. CONCLUSION

In a stylish animadversion, Walker (1969) concluded that "glue"—i.e., the concept of reinforcement—was superfluous. His analysis of the pertinent logic and evidence left him no reason to suppose that reinforcement was necessary for learning, or that the response consequences usually called *reinforcers* have any function beyond that of an incentive.

A glance at recent journals shows that Walker's arguments have not yet purged the psychological vocabulary. The pockets of resistance even contain the makers of Webster's New Collegiate Dictionary. The 1950 volume defined reinforcement and its cognates in terms of strengthening by means of the addition of something new, strictly in the sense of engineering or of military forces. A quarter century later, the same dictionary—now endorsed by the publication manual of the American Psychological Association—defined *reinforcer* as a stimulus effective in operant conditioning because it regularly follows a desired response. But it also defined *incentive* as something that incites to action. It thereby seemed to echo Walker's contention that the two terms, *reinforcer* and *incentive*, have only one referent.

The present chapter has added some arguments that favor Walker's conclusion concerning the superflous nature of glue. The evidence reviewed above reveals no immediate response consequence as such that increases the rate of the preceding response. Moreover, theory backed by experimental evidence denies the possibility that any such consequence could exist. There is little to be gained by calling a response consequence a reinforcer, and much to be gained by calling it what it is: response-contingent food, water, access to math problems, etc. If a schedule does increase the rate of the instrumental response, with what justification can one attribute that effect to the response-contingent food pellet, as one does implicitly by calling the food a *reinforcer*? One might with equal reason say that the reinforcer was the paired base point, the slope of the schedule constraint line or, better yet, the relation between the base point and the schedule requirements. Of course, there is good reason to call none of those items *the reinforcer*. A reinforcer is a stimulus, but none of those items is.

What, then, is the nature of reinforcement? Perhaps it is, after all, the chimera of Walker's contention: the fantastical One Ring that gives its user mastery of all creatures. Even if it proves to be more substantial that that, it still seems destined for a smaller role, and not a larger one, in theoretical accounts of learning and performance.

REFERENCES

Allison, J. (1976). Contrast, induction, facilitation, suppression, and conservation. *Journal of the Experimental Analysis of Behavior, 25,* 185–198.

Allison, J. (1977a, May). *Economics and operant conditioning.* Paper presented at the meeting of the Midwestern Psychological Association, Chicago, IL.

Allison, J. (1977b, July). *Economics of food consumption in normal and hyperphagic rats.* Paper presented at the Sixth International conference on the Physiology of Food and Fluid Intake, Paris, France.

Allison, J. (1979). Demand economics and experimental psychology. *Behavioral Science, 24,* 403–415.

Allison, J. (1981). Economics and operant conditioning. In P. Harzem & M. D. Zeiler (Eds.), *Advances in analysis of behaviour: Vol. 2. Predictability, correlation, and contiguity* (pp. 321–353). Chichester: Wiley.

Allison, J. (1982). Constraints on performance in two elementary paradigms. In M. L. Commons, R. J. Herrnstein, & H. Rachlin (Eds.), *Quantitative analyses of behavior: Vol. 2. Matching and maximizing accounts* (pp. 523–548). Cambridge, MA: Ballinger.

Allison, J. (1983). *Behavioral economics.* New York: Praeger.

Allison, J., Buxton, A. & Moore, K. E. (1987). Bliss points, stop lines, and performance under schedule constraint. *Journal of Experimental Psychology: Animal Behavior Processes, 13,* 331–340.

Allison, J., & Castellan, N. J., Jr. (1970). Temporal characteristics of nutritive drinking in rats and humans. *Journal of Comparative and Physiological Psychology, 70,* 116–125.

Allison, J., Miller, M., & Wozny, M. (1979). Conservation in behavior. *Journal of Experimental Psychology: General, 108,* 4–34.

Allison, J., & Moore, K. E. (1985). Lick-trading by rats: On the substitutability of dry, water, and saccharin tubes. *Journal of the Experimental Analysis of Behavior, 43,* 195–213.

Allison, J., Moore, K. E., Gawley, D. J., Mondloch, C. J., & Mondloch, M. V. (1986). The temporal pattern of unconstrained drinking: Rats' responses to inversion and identity constraints. *Journal of the Experimental Analysis of Behavior, 45,* 5–13.

Allison, J., & Timberlake, W. (1973). Instrumental and contingent saccharin-licking in rats: Response deprivation and reinforcement. *Bulletin of the Psychonomic Society, 2,* 141–143.

Allison, J., & Timberlake, W. (1974). Instrumental and contingent saccharin-licking in rats: Response deprivation and reinforcement. *Learning and Motivation, 5,* 231–247.

Allison, J., & Timberlake, W. (1975). Response deprivation and instrumental performance in the controlled-amount paradigm. *Learning and Motivation, 6,* 122–142.

Awh, R. Y. (1976). *Microeconomics: Theory and applications.* Santa Barbara, CA: Wiley/Hamilton.

Birch, L. L., Birch, D., Marlin, D. W., & Kramer, L. (1982). Effects of instrumental consumption on children's food preference. *Appetite: Journal for Intake Research, 3,* 125–134.

Blodgett, H. C. (1929). The effect of the introduction of reward upon the maze performance of rats. *University of California Publications in Psychology, 4,* 113–134.

Collier, G. H., Johnson, D. F., Hill, W. L., & Kaufman, L. W. (1986). The economics of the law of effect. *Journal of the Experimental Analysis of Behavior, 46,* 113–136.

Danaher, B. G. (1974). Theoretical foundations and clinical applications of the Premack principle: A review and critique. *Behavior Therapy, 5,* 307–324.

Deci, E. L. (1975). *Intrinsic motivation.* New York: Plenum.

Domjan, M., & Burkhard, B. (1986). *The principles of learning and behavior* (2nd ed.). Monterey, CA: Brooks/Cole.

Dougher, M. J. (1983). Clinical effects of response deprivation and response satiation procedures. *Behavior Therapy, 14,* 286–298.

Dunham, P. J. (1977). The nature of reinforcing stimuli. In W. K. Honig & J. E. R. Staddon (Eds.), *Handbook of operant behavior* (pp. 98–124). Englewood Cliffs, NJ: Prentice-Hall.

Eisenberger, R., Karpman, M., & Trattner, J. (1967). What is the necessary and sufficient condition for reinforcement in the contingency situation? *Journal of Experimental Psychology*, *74*, 342–350.

Gawley, D. J. (1986). *Local and molar mechanisms in behavior regulation*. Unpublished doctoral dissertation, Indiana University, Bloomington, IN.

Gawley, D. J., Timberlake, W., & Lucas, G. A. (1986). Schedule constraint on the average drink burst and the regulation of wheel running and drinking in rats. *Journal of Experimental Psychology: Animal Behavior Processes*, *12*, 78–94.

Gordon, W. C., McGinnis, C. M., & Weaver, M. S. (1985). The effect of cuing after backward conditioning trials. *Learning and Motivation*, *16*, 444–463.

Green, L., Kagel, J. H., & Battalio, R. C. (1982). Ratio schedules of reinforcement and their relation to economic theories of labor supply. In M. L. Commons, R. J. Herrnstein, & H. Rachlin (Eds.), *Quantitative analyses of behavior: Vol. 2. Matching and maximizing accounts* (pp. 395–429). Cambridge, MA: Ballinger.

Hanson, S. J., & Timberlake, W. (1983). Regulation during challenge: A general model of learned performance under schedule constraint. *Psychological Review*, *90*, 262–282.

Hearst, E. (1987). Extinction reveals stimulus control: Latent learning of feature-negative discriminations in pigeons. *Journal of Experimental Psychology: Animal Behavior Processes*, *13*, 52–64.

Heth, C. D., & Warren, A. G. (1978). Response deprivation and response satiation as determinants of instrumental performance. *Animal Learning and Behavior*, *6*, 294–300.

Hursh, S. R. (1980). Economic concepts for the analysis of behavior. *Journal of the Experimental Analysis of Behavior*, *34*, 219–238.

Hursh, S. R. (1984). Behavioral economics. *Journal of the Experimental Analysis of Behavior*, *42*, 435–452.

Klajner, F. (1975). *The relations among instrumental performance, reinforcement, and contingent-response deprivation in the instrumental conditioning paradigm*. Unpublished doctoral dissertation, University of Toronto.

Konarski, E. A., Jr. (1985). The use of response deprivation to increase the academic performance of EMR students. *The Behavior Therapist*, *8*, 61.

Konarski, E. A., Jr., Crowell, C. R., Johnson, M. R., & Whitman, T. L. (1982). Response deprivation, reinforcement, and instrumental academic performance in an EMR classroom. *Behavior Therapy*, *13*, 94–102.

Konarski, E. A., Jr., Johnson, M. R., Crowell, C. R., & Whitman, T. L. (1980). Response deprivation and reinforcement in applied settings: A preliminary analysis. *Journal of Applied Behavior Analysis*, *13*, 595–609.

Krebs, J. R., & Davies, N. B. (Eds.). (1984). *Behavioural ecology: An evolutionary approach* (2nd ed.). Sunderland, MA: Sinauer.

Lea, S. E. G. (1978). Psychology and economics of demand. *Psychological Bulletin*, *85*, 441–466.

Machlis, L. (1977). An analysis of the temporal patterning of pecking in chicks. *Behaviour*, *63*, 1–70.

Matzel, L. D., Schachtman, T. R., & Miller, R. R. (1985). Recovery of an overshadowed association achieved by extinction of the overshadowing stimulus. *Learning and Motivation*, *16*, 398–412.

Mazur, J. E. (1975). The matching law and qualifications related to Premack's principle. *Journal of Experimental Psychology: Animal Behavior Processes*, *4*, 374–386.

Meehl, P. E. (1950). On the circularity of the law of effect. *Psychological Bulletin*, *47*, 52–75.

Podsakoff, P. M. (1982). Effects of schedule changes on human performance: An empirical test of the contrasting predictions of the law of effect, the probability-differential model, and the response-deprivation approach. *Organizational Behavior and Human Performance*, *29*, 322–351.

Premack, D. (1959). Toward empirical behavior laws: I. Positive reinforcement. *Psychological Review*, *66*, 219–233.

Premack, D. (1962). Reversibility of the reinforcement relation. *Science*, *136*, 255–257.

Premack, D. (1965). Reinforcement theory. In D. Levine (Ed.), *Nebraska symposium on motivation, 1965* (pp. 123–180). Lincoln: University of Nebraska Press.

Rachlin, H. C., Battalio, R., Kagel, J., & Green, L. (1981). Maximization theory in behavioral psychology. *Behavioral and Brain Sciences*, *4*, 371–417.

Rachlin, H., Green, L., Kagel, J. H., & Battalio, R. C. (1976). Economic demand theory and psychological studies of choice. In G. H. Bower (Ed.), *The psychology of learning and motivation: Vol. 10* (pp. 129–154). New York: Academic Press.

Rachlin, H., & Burkhard, B. (1978). The temporal triangle: Response substitution in instrumental conditioning. *Psychological Review, 85*, 22–47.

Samuelson, P. A. (1976). *Economics* (10th ed.). New York: McGraw-Hill.

Shettleworth, S. J. (1985). Handling time and choice in pigeons. *Journal of the Experimental Analysis of Behavior, 44*, 139–155.

Skinner, B. F. (1938). *The behavior of organisms.* New York: Appleton-Century-Crofts.

Staddon, J. E. R. (1979). Operant behavior as adaptation to constraint. *Journal of Experimental Psychology: General, 108*, 48–67.

Thorndike, E. L. (1911). *Animal Intelligence.* New York: Macmillan.

Timberlake, W., & Allison, J. (1974). Response deprivation: An empirical approach to instrumental performance. *Psychological Review, 81*, 146–164.

Walker, E. L. (1969). Reinforcement—"the one ring." In J. T. Tapp (Ed.), *Reinforcement and behavior* (pp. 47–62). New York: Academic Press.

Webster's new collegiate dictionary. (1950). Springfield, MA: Merriam.

Webster's new collegiate dictionary. (1975). Springfield, MA: Merriam.

Wozny, M. C. (1979). *Models and microeconomics of performance under fixed ratio schedules.* Unpublished doctoral dissertation, Indiana University, Bloomington, IN.

3 Theories of Timing Behavior

Russell M. Church
Brown University

Events in the life of an animal occur in some temporal sequence. Events in the past are a basis for current memory, and temporal regularities among events in the past are a basis for anticipation of the future and for learning. In his influential textbook, James (1890) wondered what the consequences would be "if the constitution of consciousness were that of a string of bead-like sensations and images, all separate." He wrote "Our consciousness would be like a glow-worm spark, illuminating the point it immediately covered, but leaving all beyond in total darkness" (p. 606). He considered this hypothesis to be fanciful since he believed that consciousness had the continuity of a stream and that knowledge of the present (perception) was always mixed in with knowledge of the past (memory) and anticipation of the future. But he speculated that it was possible for individuals to act in a rational way without any conscious representation of the past or future. Since the behavior of an animal conscious of the past and present could not be distinguished from the behavior of an animal that was unaware of the time of events, the study of the mental life of animals languished. Although there have been some attempts to reintroduce the concept of animal awareness into the study of animal behavior (Griffin, 1981, 1984), it has not had much influence on the study of animal cognition (Roitblat, 1987). One of the positive accomplishments of the behavioristic movement (Watson, 1924) was to change the basic problem of psychology. The problem was no longer to describe the contents of conscious life, but to identify the determinants of behavior. This led to a great deal of information about the determinants of animal timing behavior, some of which is described below. These facts may be explained as specific instances of more general principles, or they may be explained by biological or psychological process models. The psychological process models involve mental concepts (such as memory and attention), but they do not require that the mental processes be conscious. This chapter may be considered to be about timing behavior organized by types of explanation, or it may be considered to be a chapter about types of explanation with examples of animal timing. It can be read with either emphasis.

I. TWO TYPES OF EVIDENCE FOR TIMING

Timing behavior refers both to time perception and time production. Time perception refers to the ability of animals to discriminate the duration of an event. By definition, studies of time perception involve nontemporal measures of responding. For example, a rat can learn to press a left lever following a short-duration noise and a right lever following a longer-duration noise. Thus, the temporal characteristics of a stimulus can serve as a discriminative stimulus. Time production refers to the ability of animals to perform a response at a relatively fixed time. Animals can learn to anticipate the time of occurrence of an event. By definition, studies of time production involve temporal measures of responding. For example, a rat can be trained to press a lever after a relatively constant interval of nonresponding. Thus, the temporal characteristics of a response can be selected by differential reinforcement. On the basis of extensive data from many different procedures, it is clear that animals can learn to discriminate between stimuli on the basis of their durations and that they can learn to respond at appropriate times. Although some investigators believe there are fundamental differences between the processes involved in time perception and time production, most investigators are impressed by the similarity of the conclusions based on these different methods.

Time Perception

The duration of a stimulus has been used as the basis for a discrimination in several different procedures. In a temporal discrimination procedure, pigeons were trained to peck a translucent panel illuminated by a light of one color following a short interval and to peck another translucent panel illuminated by a light of a different color following a long interval (Stubbs, 1968) (see Fig. 3.1). A trial began with illumination of the center panel with a white light. When the pigeon pecked the center panel, this panel became dark and then, after an interval of 1, 2, 3, 4, 5, 6, 8, 10, 15, or 30 seconds, one of the two side panels was illuminated with a green light and the other was illuminated with a red light. An attempt was made to randomize the panel that would be illuminated with a particular color, so that the pigeon did not decide upon a response to make until the interval was complete. For a particular pigeon, a response to the green light following one of the five short intervals, or a response to the red light following one of the five long

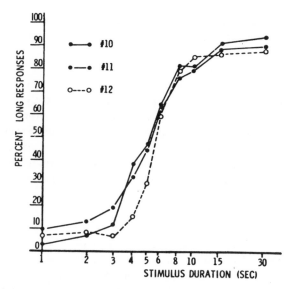

FIG. 3.1.   Median percent of long responses of three pigeons as a function of stimulus duration. From Stubbs (1968).

intervals, was a correct response that produced food and the intertrial interval. An incorrect response (a response to the green light following one of the five long intervals, or a response to the red light following one of the five short intervals) did not produce food but simply led to the intertrial interval. (Other pigeons were reinforced following a peck to the red panel following a short signal and following a peck to the green panel following long signal.) The median percentage of long responses increased as a function of stimulus duration. The function was an S-shaped curve that was reasonably symmetrical when duration was plotted on a logarithmic scale.

In this temporal discrimination procedure, a stimulus of some duration is presented and the animal classifies it as short or long by making one response or another. In a temporal generalization procedure, a stimulus of some duration is presented and, if it is of a particular duration, a response is reinforced (Church & Gibbon, 1982). The mean probability of a response is greatest near the reinforced duration, and less at shorter and longer durations. Thus, in a temporal generalization procedure, a stimulus of some duration is presented and the animal classifies it as correct or incorrect by responding or not responding. In a temporal comparison procedure, two stimuli are presented and the reinforced response depends on the relationship between the two stimuli (Fetterman, 1987). For example, one response is reinforced if the second stimulus is longer and another response is reinforced if the second stimulus is shorter. In a time left procedure, animals compare a fixed time to an elapsing comparison time (Gibbon & Church, 1981). Results from temporal discrimination, temporal generalization, temporal comparison, and time left procedures demonstrate that animals can compare the duration of a stimulus to a criterion duration.

Time Production

In the description of a time production procedure, the three basic terms are stimulus, response, and outcome. A stimulus refers to some experimenter-controlled event; a response refers to some subject-controlled observable event; an outcome refers to a reinforcement. The reinforcement can either be experimenter-controlled or subject-controlled. The general principle is that temporal regularity between any of these terms and outcome produces a regularity in the time of occurrence of some response.

Stimulus and outcome. A temporal regularity between a stimulus and an experimenter-controlled reinforcement occurs in many classical conditioning procedures. In classical conditioning, the stimulus is called a conditioned stimulus and the experimenter-controlled reinforcement is called the unconditioned stimulus. The unconditioned stimulus can be appetitive (like food) or aversive (like shock). If the interval between the onset of the conditioned stimulus and the onset of the unconditioned stimulus is constant, as it usually is, the magnitude of the conditioned response usually rises throughout the interval to be maximal near the time of the unconditioned stimulus. The recognition that a time interval can be a conditioned stimulus has been attributed to research in Pavlov's laboratory conducted between 1907 and 1916. (For a review of this research, see Dmitriev and Kochigina, 1959, an English translation of an article first published in Russian in 1955). This research identified some critical variables, but it did not meet modern standards. The treatment was not completely standard, control conditions were omitted, and data were incompletely reported and analyzed. There is even concern about experimenter cues in some of these experiments. The general conclusion was that the laws of classical conditioning apply when time is the conditioned stimulus. This conclusion is still regarded as essentially correct.

Another example of a temporal regularity between a stimulus and an experimenter-controlled reinforcement comes from autoshaping of pigeons (see Tomie, Brooks, & Zito, 1989). Prior to the study of Brown and Jenkins (1968), the identification of the peck of a key by a pigeon as a conditioned response was not seriously considered. The normal training procedure was to place a pigeon in a box, illuminate the key and, if a key-peck response was made, the food hopper was presented. The lighting of the key was defined as the discriminative stimulus, the peck was defined as the operant response, and the presentation of the food was identified as the reinforcer. The difference between a classical conditioning procedure and an instrumental training procedure is whether or not the presentation of the reinforcer is dependent upon the occurrence of a response.

In a classical conditioning procedure, the reinforcer (US) is independent of the occurrence of a response; in an instrumental conditioning procedure, the reinforcer is dependent, at least in part, on such a response. Brown and Jenkins found that pigeons developed a key-pecking response when the occurrence of food was related to the occurrence of a lighted key and there was no response requirement. This result made it clear that key-pecking of pigeons could be a conditioned response. Williams and Williams (1969) provided an even more dramatic demonstration that the pecking of the lighted key did not occur because the food followed this response. They presented food following the termination of a lighted key only if the pigeon refrained from pecking the key during the time the key was lighted. Even under these conditions, which they called "negative automaintenance," the pigeon learned to peck the key and continued to do so, although at a lower rate than under more favorable conditions.

In standard autoshaping, after an intertrial interval, a translucent key is illuminated for 10 sec and, at the end of the 10 sec, food is presented to the pigeon regardless of its behavior. The mean number of pecks at the illuminated key increases with trials, and this is called autoshaping. If the pigeon learned to expect food at the end of the 10-sec interval, it might have a greater tendency to respond toward the end of the interval than at the beginning. Especially when partial reinforcement was employed, the mean proportion of responses increased as a function of successive seconds of a trial (Gibbon & Balsam, 1980).

Similar functions have been obtained with other unconditioned stimuli and other species of animals. In classical heartrate conditioning, the latency of the heart rate increases as the interval between conditioned stimulus and unconditioned stimulus increases (Church & Black, 1958). In the standard conditioned emotional response procedure with a conditioned stimulus of fixed duration and shock at the end of the stimulus, the magnitude of the response suppression increases as the time of the next shock approaches (Libby & Church, 1975).

A temporal regularity between a stimulus and a subject-controlled reinforcement occurs in many instrumental training procedures. In instrumental training, the stimulus is called a discriminative stimulus and the reinforcement is controlled by the subject. In a discrete-trial, fixed-interval schedule of food reinforcement, the first response after some fixed interval is followed by food. The mean response rate of an animal trained on such a fixed-interval procedure gradually increases as time in the interval progresses. In an important modification of the fixed-interval procedure, some additional trials were interspersed in which there was no reinforcement and the discriminative stimulus remained on for some additional time. Figure 3.2 shows the mean response rate of a pigeon on nonreinforced trials that were interspersed with 10-sec fixed-interval trials (Catania, 1970). The time of the maximum response rate was near the time of the reinforced response, and it was not affected by the probability of reinforcement. The maximum response rate was affected by the probability of reinforcement. Similar functions have been obtained with rats and, over some range, the maximum response rate was not affected by the time of the reinforced response (Roberts, 1981).

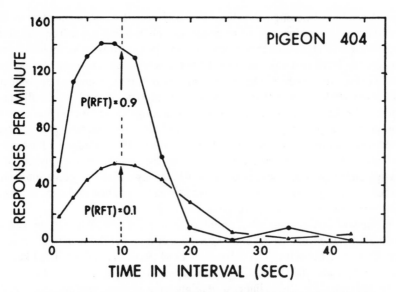

FIG. 3.2.   Response rate of a pigeon as a function of time since the trial began and probability that the first peck after 10 sec is followed by reinforcement. From Catania (1970).

Response and outcome.   A temporal regularity between a response and an experimenter-controlled reinforcement occurs in studies of delay of reinforcement. In these studies the latency of a response increases with the interval between response and reinforcement. For example, a rat in a straight alley takes longer to leave the start box if the interval between its reaching the goal box and being given the reinforcement is increased (Logan, 1960). This is normally considered to be due to a reduction in the amount of learning or motivation, but it is possible that the performance reflects timing of the response-outcome interval. Similarly, in studies of delay of punishment, the effectiveness of an electric shock is inversely related to the time between response and punisher (Church, 1969).

A temporal regularity between a response and an experimenter-controlled reinforcement also occurs in Sidman avoidance. In one standard condition, a lever response of a rat guarantees a 20-sec interval without shock. The response rate increases as a function of time, and it is related to the duration of the shock-free interval (Sidman, 1966). In avoidance learning, the mean latency of an avoidance response is proportional to the interval between the conditioned stimulus and the unconditioned stimulus (Church, Brush, & Solomon, 1956). This procedure involves both temporal regularity between stimulus and experimenter-controlled reinforcement as well as between response and experimenter-controlled reinforcement.

A temporal regularity between a response and a subject-controlled reinforcement occurs in studies of differential reinforcement of long-latency (DRL) responses (Wilson & Keller, 1953). If the first response after a wait of T sec is followed by reinforcement, the maximum of the distribution of interresponse times is near the time of reinforcement. The timing that occurs with the DRL schedule is clearer when the data are plotted in terms of the response rate as a function of time since the last response.

A temporal regularity in the duration of a response and a subject-controlled reinforcement also leads to accurate time production. A response can be described in terms of its attributes, such as force, location, topography, and duration. The duration of a response, like other attributes, can be selected by differential reinforcement. That is, if a lever response of a rat is reinforced only if it is longer than some duration (.4, .8, 1.6, 3.2, or 6.4 sec), response duration increases in a proportional manner (Platt, Kuch, & Bitgood, 1983). If the flight of a homing pigeon from one perch to another is reinforced only if the pigeon remained on the first perch at least for some criterion duration, the pigeon will learn to stay on the perch for an extended period of time. (Lejeune & Jasselette, 1986). The accuracy of time production is better for some responses than others. Homing pigeons produced more accurate times of sitting on a perch than of spaced responding on a treadle.

Outcome and outcome.   A temporal regularity between experimenter-controlled reinforcements occurs in fixed-time schedules of reinforcement. In a fixed-time schedule of reinforcement, there is a constant time between successive reinforcements. The behavior of the animal is recorded but it has no effect on the occurrence of the reinforcement. Typically, behavior changes in a regular way as the time to the next reinforcer approaches. This procedure has also been called temporal conditioning (Pavlov, 1927). If food powder (an unconditioned stimulus) is placed in the mouth of a food-deprived dog, salivation (an unconditioned response) occurs. If the food powder is presented at regular intervals, for example every 30 min, salivation continues to occur when the food powder is presented. Thus, food powder continues to be an unconditioned stimulus and salivation continues to be an unconditioned response. But, in addition, with a regular presentation of the unconditioned stimulus, salivation also begins prior to the presentation of the unconditioned stimulus. This defines some time interval as the conditioned stimulus and the anticipatory salivation as the conditioned response. Research in Pavlov's laboratory (Dmitriev & Kochigina, 1959; Pavlov, 1927) suggested that the conditioned response to time was formed more rapidly when time was the only stimulus than when time was confounded with an auditory stimulus. The investigator, Feokritova, assumed this was because the strong auditory stimulus overshadowed the weaker temporal stimulus.

When food is delivered at fixed intervals to a pigeon independent of its behavior, the pigeon develops stereotypical activity. One interpretation is that responses that happen to occur shortly before the delivery of the food are strengthened by the food and, thus, are more likely to occur again. Such stereotypical acts could be called superstitious (Skinner, 1948). Some of the responses appear to be related to the occurrence of the last reinforcer, some occur between reinforcers, and some occur near the time that the next reinforcer is expected (Staddon & Simmelhag, 1971). The activity of the pigeon increases and then decreases in the interval between successive reinforcements. As shown in Fig. 3.3, the function relating the proportion to the total activity to the proportion of the interval is approximately the same for intervals of 24, 60, and 120 sec (Killeen, Hanson, & Osborne, 1978).

Presentation of an electric shock at regular temporal intervals leads to a temporal gradient of responding. For example, a food-deprived rat can be trained to make a lever response that is reinforced on a 1-min random interval schedule of reinforcement. On such a schedule, on the average of once a minute, the next lever press of the rat will be followed by food. The probability of food being primed at any instant is a constant, so the time between successive primings is an exponential waiting-time distribution, and the response rate is relatively constant. Then an aversive stimulus (an electric shock of moderate intensity) is presented regularly at 60-sec intervals. After exposure to this shock, the response rate of the rat was rapid immediately after the shock and then it decreased in a regular manner (LaBarbera & Church, 1974). This observation alone is insufficient to demonstrate that the rats were responsive to the time interval between shocks. It is possible that they merely reacted to the shock with a burst of responses that

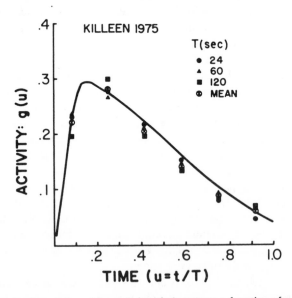

FIG. 3.3. Proportion of the activity of pigeons as a function of proportion of the interval between successive presentations of food for intervals of 24, 60, and 120 sec. From Gibbon (1977) as based on Killeen (1975).

gradually decreased as a function of time from the last shock. To rule out this possibility, the performance of the rats with fixed 1-min intervals between shocks were compared with the performance of rats with fixed 2-min intervals between shocks. The response rate of the rats with regular shocks every 2 min was also rapid immediately after the shock and then it decreased in a regular manner. If the rats on the 1- and 2-min fixed schedules of shock were merely reacting to each shock with an increase in response rate that gradually decayed in time, the two functions would be identical when plotted in terms of number of seconds since the shock occurred. In fact, the two functions were similar when plotted in terms of the proportion of the fixed interval between shocks. This is one of many examples of what may be called "the superposition result." It suggests that the performance of the rats was controlled not simply by the occurrence of the shocks but by the interval between successive shocks. And it suggests that the relevant time interval is not seconds but proportion of the interval.

The temporal gradients of responding that are observed when the aversive stimulus is presented at regular temporal intervals are not present when the aversive stimulus is presented at irregular intervals (LaBarbera & Church, 1974). In fact, if shocks were presented at random intervals that averaged 1 min (exponentially distributed waiting times), the response rate between successive shocks was relatively constant. The shock level necessary to produce intermediate levels of response suppression with random shocks was much lower than the shock level necessary to produce intermediate levels of response suppression with fixed shocks. This is consistent with the results that have shown that unpredictable shocks are more aversive than predictable ones (e.g., Maier, Seligman, & Solomon, 1969).

A temporal regularity between subject-controlled reinforcements occurs in fixed-interval schedules in free-responding situations. In such a schedule, food follows the first response after some fixed interval. Under some conditions, the response rate on individual trials appears to increase gradually throughout the interval (Dews, 1970; Skinner, 1938), but often there is an abrupt transition from a relatively constant low response rate at the beginning of the interval to a relatively high rate toward the end of the interval (Schneider, 1969). This pattern has been called the break-run pattern, and the location of the abrupt transition appears to be about two-thirds of the interval, for fixed intervals between 16 and 512 sec.

Summary

Studies of time perception and production demonstrate that animals are sensitive to the durations of stimuli and to the time intervals between stimuli, responses, and outcomes. The examples in this section came from many experimental procedures and several species. Although most of the research has been conducted with rats and pigeons, some studies of timing have been conducted with many other species (Richelle & Lejeune, 1984). In the range of seconds to minutes, most investigators have been more impressed by the similarities than the differences among species in their time perception and production.

Time as an Attribute of Stimuli and Responses

In time perception experiments, time is an *attribute* of the stimulus, not a stimulus. Visual, auditory, and tactile stimuli may be described, in part, by their durations, but a duration without reference to some modality cannot be a stimulus. Thus, time is not coordinate with vision, audition, or touch. Durations are more closely related to attributes such as frequency, number, location, and intensity. Stimuli that differ in only one attribute are perceived to be similar. In the case of frequency, duration, number, location, and intensity, this is known as "generalization." In the case of modality, it is known as "cross-modal transfer." Evidence for generalization comes from experiments in which a particular response occurs in the presence of a stimulus and a slightly less strong response occurs in the presence of a stimulus that differs in one attribute. This leads to frequency generalization, duration generalization, number generalization, location generalization, or intensity generalization, depending upon the attribute that is changed. If a similar response occurs when the modality is changed, cross-modal transfer occurs.

There is substantial evidence that animals learn the duration of a signal independent of its modality(Meck & Church, 1982; Roberts, 1982). This is cross-modal transfer of duration. For example, rats that learned to make a left response after a 2-sec noise and a right response after an 8-sec noise were more likely to make a left response after a 2-sec light and a right response after an 8-sec light. Duration was separable from the stimulus modality.

II. TYPES OF EXPLANATIONS OF TIMING BEHAVIOR

Our goal is to explain animal timing, both time perception and production. First, it is useful to consider the meaning of the term "explanation." (This section is based on Church, 1985.) Hempel (1965) wrote that an explanation is an answer to a question about why a particular empirical statement is true. The explanation is a deduction of predictions from various facts and laws.

Explanation and the organization of a research report

An article that describes the results of an experimental study in psychology normally has separate sections that correspond to these three parts of an explanation. (See Table 3.1.) Such articles are normally written in a stylized manner, following the Publication Manual of the American Psychological Association

TABLE 3.1
Correspondence of Parts of a Report With Parts of an Explanation

Explanation	Report
Facts	Methods
Laws	Discussion
Prediction	Results

(1983). Following an introduction, this style manual requires that articles have three separate sections for Methods, Results, and Discussion. Most sentences can be unambiguously assigned to one of these sections.

The Methods section contains sentences about what was done: a description of the subjects, apparatus, procedure, and data analysis. It corresponds to the facts of an explanation. The Discussion section may be used for many purposes: to summarize the results, make general conclusions, qualify the results and conclusions, and to compare them to those of others. It is a place to suggest applications of the results and to propose research that should be conducted in the future. In addition, it may contain "if...then" propositions in which some antecedent statements correspond to statements in the Method section and some consequent statements correspond to statements in the Results section. If the discussion section contains such propositions, the article includes an attempt to explain the results. The Results section contains sentences about what was found. It corresponds to the predictions of an explanation.

Thus, from the facts in the methods section and the laws in the discussion section, predictions are generated by standard inference rules, and the predictions are compared to the obtained results. The results that correspond to the predictions are explained.

Types of Explanations

Three types of explanations are considered: behavioristic, biological, and psychological. All of them deal with the same input (the method of the experiment or facts of the explanation), and all of them deal with the same output (the results of the experiment or the predictions of the explanation). They differ on the basis for making the deductions. That is, they differ in the discussion of the experiments or the laws of the explanation. The behavioristic laws will be general principles. The biological laws will be process models with physiological mechanisms to account for the input-output regularities. The psychological laws will be process models with mental mechanisms to account for the input-output regularities.

These three types of explanations do not exhaust the alternatives, but they are the ones that are most fully developed. Some process models may be purely formal without specific identification with either mental or physiological mechanisms. One major type of explanation that has not been sufficiently developed to account for animal timing is the historical. This includes explanations in terms of individual development through maturation, or of species development through evolutionary and genetic mechanisms.

Evaluation of an Explanation

The explanations of animal timing are currently being developed, and they are far from a completed state. There are two bases for evaluating an explanation in psychology. Some criteria depend only on formal aspects of the theory and depend not at all on the data; some refer to the predictive value of the theory.

Formal characteristics of an explanation.   The explanation should be clear, internally consistent, and simple. Not all explanations of animal timing are clear. Ambiguity is a defense against refutation and it provides versatility. But an explanation that is not clear cannot be further evaluated. A clear explanation can be checked for any contradictions and then compared with alternatives with respect to simplicity. A simple theory contains few concepts and principles, and few parameters to be estimated by the data. The principles should be reasonable, and they should not involve higher mental processes if a lower one is sufficient (Morgan, 1894). Simplicity can sometimes be in conflict with the predictive characteristics and, in such cases, the choice between explanations is a matter of personal preference.

Predictive characteristics of an explanation.   The explanation should be testable, accurate, and general. It is necessary to be able to identify an objective measure for each concept and to develop the implications of the theory with direct calculation or computer simulations rather than with verbal arguments which often contain omissions, ambiguities, incompatible propositions, or other flaws that are clearly revealed by calculation or simulation. In a comparison of the predictions of the theory to actual results, it is desirable if the theory accounts for the quantitative results, not simply the direction of the differences. The theory should account for a high proportion of the variance and there should be no systematic deviation of the observations from the theory. The theory should account for a large number of different facts, not simply many repetitions of the same fact. Parameter values should remain constant in different experimental procedures. In many cases the data are consistent with more than one theoretical explanation. In fact, there may always be alternative explanations for any experimental observation. With additional experimental results, however, the constraints on an adequate theory increase. It is much more difficult to devise alternative explanations for multiple results than for a single result. One sign that a theoretical analysis is likely to be good is when it is generally applicable and accounts for the currently known facts. Another is when current theory precedes results it accurately predicts, especially surprising ones.

III. BEHAVIORISTIC EXPLANATIONS OF ANIMAL TIMING BEHAVIOR

General Characteristics of a Behavioristic Explanation

A behavioristic explanation, as the term is used here, is the application of input-output analysis to the study of behavior. This approach has been essential for progress in all the empirical sciences. It is necessary to identify critical observations to be explained (the dependent variables), to identify conditions that affect these dependent variables (the independent variables), to establish functional relationships between the independent and dependent variables, and to establish general principles based on these functional relationships.

The input-output explanations in this section do not make any reference to an unobserved physiological process, or to an unobservable psychological or hypothetical intervening process between the input and output variables. Some psychologists believe that the attempt to postulate such inner causes has not been useful, most notably Skinner (1953). The position is as follows: Our knowledge of neural mechanisms has not advanced to the point that is useful for the explanation of behavior. And while biological analysis has not yet provided much useful information, mental mechanisms never will be able to do so. If a statement about a psychological process or a hypothetical intervening process is meaningful, it can be restated in terms of the behavior to which it refers. Thus, psychic causes of behavior may be regarded to be "merely redundant descriptions" (Skinner, 1953).

Superposition

In time perception equal duration ratios are approximately equally discriminable, but equal duration differences are not. For example, the discriminability of 1 sec vs. 2 sec (a ratio of 2 and a difference of 1 sec) is approximately equal to the discriminability of 8 sec vs. 16 sec (a ratio of 2) and it is much greater than the discriminability of 8 sec vs. 9 sec (a difference of 1 sec). In one experiment, rats were trained to press a left lever following a 2-sec stimulus and a right level following an 8-sec stimulus (Church & Deluty, 1977). Testing began with half the trials the same as during training and the remaining trials were unreinforced trials with stimuli of intermediate durations. This procedure is closely related to the one shown in Fig. 3.1, except that there was no differential reinforcement for a particular response to the intermediate duration stimuli. Although rats may be trained to divide a stimulus continuum at an arbitrary duration, how the rats classified these intermediate duration stimuli without differential reinforcement provides information about the apparent duration of these stimuli. On successive blocks of sessions the rats were trained on other pairs of stimulus durations (1 vs. 4 sec, 2 vs. 8 sec, 3 vs. 12 sec, and 4 vs. 16 sec). The proportion of "long" responses (responses on the right lever) is shown as a function of stimulus duration in logarithmic units in Fig. 3.4. There are three important features of this figure. First, the psychophysical functions for the different stimulus ranges are very similar when plotted as a function of relative stimulus duration, but very different when plotted as a function of absolute stimulus duration. This has been called the superposition result, and it occurs under many conditions. Second, the duration the rats classified as long half the time (the point of indifference) was approximately at the middle of a logarithmic scale between the trained durations (the geometric mean) and much below the arithmetic mean. The subjective middle has often been found to be approximately at the geometric mean. Third, the psychophysical function was more symmetrical with signal duration on a logarithmic scale than on an arithmetic scale.

When plotted with respect to absolute time (seconds), the point of indifference and the slopes of the psychophysical functions (a measure of sensitivity to time) varied. But, when plotted with respect to relative time (seconds divided by the reinforced short duration), the points of indifference and the slopes of the psychophysical functions were relatively constant. The statement that a dependent variable (proportion long responses) is not related to an independent variable (range of signals) on an absolute time scale contains less information than a statement that the dependent variable is related to the independent variable on a relative time scale. Two functions may differ in many ways, but they can be identical only in one way.

Time production also is described more simply in terms of relative than absolute time. In a fixed-interval schedule of reinforcement the response rate of pigeons relative to the maximum response rate is about the same at different porportions of the interval, for intervals of 30, 300, and 3000 sec (Dews, 1970); when shocks were presented at fixed times, the lever response rate of rats were about the same at different proportions of the interval, for intervals of 60 and 120 sec; in an avoidance schedule the probability of a response being longer than a particular time was approximately the same for responses that delay shock by 5, 10, 15,

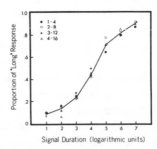

FIG. 3.4.   Mean proportion of long responses as a function of signal duration for signal ranges from 1-4, 2-8, 3-12, and 4-16 sec. Signal duration is drawn in relative logarithmic units. From Church and Deluty (1977).

or 20 sec. To obtain the superposition result, it is sometimes necessary to subtract a small constant from all times before converting to ratios. This was done in the third panel of Fig. 3.5, and it probably represents a fixed latency to begin timing. In other cases, to obtain the superposition result it is necessary to divide by the time of the maximum response (subjective time) rather than the time of the reinforced response (physical time).

Specific experiments are explained as an instance of more general principles, such as the subjective middle is at the geometric mean and the ratio of the standard deviation to the mean is approximately constant (Weber's law). Such principles can be deduced from psychological process model, such as Scalar Timing Theory.

IV. BIOLOGICAL EXPLANATIONS OF TIMING BEHAVIOR

Characteristics of a Biological Explanation

A biological explanation, as the term is used here, involves the use of intervening brain mechanisms. These include concepts from anatomy, physiology, and neuropharmacology. Biological explanations, like behavioristic explanations, are based on objective measures of input and output. In both cases, the input consists of current conditions of stimulation and past experience and in both cases the output consists of behavior. In addition, in a biological explanation, the effects of the input on brain structures and processes and the interrelationships among

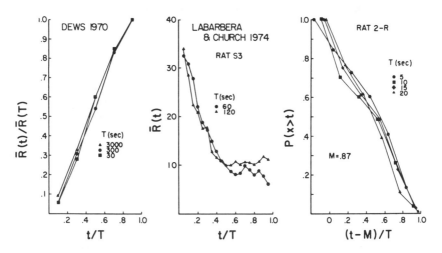

FIG. 3.5.   Three examples of superposition, as described in the text. From Gibbon (1977).

brain processes are identified. Both types of explanations can be tested by an examination of the behavioral results. In addition, the physical nature of the anatomical parts and their electrical and chemical activity makes it possible to test some aspects of a biological explanation more directly. Recording, stimulation, and lesioning are the main methods. They may be done either chemically or electrically and they may be done either at large or small areas of the brain.

Neuropharmacology

Dopamine. A phasic shift in a temporal discrimination function is one that occurs immediately on the application of the treatment, that is no longer present after repeated exposure to the treatment, and that reappears to an equal extent but in the opposite direction immediately when the treatment is removed. Dopaminergic treatments often result in phasic shifts in a temporal discrimination function.

In a time production procedure, a differential reinforcement of low rate procedure, the first response after a fixed period of nonresponding is reinforced. This leads to an increase in the probability of interresponse times greater than the fixed time. Amphetamine and related drugs, such as methamphetamine, shift the distribution of interresponse times to the left. (See Maricq, Roberts, & Church, 1981, for a list of references.) That is, the short interresponse times are relatively more frequent and the long interesponse times are less frequent. To understand why there is a relationship between a particular biological manipulation and behavioral outcome, it is useful to understand what it is that the behavior measures. The leftward shift may be related to an increase in clock speed produced by amphetamine, and that possibility is discussed further in the section on psychological explanations. There are other possibilities. For example, at low doses amphetamine increases response rate, and an increase in the response rate would also produce a leftward shift in the function.

In another time production procedure, a fixed interval procedure, the first reponse after a fixed period is reinforced. Amphetamine leads to an increase in response rate early in the interval. As in the case of the leftward shift in the differential reinforcement of low rate procedure described in the paragraph above, to understand why there is a relationship between a biological manipulation and a behavioral outcome, it is useful to understand what the behavior measures. It may be that the increase in responding early in the interval is related to an increase in clock speed produced by amphetamine, but again there are other possibilities. At low doses amphetamine may reduce inhibition and a reduction of inhibition would increase response rate early in the interval.

The use of a time perception procedure, with qualitatively different responses to indicate stimulus duration, avoids some of the interpretive problems of measures from time production procedures. Methamphetamine shifted the psychophysical function relating the percentage of long responses to signal duration to the left about 10% (Maricq et al. 1981). This percentage was approximately constant for different stimulus ranges (1 vs. 4, 2 vs. 8, and 4 vs. 16 sec).

Methamphetamine was found to produce an immediate leftward shift in the psychophysical function relating percentage long response to the physical duration of the signal. This effect was eliminated after further training under the drug, and termination of chronic methamphetamine produced an immediate rightward shift in the psychophysical function. (See upper left panel of Fig. 3.6.)

Stimulant drugs, like amphetamine and methamphetamine, increase the level of dopamine in the synaptic cleft by increasing the release of dopamine and inhibiting its reuptake. But they also have many other effects. To determine whether or not the dopaminergic effects are responsible for the phasic leftward shift, more selective drugs will need to be used.

If an increase in the effective level of dopamine produces a phasic leftward shift in temporal discrimination functions, it is plausible that a neuroleptic (like haloperidol) that blocks postsynaptic dopamine receptors would produce a phasic rightward shift. This has been found in temporal discrimination experiments (Maricq & Church, 1983; Meck, 1983). That is, haloperidol produced an immediate rightward shift in the psychophysical function relating perceived duration (percent long response) to the physical duration of a signal; this effect was eliminated after further training under the drug; and the termination of chronic

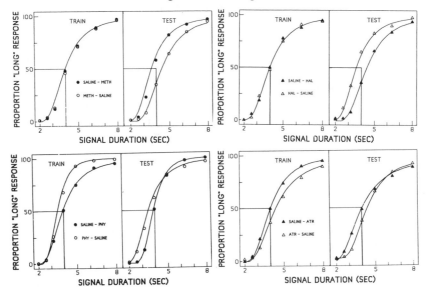

FIG. 3.6.   Median proportion long responses as a function of signal duration during the last three sessions of training and the first three sessions of testing. The treatments were saline, methamphetamine (METH), haloperidol (HAL), physostigmine (PHY) and atropine (ATR). The drug used during training is listed before the hyphen and the drug used during testing is listed after the hyphen. From Meck (1983).

haloperidol produced an immediate leftward shift in the psychophysical function. (See upper right panel of Fig. 3.6.) When the effectiveness of five different neuroleptics was compared, the dose necessary to produce a rightward shift of 15–20% was closely related to the binding affinity of the neuroleptic to the dopmine D_2 receptor (Meck, 1986). Of course, each of these drugs has multiple effects so that experiments with more selective drugs would be desirable to test the dopaminergic interpretation of the change in clock speed.

Nutrients, as well as drugs, can modify brain neurotransmitter levels (Wurtman, Hefti, & Melamed, 1980). In one experiment, rats were maintained on a balanced diet with an added source of protein or carbohydrate 20 min prior to testing to determine whether this would produce phasic shifts. A protein snack produced a phasic leftward shift and a carbohydrate snack produced a phasic rightward shift (Meck & Church, 1987b). The mechanism through which dietary protein and carbohydrate differentially affect brain neurotransmitters is controversial.

Acetylcholine.   A chronic shift in a temporal discrimination function is one that occurs gradually after training under application of the treatment, that remains as long as the training under treatment continues, and that is gradually eliminated when training without treatment is given.

Drugs that differentially affect central cholinergic systems, such as physostigmine and atropine, produce chronic shifts in both time perception and time production experiments (Meck, 1983; Meck & Church, 1987a). Physostigmine, an anticholinesterase that inhibits the acetylcholine degrading enzyme thus increasing the amount of transmitter in the synaptic cleft, shifted the psychophysical function relating the probability of a long response to stimulus duration to the left. (See lower left panel of Fig. 3.6.) Atropine, a drug that blocks the postsynaptic acetylcholine receptors, shifted the psychophysical function relating probability of a long response to stimulus duration to the right. (See lower right panel of Fig. 3.6.)

Physostigmine administered intraperitoneally to rats shifted peak times chronically leftward on the time scale in a dose-dependent fashion (0, .01, .03, and .09 mg/kg). Neostigmine, an anticholinesterase that does not readily cross the blood-brain barrier, did not produce this effect. Atropine administered intraperitoneally shifted peak times chronically rightward on the time scale in a dose-dependent fashion (0, .05, .15, and .45 mg/kg). Methyl-atropine, a cholinergic receptor blocker that does not readily cross the blood-brain barrier, did not produce this effect (Meck & Church, 1987a).

Dietary intake of choline can lead to an increase in brain choline concentrations and probably an enhancement of acetylcholine release (Wurtman et al., 1980). In one experiment, rats were maintained on a balanced diet with an added choline snack 20 min prior to testing (Meck & Church, 1987b). This produced a chronic leftward shift in the temporal discrimination function similar to that produced by physostigmine.

Drugs that affect the central cholinergic system, such as physostigmine and atropine, have effects on timing other than the chronic shift of the function. Physostigmine increased the speed of acquisition of the temporal discrimination and atropine decreased it (Meck, 1983). Physostigmine decreased the variability of performance relative to a saline control group and atropine increased it (Meck & Church, 1987a). Atropine also changed the stimulus that is used for timing when a gap in the signal occurs. After rats had learned to time a signal with a peak procedure, some signals were presented with gaps. No reinforcement was available on trials in which there were gaps in the signal. For example, there might be 10 sec of signal, a 5-sec gap, and then a continuation of the signal. The behavior of saline conrol rats was controlled by the total signal duration— they had a maximum response rate approximately 5 sec later than usual with a 5-sec gap. Under the same conditions, the behavior of the rats with atropine was controlled only by the duration of the signal following the gap—they had a maximum response rate approximately 15 sec later than usual with a 10 sec signal prior to a 5-sec gap. (Olton, Meck, & Church, 1987).

Other neurochemicals.   There are many other neurotransmitters and the effects of most of them on timing are unknown either singly or in combination. The effect of various neuropeptides are also unknown, although vasopressin has been found to act in many ways in a manner similar to physostigmine (Meck, 1983; Meck, Church, & Wenk, 1986). Application of the neurochemicals to localized parts of the brain permits the use of substances that do not readily cross the blood-brain barrier and they can also provide more detailed knowledge.

Neuroanatomy

Nigrostriatal pathway.   Dopaminergic cell bodies in the substantia nigra project to the caudate nucleus, and they are presumably involved in phasic shifts of the timing functions. Electrical stimulation of the pathway, the same one that is a prominent location for brain reinforcement, leads to a phasic leftward shift in the timing functions (Meck, 1988). This pathway is also critical for motor performance, so there is an intimate connection between timing, reinforcement, and movement.

Cholinergic pathways.   The basal forebrain cholinergic system is often divided into two subcomponents. One of these is the nucleus basalis magnocellularis (NBM) which contains cholinergic cell bodies that project to terminal fields in the cerebral cortex; another is the medial septal area (MSA) which contains cholinergic cell bodies that project to terminal fields in the hippocampus. In temporal discrimination tasks by rats, these anatomically distinct acetylcholine pathways have different behavioral functions. Lesions produced by an excitotoxin, ibotenic acid, were placed in the NBM and MSA, and physical lesions were placed in the frontal cortex (FC), a target area of fibers arising from the NBM, and in the fimbria fornix, the pathway for fibers from the MSA to the hippocampus. The time of maximum response rate of control rats with sham lesions remained at approximately at the time of scheduled reinforcement (40s), but the maximum response rate of rats with lesions in the NBM or frontal cortex gradually increased to be reliably later than the time of scheduled reinforcement. In contrast, the maximum response rate of rats with lesions in the MSA or fimbria fornix gradually decreased to be reliably earlier than the time of scheduled reinforcement (Meck, Church, Wenk, & Olton, 1988).

When a gap in the signal was introduced after a signal had begun, rats with control operations shifted the time of their maximum response rate about the duration of the gap. The time of the maximum response rate of rats with a radiofrequency lesion of the fimbria fornix increased about the duration of the gap plus the signal duration prior to the gap (Meck, Church, & Olton, 1984; Olton, Meck, & Church, 1987). The lesion produced a change in the controlling variable: for normal rats it was the time before plus time after a gap in a signal, but for rats with fimbria fornix lesions it was only the time after a gap in the signal. Rats with an ibotenic acid lesion of the medial septal area (MSA), were similar to rats with a radiofrequency lesion of the fimbria fornix. Rats with an ibotenic acid lesion of the nucleus basalis magnocellularis (NBM) were similar to rats with an aspiration lesion of the frontal cortex (FC) on this measure (Meck et al., 1988). A psychological explanation can contribute to the understanding of the change in the controlling variable in signals with gaps produced by biological manipulations.

Rats were trained on a 20-sec peak procedure with one stimulus (e.g., white noise) and a 10-sec peak procedure with a different signal (e.g., light). Then, on some trials, they were presented in a partially overlapping manner. For example, on one trial the 20-sec signal would begin and then, after a few seconds, the 10-sec signal would begin. By examining the response rate functions of the rats to the signals on nonreinforced trials, it was possible to determine whether or not the rats were effectively timing two asynchronously presented signals simultaneously. In timing a single stimulus, normal rats and those with NBM or frontal lesions performed equivalently well. Normal rats also did well on a simultaneous timing task, but rats with the NBM or frontal lesions timed only a single signal when two signals were present (Olton, Wenk, Church, & Meck, 1988).

One general conclusion is that drugs and other manipulations affecting the dopaminergic system produce phasic shifts in timing functions and that drugs and other manipulations affecting the cholinergic system produce chronic shifts in timing function. The understanding of the basis for the distinction between phasic and chronic shifts, and some of the other behavioral effects of biological manipulations, require psychological explanation.

V. PSYCHOLOGICAL EXPLANATIONS
OF TIMING BEHAVIOR

Characteristics of a Psychological Explanation

A psychological explanation, as the term is used here, involves the use of intervening mental mechanisms. These include processes of perception, attention, memory, motivation, and decision. Psychological explanations of behavior, like biological explanations, involve intervening concepts between input and output. In a psychological explanation, the intervening concepts are mental structures. Each of them is characterized by properties and by relationships with other structures.

Current psychological explanations contain concepts of clock, working memory, reference memory, and comparator. (See Fig. 3.7.) The clock is divided into three parts: a pacemaker that is a source of relatively regular pulses, a switch that can be open or closed to gate the transfer of pulses from the pacemaker to the accumulator, and an accumulator that integrates and holds the sum of the pulses. Working memory is a storage location for information that is temporarily relevant; reference memory is a storage location for storage for information that is more generally relevant. The comparator receives input from the current duration (accumulator or working memory) and from past durations (reference memory). On the basis of a comparison between these values, the output is a response decision.

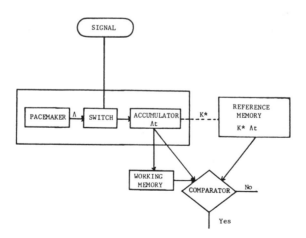

FIG. 3.7. A psychological model of timing with a clock (containing pacemaker, switch, and accumulator), working memory, reference memory, and a comparator. The pacemaker rate is Λ pulses per sec, and the memory storage constant is K^*. From Church (1984).

For time perception, the duration of a stimulus can be compared to one or more remembered durations. For example, in temporal generalization, if a particular response is reinforced following a stimulus of one duration and not following stimuli of longer or shorter durations, a representation of the duration in the accumulator is stored in reference memory. On a given trial, when a stimulus is presented for some duration, a representation of this duration is held in the accumulator, compared to the representation of the reinforced duration in reference memory and, if it is close enough, the response is made. In temporal discrimination, if one response is reinforced following a stimulus of one duration and a different response is reinforced following a stimulus of a different duration, representations of the two durations are stored in reference memory. On a given trial, when a stimulus is presented for some duration, a representation of this duration is held in the accumulator and compared to the representation of the reinforced durations in reference memory. If one of the two is close enough, that response is made; if both are close enough, one basis for resolving the conflict would be to respond to the one that is closer; if neither is close enough, one basis for continuing with new trials would be to choose one or the other according to a possibly biased random process. In the Time Left procedure, an animal has the choice between the remaining time in one stimulus or a fixed time in a second stimulus (Gibbon & Church, 1981). The animal compares the difference between a representation of a remembered duration and a duration in the accumulator, and a representation of a second remembered duration and makes the response corresponding to the shorter interval.

Clock

A clock is an instrument that measures time so, by definition, all clocks change in a regular way with time. The value of the clock is that it translates a hard-to-read input into an easy-to-read output. An animal may possess some kind of internal clock to discriminate the time of occurrence of stimuli that occur at predictable times and to respond at appropriate times. One problem is to determine the properties of the clock. A consideration of physical clocks (Landes, 1983) can contribute to the understanding of the properties of the internal clock that animals use for time perception and the timing of responses.

A sundial consists of a rigidly mounted pointer and a labeled dial. The input to a sundial is the location of the sun and the output is the location of a shadow on the dial. The output is available only when the input is available, and this excludes nighttime and periods of cloudiness. Unlike a sundial, the internal clock is not dependent upon an external driving stimulus.

A water clock (clepsydra) has an accumulation process, as well as an input and an output. The input to a water clock is a source of water in one container, and the accumulation process is the height of the water in a second container. The output can either be read from a dial calibrated in terms of the height of the water in the second container, or a float can be used with a rod attached to a geared wheel that can be read. The main problem in the design of an accurate water clock is to keep the driving energy source at a relatively fixed height and temperature so that the speed of the clock will be relatively constant. Sand clocks have similar problems, although the ones designed to time only fixed durations (like a 3-min egg timer) do not require a constant speed. An internal clock should have a relatively constant speed regardless of changes in the environment.

Mechanical clocks use digital, rather than analog, input. Unlike premechanical clocks (sundials, water clocks, and sand clocks), the input to a mechanical clock is discrete pulses from a pacemaker. The principle of the earlier clocks was to measure the amount of a continuous variable, while the principle of the mechanical clock is to count the number of discrete pulses. In any mechanical clock it is possible to identify a source of energy, a pacemaker, transmission of pulses, inhibition of transmission of pulses, maintenance of pacemaker, and output. Sources of energy that have been used are gravity, spring, and electricity. The process consists of transmission, inhibition of transmission, and maintenance of the pacemaker with escapement mechanisms. The output consists of dials that can be read or distinctive sounds or movements. Quartz clocks have now superseded the mechanical ones. They are less expensive, more rugged, and they have more versatile outputs. Although they are based on an entirely different technology, they have no new conceptual parts. The input consists of a source of energy (a battery) and a pacemaker (a quartz crystal); the process consists of an accumulation process; and the output consists of auditory and visual signals.

An internal clock used by an animal for interval timing may consist of three parts: a pacemaker to generate pulses, a switch to control whether or not the pulses are stored, and an accumulator to store the pulses. The properties of the internal clock are similar to those in a standard stopwatch (Church, 1984; Roberts, 1983; Roberts & Church, 1978; Roberts & Holder, 1984).

If the rate of the pacemaker were increased, the animal would expect an event early; if the rate of the pacemaker were decreased, the animal would expect an event late. This may contribute to the understanding of the phasic leftward and rightward shifts produced by drugs that affect dopamine metabolism. Drugs that increase the amount of dopamine in the synaptic cleft (such as methamphetamine) increase clock speed; those that block postsynaptic dopamine receptors (such as haloperidol) decrease clock speed.

The switch can be controlled by reinforcement. Thus it can transfer pulses from the pacemaker to the accumulator in the presence of one stimulus and not another. It can also operate in various modes (Roberts & Church, 1978). If there is a gap in the stimulus, the switch may be closed from the beginning to the end (run mode), the switch may be closed only during the stimulus (stop mode) or it may be closed briefly at each stimulus onset (event mode). In event mode, the interval clock can be used for number discrimination (Meck, Church, & Gibbon, 1985). Multiple clocks are apparently used to time several signals simultaneously (Meck & Church, 1984).

Working Memory

If an animal is trained on a time perception task with continuous signals and is then presented with a signal with a 5-sec gap, there are three possible rules that can be used: run, stop, or reset. That is, the clock can continue to run during the 5-sec gap; it can stop during the gap and then continue when the signal resumes; or it can start over when the signal resumes. Without specific training to the contrary, the internal clock of most normal rats stop during a gap in the signal (Roberts & Church, 1978). Thus, they report the total signal duration, rather than the time since the signal began. With specific reinforcement of the run or stop rule, rats learn to adopt the rule. Apparently, cognitive strategies as well as overt responses can be selected by differential reinforcement.

This psychological analysis now provides a way to understand the effects of cholinergic receptor blockers (like atropine) and lesions of the medial septal area to hippocampus cholinergic system on performance on trials with gaps in the signals. Control rats normally stop their clocks during a gap, but rats with reduction of this cholinergic activity reset their clocks. It is possible that they have no working memory of the duration of the signal prior to the gap and thus begin to time again after a gap.

Reference Memory

The number of pulses in the accumulator may be called the perceived time. When the perceived time is transferred into reference memory, it may be transferred with some bias, a memory storage constant that is greater or less than 1.0. (This is labeled as K^* in Fig. 3.7.) If the remembered time reliably differed from the perceived time, then an animal would regularly expect the event to occur earlier than it was scheduled (if its memory storage constant was less than 1.0), or it would regularly expect the event to occur later than it was scheduled (if its memory storage constant was greater than 1.0). Such individual differences have been observed (Church & Meck, 1988). Without a memory storage concept, the behavior of the rats that act as if they expect an event earlier or later than it regularly occurs would seem to violate the general principle of reinforcement in which differential reinforcement of responding at the correct time would eventually lead to time estimates that are accurate in the mean.

The memory storage constant provides a way to understand the effect of manipulation of the cholinergic nervous system with drugs and lesions (Church & Meck, 1988). Drugs that increase the amount of acetylcholine in the synaptic cleft (such as physostigmine) decrease the memory constant and produce a constant leftward shift; drugs that block the postsynaptic cholinergic receptors (such as atropine) increase the memory constant. Lesions of the nucleus basalis to frontal cortex cholinergic nervous system increase the memory storage constant. The memory storage constant is also related to age. It has been found to be greater when the rats were 30 months old than when they were 10 or 20 months old (Meck,

Church, & Wenk, 1986). Presumably, this is related to the reduction in the number of acetylcholine receptors in the brain.

Separation of Clock and Memory functions

Changes in clock speed produce phasic shifts in the time discrimination functions; changes in the memory constant produce chronic shifts in the time discrimination functions (Meck, 1983). Table 3.2 provides the basis for the difference based on mean values of the parameters. Five different phases of an experiment are considered: before a treatment, the initial effect of a treatment, the final effect of a treatment, the initial effect after a treatment, and the final effect after a treatment. Clock speed is represented by Λ_1 before and after treatment and by Λ_2 during the treatment; the memory constant is represented by K^*_1 before and after the treatment and by K^*_2 during the treatment. The number of pulses in the accumulator at time t is the clock speed (in pulses per sec) multiplied by t (in seconds). The number of pulses in reference memory at the time of reinforcement is the product of the number of pulses in the accumulator times the memory constant from the previous phase of the experiment. Finally, the time of the maximum response is assumed to be when the value in the accumulator equals the value in reference memory. The last column of Table 3.2 is the time (in seconds) at which the maximum response is predicted to occur.

If an independent variable affected the memory constant, but not the clock speed ($\Lambda_1 = \Lambda_2$), then the chronic pattern would occur: there is no immediate change when a treatment is begun, the effect emerges and remains as long as the treatment is administered, there is no immediate change when the treatment is terminated, but the original performance is restored and maintained indefinitely. In contrast, if an independent variable affected clock speed, but not the memory constant ($K^*_1 = K^*_2$), then the phasic pattern would occur: there is an immediate change when a treatment is begun, the effect disappears with continued treatment, there is an immediate change of equal magnitude and in the opposite direction when the treatment is terminated, and this effect disappears with continued training.

The phasic changes characteristic of changes in clock speed are related to changes in dopaminergic function; the chronic changes characteristic of changes in the memory constant are related to changes in cholinergic function.

Attention

The term "attention" is used in two different ways. General attention refers to the tendency of the animal to respond on the basis of the relevant dimension; selective attention refers to the tendency of the animal to respond differentially to one stimulus rather than another.

Although the information processing model characterizes many trials in a time

TABLE 3.2
Separation of Clock and Memory Functions

	Clock Speed	Accumulator	Memory Constant	Reference Memory	Maximum Response
Before Treatment	Λ_1	$\Lambda_1 t$	K^*_1	$K^*_1\Lambda_1 t_{rf}$	$K^*_1 t_{rf}$
During Treatment					
Initial	Λ_2	$\Lambda_2 t$	K^*_2	$K^*_1\Lambda_1 t_{rf}$	$(\Lambda_1/\Lambda_2)K^*_1 t_{rf}$
Final	Λ_2	$\Lambda_2 t$	K^*_2	$K^*_2\Lambda_2 t_{rf}$	$K^*_2 t_{rf}$
After Treatment					
Initial	Λ_1	$\Lambda_1 t$	K^*_1	$K^*_2\Lambda_2 t_{rf}$	$(\Lambda_2/\Lambda_1)K^*_2 t_{rf}$
Final	Λ_1	$\Lambda_1 t$	K^*_1	$K^*_1\Lambda_1 t_{rf}$	$K^*_1 t_{rf}$

discrimination task, on some trials the animal appears to respond independently of the signal duration. Quantitative fits of performance are often improved if it is assumed that, with some probability, the animal responds on the basis of signal duration and, on the remainder of the trials the animal responds without respect to signal duration. On these trials the animal selects the response on the basis of some constant bias (Heinemann, Avin, Sullivan, & Chase, 1969). In temporal generalization (Church & Gibbon, 1982) most of the variance was accounted for by parameters for the probability of inattention and responsiveness given attention. Selective attention to a stimulus can be produced by overall probability during a session of a stimulus from a particular modality (light or sound) or by its local probability on a trial (Meck, 1984). Presumably, an animal attends to highly probable stimuli. The latency to begin timing a light was affected by the probability of a light, but the latency to begin timing a sound was not affected by the probability of a sound. This suggests that lights to which attention is directed may be timed but that sounds are timed automatically.

Scalar Timing Theory

Scalar timing theory provides a quantitative version of the psychological explanation of animal timing. There are several sources of variance: clock, switch, memory storage, and decision. The basic assumption of scalar timing theory is that at least one of these sources of variance must be scalar and that the scalar sources of variance must be large relative to other sources of variance. A scalar source of variance is one in which the standard deviation of the process increases linearly with the mean of the process. The theory has been applied to time estimation and production experiments (Gibbon, 1977; Gibbon & Church, 1984; Gibbon, Church, & Meck, 1984) and to the preference between reinforcements scheduled to occur at different fixed or random times (Gibbon, Church, Fairhurst, & Kacelnik, 1988). The theory is still under development, but it now accounts for well over 95% of the variance in the animal timing experiments to which it has been applied.

VII. CONCLUSION

Timing is an essential component of psychological processes involved in perception, cognition, and performance. The perception of motion involves both space and time; working memory requires a separation of recent from remote experience; and locomotion involves a timed sequence of movements. For echolocation a bat must be sensitive to differences in the microsecond range; for migration some birds must be sensitive to circadian and circannual times. This chapter concentrated on timing in the range of seconds to minutes. Presumably, animals would not have this capacity if it was never of functional value. Some animals undoubtedly make use of timing in the second to minute range in foraging for food. Estimates of the value of a foraging in a particular place involves time, number, amount, and combinations of these dimensions. To avoid predators, some estimate of the time spent in a particular location is probably useful.

A functional explanation of animal timing would deal with the survival value of timing, and the evolution of timing in different species. A developmental explanation of animal timing would deal with the maturation of learning of timing that occurs in the life of an individual. This chapter has restricted itself to process explanations of animal timing. In a process explanation, the effects of input variables on output variables can be explained with general principles, biological processes, or psychological processes. Whenever it is possible to develop both a biological and a psychological explanation for the same input-output observations, there is a plausible basis for a connection between specific biological and psychological concepts. This is an empirical approach to the mind-body problem.

REFERENCES

Brown, P. L., & Jenkins, H. M. (1968). Autoshaping of the pigeon's keypeck. *Journal of the Experimental Analysis of Behavior, 11*, 1–8.

Catania, A. C. (1970). Reinforcement schedules and psychophysical judgments: A study of some temporal properties of behavior. In W. N. Schoenfeld, *The Theory of Reinforcement Schedules* (pp. 1–42). New York: Appleton-Century-Crofts.

Church, R. M. (1969). Response suppression. In B. A. Campbell & R. M. Church (Eds.), *Punishment and aversive behavior* (pp. 111–156). New York: Appleton-Century-Crofts.

Church, R. M. (1984). Properties of the internal clock. In J. Gibbon & L. G. Allan (Eds.), Timing and time perception. *Annals of the New York Academy of Sciences, 423*, 566–582.

Church, R. M. (1985). Approaches to the study of behavior: Examples from behavioral pharmacology. In F. R. Brush & J. B. Overmier (Eds.), *Affect, conditioning, and cognition: essays on the determinants of behavior* (pp. 163–182). Hillsdale, NJ: Lawrence Erlbaum Associates.

Church, R. M., & Black, A. H. (1958). Latency of the conditioned heart rate as a function of the CS-US interval. *Journal of Comparative and Physiological Psychology, 51*, 478–482.

Church, R. M., Brush, F. R., & Solomon, R. L. (1956). Traumatic avoidance learning: The effects of CS-US interval with a delayed-conditioning procedure in a free-responding situation. *Journal of Comparative and Physiological Psychology, 49*, 301–308.

Church, R. M. & Deluty, M. Z. (1977). Bisection of temporal intervals. *Journal of Experimental Psychology: Animal Behavior Processes, 1977, 3*, 216–228.

Church, R. M., & Gibbon, J. (1982). Temporal generalization. *Journal of Experimental Psychology: Animal Behavior Processes, 8*, 165–186.

Church, R. M., & Meck, R. M. (1988). Biological basis of the remembered time of reinforcement. In M. L. Commons, R. M. Church, J. Stellar, & A. R. Wagner (Eds.), *Quantitative analysis of behavior: Biological determinants of behavior* (Vol 7). Hillsdale, NJ: Lawrence Erlbaum Assoicates.

Dews, P. B. (1970). The theory of fixed-interval responding. In W. N. Schoenfeld (Ed.). *The theory of reinforcement schedules* (pp. 43–61). New York: Appleton-Century-Crofts.

Dmitriev, A. S., & Kochigina, A. M., (1959). The importance of time as a stimulus of conditioned reflex activity. *Psychological Bulletin, 56*, 106–132.

Fetterman, J. F. (1987). Same-different comparison of duration. *Animal Learning & Behavior, 15*, 403–411.

Gibbon, J. (1977). Scalar expectancy theory and Weber's Law in animal timing. *Psychological Review*, *84*, 279–325.

Gibbon, J., & Balsam, P. (1980). Spreading association in time. In C. M. Locurto, H. S. Terrace, & J. Gibbon (Eds.), *Autoshaping and conditioning theory*. New York: Academic Press.

Gibbon, J., & Church R. M. (1981). Time left: Linear versus logarithmic subjective time. *Journal of Experimental Psychology: Animal Behavior Processes*, *7*, 87–108.

Gibbon, J., & Church, R. M. (1984). Sources of variance in an information processing theory of timing. In H. L. Roitblat, T. G. Bever, & H. S. Terrace (Eds.), *Animal cognition* (pp. 465–488). Hillsdale, NJ: Lawrence Erlbaum Associates.

Gibbon, J., Church, R. M., Fairhurst, S., & Kacelnik, A. (1988). Scalar expectancy theory and choice between delayed rewards. *Psychological Review*, *95*, 102–114.

Gibbon, J., Church, R. M., & Meck, W. H. (1984). Scalar timing in memory. In J. Gibbon & L. Allan (Eds.), *Timing and time perception. Annals of the New York Academy of Sciences*, *423*, 52–77.

Griffin, D. R. (1981). *The question of animal awareness: Evolutionary continuity of mental experience*. New York: Rockefeller University Press.

Griffin D. R. (1984). *Animal thinking*. Cambridge, MA: Harvard University Press.

Heinemann, E. G., Avin, E., Sullivan, M. A., & Chase, S. (1969). Analysis of stimulus generalization with a psychophysical method. *Journal of Experimental Psychology*, *80*, 215–224.

Hempel, C. G. (1965). Aspects of scientific explanation. In C. G. Hempel (Ed.), *Scientific explanation* (pp. 331–495). New York: Free Press.

James, W. (1890). *Principles of psychology*. London: Macmillan.

Killeen, P. R. (1975). On the temporal control of behavior. *Psychological Review*, *82*, 89–115.

Killeen, P. R., Hanson, S. J., & Osborne, S. R. (1978). Arousal: Its genesis and manifestation as response rate. *Psychological Review*, *85*, 571–581.

LaBarbera, J. D., & Church, R. M. (1974). Magnitude of fear as a function of expected time to an aversive event. *Animal Learning and Behavior*, *2*, 199–202.

Landes, D. S. (1983). *Revolution in time*. Cambridge, MA: Harvard University Press.

Lejeune, H., & Jasselette, P. (1986). Accurate DRL performance in the pigeon: Comparison between perching and treadle pressing. *Animal Learning & Behavior*, *14*, 205–211.

Libby, M., & Church, R. M. (1975). Fear gradients as a function of the temporal interval between signal and aversive event in the rat. *Journal of Comparative and Physiological Psychology*, *88*, 911–916.

Logan, F. (1960). *Incentive*. New Haven: Yale University Press.

Maier, S. F., Seligman, M. E. P., & Solomon, R. L. (1969). Pavlovian fear conditioning and learned helplessness. Effects on escape and avoidance behavior of (a) the CS-US contingency and (b) the independence of the US and voluntary responding. In B. A. Campbell & R. M. Church (Eds.), *Punishment and aversive behavior* (pp. 299–342). New York: Appleton-Century-Crofts.

Maricq, A., & Church, R. M. (1983). The differential effects of haloperidol and methamphetamine on time estimation in the rat. *Psychopharmacology*, *79*, 10–15.

Maricq, A., Roberts, S., & Church, R. M. (1981). Methamphetamine and time estimation *Journal of Experimental Psychology: Animal Behavior Processes*, *9*, 171–201.

Meck, W. H. (1983). Selective adjustment of the speed of internal clock and memory processes. *Journal of Experimental Psychology: Animal Behavior Processes*, *9*, 171–201.

Meck, W. H. (1984). Attentional bias between modalities: Effect on the internal clock, memory, and decision stages used in animal time discrimination. In J. Gibbon & L. Allan (Eds.), *Timing and time perception*, New York Academy of Science, *423*, 528–541.

Meck, W. H. (1986). Affinity for the dopamine D_2 receptor predicts neuroleptic potency in decreasing the speed of an internal clock. *Pharmacology, Biochemistry & Behavior*, *25*, 1185–1189.

Meck, W. H. (1988). Internal clock and reward pathways share physiologically similar information-processing stages. In M. L. Commons, R. M. Church, J. R. Stellar, & A. R. Wagner (Eds.), *Quantitative analyses of behavior: vol 7. Biological determinants of reinforcement*. Hillsdale, NJ: Lawrence Erlbaum Associates.

Meck, W. H., & Church, R. M. (1982). Abstraction of temporal attributes. *Journal of Experimental Psychology: Animal Behavior Processes, 8*, 226–243.

Meck, W. H., & Church, R. M. (1984). Simultaneous temporal processing. *Journal of Experimental Psychology: Animal Behavior Processes, 10*, 1–29.

Meck, W. H., & Church, R. M. (1987a). Cholinergic modulation of the content of temporal memory. *Behavioral Neuroscience, 101*, 457–464.

Meck, W. H., & Church, R. M. (1987b). Nutrients that modify the speed of internal clock and memory storage processes. *Behavioral Neuroscience, 101*, 465–475.

Meck, W. H., Church, R. M., & Gibbon, J. (1985). Temporal integration in duration and number discrimination. *Journal of Experimental Psychology: Animal Behavior Processes, 11*, 591–597.

Meck, W. H., Church, R. M., & Olton, D. S. (1984). Hippocampus, time, and memory. *Behavioral Neuroscience, 98*, 3–22.

Meck, W. H., Church, R. M., & Wenk, G. L. (1986). Arginine vasopressin inoculates against age-related increases in sodium-dependent high affinity choline uptake and discrepancies in the content of temporal memory. *European Journal of Pharmacology, 130*, 327–331.

Meck, W. H., Church, R. M., Wenk, G. L., & Olton, D. S. (1988). Nucleus basalis magnocellularis and medial septal area lesions differentially impair temporal memory. *The Journal of Neuroscience, 7*, 3505–3511.

Morgan, C. L. (1894). *An introduction to comparative psychology.* London: Scott.

Olton, D. S., Meck, W. H., & Church, R. M. (1987). Separation of hippocampal and amygdaloid involvement in temporal memory dysfunctions. *Brain Research, 404*, 180–188.

Olton, D. S., Wenk, G. L., Church, R. M., & Meck, W. H. (1988). Attention and the frontal cortex as examined by simultaneous temporal processing. *Neuropsychologia, 26*, 307–318.

Pavlov, I. (1927). *Conditioned reflexes.* Oxford: Oxford University Press.

Platt, J. R., Kuch, D. O., & Bitgood, S. C. (1983). Rats' lever-press durations as psychophysical judgments of time. *Journal of the Experimental Analysis of Behavior, 19*, 239–250.

Publication Manual of the American Psychological Association. (1983). Washington: American Psychological Association.

Richelle, M., & Lejeune, H. (1984). Timing competence and timing performance. A cross-species approach. In J. Gibbon & L. Allan (Eds.), *Timing and time perception.* Annals of the New York Academy of Sciences, *423*, 254–268.

Roberts, S. (1981). Isolation of an internal clock. *Journal of Experimental Psychology: Animal Behavior Processes, 7*, 242–268.

Roberts, S. (1982). Cross modal use of an internal clock. *Journal of Experimental Psychology: Animal Behavior Processes, 7*, 242–268.

Roberts, S. (1983). Properties and function of an internal clock. In R. L. Mellgren (Ed.), *Animal cognition and behavior.* New York: North-Holland.

Roberts, S., & Church, R. M. (1978). Control of an internal clock. *Journal of Experimental Psychology: Animal Behavior Processes, 4*, 318–337.

Roberts, S., & Holder, M. (1984). The function of time discrimination and classical conditioning. In J. Gibbon & L. Allan (Eds.), *Timing and time perception.* New York Academy of Sciences, *423*, 228–241.

Roitblat, H. L. (1987). *Introduction to comparative cognition.* New York: Freeman.

Schneider, B. A. (1969). A two-state analysis of fixed-interval responding in the pigeon. *Journal of the Experimental Analysis of Behavior, 12*, 677–687.

Sidman, M. (1966). Avoidance behavior. In W. K. Honig (Ed.), *Operant behavior: Areas of research and application* (pp. 448–498). New York: Appleton-Century-Crofts.

Skinner, B. F. (1938). *The behavior of organisms.* New York: Appleton-Century-Crofts.

Skinner, B. F. (1948). "Superstition" in the pigeon. *Journal of Experimental Psychology, 38*, 168–172.

Skinner, B. F. (1953). *Science and human behavior.* New York: Macmillan.

Staddon, J. E. R., & Simmelhag, V. L. (1971). The "superstition" experiment: a reexamination of its implications for the principles of adaptive behavior. *Psychological Review, 78*, 3–43.

Stubbs, A. (1968). The discrimination of stimulus duration by pigeons. *Journal of the Experimental Analysis of Behavior, 11*, 223–238.

Tomie, A., Brooks, W., & Zito, B. (1989). Sign tracking: The search for reward. In S. B. Klein & R. R. Mowrer (Eds.), *Contemporary learning theories: Pavlovian conditioning and the status of traditional learning theory.* Hillsdale, NJ.: Lawrence Erlbaum Associates.

Watson, J. B. (1924). *Behaviorism.* Chicago: University of Chicago Press.

Williams, D. R., & Williams, H. (1969). Auto-maintenance in the pigeon: Sustained pecking despite contingent non-reinforcement. *Journal of the Experimental Analysis of Behavior, 12*, 511–520.

Wilson, M. P., & Keller, F. S. (1953). On the selective reinforcement of spaced responses. *Journal of Comparative and Physiological Psychology, 46*, 190–193.

Wurtman, R. J., Hefti, F., & Melamed, E. (1980). Precursor control of neurotransmitter synthesis. *Pharmacological Reviews, 32*, 315–332.

4 Learned Helplessness: Event Covariation and Cognitive Changes

Steven F. Maier
University of Colorado, Boulder

It has been 20 years since the learned helplessness enterprise began. It was in 1967 that Bruce Overmier and Martin Seligman first reported that dogs exposed to inescapable and unavoidable electric shocks in a Pavlov harness later failed to learn to escape and avoid shock in a shuttlebox where escape and avoidance was possible. It was also in 1967 that Seligman and I began to pursue the explanation and implications of this failure to learn and first published the learned helplessness explanation of its occurrence. These 20 years have witnessed a bewilderingly large amount of research concerning this phenomenon and theory. This research has gone in three very different directions which we have called inward, downward, and outward. First, inward to the unraveling of the basic processes involved in the phenomenon. Second, downward to the biological processes that underlie learned helplessness. Third, outward towards an understanding of the manner in which learned helplessness might contribute to an understanding of important human problems such as depression, aging, school failure, and the like.

The purpose of this chapter is not to review all of these developments. Although work on learned helplessness grew out of the study of animal learning and learning theory, much of the research and theorizing that has followed is not really germane to animal learning and learning theory and is thus beyond the scope of this volume. Instead, this chapter focuses on those aspects of learned helplessness that were important for the psychology of learning and that are still topics of study today. The chapter first describes learned helplessness and learned helplessness theory, then discusses the relationship between the assertions of learned helplessness theory and the principles of the psychology of learning current at the time it was proposed, and finally, evaluates the current status of these assertions in the context of modern learning theory.

I. WHAT IS LEARNED HELPLESSNESS?

The study of learned helplessness arose in the context of research designed to test two-process theories of avoidance learning (see Levis, 1989). The aim was to examine the relationship between Pavlovian fear conditioning and instrumental escape and avoidance learning. The desire was to examine the impact of Pavlovian CSs for electric shock on the performance of instrumental shock avoidance responding. The question was whether an independently established CS for shock would control and energize the avoidance response, thereby suggesting that Pavlovian conditioned fear is the motivator of avoidance learning. In the course of performing such experiments Overmier and Leaf (1965) noted that this sort of experiment was easy to accomplish only if the avoidance training was carried out before the Pavlovian conditioning. If the Pavlovian conditioning was conducted first the dogs were poor at learning to escape and avoid, and so the impact of the CS on avoidance responding was difficult to assess.

Of course, this is an annoying nuisance if one wants to study the effect of Pavlovian CSs on avoidance. However, we were fascinated by this nuisance and decided to study it in its own right. Pavlovian fear conditioning involves the temporal pairing of a CS such as a tone or a light with shock. Because it is Pavlovian conditioning the UCS, here electric shock, is not modifiable by the subject—it is inescapable and unavoidable. The first question was which aspect of this procedure was responsible for the dog's later inability to learn to avoid shock. The answer was that Pavlovian conditioning as such was not essential. The impairment of learning occurred even if there was no CS paired with the shock. All that was necessary was that the dog be exposed to a series of shocks and that the shocks be inescapable. If the dog was allowed to terminate each of the initial shocks by means of some response (e.g., pressing a panel with its nose while restrained in the Pavlov harness), later failure to learn to escape and avoid did not occur (Seligman & Maier, 1967).

We called this failure to learn the "learned helplessness effect," because it occurred only after exposure to shocks which the dog could do nothing to modify and so was helpless. More generally, any behavioral outcome that depends on the escapability or controllability of an aversive event rather than on exposure to the event per se has come to be called a learned helplessness effect. The explanation that we provided for this effect came to be called the learned helplessness hypothesis or theory. It was quite simple and seemed obvious. We (Maier, Seligman, & Solomon, 1969; Seligman, Maier, & Solomon, 1970) argued that when shock is inescapable the dog learns that it is unable to exert *control* over the shock by means of voluntary behavior, that the dog would expect that this would also be so in the future, and that this expectation of uncontrollability causes the failure to escape. We argued that the expectancy would do two things. First, reduce the dog's incentive to attempt to escape, thereby producing a *response initiation deficit*. Second, interfere with the learning of response-shock termination relationships, thereby producing a *cognitive deficit*.

II. WHY WAS LEARNED HELPLESSNESS IMPORTANT FOR THE PSYCHOLOGY OF LEARNING AND WHY WAS THERE A FUSS?

These ideas provoked intense controversy when they were proposed. The modern reader might have difficulty understanding why. A major reason was that the learned helplessness hypothesis conflicted with many of the traditional principles of the psychology of learning circa the late 1960s. To see this the theory will have to be explicated a bit more fully. The theory has components at three levels: (1) critical environmental conditions; (2) translation of these into expectations; and (3) psychological processes altered by these expectations. Each is discussed in turn.

The Theory

1. Control, Contiguity, and Contingency. Although it might seem obvious that organisms ought to be able to learn the degree of control that they have over environmental events, traditional S–R learning theory did not allow for this to be learned. For S–R theory motor responses were learned and their connections to stimuli strengthened by reinforcement (see Chapter 1 of this volume by Mowrer & Klein). Learning could occur only when responses occurred, and the strength of the learning of the response was governed by the frequency or probability with which reinforcement or reward followed. One conditional probability, the conditional probability of reinforcement given that a response occurred, $P(Rft/R)$, governed all of instrumental learning. However, to learn that one has no control over a reinforcer requires that the organism be sensitive to what happens when the response has *not* been made, as well as what happens when the response has occurred. The organism must be sensitive to the conditional probability of reinforcement given that the response has not been made, $P(Rft/No\ R)$, as well as $P(Rft/R)$. To learn that one has no control the organism must be sensitive to both of the probabilities and their *relationship*, because the absence of control is defined by the equality of these two probabilities. To say that one has no control is to say that the outcome is the same whether or not a response occurs. When there is no control the probability of reinforcement is not zero, the shock does go off on every trial. The crucial feature is that whatever this probability is, it is independent of the organism's behavior. It is only by comparing the value of $P(Rft/R)$ with $P(Rft/No\ R)$ that an organism could *know* that it does or does not have control. The greater the *difference* between these two probabilities the greater the degree of behavioral control.

We argued that the traditional view that instrumental learning was governed by the temporal contiguity between response and reinforcement was inadequate, and that instead the contingency or correlation between response and reinforcement was crucial. We defined contingency as the conjoint variation of $P(Rft/R)$

and P(Rft/No R). The difference between contingency and contiguity views is deeper than it might appear. The contiguity position views the organism as being trapped by momentary cooccurrences of events—if a response is followed by a reinforcer it is strengthened even if there is no *real* relation between them and the cooccurrence is only accidental. Here events that occur in the absence of the particular response under discussion have no impact on the learning of that response. In contrast, learned helplessness theory proposed that the organism performs a causal analysis and has the means to separate momentary and spurious relations from more enduring ones.

2. Representation, Expectation, and Perception.   We argued more than that the organism is sensitive to the degree of contingency between behavior and outcomes. We argued that environmental evidence about contingency or control can be transformed into a cognitive representation. It is this representation that was seen to initiate the events that cause the later behavioral consequences of exposure to inescapable shock.

Although we were vague about this process, it must involve at least two steps. First, the immediately present contingency must be registered and learned about. Second, the organism must form an expectation about future contingency or noncontingency. It is the expectation that we claimed to be the critical mediating cognitive event in learned helplessness and to be responsible for phenomena such as later failure to learn to escape.

3. Psychological Processes.   We argued that the organism's expectation that an aversive event is uncontrollable should lead to alterations in at least three psychological processes. It is these processes which were seen as directly responsible for the behavioral changes that follow exposure to uncontrollable aversive events such as inescapable shock.

   a. *Incentive Motivation.*   Learning that responding and outcomes are independent cannot by itself produce later phenomena such as failure to learn to escape. We argued that the expectation that shock cannot be controlled would alter two processes involved in the acquisition of instrumental tasks, one motivational and the other cognitive. The motivation to respond is thought to be partly determined by incentive (Mowrer, 1960), which roughly means the anticipation of reinforcement. If the motivation to respond is determined by the anticipated reward for doing so, it should be obvious that the expectation of a noncontingent relationship between response and reinforcement would undermine the motivation to respond. If responding is not expected to alter the probability of reinforcement, why try? So we proposed that exposure to inescapable shock reduces subsequent incentive to respond, thereby producing a *response initiation deficit*.

   b. *Cognition.*   We argued that exposure to inescapable shock produces a cognitive deficit in addition to alterations in response initiation processes. Here there is an interference with what the organism actually learns from exposures to relationships between its own behavior and shock termination, a change in how information concerning the learning task is processed.

The initial statements made by Seligman and I were quite vague about how this cognitive change comes about, but there are several obvious possibilities. First, previously inescapably shocked subjects may not perceive or register the contiguity between their responses and shock termination. This could happen in a number of ways that are discussed later. Alternatively, inescapably shocked subjects might accurately register the cooccurrence of their behavior and shock termination, but might not expect that the relationship will recur reliably in the future. Here, contiguity between the escape response and shock offset is noted, but the organism simply does not expect that this relationship wil be maintained on future trials—an expectational bias rather than a perceptual interference. After all, during inescapable shock particular responses must have accidentally occured at the moment of shock termination, but these relationships were never real or enduring. Performance of such a response on the next trial would, of course, not produce shock termination. Thus, why should the organism attribute significance to a *perceived* cooccurrence of responding and shock termination in the new situation?

c. *Emotion.* Finally, we argued that the experience of uncontrollability produces emotional changes—anxiety followed by depression. Learning that one has no control over aversive events was seen as first leading to anxiety and then to depression if the experience continued or became chronic (Maier & Seligman, 1976). This aspect of learned helplessness is beyond the scope of the present chapter and is not further discussed or evaluated.

The Controversy

The publication of the learned helplessness hypothesis was quickly followed by the proposal of a variety of alternative explanations for why animals exposed to inescapable shock later fail to learn to escape shock in different situations. There were two types of explanation offered—behavioral and neurochemical. The behavioral explanations all argued that

1. the subject in a learned helplessness experiment acquires a motor response during exposure to inescapable shock;

2. the presence of shock in the test situation mediates the transfer of this motor response from the inescapable shock to the test situation so that the animal now performs this response; and

3. that this motor response is incompatible with the escape response to be learned in the sense that the two responses cannot be performed at the same time.

Thus, the subject fails to learn to perform the escape response because it is performing this other motor response. Here there is only a *performance* deficit, rather than a motivational and cognitive impairment. The animal is seen as adequately motivated and perfectly able to learn, it simply does not emit the required response because it is engaged in a competing behavior. This competing behavior was generally seen as involving inactivity or the cessation of movement. The theories of this type differed among themselves with regard to the mechanism by which the competing motor response is acquired during exposure to inescapable shock. For example, perhaps it hurts more to move than to remain still during inescapable shock, thereby reinforcing inactivity (Bracewell & Black, 1974). Detailed descriptions can be found in Alloy and Seligman (1969) and Maier and Jackson (1979).

The neurochemical views most often maintained that inescapable shock is a severe stressor and depletes neurotransmitters thought to be involved in the production of movement. The inescapably shocked animal later fails to learn because it cannot move enough to meet the response requirements of the escape learning task. Weiss and his associates (e.g., Weiss, Glazer, & Pohorecky, 1975) focused on norepinephrine, while Anisman (1975) has argued for dopaminergic and cholinergic involvement as well. Although these views are at a different level of analysis than the incompatible motor response learning theories, they also argue that inescapable shock interferes with later escape learning because it affects motor processes rather than cognitive processes.

Why the Controversy

Not only were many alternative explanations offered, but the literature was soon filled with many papers attacking the other position, defending positions, etc. Why was there so much controversy about a seemingly simple idea like learned helplessness? It was because the learned helplessness hypothesis contained a number of assumptions that were incompatible with the assumptions of the then dominant S–R theories of learning. The disagreements concerning the explanation of why inescapable shock produces later failure to learn to escape shock can be seen as forming a part of the larger Cognitive versus S–R debate (see Chapter 1 in this volume by Mowrer and Klein). The alternative explanations that were offered assumed only processes contained in traditional S–R theory—the reinforcement of motor responses, generalization of these learned motor responses to situations containing similar stimuli, and the mechanical interaction of elicited motor responses.

Learned helplessness was at odds with 4 assumptions often made by S–R theory.

1. *Contiguity.* S–R theories assumed that contiguity between events is the critical relation producing learning. However, the helplessness hypothesis was phrased in terms of contingency rather than contiguity.

2. *Automatic strengthening and simplicity of the associative process.* The strengthening effect of reinforcement or contiguity was seen as being direct, in-

evitable, and independent of the cognitive processes of the organism. Performance rules which translate associations into behavior were sometimes seen as complex, but the basic hooking together process was viewed as simple. However, learned helplessness argued that learning cannot be viewed as a simple outcome of the conjunction of response and reinforcer. Rather, it held that the organism compares $P(Rft/R)$ with $P(Rft/No\ R)$. The temporal conjunction of R and Rft were not seen as sufficient to produce learning. Instead, the organism engages in a causal analysis of its' environment. Moreover, the hypothesis argued that what was learned about a conjunction of R and Rft depended on the subject's ongoing expectations.

3. *Responses.* S–R theory maintained that the organism learned motor responses and that transfer between situations was based on the mechanical interaction of motor responses. On the other hand, learned helplessness theory argued that expectations were learned and that the later failure to learn (transfer) was produced by this cognition rather than by a transfered motor response.

4. *Breadth of transfer.* Most theories assumed that what was learned about a given stimulus or response remained specific to that stimulus or response. Only stimulus or response generalization along a dimension of physical similarity allowed transfer to new situations. However, for us the expectation generalized and the expectation of response-reinforcer independence was not limited to the responses attempted in the situation. We assumed that the organism makes an inference to physically dissimilar responses after learning that a certain number are independent of shock termination.

In sum, the learned helplessness hypothesis differed from then traditional views concerning the fundamental issues of how to describe what is learned, what is learned about, and what leads to transfer. It was a *cognitive* theory proposed at a *noncognitive* time. Now its assumptions do not seem radical, but they once were. This then is learned helplessness and its place in the history of the Psychology of Learning. I turn now to a more detailed evaluation of the current status of its major assertions. How has it fared?

III. CONTIGUITY AND CONTINGENCY

As has been seen learned helplessness theory differed from traditional views by asserting that the contingency between response and reinforcer rather than their contiguity regulated instrumental learning. For learned helplessness the organism compares $P(Rft/R)$ with $P(Rft/No\ R)$, and the difference between the two determines instrumental responding. What is the evidence?

Contingency

1. Support—the empirical reality of contingency. The contingency view has two obvious requirements. First, organisms must discriminate the occurrence of reinforcing events which are and which are not dependent on their behavior. If they cannot, P(Rft/R) versus P(Rft/No R) can have no psychological impact. Second, changes in contingency must produce changes in behavior. That is, the *relationship* between the two conditional probabilities should control behavior. Here the experiment must be conducted in such a way that contiguity does not also change as the contingency is varied. Both requirements have been investigated.

a. *Discrimination.*   In an important series of experiments, Killeen (1978; Killeen & Smith, 1984) asked whether pigeons could distinguish response-dependent from response-independent outcomes. The pigeons were trained to peck a lit response key. Each peck darkened the key with a probability of .05. That is, 1 out of 20 pecks was followed by the outcome of key darkening, but the pigeon had no means to predict which peck it would be since each peck independently sampled the probability distribution. At the same time, a computer generated "computer pecks" at the same rate at which the pigeon had recently been pecking. These computer pecks were also followed by key darkening with a probability of .05. Thus, some key darkenings were dependent on the pigeon's peck, and some were independent of the pigeon's peck but rather were dependent on the computer's peck. When the key darkened, two side keys were illuminated. The pigeon's job was then to peck the left side key if its behavior had produced darkening of the center key, and the right side key if the darkening had been independent of its behavior. Correct reports were, of course, followed by food.

The pigeons were very good at this task and were able to correctly report whether or not it was their behavior that had darkened the key. A little thought will reveal that there must have been instances in which the computer peck coincided in time with the pigeon's own pecks, since the computer pecks were unconstrained by the animal's behavior. Clearly, if the two coincided exactly it would be impossible for the pigeon to make the discrimination. It is thus possible to ask precisely how good the pigeon is at this task. How close can the response-independent change be to the pigeon's own peck and still allow the pigeon to say "response-independent"? Killeen has estimated the just noticeable difference (jnd) as roughly 1/20 of a second!

b. *Behavior Varies with Contingency.*   The essence of the contingency notion is that behavior should vary with both the traditional dimension, P(Rft/R), and with the P(Rft/No R). More specifically, responses should be learned only if P(Rft/R) does not equal P(Rft/No R), and the response should be stronger the greater the difference in the probabilities. For any P(Rft/R) the response should weaken as the P(Rft/No R) increases from zero to the value of P(Rft/R). It is just this result that would be directly antagonistic to contiguity theory, since the degree of contiguity or number of response-reinforcer pairings would not change.

Unfortunately, it is not easy to think of ways to do this experiment. The experiment requires the manipulation of the value of P(Rft/No R), but it is not obvious how to calculate this probability and arrange for its occurrence? It is easy to arrange any specified P(Rft/R) because instances of R are easy to identify. To arrange for a .5 probability a reinforcer is delivered for half of the observed responses. But how can a P(Rft/No R) of .5 be arranged? How is it possible to identify instances of No R? If R does not occur for 10 sec how many No Rs have occurred in this period of time?

Hammond (1980) provided a clever solution to this dilemma. He developed a probabilistic reinforcement schedule. The schedule determined whether or not to deliver a reinforcer every t sec, depending on whether one or more responses had occurred in that period of time. He placed rats in a situation in which P(Rft/R) each 1 sec was held constant at .12. The response was lever pressing and the reinforcer was water. Thus, every 1 sec a determination was made as to whether a lever press had occurred in the last sec, and if so water was delivered with a probability of .12. It is now possible to manipulate P(Rft/No R) by focusing on the same time interval as for R, namely 1 sec. If no lever press had occurred during a 1-sec interval than that was taken as a single instance of No R. Thus, each 1-sec interval could be examined for instances of R or No R and P(Rft/No R) varied. Hammond found that lever pressing fell as P(Rft/No R) was progressively increased from 0 to .12! As predicted by contingency theory, behavior did vary systematically with P(Rft/No R). A similar conclusion emerges from a parallel study by Tomie and Loukas (1983) using position in an open field as the response and brain stimulation as the reinforcer. At an empirical level then, the contingency between response and reinforcer does control behavior.

2. Problems with the contingency formulation.

a. *Vagueness.*   Our contingency proposal was vague and unspecified in a variety of ways. Most seriously, perhaps, the very notion of contingency requires more definition than we gave it. To see the problem it is first necessary to realize that the organism does not directly encounter conditional probabilities in its environment. Such probabilities are abstractions that can be calculated only from information which the organism receives—its own actions, events in the environment, and the time between these. Responses, environmental events, and the conjunction of responses and events occur with certain *frequencies*, and probabilities are calculated from these frequencies.

There are 4 relevant frequencies which form a 2 × 2 contingency matrix as shown in Table 4.1. The 4 cells are the possible conjunctions of R, No R, Rft, and No Rft. Cell "a" represents instances in which a response is closely followed by a reinforcer, cell "b" instances in which a response is not closely followed by a reinforcer, cell "c" instances in which the nonoccurrence of the response is followed by a reinforcer, and cell "d" instances in which a nonresponse is not followed closely by a reinforcer. The entries in this matrix are the number of times that these conjunctions occur.

These are the data that the organism actually encounters and are the basis for computing probabilities. For example, P(Rft/R) = a/a+b and P(Rft/No R) =

TABLE 4.1
Contingency matrix representing the occurrence or nonoccurrence
of Rft after a R or No R

	Rft	*No Rft*
R	a	b
No R	c	d

c/c+d. We implicitly assumed that the organism asseses contingency by computing these two ratios and their difference. But there are many other ways to calculate contingency from the matrix, and the organism could be using any of these other metrics (see Hammond & Paynter, 1983, for a discussion). For example, the organism could be computing the phi correlation coefficient, a suggestion made by Gibbon, Berryman, and Thompson (1974). The phi coefficient here would equal (a/a+b − c/c+d) (a/a+c − b/b+d). Moreover, there are many other possible metrics that the organism could be using to integrate event frequency information.

We proposed a particular metric, but were not fully aware of the other metrics that could be used to integrate contingency information and had no very good reason for choosing the one that we did. We simply wished to argue for the importance of contingency in general terms, and argued for the metric that seemed most obvious. But the organism could be using any of a number of computations, and they embody different theories.

Then why not simply conduct the appropriate experiments to determine how the organism calculates contingency? To determine which metric best predicts behavior as some parameter is manipulated it is necessary to be able to calculate the degree of contingency for each of the metrics. Here, a second poorly specified aspect of contingency theory becomes apparent. The theory does not say how close a reinforcer has to come to a response to count as a cell "a" entry. The same is true for the other cells. Clearly, the events representing the 4 cells of the contingency matrix must be classified in relation to some temporal unit, *t*, just as in the Hammond (1980) experiment. Classification will then occur by examining every *t* interval and seeing whether it contains a R, No R, Rft or No Rft. This is not problematic. What is problematic is that a given metric will yield a different contingency estimate for the same experimental treatment for different values of t. Of course, the value of t is arbitrary, and then so are the contingency estimates. It might seem that ordinal predictions would still be possible, but the different metrics respond very differently to variations in t. Which metric best fits the data will thus vary with t. This makes it difficult to assess exactly how the organism construes contingency.

b. *Reinforcer Advance and Delay Experiments.* The problem of how to treat time in contingency theory is nowhere more apparent than in the analysis of experiments in which the organism's response determines not whether reinforcers will occur, but only *when*. For example, Thomas (1981) exposed rats to a schedule divided into consecutive 20 sec segments. The rats were given food every 20 sec regardless of whether they responded or not. If no lever press response had occurred by the end of the 20-sec interval food was delivered at that point. However, the first lever press in a 20-sec interval was immediately followed by food. So, the only consequence of pressing the lever was to move the food presentation for that interval from the 20-sec point to the point at which the response occurred. Thomas found that this procedure led to the acquisition and stable performance of regular lever pressing.

It might seem that these results favor the contiguity principle because the food was contiguous with lever pressing. However, this aspect of the procedure is not essential. Hineline (1970) developed a schedule in which an electric shock was delivered in every 20-sec interval. If the rat did not press a lever the shock occurred at the 8-sec point of the 20-sec interval; if it did respond the shock was postponed to the end of the 20-sec interval. Performance of the response did not avoid shock, it merely delayed it. Here there is no obvious contiguity, but the response was still acquired. Parallel results in humans to both the Thomas and Hineline experiments have been reported by Wasserman and Neunaber (1986).

Is there a response-reinforcer contingency in these experiments? The answer is totally dependent on t. Consider the Thomas experiment. If t is taken to be the cycle length of 20 sec there is no contingency, here the probability of reinforcement is the same (1.0) whether or not a lever press occurs. The animal cannot here affect the overall probability of reinforcement. However, there are values of t for which there would be a positive contingency between lever pressing and reinforcement. This is not a satisfactory state of affairs.

Causality

The foregoing discussion indicates that the contingency view is supported in a general sort of way in that the organism does appear to integrate information about what happens after R and No R. But the conditional probability analysis that we proposed encounters a variety of difficulties. Can this be resolved?

A consideration of the concept of causality may help. Indeed, principles of association and contiguity arose in the context of attempting to specify circumstances under which people infer that there is a causal relationship between events.

In *A Treatise of Human Nature* (1739, 1962) David Hume proposed three principles which he believed gave humans the impression of a cause-effect relation: (a) temporal precedence, causes must precede effects; (b) temporal and spatial contiguity, causes and effects must occur close together in space and time; and (c) constant conjunction, effects must regularly follow causes.

Causality is not an easy concept. An event can have many different kinds of "causes" (proximate cause, material cause, ultimate cause, etc.), and it is not even entirely clear what "to cause" means at any of these levels. Causality does not inhere in physical events, it is a label that we sometimes give to some orderly relations between events and not to others. It is important to understand that Hume held causation to be a psychological, not a physical phenomenon. It was seen as a relation between *experiences*, not a unique connection between physical events. There are many orderly relationships between physical events that we do not often call causal. Is the position of a planet at one point in time the cause of its moving to a different location? Nor will any particular juxtaposition of necessary and/or sufficient conditions lead to a unique combination for making causal inferences. For example, does birth cause death? Most of us would say not, yet birth is both necessary and sufficient for death. However, we sometimes do ascribe causality to a relation, and that ascription seems to have special properties (Michotte, 1963).

It is interesting in this regard that a similarity between principles of causal inference and the laws of learning have sometimes been noted (Testa, 1975). Temporal precedence, spatial and temporal contiguity, and constant conjunction are all factors crucial for the occurrence of classical conditioning and instrumental learning. Response must precede reinforcer, and learning is retarded if there is a temporal delay between them. Spatial contiguity between response and reinforcer facilitates learning (Boakes, 1977), and the correlation between response and reinforcement is indeed critical (Hammond, 1980). It thus may be quite reasonable to consider learning phenomena in the context of the perception of causality.

How does this bear on learned helplessness? It may help to step back and consider what we were trying to say in 1967, rather than focusing on the specifics of our proposal. What we wished to develop was a formulation that allowed us to say that the subject learned that its behavior did not cause the shock to terminate. We viewed the organism as searching for the causes of events, because knowing the cause of an event would aid in future adaptive behavior with respect to that event. This analysis had to allow the distinction between chance conjunctions and *true* relations. Thus, we had to develop a scheme that allowed the organism to use information both with regard to sufficiency (if I respond what happens) and necessity (if I don't respond what happens), even though necessity and sufficiency do not by themselves lead to causal impressions.

Because of the nature of the actual experimental procedure that we were using we stated our position in terms of conditional probabilities. But this focus on conditional probabilities was only accidental. Our experimental procedure involved events going on and off either contingent on a response or not, and so we talked about the probabilities of events going on or off given a response or not. But if responding in our initial experiments had brought events sooner or later, we would probably have translated our view into something other than P(Rft/R) and P(Rft/No R). And it may be that many of the problems with our contingency theory noted above as well as with other contingency theories might have more to do with the translation into conditional probabilities than with the kernel concepts.

Consider the experiments described above in which responding does not change the overall probability of reinforcement but only moves the reinforcer to an earlier point in time. Wasserman and Neunaber (1986) explain these results by arguing that organisms compare the relative delay of reinforcement which follows R and No R. Since organisms do not like reinforcers to be delayed, R will be performed it if results in less delay than No R. They further argue that the relative delay principle can explain many of the findings which have been taken to support the conditional probability statement of contingency theory. In the Hammond (1980) experiment, for example, increasing P(Rft/No R) reduces the average delay between No R and reinforcement, and when the two probabilities are equal so are the average delays to reinforcement for R and No R.

Wasserman and Neunaber go on to argue for the primacy of delay, and suggest that this might be intimately tied to perceptions of causality. Perhaps to cause an event to occur or not to occur means moving that event forward or backward in time. They further argue that this sort of experiment and their analysis supports contiguity theory since time is seen to be critical, and weighs against contingency views. But is this so? Contiguity theories did not merely assert that time is an important dimension. They typically viewed learning as being produced by the automatic strengthening effect of reward on immediately preceding responses and did not allow for a comparison process. However, contingency theory explicitly focused on a comparison between what happens after R and No R, although the comparison was of probabilities of reinforcement. Here the argument is that the organism compares delays after R and No R, a position which seems entirely in the spirit of contingency rather than contiguity theory.

The reinforcer advance and delay experiments may be consistent with a more general contingency view which is not tied to conditional probabilities of event occurrence. The subjects in the reinforcer advance and delay experiments *do* have control, but not over the overall probabilities of event occurrence—they have control over the time at which the reinforcer will occur.

As already noted, the organism does not experience probabilities. It experiences action, events in the environment, characteristics of the events (quality, intensity, etc.), and time. Probabilities are constructed from this information, but there is no reason to think that they are primary. Nor is there reason to believe that time is primary. To see this let us conduct a thought experiment. Let's allow the organism's response to change the intensity of a reinforcer. The probability that the reinforcer will occur and the exact time at which it occurs will not be affected by the subject's behavior, only the intensity. Is there any question that the organism will learn to perform the response under appropriate conditions? Indeed, Bersh and Alloy (1978) found that rats will learn to press a lever to reduce the intensity of a later shock.

Our intent was to argue that organisms analyze the consequences of their actions and learn the degree to which their actions have consequence and causal impact. Some philosophers have argued (e.g., von Wright, 1974) causal efficacy to mean interference with the flow of events. Shultz (1982) has somewhat similarly argued that causal relations are characterized by "generative transmission." This could be with regard to event probabilities, event delay, event intensity, etc. Clearly, a contingency analysis can be applied to dimensions other than event probability. Indeed, event probability must be derived from more basic data, and may be of less importance. If the theory is so-broadened, the experiments that seem to contradict contingency theory lose their force. The problems with how to treat time might also diminish. It would not do violence to our view to acknowledge that the organism in learned helplessness experiments might not be computing probabilities but comparing the delay to shock termination following a response with the delay to shock termination in the absence of that response.

Another Problem—Is No R Merely No R?

As already discussed, the essence of the contiguity model is that learning about R only occurs at the moment of R or shortly thereafter. R, or the stimulus consequences of R, have to be physically present for the occurrence of some other event such as a reinforcer to change R. On the other hand, the contingency model asserts that the organism compares what happens after R with what happens after No R. Thus it differs from the contiguity model in the fundamental way that R does not have to be present for an event to alter R.

The finding (e.g., Hammond, 1980) that $P(Rft/No R)$ systematically alters the performance of R would seem to indicate that R does not have to be present for the occurrence of events to alter R. But, is this really so? An exactly parallel debate has occurred in the realm of Pavlovian conditioning. Rescorla (1968) demonstrated that conditioning to a CS varied not only with $P(UCS/CS)$, but also with $P(UCS/No CS)$. That is, the greater the number of occurrences of the UCS in the absence of the CS the less the conditioning that accrued to the CS. Indeed, this finding was originally taken to support a contingency analysis of Pavlovian conditioning. Clearly, conditioning to the CS changed when the CS was not present, and it seemed as if the subject compared what happened after CS and No CS.

However, it turned out to be easy to develop an explanation of the effectiveness of $P(UCS/No CS)$ without assuming that conditioning to the CS changed without the CS being present. The argument was that the UCSs that occurred in the absence of the CS occurred in the presence of background or contextual cues (the ambient illumination, noise, odors, etc.). The background cues would therefore be assumed to acquire associative strength, and the greater P(UCS/No CS) the greater ought to be the associative strength acquired by the background. It only needed to be added that when the CS does occur it does not occur by itself, but rather in compound with these very same background cues. After all, these stimuli do not disappear at CS onset. This is now a "blocking" paradigm (see Durlach, 1989, and Baker and Mercier, 1989) and the background cues should compete with the CS. Thus the CS should accrue less conditioning the greater the associative strength of the background or the greater P(UCS/No CS) (Rescorla & Wagner, 1972). But notice that here the organism does not make a comparison between what happens after CS occurrence with what happens at other times. The associative strength of the CS changes only as a result of events *concomitant with the presentation of the CS*. P(UCS/No CS) alters the associative strength of the CS only because it determines the associative strength of other stimuli present at the same time as the CS.

How does this apply to instrumental learning situations such as the Hammond (1980) experiment? Can the operation of P(Rft/No R) be explained by a parallel contiguity argument to that made for Pavlovian conditioning? At first blush this would appear to be a difficult task. It is one thing to hypothesize the operation of background stimuli during Pavlovian conditioning, but it is more difficult to conceptualize *background responses* that would be present during the occurrence of reinforcers in the absence of R and which would later be in compound with the instrumental response being trained. However, the requirement that there be background responses assumes that Pavlovian and instrumental learning are really a reflection of different processes and that stimulus and response learning are independent and do not interact. Such a view may well be erroneous. Both Pavlovian and instrumental learning can be viewed as reflecting the operation of the very same process in which the organism learns about the relationships between *events* which occur in its environment. The events could be stimuli or responses, and indeed, there is abundant evidence that stimuli and responses do not remain separate from each other and interact just as two stimuli might. For example, a stimulus can block the acquisition of a response that produces a reinforcer if it is more highly correlated with the reinforcer and is presented in compound with the response (Pearce & Hall, 1978).

If stimuli and responses interact in the same manner as do compounds of stimuli, then a contiguity explanation of the operation of P(Rft/No R) is easy to construct. These reinforcers augment the associative strength of background *stimuli* which are, of course, present at the same time as R. These stimuli then compete with R for associative strength and interfere with R, the interference increasing with the magnitude of P(Rft/No R).

Selective Attribution of Causality

Indeed, Dickinson and Shanks (1985) have made exactly this proposal (see Dickinson, 1989). Their argument is stated in terms of attributions of causality rather than conditioning, although the model they propose is an associative one. Their view is that Pavlovian and instrumental learning can be conceptualized as instances in which the organism attempts to determine the causes of important events in its environment. In their experimental task human subjects observe a video screen and are asked to make judgments concerning the effectiveness of a new shell in destroying tanks. A tank moves across the screen on each trial and the subject can fire a shell (the response or action, A) at the tank or not fire (No A) on that trial. The subject is told to fire when the tank passes through a "gunsight" and is immediately informed as to whether the shell will hit the tank. The subjects become good at this and all shell firings become hits. On a given trial the tank either blows up (the outcome, O) or it does not. Subjects are also told that the tank is crossing a minefield on each of the trials, and so any tank destruction could be due to a fired shell or a mine. They are also told that different shells from different firings take different times to reach the tank so that when the tank blows up as it moves across the screen is not a cue to whether the shell was effective.

The subject's task is to judge the effectiveness of the shell after experiencing a number of trials on which firing (A) and no firing occurred. Here the contingency between A and O can be varied since both P(O/A) and P(O/No A) can be independently manipulated. As in the animal contingency experiments humans are sensitive to contingency—the shell was judged less effective as P(O/No A) increased. But Dickinson and Shanks argue that this is so because the greater P(O/No A) the more likely the subject is to attribute the tank destruction to the minefield. That is, the minefield is present on every trial, and so when the tank is destroyed when no firing occurs, the tank is destroyed in the presence of the minefield. Thus the greater is P(O/No A) the greater is the assumed density of the minefield. Of course, when the tank passes across the screen after a firing (A) the minefield is simultaneously present and competes with the firing as a potential cause of the tank destruction, thereby decreasing its assessed effectiveness. Indeed, Dickinson and Shanks have conducted a variety of experiments supporting the idea that with their procedure P(O/No A) alters judgments of the effectiveness of A because of the subjects attributions of cause to the "background" minefield (Dickinson, Shanks, & Evenden, 1985; Shanks, 1985).

Dickinson and Shanks essentially argue for the Rescorla-Wagner associative rule (see Durlach, 1989), but transposed into the realm of causal judgment. More formally, they propose that judgments of the effectiveness of some target event A, J_a, is determined by the strength of the expectation of the outcome given the occurrence of A and other simultaneously present events (V_{ax}), minus the strength of the expectation produced by the other events (V_x). Thus, $J_a = V_{ax} - V_x$. When there are no obvious X events, the X is assumed to be the background cues or "causal context."

Two questions concerning this selective causal attribution argument come immediately to mind. First, how does this idea differ from what was proposed by learned helplessness? Second, how plausible is the idea? At first glance learned helplessness and selective causal attribution are quite similar. After all, both view humans and animals as learning about the degree to which their behavior and other events cause important outcomes in the environment. Importantly, both allow for changes in the evaluation of the target behavior or event without the event itself occurring. While Va changes only when A occurs, Ja will change when either Vax or Vx changes. Thus, what happens when only X occurs will change Ja. Moreover, both agree that in the crucial situation in which an outcome is independent of behavior the organism can learn or make judgments about this independence. On the other hand, the selective attribution idea argues that the judgment of independence can only be made because there are events that occur concommitantly with the target event that carry causal strength. For learned helplessness the organism is able to weigh what happens after the presence and absence of the target event without the necessity of mediation by a jointly present event. Learned helplessness does not deny that such events can operate, but only that this sort of mediation is not necessary for the organism to be sensitive to what happens in the absence of the event.

There is no obvious experimental evidence that favors one of these ideas over the other. However, most experiments that examine either causal attribution or covariation judgments do not provide a likely alternative cause (i.e., the minefield) that is present during instances of outcomes that occur in the absence of the action being judged. That is, a typical experiment allows the subject to perform a response, say pushing a button, or to refrain from responding, and an event, say a light, comes on or not. Probabilities of the light coming on after R and No R are varied and the subject is asked to make judgments about the effectiveness of the response in producing the light. Alternative causes for the light are not provided.

Here, Dickinson and Shanks (1985) argue that static background cues in the situation function as the alternative cause to which the event is then attributed and which then competes with the action for causal strength. Dickinson and Shanks seem to implicitly assume that subjects will always attribute an event to some cause that they can identify in the situation. Is this plausible? Is it reasonable to assume that static background cues will operate and influence causal judgments in the same way as an explicitly provided alternative cause such as the minefield?

There is an extensive literature concerning the conditions which influence whether a person is likely to judge some event as the probable cause of another event. In an excellent recent review, Einhorn and Hogarth (1986) argue that four major factors are involved: (1) the causal field or context; (2) cues-to-causality; (3) judgmental strategies used to combine the causal field with cues-to-causality; and (4) the discounting of causal strength by alternative explanations.

The causal field or context is important in a number of ways. First, it defines the factors that might be relevant as causes. Any event has as many potential causes as it has potential explanations. Consider the death of the astronauts in the explosion of the space shuttle. What caused the deaths? A physician might judge the cause as shock or heat, an engineer might judge the cause as a seal with certain inadequate features, a member of Congress might judge the cause as a space program operating under poor leadership, and a lawyer might judge the cause as negligence by one or more of the manufacturers of the equipment. It is the context in which judgments are made that determines the field of potential causes.

Context is important in a second way. Causes are generally seen as a *difference-in-a-background* (Mackie, 1974). Factors that are part of the background or "causal field" are *not* seen as causes. An example from Einhorn and Hogarth, already referred to, may be useful. Does birth cause death? Most people do not see birth as a cause of death even though it is both a necessary and sufficient condition. The reason is that birth is a part of the causal field and not a difference-from-a-background. Moreover, not all differences-from-a-background are typically judged as causal. Factors that are seen as causal tend to be events rather than standing conditions, and intrusive or abnormal (Mackie, 1974). For these reasons it would seem unlikely that background contextual cues would acquire causal strength and compete with the target event.

Where Does This Leave Us?

Event or response-reinforcer covariation is clearly an important dimension governing behavior, but the issue of whether a contingency model is necessary and whether a contiguity model might not suffice is not resolved. Perhaps it has been a mistake to view these as *either-or* alternatives. Perhaps contiguity and contingency should be viewed as different cues-to-causality, both of which are used by the organism. Indeed, contiguity might be a factor which makes contingencies more obvious. Of course, these are not the only cues which organisms use to judge cause—temporal order (causes preceed effects) and similarity (physical resemblance and congruity of strength and duration) are others.

IV. REPRESENTATION AND EXPECTATION

Learned helplessness theory not only claimed that contingency is important, but also that exposure to inescapable shock leads organisms to represent the noncontingency between their behavior and shock termination and to expect that noncontingency will hold true in the future. This key assertion has been difficult to test. It is not easy to see how to ask questions about representations and expectations that are formed by animals. The most obvious approach would be to investigate the existence of the behavioral products which should follow from such representations and expectations. We have argued that the representation and expectation of shock uncontrollability leads to response initiation deficits and cognitive deficits, which in turn produce poor learning in escape tasks such as the shuttlebox. However, inactivity theories can also account for poor performance in escape learning tasks, and so these learning deficits cannot be taken as evidence for representation and expectation. Moreover, response initiation and activity are so tightly related that this sort of deficit cannot be taken to support either view. It is the cognitive deficit that distinguishes the theories. Learned helplessness argues for a cognitive interference in addition to any activity deficits which might occur. The competing motor response theories see the learned helplessness effect as purely a performance deficit, while the learned helplessness hypothesis insists on both a true cognitive, as well as a performance deficit.

The Cognitive Deficit

At first glance, poor learning to escape constitutes evidence for a cognitive deficit. However, the escape tasks typically used confound any potential cognitive changes with inactivity produced by sources other than cognition. Poor escape performance in tasks such as shuttleboxes and lever pressing could result either from interference with the learning process or from simple reduced activity. To make matters even more complicated, inescapably shocked subjects frequently fail to respond at all on a given trial in these situations. They are thus exposed to the escape contingency less often than control subjects, making it difficult to show that differences in performance are caused by differential sensitivity to the escape contingency. Add to this that inescapably shocked subjects begin at a different level of performance than other subjects, and the situation becomes a hopeless one for infering conclusively that a cognitive deficit is present.

A clear demonstration of an inescapable shock produced cognitive deficit requires interference with learning in a task in which three conditions are met. The task must be one in which activity level and shock escape are either uncorrelated or negatively correlated. Second, inescapably shocked and control subjects must receive equal exposure to the escape contingency. Finally, all subjects must begin at the same level of escape performance. Although these requirements might seem quite stringent, several tasks actually do meet them. One is signaled punishment, but space does not permit a discussion here (see Baker, 1976; and Jackson, Maier, & Rapaport, 1978). A *choice* task in which shock is escaped by choosing the correct response from a number of alternatives seemed another possibility. Here escape learning is assessed by the *accuracy* of the subject's choices rather than by response speed. High levels of activity should not necessarily lead to accurate choices nor should low levels lead to poor choice performance, provided that enough activity is present for choices to occur. In any case, both response speed and accuracy can be measured and their correlation assessed.

Jackson, Alexander, and Maier (1980) developed a Y-maze escape task. The apparatus was quite small so that not much movement was required for the rat to choose one of the arms. The three 22.5 cm arms were at a 120° angle to each other and connected to a small central section in the shape of an equilateral triangle measuring 11 cm on a side. The rat only had to move 12 cm into an arm to register a response. The arms were all identical, and the maze was housed in a dark room to minimize the possibility of using cues outside the maze.

The interval between trials was spent in darkness. A trial began with the simultaneous onset of lights behind the end walls of the 3 arms and shock to the grids. The shock and lights terminated if the rat entered the arm to the left of where it was when the trial started. If the rat made a right turn a left turn was still required before the trial would terminate. If another right turn occurred, the rat then had to move into the arm to the left of this arm, etc. A trial terminated only if a left turn occurred, and so any number of incorrect choices were possible before a correct turn. Shock automatically terminated if a correct choice had not been made after 60 sec. The rat was free to move about between trials, and its position at the beginning of the trial defined its starting point.

Rats were given either escapable shock, yoked inescapable shock, or no shock in an apparatus very different from the Y-maze, followed by 100 trials of escape training in the Y-maze 24 hr later. The results of this experiment can be seen in Fig. 4.1, which presents the mean percentage of trials on which one or more errors (right turns) occurred across blocks of 10 trials. This measure represents the accuracy of the organism's responses rather than the speed with which they are made. As can be seen, all groups began by choosing the correct arm of the maze at a chance level. However, the performance of the groups quickly diverged. The nonshocked and escapably shocked animals soon eliminated errors and were making errors on only 10% of the trials by the end of the training session. In contrast, the inescapably shocked rats remained at random choice for 40 trials and were still beginning 30% of the trials with an incorrect choice by the end of training.

The difference between the inescapably shocked and other subjects was *not* caused by failures to respond. There were virtually no failures to terminate a

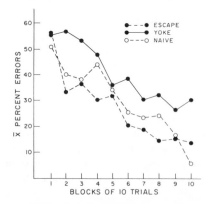

FIG. 4.1.   Mean percent of trials with an error across blocks of 10 Y-maze trials.

trial with a correct response. The error data thus indicate that the inescapably shocked rats made more errors than did the others, not that they responded less often. The animals did not fail to respond and choose an arm of the maze, they simply chose incorrectly. Thus, the Y-maze results reveal an interference with learning under conditions in which the subjects were exposed to the correct contingency on every trial. The inescapably shocked subjects continued to run and choose arms until a correct response finally occurred, but they made a large number of errors.

It should be noted that the inescapably shocked animals did respond more slowly and take more time to make their first choice on a trial. However, this difference in response speed is not capable of explaining the poor choice learning. There was no correlation between response speed and choice accuracy either within or across groups. Nor did statistically controlling for response speed by using it as a covariate change the response accuracy results. In addition, the independence of response vigor and accuracy of choice is supported by the finding that it is possible to produce poor choice escape without producing slow responding. Jackson et al. (1980) found that with increased Y-maze shock intensities speed increased but choice accuracy did not. Conversely, it is possible to produce slow responding without poor choice performance. Minor, Pellymounter, and Maier (1988) found that exposure to a number of inescapable shocks (40) normally insufficient to produce learned helplessness failed to produce a choice accuracy deficit but still produced slow responding.

The Y-maze thus reveals an escape deficit that cannot be explained by reduced activity and suggests a true cognitive deficit. Moreover, this interference with choice learning seems to have generality. Rosellini, DeCola, and Shapiro (1982) found that inescapable shock interferes with learning to choose between two responses to acquire food. Here learning impairment was found under conditions in which differential activity was not even present.

Nature of the Cognitive Deficit

The foregoing results clearly indicate a change in the learning process produced by inescapable shock, but they do not indicate the nature of the change. It is possible that inescapable shock alters what the subject learns from a given exposure to the contingency between its behavior and the reinforcing event. The possibilities here can be organized around whether inescapable shock alters some aspect of processing related to the response, the reinforcer, or the machinery that associates them. On the reinforcer side, for example, shock termination might be less likely to initiate the processing steps necessary for learning (Kamin, 1969) in inescapably shocked subjects. With regard to behavior, inescapably shocked subjects might be less likely to attend to, encode, remember, or otherwise process the behavior that now leads to shock termination. With regard to the associative machinery, response events might be fully processed and shock termination might be effective in initiating the necessary associative processing steps, but these processes themselves might be altered. Alternatively, inescapably shocked organisms might learn about the trial events in a normal fashion, but might have an expectational bias. Here, the subject accurately registers the events of a given trial, but does not expect the contingency to hold on future trials.

A series of experiments reported by Minor, Jackson, and Maier (1984) supports the notion that inescapable shock interferes with what is learned on a given trial rather than biasing expectations. Moreover, the experiments suggest that the processing of the response is altered, and that the source of the difficulty is attentional. They began by noting that the choice accuracy deficit became difficult to obtain when the Y-maze was fully automated. In their original studies Jackson et al. observed the rats in the Y-maze and depressed switches to record the rat's movement from arm to arm as they broke the photocell beam in each arm. Eventually a computer was added to conduct the experiment and a human observer was no longer needed, and the phenomenon disappeared! With the computer-run-fully-automated-and-personless procedure, inescapably shocked animal learned brilliantly and no longer chose poorly. What could have been the role of the human? Since the human had to press a button to record the rat's breaking a photobeam there must have been a small delay between a correct response and shock termination. Computers are faster. But there was also a more subtle possibility. We had been careful to construct a maze with no external cues to differentiate the arms and even kept the maze dark between trials. But the human could have functioned as a cue. The human must have given off odors, made some noise, etc. The human stood in a fixed position relative to the maze, behind one of the arms. Thus depending on the rat's position at the beginning of a trial, the human was sometimes behind the rat's starting arm, sometimes behind the correct choice, and sometimes behind the incorrect choice. This means that the human was an *irrelevant* cue because the use of the position of the human to guide responding could not have led to problem solution—either approaching or avoiding the human would lead to only chance performance.

Minor et al. (1988) began by investigating the delay factor. The computer arranged for slight delays in shock termination following the correct choice which averaged 350 ms, an approximation of human reaction time. Inescapably shocked subjects still learned beautifully. They next eliminated the delay but now placed a human in the room behind one arm of the maze. The human was not able to intervene in the experiment, it was still run by the computer. Inescapably shocked animals now showed a learning deficit, but it was not reliable. Undaunted, Minor et al. combined these two factors—shock termination was slightly delayed and a human stood in the room. The results can be seen in Fig. 4.2. Now an enormous deficit in choice escape learning appeared! Animals who had first received no shock were unaffected by the slight delay and presence of the person in the room, they learned well under all conditions. However, rats inescapably shocked 24 hr earlier were profoundly disrupted if there was a delay and a person in the room. It is not that they failed to respond and choose—response levels remained normal. They simply did not learn to choose correctly.

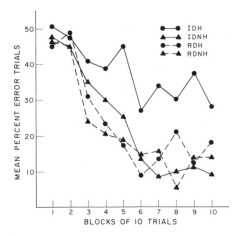

FIG. 4.2. Mean percent of trials with an error across blocks of 10 Y-maze trials. The groups had received either inescapable shock (I) or restraint (R) 24 hr earlier, and either had a delay of shock termination and a human present during testing (DH), or had a delay but no human (DNH).

If the function of the human is really to provide an irrelevant cue, stimuli such as lights and tones ought to be able to disrupt the choice learning of inescapably shocked subjects. Minor et al. therefore tested animals under conditions in which the light behind one of the arms of the maze was lit at the beginning of each trial (an average delay of shock termination of 350 ms was still in effect). The particular arm that was illuminated varied randomly from trial to trial and was unrelated to the animal's position, and so was an irrelevant cue. Escapably shocked and nonshocked rats were not influenced by the light cue. However, inescapably shocked animals were profoundly impaired.

The role of the delay in shock termination is reasonably clear. There is no reason why a 350 ms delay should affect whether the animal expects that a contingency it has registered will remain in effect on succeeding trials. However, a delay would make the contingency on a trial harder to notice, and could thus magnify any effect that inescapable shock has on this *noticing* process. But what of the irrelevant cue. Why is it necessary?

The most obvious possibility is that it operates to distract the subject, and perhaps inescapable shock makes the organism more distractable. However, recall that the normal procedure without the cue involves darkness between trials and all three arms becoming illuminated at the beginning of a trial. Here even more light comes on than in the irrelevant cue condition and should be even more distracting. However, inescapably shocked animals do not show interference with learning. It is only when the light is a *differential* cue that can be used to guide behavior that interference occured.

The critical importance of an irrelevant external cue strongly supports an interference with the processing of the contingency information on a given trial rather than a biasing of the expectational process. Moreover, it points to an alteration in attention. The data are consistent with the following argument. During inescapable shock the organism learns that its own behavior, or stimuli such as proprioceptive feedback from its behavior, are not correlated with shock termination. Expecting that this condition holds true in the Y-maze situation has a variety of consequences including reduced salience of responses or of response produced cues. The organism is thus less likely to attend to such cues and therefore less likely to associate them with shock termination. However, this reduced salience of response-related cues might not have much effect if the contingency is very obvious and if there is nothing else to attend to. Other things being equal a reduction in attention to internal behavior-related cues should increase attention to external cues such as lights, odors, etc. Thus, inescapably shocked animals should show increased attention to such cues, and this should interfere with learning if these cues are present and irrelevant. These are just the results obtained.

It should be carefully noted that this perspective suggests that labeling the cognitive change produced by inescapable shock as a *deficit* is misleading. It suggests that these organisms process trial information differently and are biased towards attention to external rather than internal cues, but this could lead to *improved* learning under some conditions. What if the light cue in the Y-maze was made *relevant* rather than irrelevant? That is, what if it defined which arm was the correct one? Our argument would have to predict that inescapably shocked animals would now learn faster than controls!

This interesting possibility has recently been examined by Robert Lee and myself. An escape from water task was used rather than the Y-maze, and is depicted in Fig. 4.3. On each trial the rat is placed at the "start" end of a rectangular tank. Although the water is at room temperature and thus not highly aversive, rats are still motivated to get out of the water. The far end of the tank is divided into two compartments, with a piece of plastic in front of each compartment and coming down to the level of the water. The rat can swim under either of these, but cannot go directly from one compartment to the other. To go from one compartment into the other the rat must first swim out of the compartment in which it is in and then to the other side.

In our first experiment we asked whether inescapable shock would interfere with the later acquisition of a left-right discrimination to escape the water. On each trial there was a platform extending above the water in one of the compartments. Thus the rat could escape the water on that trial by choosing the correct compartment. One of the compartments had a black stimulus at its entrance and the other had a white stimulus, with the stimuli shifting from side to side randomly on each trial. The platform was always in either the left or the right compartment, and care was taken to eliminate the possibility that cues external to the maze could be used to identify the right and left sides. Thus, the rat had to use proprioceptive or response based cues correlated with left and right to solve this problem. The results can be seen in Fig. 4.4, which shows the mean number

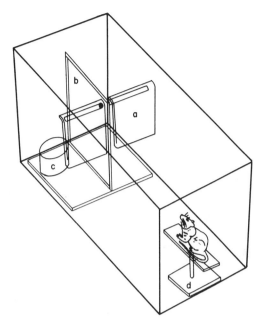

FIG. 4.3.   Diagram of the water maze. Taken from Rudy and Castro (1987).

of trials on which an error occurred. As with the Y-maze, prior exposure to inescapable shock interfered with learning.

In the crucial experiment *all* aspects of the task remained the same—the motivational conditions, the stimuli present, etc. The only difference was that the external black-white stimulus was made a relevant instead of an irrelevant cue. Instead of going to the left or the right to solve the problem the rat now had to learn to go to the compartment with the black or the white door. The black and white stimulus still changed from side to side randomly, but now the platform was always behind one of these stimuli rather than always being on the left or right side. The results are shown in Fig. 4.5. Now the inescapably shocked subjects learned more rapidly than did the restrained controls! Thus, inescapable shock either interfered with or actually improved learning depending only on which stimulus led to problem solution. It might be noted that this difference cannot be explained by arguing that inescapable shock exposure will only interfere with the performance of complex hard to learn tasks or ones that require a more sustained motor output (Anisman, DeCatanzaro, & Remington, 1978). The black–white problem was actually much more difficult than the left-right problem and took many more trials to solve. Moreover, this argument cannot explain why inescapable shock augmented performance when black-white was the relevant cue. These data would seem to provide strong support for the notion that inescapable shock alters the direction of the subject's attention away from cues from

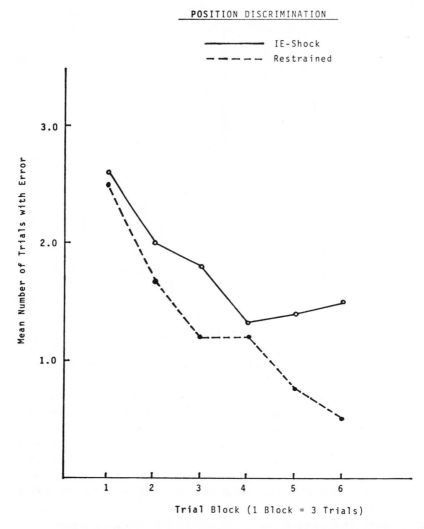

FIG. 4.4.   Mean number of trials with an error across blocks of 3 water maze position discrimination trials.

its own responding and toward external cues in the environment. Here the change in learning cannot be argued to have occurred because inescapable shock makes the reinforcer (escape from water) less effective or interferes with the organism's ability to associate.

Overshadowing and Potentiation

A second line of research exploring the attention idea capitalized on the finding that stimulus-reinforcer associations can *overshadow* response-reinforcer associations (Mackintosh & Dickinson, 1979). Here the acquisition/maintenance of an instrumental response is disrupted if an exteroceptive stimulus such as a light or tone precedes the occurrence of the reinforcer (Pearce & Hall, 1978; St. Clair-Smith, 1979). The explanation proposed was that the exteroceptive cues compete with the response for associative strength, just as they would with other stimuli. To the extent that the external cue is better correlated with reinforcement than are the response-produced cues, it will gain associative strength at the expense of the response-produced cues and interfere with instrumental learning (but see Tarpy, Lea, & Midgley, 1983, for an alternative explanation).

If an exteroceptive stimulus that is strongly correlated with reinforcement tends to overshadow response-produced cues, this overshadowing effect might be expected to be particularly potent in animals that already do not attend to such cues. However, a recent study by Mitchell, Channell, and Hall (1985) on the effects of caudate-putamen lesions suggests the opposite possibility. Lesions of this region of the brain impair instrumental learning and are believed to do so because they interfere with the organism's ability to make use of feedback information from motor responses (Potegal, 1982). Mitchell et al. (1985) wished to further test this hypothesis by examining the effect of caudate-putamen lesions on the ability of exteroceptive cues to overshadow instrumental response learning. Rats were trained to press a lever on a variable-interval schedule with a .5 sec delay between the criterion response and the presentation of food. The delay interval was either filled with a light or not filled. As expected, the light stimulus interfered with the lever press performance of control subjects—overshadowing occurred. Surprisingly, the light did not produce greater overshadowing in caudate-putamen lesioned subjects. Rather the light had the direct opposite effect and *enhanced* the lever press performance of caudate-putamen lesioned subjects, a phenomenon called "potentiation" (Rusiniak, Hankins, Garcia, & Brett, 1979).

Mitchell et al. (1985) explained this unexpected facilitory effect of the light stimulus by arguing that when the ability to attend to or use response-produced cues is weak, the provision of an external stimulus soon after or contemporaneous with the response might draw attention to these cues and/or preserve their representation in short-term memory. This would make these cues more available for association with reinforcement (Thomas, Lieberman, McIntosh, & Ronaldson, 1983). The enhanced attention to the response-produced cues brought about by the external cue somehow overcomes the usual tendency of such stimuli to overshadow responding.

In sum, the Mitchell et al. (1985) experiments suggest the interesting possibility that exteroceptive cues correlated with reinforcement potentiate rather than overshadow response learning in animals which do not attend to or use response-produced cues. Inescapably shocked animals are poor at learning in tasks such as lever press and shuttlebox escape. If this interference with escape learning occurs because inescapable shock reduces attention to response-produced cues, the addition of an external cue contemporaneous with the escape response might then be expected to enhance performance rather than interfere with it.

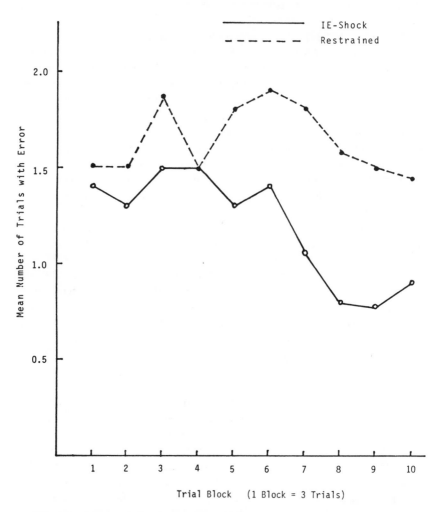

FIG. 4.5.   Mean number of trials with an error across blocks of 3 water maze brightness discrimination trials.

In our first experiment (Maier, Jackson, & Tomie, 1986) rats were given escapable shock, yoked inescapable shock, or only restraint and tested in a FR-2 shuttlebox escape task 24 hr later. In this task unsignaled shocks appear on the average of every minute and can be terminated by two crossings of the shuttlebox. Shocks terminate automatically if an FR-2 escape response has not occurred by 40 sec. Thus latencies near 40 sec indicate a preponderance of trials in which failure to escape occurred. The animals were either given a brief signal (.75 sec offset of the houselight) after each crossing of the FR-2 or were not given sig-

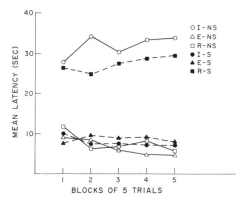

FIG. 4.6.   Mean latency to escape shock in a shuttlebox for rats previously given escapable shock (E), yoked inescapable shock (I), or restraint
(R), and either a lights-out stimulus after each shuttlebox response (S)
or no stimulus after responding (NS).

nals. The results can be seen in Fig. 4.6 which shows the mean escape latencies
across blocks of 5 trials. The animals that did not receive an external signal concomitant with the escape response showed the usual learned helplessness effect—
prior inescapable shock interfered with performance but escapable shock did not.
The addition of the external signal after responding had a dramatically different
effect on animals which had different prior shock experience. The signal had no
effect on escapably shocked subjects, interfered with the performance of rats that
had not previously received shock (overshadowing), and improved the performance of inescapably shocked rats (potentiation). Indeed, the external signal completely eliminated the learned helplessness effect and improved the performance
of inescapably shocked subjects to nonshocked control levels.

This effect appears to be a general one. Figure 4.7 shows the results of a similar experiment conducted with a FR-3 lever press escape task and a 350 msec
white noise burst as the response-dependent signal. Here the subject must press
a lever 3 times to escape shock. As can be seen inescapable shock interfered with
escape learning in the absence of stimulus feedback. However, adding a signal
consequent upon responding interfered with responding in non-shocked controls
and augmented responding in inescapably shocked subjects.

The overshadowing in control subjects and potentiation in inescapably shocked
subjects might depend on different functions of the external stimulus. Overshadowing is generally thought to depend on the association of the overshadowing stimulus
with reinforcement, here shock termination. If the potentiation effect in the inescapably shocked subjects occurs because the stimulus draws attention to the escape response, then the potentiation effect should not be particularly dependent
on the association of the stimulus with shock termination. Our next experiment
thus explored the importance of the contiguity between the external stimulus and
shock termination and the relationship between the stimulus and the responses
of the FR-3 lever press. For some groups the stimulus was produced by the

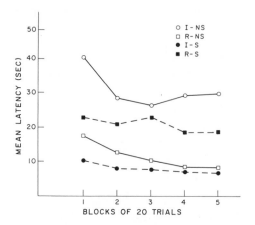

FIG. 4.7. Mean lever press FR-3 escape latencies for groups previously
given inescapable shock (I) or restraint (R), and a stimulus after each
response of the FR-3 (S) or no stimulus after responding (NS).

response that immediately preceded shock termination and so was contiguous with
reinforcement, and for other groups it was not. The external stimulus occurred
after only one of the three responses (either the first, second, or third), after two
of the responses (either the first and second, second and third, or first and third),
or after all three responses of the FR-3.

  For simplicity the results are presented separately for previously inescapably
shocked and restrained-control subjects. The escape performance of the control
subjects can be seen in Fig. 4.8 and the inescapably shocked subjects in Fig. 4.9.
The groups are designated by what happened after each of the responses of the
FR-3, either no signal (−) or a signal (S). Thus, for example, the group designated as S-S received a signal after the first and third response of the FR-3 but
not after the second. The results are rather complex. Table 4.2 summarizes them
and may make them easier to digest. If one stares at the figures and table for
a while a very clear pattern emerges. Control subjects showed either overshadowing or no effect, never potentiation. Moreover, overshadowing occurred in all
cases in which the third response of the FR-3 produced the signal. That is, over-

TABLE 4.2
Effect of signal conditions on the escape performance of inescapably
shocked and control subjects

	S--	-S-	--S	S-S	SS-	-SS	SSS
Control	NE	NE	OS	OS	NE	OS	OS
Inescapable Shock	NE	NE	NE	PO	PO	PO	PO

NE = No Effect
OS = Overshadowing
PO = Potentiation

shadowing occurred only when the stimulus was paired with the termination of shock. The pattern is quite different for inescapably shocked subjects. Here either potentiation or no effect occurred. But here pairing with shock termination was not relevant. Potentiation occurred when any two or more responses of the FR-3 produced a stimulus, and it did not matter which two.

Because exposure to inescapable shock led to potentiation rather than overshadowing, understanding the processes and conditions involved in determining whether a stimulus will lead to either overshadowing or potentiation ought to tell us something about learned helplessness. Moreover the conditions that determine whether overshadowing or potentiation will occur are important to understand because potentiation is unusual and is unexpected by most theories of associative learning. In our experiments the identical stimulus arrangement produced overshadowing in control subjects for whom learning proceeded rapidly in the absence of the added stimuli, and potentiation in the inescapably shocked subjects for whom learning proceeded poorly in the absence of the stimuli. This suggests that whether overshadowing or potentiation occurs might depend on how well the target association is learned without the added stimuli, potentiation occurring when learning would otherwise be poor. Indeed, Bouton, Jones, McPhilips, and Swartzentruber (1986) have recently argued that most or all cases of potentiation have occurred under conditions where the target association was weak. Moreover, overshadowing in our experiments depended on the association or close temporal relationship between the stimulus and the reinforcer, while potentiation did not. This suggests that potentiation and overshadowing might depend on fundamentally different functions of the stimulus.

Even if this principle is correct, it does not by itself provide insight into the processes involved. Various explanations of how stimuli potentiate learning have been proposed. A useful hint may come from the fact that potentiation seems

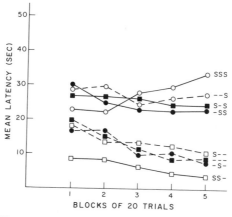

FIG. 4.8. Mean lever press FR-3 escape latencies for groups not previously shocked. S indicates the occurrence of a stimulus after a response and − indicates no stimulus. The position of the S and − correspond to the 3 responses of the FR-3.

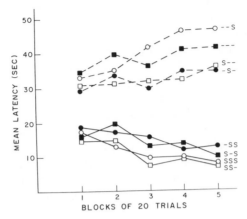

FIG. 4.9.   Mean lever press FR-3 escape latencies for groups previously given inescapable shock. S and − have the same meaning as in Fig. 4.8.

to be independent of the association between the potentiating stimulus and the reinforcer (Kiefer, Rusiniak, & Garcia, 1982; Lett, 1984). This has led several investigators to adopt the view that the potentiating stimulus increases the strength of a *direct association* between the target event and the reinforcer or UCS. One way the potentiating stimulus might accomplish this function is by causing the subject to devote more processing or attention to the target stimulus, thus making it more available in memory for association (e.g., Lett, 1984; Rusiniak, Hankins, Garcia, & Brett, 1979). Such accounts seem similar to a superficially different phenomenon called "temporal marking." Lieberman, Thomas, and their colleagues (Lieberman, Davidson, & Thomas, 1985; Lieberman, McIntosh, & Thomas, 1979; Thomas et al., 1983) studied instrumental learning under conditions of delayed reinforcement. Again learning was made weak, here by the interposition of a long delay (30–120 sec) between the occurrence of a choice response and the delivery of reinforcement for a correct choice. The provision of a brief external "marking" stimulus (a light, a tone, handling, etc.) after the choice response facilitated choice learning. Indeed, it allowed learning to occur where none occurred otherwise. Here, too, the facilitory effect did not depend on the temporal association of the marking stimulus and the food reinforcer. Learning of the correct choice response across the delay was facilitated if the stimulus was not presented again before reinforcement but only occurred after the choice response. Moreover, the stimulus was given after *both* correct and incorrect choices and so was not strongly correlated with reinforcement. The marking stimulus thus preceded reinforcement by 30 to 120 sec and was not correlated with it, yet facilitated learning. All that was required was that the stimulus be salient and follow a choice response.

Lieberman and Thomas argued that salient events such as their marking stimuli lead organisms to search memory for recent events which may predict them. Processing these antecedents *marks* them in memory, making it more likely that they will be available in memory for association with the reinforcer when it subsequently occurs. Potentiation and temporal marking might represent the same phenomenon and be produced by the same processes. Most cases of potentiation involve a target association that is weak under normal circumstances. These target associations were not weak because the USCs and reinforcers were inadequate to promote learning. Rather, they were weak because of the CS–UCS combination, the temporal delay interval, etc. These experimental arrangements may have made it unlikely that the representation of the CS was available at the time of reinforcer occurrence for "joint processing" with the reinforcer or UCS representation (Wagner, 1981). Perhaps potentiation occurs as marking is envisioned by Lieberman and Thomas—the potentiating stimulus was always highly salient and thus may have initiated processing which forced attention to and memory of the occurrence of the target stimulus or response. Thus at the time of UCS occurrence or reinforcement, the representation of the target event would be available for associative learning. What of cases in which the addition of a salient stimulus after an event reduces memory of the event (Wagner, Rudy, & Whitlow, 1973)? These case have all been ones in which the target event was highly attended to and remembered. Thus competition may occur when an event is strongly represented, but augmentation when the event is either weakly or not at all represented.

What of overshadowing? Overshadowing does seem to depend on the associative relation between the overshadowing stimulus and the UCS or reinforcer. In our experiments overshadowing occurred only when the terminal response of the FR-3 produced the stimulus. Overshadowing may well involve just the sort of process envisaged by associative theories in which the elements compete for associative strength (Mackintosh, 1978). From this viewpoint there is no contradiction between the same stimulus or arrangement being able to produce both potentiation and overshadowing. This is because they depend on *different* aspects of the stimulus, potentiation depending on the ability of the cue to deploy attention to target learning, and overshadowing depending on the associative strength of the cue. It is not hard to see that which of these functions will predominate will depend on the strength of the target association or the associability of the CS or response with the UCS or reinforcer. If the target CS or response is already strongly attended to, remembered, and retrieved at the time of UCS or reinforcer presentation, then marking can have little or no impact and the associative competition function will be unopposed. It is only when the stimulus or response is not attended to, etc., that bringing attention to it can augment conditioning.

What about learned helplessness? The present results follow naturally from the view that inescapable shock does alter cognitive processes involved in instrumental learning rather than only motor performance. There is no obvious reason why providing brief cues consequent on responding should alter inactivity produced by either a transfer of competing motor responses or neurochemical depletions. It might seem that the stimuli used could have a direct motor-enhancing effect, but we ruled this out in a further study (Maier et al., 1986). If inescapably shocked animals later learn poorly because they do not attend to their own responses or cues coming from their own responses, then the argument concerning potentiation just made would expect exactly those results obtained. The strong impact of response-dependent stimuli is most consistent with the argument that some aspect of response processing is altered by inescapable shock. Potentiation seems to occur when the target stimulus or response is only weakly associable with the reinforcer, and potentiation occurs in inescapably shocked subjects suggesting that responding in these animals is indeed not strongly associable with shock termination. The most obvious possibility is that these animals do not attend to their own behavior or cues from their own behavior as predictors of shock termination. Animals with caudate-putamen lesions are known to be poor at using such cues, and here, too, feedback stimuli potentiated instrumental responding.

V. CONCLUSION

The purpose of this chapter was to review the manner in which learned helplessness theory and research has related to the general field of animal learning and motivation and to evaluate the current status of those parts relevant to learning theory. How has learned helplessness theory fared since it was proposed in 1967 and 1968? Quite well I would argue, given the usual half-life of any theory, and given the minimal data on which we then proposed it. It is still alive in 1988 with numerous investigators using it to organize and guide their research. The central phenomena have been robust. The basic learned helplessness effect in animals has been replicated by at least 20 independent laboratories, and more particular findings such as the "therapy" and "immunization" effects by half a dozen. Occasional failures have been reported, but the conditions used have generally been quite different than those which we have established. At a more theoretical level, the contingency between behavior and outcome does control behavior, and the pattern of learning alterations produced by inescapable shock cannot be explained without cognition. However, there are uncertainties at each of the stages of the theory.

1. Contingency and Control. It is clear that variation in contingency leads to variation in behavior. However, the fact that the organism responds sensitively to contingency does not mean that it is extracting degree of contingency and representing it cognitively. A more molecular model which does not refer to contingency at all might be able to account for behavioral sensitivity to contingency with contiguity mechanisms. Moreover, even if degree of contingency is psychologically real, a model is needed that specifies how contingency is computed from the data which the organism has at hand. Contingency is not present in momentary sensory data but can only be derived by computation of event relationships across long periods of time.

Similarly, the controllability of an event is critical in determining the outcome of experiencing that event. But is it control per se, or some more molecular process that is responsible for the apparent effects of control? There are numerous possibilities, but several have been argued in the literature. The predictability as well as the controllability of events modulates the impact of those events, and it has been suggested that the effects of control might be mediated by prediction (Overmier, Patterson, & Wielkiewicz, 1979). The idea is that having control over an event inherently adds predictability concerning the event. In the case of escapability, the argument is that the ability to escape allows the organism to predict when shock will terminate.

Another potential mediating factor may be fear, anxiety, or stress. Uncontrollable shock does produce more fear than controllable shock, and this intense fear rather than control per se may be responsible for some of the sequalae of uncontrollable aversive events (Minor & LoLordo, 1983). Thus, anything that produces intense fear may produce some of these behavioral effects, whether it involves uncontrollability or not.

2. Cognition. Here uncertainties exist at several levels. First, the mechanism by which cognitive processing is altered is poorly understood. I have presented evidence indicating that attention is altered, but the details of how this occurs are not known. Moreover, this does not imply that expectational biasing fails to occur. Second, it is not clear which of the behavioral consequences of uncontrollable aversive events are directly produced by the cognition of no control and which are produced by other consequences (motivational, motor, emotional, neurochemical, etc.). For example, maternal behavior is altered by exposure to inescapable shock (Williams, 1984). Is maternal behavior disrupted because of the cognition of no control or because inescapable shock has induced some other change?

3. Behavior. Here there seem to be two areas of greatest ignorance. The first concerns the limits of uncontrollable shock effects. Where do they stop? The second is related to 2 above. Are the behavioral changes which occur reducible to a single cause, or are the various behavioral changes produced by different processes induced by inescapable shock? If there are multiple causes, then what are they and how do they map into behavior?

ACKNOWLEDGMENT

The preparation of this chapter was supported by National Science Foundation Grant BNS 85–07451 and RSDA 00324. I would like to thank Don Warren for helpful comments.

REFERENCES

Alloy, L. B., & Seligman, M. E. P. (1979). On the cognitive component of learned helplessness and depression. In G. H. Bower (Ed.), *The psychology of learning and motivation, Vol. 13* (pp. 219–270). New York: Academic Press.

Anisman, H. (1975). Time-dependent variations in aversively motivated behaviors: Non-associative effects of cholinergic and catecholaminergic activity. *Psychological Review, 82,* 359–385.

Anisman, H., deCatanzaro, D., & Remington, G. (1978). Escape performance following exposure to inescapable shock: Deficits in motor response maintenance. *Journal of Experimental Psychology: Animal Behavior Processes, 4,* 197–218.

Baker, A. G. (1976). Learned irrelevance and learned helplessness: Rats learn that stimuli, reinforcers, and responses are uncorrelated. *Journal of Experimental Psychology: Animal Behavior Processes, 2,* 130–142.

Baker, A. G., & Mercier, P. (1989). Attention, retrospective processing and cognitive representations. In S. B. Klein & R. R. Mowrer (Eds.), *Contemporary learning theories: Pavlovian conditioning and the status of traditional learning theory.* Hillsdale, NJ: Lawrence Erlbaum Associates.

Bersh, P. J., & Alloy, L. B. (1978). Avoidance based on shock intensity reduction with no change in shock probability. *Journal of the Experimental Analysis of Behavior, 30,* 293–300.

Boakes, R. A. (1977). Performance on learning to associate a stimulus with positive reinforcement. In H. Davis & H. M. B. Hurwitz (Eds.), *Operant-Pavlovian interaction* (pp. 67–97). Hillsdale, NJ: Lawrence Erlbaum Associates.

Bouton, M. E., Jones, D. L., McPhillips, S. A., & Swartzentruber, D. (1986). Potentiation and overshadowing in odor-aversion learning: Role of method of odor presentation, the distal-proximal cue distinction, and the conditionability of odor. *Learning and Motivation, 17,* 115–138.

Bracewell, R. J., & Black, A. H. (1974). The effects of restraint and noncontingent preshock on subsequent escape learning in the rat. *Learning and Motivation, 5,* 53–69.

Dickinson, A. (1989). The expectancy theory of animal conditioning. In S. B. Klein & R. R. Mowrer (Eds.), *Contemporary learning theories: Pavlovian conditioning and the status of traditional learning theory.* Hillsdale, NJ: Lawrence Erlbaum Associates.

Dickinson, A., & Shanks, D. R. (1985). Animal conditioning and human causality judgment. In L. G. Nilsson & T. Archer (Eds.), *Perspectives on learning and memory.* Hillsdale, NJ: Lawrence Erlbaum Associates.

Dickinson, A., Shanks, D. R., & Evenden, J. (1984). Judgment of act-outcome contingency: The role of selective attribution. *Quarterly Journal of Experimental Psychology, 36A,* 29–50.

Durlach, P. (1989). Learning and performance in Pavlovian conditioning: Are failures of contiguity failures of learning or performance. In S. B. Klein & R. R. Mowrer (Eds.), *Contemporary learning theories: Pavlovian conditioning and the status of traditional learning theory.* Hillsdale, NJ: Lawrence Erlbaum Associates.

Einhorn, H. J., & Hogarth, R. M. (1986). Judging probable cause. *Psychological Bulletin, 99,* 3–20.

Gibbon, J., Berryman, R., & Thompson, R. L. (1974). Contingency spaces and measures in classical and instrumental conditioning. *Journal of the Experimental Analysis of Behavior, 21,* 585–605.

Hammond, L. J. (1980). The effect of contingency upon the appetitive conditioning of free-operant behavior. *Journal of the Experimental Analysis of Behavior, 34,* 297–304.

Hammond, L. J., & Paynter, W. E., Jr. (1983). Probabilistic contingency theories of animal conditioning: A critical analysis. *Learning and Motivation, 14,* 527–550.

Hineline, P. N. (1970). Negative reinforcement without shock reduction. *Journal of the Experimental Analysis of Behavior, 14,* 259–268.

Hume, D. (1962). A treatise of human nature. In A. Flew (Ed.), *On human nature and the understanding.* New York: Collier. (*A treatise of human nature* was originally published in 1739).

Jackson, R. L., Alexander, J. H., & Maier, S. F. (1980). Learned helplessness, inactivity, and associative deficits: Effects of inescapable shock on response choice escape learning. *Journal of Experimental Psychology: Animal Behavior Processes, 6,* 1–20.

Jackson, R. L., Maier, S. F., & Rapaport, P. M. (1978). Exposure to inescapable shock produces both activity and associative deficits in the rat. *Learning and Motivation, 9,* 69–98.

Kamin, L. J. (1969). Predictability, surprise attention, and conditioning. In B. Campbell & R. Church (Eds.), *Punishment and aversive behavior* (pp. 279–296). New York: Appleton-Century-Crofts.

Kiefer, S. W., Rusiniak, K. W., & Garcia, J. (1982). Flavor-illness aversions: Gustatory neocortex oblations disrupt taste but not taste-oriented odor cues. *Journal of Comparative and Physiological Psychology, 96,* 540–548.

Killeen, P. R. (1978). Superstition: A matter of bias, not detectability. *Science, 199,* 88–90.

Killeen, P. R., & Smith, J. P. (1984). Perception of contingency in conditioning: Scalar timing, response bias and erasure of memory by reinforcement. *Journal of Experimental Psychology: Animal Behavior Processes, 10,* 333–346.

Lett, B. T. (1984). Extinction of taste aversion does not eliminate taste potentiation of odor aversion in rats or color aversion in pigeons. *Animal Learning & Behavior, 12,* 414–420.

Levis, D. J. (1989). The case for a return to a two-factor theory of avoidance: The failure of non-fear interpretations. In S. B. Klein & R. R. Mowrer (Eds.), *Contemporary learning theories: Pavlovian conditioning and the status of traditional learning theory.* Hillsdale, NJ: Lawrence Erlbaum Associates.

Lieberman, D. A., Davidson, F. H., & Thomas, G. V. (1985). Marking in pigeons: The role of memory in delayed reinforcement. *Journal of Experimental Psychology: Animal Behavior Processes, 11,* 611–624.

Lieberman, D. A., McIntosh, D. C., & Thomas, G. V. (1979). Learning when reward is delayed: A marking hypothesis. *Journal of Experimental Psychology: Animal Behavior Processes, 5,* 224–242.

Mackie, J. L. (1974). *The cement of the universe: A study of causation.* Oxford, England: Clarendon Press.

Mackintosh, N. J. (1978). Cognitive or associative theories of conditioning: Implications of an analysis of blocking. In H. Fowler, W. K. Honig, & S. H. Hulse (Eds.), *Cognitive processes in animal behavior* (pp. 155–175). Hillsdale, NJ: Lawrence Erlbaum Associates.

Mackintosh, N. J., & Dickinson, A. (1979). Instrumental (Type II) conditioning. In A. Dickinson & R. A. Boakes (Eds.), *Mechanisms of learning and motivation: A memorial volume to Jerzy Konorski.* Hillsdale, NJ: Lawrence Erlbaum Associates.

Maier, S. F., & Jackson, R. L. (1979). Learned helplessness: All of us were right (and wrong): Inescapable shock has multiple effects. In G. H. Bower (Ed.), *The psychology of learning and motivation, Vol. 13,* (pp. 155–218). New York: Academic Press.

Maier, S. F., Jackson, R. L., & Tomie, A. (1987). Potentiation, overshadowing, and prior exposure to inescapable shock. *Journal of Experimental Psychology: Animal Behavior Processes, 13,* 260–272.

Maier, S. F., & Seligman, M. E. P. (1976). Learned helplessness: Theory and evidence. *Journal of Experimental Psychology: General, 105,* 3–46.

Maier, S. F., Seligman, M. E. P., & Solomon, R. L. (1969). Pavlovian fear conditioning and learned helplessness: Effects on escape and avoidance behavior of (a) the CS–US contingency, and (b) the independence of the US and voluntary responding. In B. A. Campbell & R. M. Church (Eds.), *Punishment.* New York: Appleton-Century-Crofts.

Michotte, A. (1963). *The perception of causality.* New York: Basic Books.

Minor, T. R., Pelleymounter, M. A., & Maier, S. F. (1988). Uncontrollable stress, forebrain norepinephrine, and stimulus selection during choice escape learning. *Psychobiology,* in press.

Minor, T. R., Jackson, R. L., & Maier, S. F. (1984). Effects of task irrelevant cues and reinforcement delay on choice escape learning following inescapable shock: Evidence for a deficit in selective attention. *Journal of Experimental Psychology: Animal Behavior Processes, 10,* 543–556.

Minor, T. R., & LoLordo, V. M. (1984). Escape deficits following inescapable shock: The role of contextual odor. *Journal of Experimental Psychology: Animal Behavior Processes, 10,* 168–181.

Mitchell, J. A., Channell, S., & Hall, G. (1985). Response-reinforcer associations after caudate-putamen lesions in the rat: Spatial discrimination and overshadowing-potentiation effects in instrumental learning. *Behavioral Neuroscience, 99,* 1074–1088.

Mowrer, O. H. (1960). *Learning theory and behavior.* New York: Wiley.

Overmier, J. B., & Leaf, R. C. (1965). Effects of discriminative Pavlovian fear conditioning upon previously or subsequently acquired avoidance responding. *Journal of Comparative and Physiological Psychology, 60,* 213–218.

Overmier, J. B., Patterson, J., & Wielkiewicz, R. M. (1979). Environmental contingencies as sources of stress in animals. In S. Levine & H. Ursin (Eds.), *Coping and Health* (pp. 1–38). New York: Plenum Press.

Pearce, J. M., & Hall, G. (1978). Overshadowing the instrumental conditioning of a lever-press response by a more valid predictor of the reinforcer. *Journal of Experimental Psychology: Animal Behavior Processes, 4,* 356–367.

Potegal, M. (1982). Vestibular and neostriatal contributions to spatial orientation. In M. Potegal (Eds.), *Spatial abilities: Development and physiological foundations* (pp. 361–387). New York: Academic Press.

Rescorla, R. A. (1968). Probability of shock in the presence and absence of CS in fear conditioning. *Journal of Comparative and Physiological Psychology, 66,* 1–5.

Rescorla, R. A., & Wagner, A. R. (1972). A theory of Pavlovian conditioning: Variations in the effectiveness of reinforcement and non-reinforcement. In A. H. Black & W. F. Prokasy (Eds.), *Classical conditioning II. Current research and theory.* New York: Appleton-Century-Crofts.

Rosellini, R. A., DeCola, J. P., & Shapiro, N. K. (1982). Cross-motivational effects of inescapable shock are associative in nature. *Journal of Experimental Psychology: Animal Behavior Processes, 8,* 376–388.

Rusiniak, K. W., Hankins, W. G., Garcia, J., & Brett, L. P. (1979). Flavor-illness aversions: Potenttaition of odor by taste in rats. *Behavioral and Neural Biology, 25,* 1–17.

Rudy, J. W., & Castro, C. A. (1987). A developmental analysis of brightness discrimination learning in the rat: Evidence for an attentional deficit. *Psychobiology, 15,* 79–86.

Seligman, M. E. P., & Maier, S. F. (1967). Failure to escape traumatic shock. *Journal of Experimental Psychology, 74,* 1–9.

Shanks, D. R. (1985). Forward and backward blocking in human contingency judgment. *Quarterly Journal of Experimental Psychology, 37B,* 1–21.

Shultz, T. R. (1982). Rules of causal atrribution. *Monographs of the Society for Research in Child Development, 47,* 1–51.

St. Clair-Smith, R. (1979). The overshadowing of instrumental conditioning by a stimulus that predicts reinforcement better than the response. *Animal Learning and Behavior, 7,* 224–228.

Tarpy, R. M., Lea, S. E. G., & Midgley, M. (1983). The role of response–US correlation in stimulus-response overshadowing. *Quarterly Journal of Experimental Psychology, 35B,* 53–65.

Testa, T. J. (1975). Effects of similarity of location and temporal intensity pattern of conditioned and unconditioned stimuli on the acquisition of conditioned suppression in rats. *Journal of Experimental Psychology: Animal Behavior Processes, 1,* 114–121.

Thomas, G. V. (1981). Contiguity, reinforcement rate and the law of effect. *Quarterly Journal of Experimental Psychology, 33B,* 33–43.

Thomas, G. V., Lieberman, D. A., McIntosh, D. C., & Ronaldson, P. (1983). The role of marking when reward is delayed. *Journal of Experimental Psychology: Animal Behavior Processes, 9,* 401–411.

Tomie, A., & Loukas, E. (1983). Correlations between rats' spatial location and intracranial stimulation administration affects rate of acquisition and asymptotic level of time allocation preference in the open field. *Learning and Motivation, 14,* 471–491.

Von Wright, G. H. (1974). *Causality and determinism.* New York: Columbia University Press.

Wagner, A. R. (1981). SOP: A model of automatic memory processing in animal behavior. In N. E. Spear & R. R. Miller (Eds.), *Information processing in animals: Memory mechanisms* (pp. 5–47). Hillsdale, NJ: Lawrence Erlbaum Associates.

Wagner, A. R., Rudy, J. W., & Whitlow, J. W. (1973). Rehearsal in animal conditioning. *Journal of Experimental Psychology Monograph, 97,* 407–426.

Wasserman, E. A., & Neunaber, D. J. (1986). Reporting and responding to causal relations by college students: The role of temporal contiguity. *Journal of the Experimental Analysis of Behavior, 46,* 15–35.

Weiss, J. M., Glazer, H. J., & Pohorecky, L. A. (1975). Coping behavior and neurochemical changes: An alternative explanation for the original "learned helplessness" experiments. In *Relevance of the psychopathological animal to the human.* New York: Plenum Press.

Williams, J. L. (1984). Influence of postpartum shock controllability on subsequent maternal behavior in rats. *Animal Learning and Behavior, 12,* 209–216.

5 Biological View of Reinforcement

Franco J. Vaccarino
Bernard B. Schiff
University of Toronto

Stephen E. Glickman
University of California, Berkeley

During that time when the study of animal learning occupied center stage in American psychology, the nature of reward/reinforcement was a core issue in theoretical debate. Two problems dominated psychological attention: (1) defining reinforcing stimuli, and (2) specifying the role of such stimuli in the learning process. From Thorndike's earliest writings, the problem of circularity haunted reinforcement theorists. The law of effect suggested that actions that led to a "satisfying state of affairs" would be repeated. But how were we to recognize this satisfying state of affairs? Because the animal repeated the responses. This circular definitional situation produced an unsatisfying state of affairs for many psychologists. Several broad classes of solution emerged. The first, perhaps best exemplified by B. F. Skinner (1958) was a route of simple empiricism: use whatever works. The second range of solutions involved attempts to stipulate independently the characteristics of reinforcing stimuli. One could work close-to-the-data and rely on transsituational generality (what works in one reinforcement situation is predicted to work in other situations involving different instrumental responses; Meehl, 1950). Alternately, it was possible to derive many more precise predictions using the empirically based system developed by David Premack (1965). Within this framework, independent measures of response probability in particular stimulus situations were used to predict which stimuli could be employed to reinforce which responses. Positive reinforcement effects were to be found only under conditions where the performance of a high probability behavior was contingent on the prior performance of a behavior with a lower probability of occurrence (see Chapter 2 by Allison for a review of this literature).

Other theorists were more ambitious. In line with Thorndike's original goal, they wished to define reinforcers in terms of actions within the organism. Clark

111

Hull (1943) discussed reinforcement in terms of drive or tension-reduction. P. T. Young (1959) and Carl Pfaffman (1960) emphasized the ability of reinforcing stimuli (e.g., sweet foods) to activate particular sensory pathways (e.g., taste) with access to a positive hedonic system. Still other theorists suggested that any stimuli would function as reinforcers if they produced an optimal state of arousal or activation (Berlyne, 1967; McClelland, Atkinson, Clark, & Lowell, 1953). Finally, a set of theorists appeared who argued that any stimuli eliciting species-characteristic consummatory responses would serve as reinforcing stimuli (Sheffield, 1966; Tinbergen, 1951). Each of these theoretical positions had a favorite domain of data (Glickman, 1973), but no position ever achieved clear dominance. In recent years, learning psychologists have tended to ignore the entire question of independent stipulation of reinforcement, perhaps discouraged by the historical record.

The second major problem area for psychologists dealing with reinforcement concerned the potential role of reinforcement in the learning process. The question assumed several forms. Was the presence of a reinforcing stimulus essential for association formation? Alternately, if a clear reinforcing stimulus was appropriately positioned in the situation, would it strengthen the association bond? In the course of long debates between the followers of Hull and Tolman over the existence of (nonreinforced) latent learning, the preponderance of evidence tended to favor an answer of *no* (Thistlethwaite, 1951), the presence of a clear reinforcing stimulus was not necessary for association formation. On the face of the argument, the occurrence of sensory preconditioning, presumably an example of nonrewarded pure sensory–sensory associations (Brogden, 1939), was also in accord with this view. However, definitions of reinforcement were sufficiently fuzzy that a devoted advocate of the reinforcement-is-essential position could always find a glimmer of reward in any learning situation; a state of affairs which surely discourages psychologists with further concern with this issue as well. Finally, the idea that reinforcing stimuli had some special ''glue'' function, strengthening the associative bond, seemed to lack solid evidence (Walker, 1969) and further research on this problem tended to disappear from the learning literature.

We therefore have a situation in which a set of classic questions of reinforcement theory were apparently abandoned, not because they were solved, but because people had reached a theoretical dead end. However, modern research in biological psychology suggests that these problems may profitably be reopened. If we can begin to stipulate the actual neural events associated with reinforcement, that is a substantial improvement over such phrases as ''a satisfying state of affairs'' or ''drive-reduction,'' which had no clear, independent reference points. Moreover, in this biological tradition, new entry points are provided for the study of reinforcing effects on associative processes per se. The remainder of this paper is concerned with a reexamination of reinforcement from a physiological vantage point , supplemented where appropriate by references to relevant data developed in an ethological, naturalistic framework.

The bulk of our discussion involves positively reinforced behavior in the context of instrumental learning.

I.   NEURAL SUBSTRATES OF REWARD

In 1954, Olds and Milner discovered that rats could be easily trained to perform an operant response in order to receive trains of electrical stimulation into discrete brain regions. This finding marked the beginning of a multitude of studies aimed at characterizing the nature of the neural substrates mediating brain stimulation reward (BSR). The fact that the reinforcer in this case was the electrical stimulation of discrete brain areas, rather than a natural reinforcer, indicated that the brain possessed groups of neurons which, when stimulated, represented a reward to the animal. Because the activation of these neurons is rewarding to the animal it has been suggested that, under normal conditions, the activation of reward neurons by natural stimuli or behavior itself could, in principle, reinforce behavior. Thus, this represented a possible neural substrate for mediation of reinforcement. The fact that BSR was only observed in certain brain regions further suggested that reward neurons are not a general brain phenomenon and that reinforcement may be dependent on the activation of specific neural systems.

Since the original Olds and Milner (1954) finding, many experiments have been directed at trying to characterize the nature of the neural substrates mediating BSR. Although BSR can be obtained from a number of brain regions, most of the research aimed at characterizing neural substrates of BSR have focused on stimulation of the medial forebrain bundle (MFB) in the area of the lateral hypothalamus. This chapter focuses on elements of reinforcement associated with the MFB. The MFB is particularly interesting because it is a fiber system that courses through the length of the hypothalamus, a structure known to be critical for the expression of numerous fundamental behaviors important for the survival of the organism. It is important to emphasize that phylogenetically more recent structures, such as the frontal cortex and hippocampus, will also support BSR and, not surprisingly, have different properties from more primitive BSR systems (Corbett, LaFerriere, & Milner, 1982; Corbett & Stellar, 1983; Robertson, Laferriere, & Franklin, 1981; Routtenberg & Sloan, 1971; Schenk & Shizgal, 1982; van der Kooy, Fibiger & Phillips, 1977). Elements of reinforcement associated with these evolutionarily more advanced structures are not considered in this chapter.

In order to help guide the reader through subsequent sections, Fig. 5.1 presents a schematic representation of various brain sites and pathways that are referred to in text. In addition, a brief description of the reinforcement-relevant function ascribed to the various brain regions is presented.

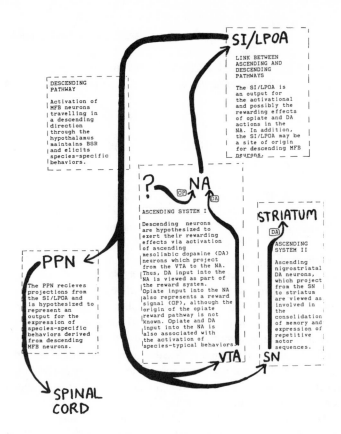

SI/LPOA

LINK BETWEEN
ASCENDING AND
DESCENDING
PATHWAYS

The SI/LPOA is
an output for
the activational
and possibly the
rewarding effects
of opiate and DA
actions in the
NA. In addition,
the SI/LPOA may be
a site of origin
for descending MFB
neurons.

DESCENDING PATHWAY

Activation of
MFB neurons
travelling in
a descending
direction
through the
hypothalamus
maintains BSR
and elicits
species-specific
behaviors.

? NA

OP   DA

ASCENDING SYSTEM I

Descending neurons
are hypothesized to
exert their rewarding
effects via activation
of ascending
mesolimbic dopamine (DA)
neurons which project
from the VTA to the NA.
Thus, DA input into the
NA is viewed as part of
the reward system.
Opiate input into the NA
also represents a reward
signal (OP), although the
origin of the opiate
reward pathway is not
known. Opiate and DA
input into the NA is
also associated with
the activation of
species-typical behaviors.

STRIATUM

DA

ASCENDING
SYSTEM II

Ascending
nigrostriatal
DA neurons,
which project
from the SN
to striatum
are viewed as
involved in
the
consolidation
of memory and
expression of
repetitive
motor
sequences.

PPN

The PPN recieves
projections from
the SI/LPOA and
is hypothesized to
represent an
output for the
expression of
species-specific
behaviors derived
from descending
MFB neurons.

VTA   **SN**

SPINAL CORD

FIG. 5.1 presents a schematic drawing of the model developed in this paper. In this model descending medial forebrain bundle (MFB) fibres which support brain stimulation reward (BSR) have three outputs. The first projects caudally to the pedunculopontine nucleus (PPN) and thence to the spinal cord and is the route whereby species-specific behaviors are expressed. The second is to the mesolimbic system (ASCENDING SYSTEM I) which projects from the ventral tegmental area (VTA) to the nucleus accumbens (NA). This is viewed as the output upon which MFB reinforcement depends. The mesolimbic system in turn is seen as facilitating the MFB via its projection to the substantia innominata/lateral preoptic area (SI/LPOA), which may be a site of origin for descending MFB neurons. Therefore, the activation of MFB neurons, whether this be by electrical stimulation or by the physiological activation of pathways subserving a particular species-typical behavior, results in the activation of the mesolimbic system which feeds back and helps to maintain the MFB activity that has produced it in the first place. Opiate activation in the NA is also seen as contributing to this process, although the origin of the NA opiate input is not known. Conceptualized this way, the neural substrate of reward is a positive feedback loop which is initiated by the activation of pathways mediating species-typical behaviors and which in turn serves to help maintain the species-specific behavior. The third output is to the nigrostriatal system (Ascending System II) which projects from the substantia nigra (SN) to the striatum. This pathway is seen as being involved in memory consolidation and repetitive, stereotyped motor sequences.

Descending MFB Fibres Mediate BSR

In recent years, techniques derived from single cell electrophysiology have been applied to characterize the neurophysiological and anatomical properties of behaviorally relevant neurons in brain stimulation studies. Studies applying these techniques to the analysis of BSR derived from the MFB have found that the refractory period of the reward-relevant neurons lies in the range of 0.4–1.2 msec. (Yeomans, 1975, 1979, 1988). Conduction velocity estimates of these neurons indicate that they propagate their action potentials at a velocity of 1.0–8.0 m/sec (Bielajew & Shizgal, 1982; Shizgal, Bielajew, Corbett, Skelton, & Yeomans, 1980; Yeomans, 1988). This suggests that the neurons mediating BSR are small and myelinated (Waxman, 1978). Further studies aimed at determining the directionality of the reward-relevant neurons suggest that BSR from the MFB is dependent on the activation of descending fibers traveling through the lateral hypothalamic region to the ventral tegmental area of the midbrain (Bielajew & Shizgal, 1986). This is consistent with earlier suggestions by Glickman and Schiff (1967).

Ascending Dopamine Neurons and Reward

Although foregoing results indicate that the directly stimulated MFB reward neurons are small, myelinated neurons which travel in a descending direction, numerous pharmacological studies investigating the neurochemical characteristics of BSR provide strong support for the involvement of ascending dopamine (DA) neurons (small and unmyelinated) in the expression of MFB BSR. It has been demonstrated that drugs that increase DAergic transmission facilitate BSR while drugs that interfere with DAergic transmission attenuate BSR (Cooper, Cott, & Breese, 1976; Koob, Fray, & Iversen, 1978; Fouriezos & Wise, 1976; Phillips, Brooks, & Fibiger, 1975; Phillips & Fibiger, 1973; Phillips & Fibiger, 1978; Wise, 1978). Electrode mapping studies have further revealed that there is a close correspondence between sites that support BSR and the presence of DAergic neural elements (e.g., Corbett & Wise, 1980). In addition, studies have found that there is an anatomical correspondence between specific reward-sensitive DA terminal sites and the location of the BSR electrode in the DA cell body region (Phillips, LePiane, & Fibiger, 1982; Porrino, 1987; Redgrave, 1978). The latter suggests that the rewarding properties of BSR may be associated with the electrode's activation (probably indirectly) of DA neuron subsets. It appears that nigrostriatal DA neurons (Ascending System II, see Fig. 5.1) and mesolimbic DA neurons (Ascending System I, see Fig. 5.1) are both important for the expression of BSR derived from the MFB (Broekkamp, Pijnenburg, Cools, & Van Rossum, 1975; Koob et al., 1978; Phillips & Fibiger, 1978; Phillips et al., 1982; Porrino, 1987; Redgrave, 1978). To explain why MFB BSR is altered by DAergic drugs, it has been suggested that BSR is dependent on the direct activation of descending non-

DAergic fibers which in turn activate ascending DA fibers (Bielajew & Shizgal, 1986; Shizgal et al., 1980; Yeomans, 1982, 1988).

Support for the involvement of the mesolimbic DA system in the mediation of reward functions comes from studies directly examining the rewarding properties of DAergic agonists.[1] Studies investigating the central substrates of cocaine and amphetamine (see Footnote 1) drug reward indicate that the ability for these drugs to increase DA transmission in the mesolimbic DA system is critical for their rewarding properties. This conclusion is derived from the following findings:

1. Animals will readily learn to self-administer (systemically) drugs such as cocaine and amphetamine and will develop a conditioned preference for a place in which they have previously been exposed to such drugs (Bozarth & Wise, 1983; Mucha, van der Kooy, O'Shaughnessy, & Bucenieks, 1982; Spyraki, Fibiger, & Phillips, 1982; Wise 1978).

2. Destruction of mesolimbic DA neurons, or selective blockade of DA receptors will attenuate the rewarding properties of these drugs as demonstrated in both self-administration and conditioned place preference paradigms (Lyness, Friedle, & Moore, 1979; Roberts, Corcoran, & Fibiger, 1977; Roberts & Koob, 1982; Spyraki et al., 1982; Wise, 1978).

3. Animals with lesions of the mesolimbic DA neurons (see Fig. 5.1) will self-administer apomorphine, a DA receptor agonist, and will show a place preference for an environment previously paired with apomorphine (Roberts & Koob, 1982; van der Kooy, Swerdlow, & Koob, 1983). This latter result indicates that DA receptor stimulation can continue to be reinforcing in rats with lesions of the DA terminals.

4. Rats will readily learn to self-administer DAergic agonists directly into the brain in DAergic terminal regions in the NA, and that such treatment will also induce a conditioned place preference (Carr & White, 1986; Hoebel et al., 1982; Monaco, Hernandez, & Hobel, 1981).

Taken together, these results demonstrate that DAergic substrates are critical for reward functions and indicate that the rewarding properties of drugs such as cocaine and amphetamine are dependent on mesolimbic DA neurotransmission. It is worth noting that the mesolimbic DA system has also been implicated in the development of responsiveness to conditioned stimuli (Beninger, 1983; Taylor & Robbins, 1984, 1986).

Ascending System I vs. Ascending System II
Involvement in Reward

The self-administration and conditioned place preference studies just described suggest that the mesolimbic DA system (Ascending System I), but not the nigro-

---

[1]DAergic agonists such as apormorphine, are drugs which mimic the effects of DA. Amphetamine and cocaine are indirect DAergic agonists in that they increase DA transmission. DAergic antagonists interfere with DA transmission.

striatal DA system (Ascending System II) is critical for reward functions. In support of this notion, destruction of striatal DA terminals has little effect on cocaine self-administration (Koob, Vaccarino, Amalric, & Bloom, 1987). By contrast, destruction of NA DA terminals attenuate intravenous cocaine self-administration and significantly reduces the fixed ratio for which rats will continue to work. Furthermore, conditioned place preferences can be observed for environments paired with intra-NA amphetamine, but not intrastriatal amphetamine microinjections (Carr & White, 1986). In addition, while rats will self-administer amphetamine into the NA, intrastriatal amphetamine self-administration is rare (Hoebel et al., 1982). Taken together these results imply that increased DA release from mesolimbic neurons represents a reward signal to the animal while increased DA release from the nigrostriatal system does not.

Although the self-administration and conditioned place preference studies promote the importance of mesolimbic DA neurons in reward system function, the nigrostriatal DA system does appear to be involved in reinforcing responding for BSR (Phillips et al., 1982; Porrino, 1987; Wise, 1981). Phillips et al. (1982) found that kainic acid (destroys cell bodies) lesions of the dorsal striatum attenuated BSR derived from the substantia nigra but not from the ventral tegmental area (VTA) (see Fig. 5.1). Furthermore, intrastriatal amphetamine can facilitate MFB BSR (Broekkamp et al., 1975). In light of the topographical correspondence between nigral cell bodies and striatal terminal regions (Fallon & Moore, 1978; Redgrave & Mitchell, 1982), these results suggest that the nigrostriatal system is involved in BSR derived from the substantia nigra or MFB. Studies examining metabolic changes in the brain associated with BSR suggest that BSR derived from the substantia nigra and VTA are distinguishable based on the different metabolic changes associated with BSR from the two sites (Porrino, 1987). Consistent with the results of Phillips et al. (1982), BSR derived from the substantia nigra, but not the VTA, was found to be associated with increased metabolic activity in the striatum.

If increased nigrostriatal DA release is not a rewarding event then why would the nigrostriatal system be involved in BSR? One possible explanation is that BSR derived from the substantia nigra is not associated with reward per se, but instead reflects some other function of the nigrostriatal system that results in the reinforcement of operant responding.

Ascending System II and the "Glue" Function of Reinforcers

A number of experiments have shown that reinforcers have the ability to facilitate memory consolidation. They have shown that the memory for 1-trial avoidance tasks and 1-trial appetitive tasks are significantly improved when the animals are exposed to positive reinforcers during a limited time period following the 1-trial learning experience. This has been shown by feeding hungry rats after a 1-trial passive avoidance (Huston, Mondadori, & Waser, 1974), and also by electrical stimulation of the MFB following 1-trial passive avoidance (Mondadori, Ornstein, Waser, & Huston, 1976), 1-trial appetitive learning (Major & White, 1978) and sensory preconditioning (Coulombe & White, 1982), and by posttrial injection of amphetamine in a variety of tasks (see Carr & White, 1984). These authors argue convincingly that the facilitation is a specific effect on memory consolidation.

Although there is no evidence regarding sites of central action for the posttrial facilitatory effects of food, it has been shown that the *glue* function of BSR and amphetamine is related to nigrostriatal activity and not to mesolimbic activity (Major & White, 1978; Carr & White, 1984). It should be noted that other researchers (Routtenberg & Holzman, 1973; Fibiger & Phillips, 1976) have produced disruption of retention with nigral stimulation. However, an analysis of experimental variables that is consistent with a consolidation hypothesis could account for these results.

A picture emerges that suggests that the two ascending dopamine systems are specialized to subserve two different functions of positive reinforcers. The mesolimbic system is involved in the motivational properties of positive reinforcement, and the nigrostriatal system is involved in the memory consolidation properties of these same reinforcers.

The view that the mesolimbic system is motivational and that the nigrostriatal system is not, is supported by the differences in elicited behaviors associated with activation of these two systems. Feeding elicited by dopaminergic activity in the mesolimbic system interacts with motivational variables such as the state of deprivation and the attractiveness of food, while feeding associated with dopaminergic activity in the nigrostriatal system does not (see section on Elicited Behavior). Systemic injections of amphetamine result in increased locomotion (which appears appetitive in nature) and motor stereotypy. The former is associated with dopaminergic activity in the mesolimbic system and the latter with dopaminergic activity in the nigrostriatal system (see section on Elicited Behavior).

The stereotyped motor behavior elicited by nigrostriatal dopamine activity has been directly related to the memory consolidation functions of the striatum. Carr and White (1984) have shown that the degree of memory improvement produced by posttrial injection of amphetamine is significantly correlated with the amount of stereotypy but not with the locomotor exploration induced by that injection.

This relationship between stereotypy and memory consolidation arising from increased dopamine in the striatum can be the basis for explaining why animals will bar press for electrical stimulation in the substantia nigra. Electrical stimulation in the substantia nigra may increase dopamine activity in the striatum, and thereby increase the probability of ongoing activity, as in the facilitation of consolidation. In self-stimulation experiments the ongoing activity that is facilitated is the bar press response which has delivered the electrical stimulation. The bar press response seen this way becomes an instance of stereotypy associated with increased dopamine activity in the striatum.

If this is the case then we should find that the topography of the bar pressing response for BSR in the nigrostriatal system should be different from the bar pressing response for BSR in the mesolimbic system. In particular, we could expect that stimulating the mesolimbic motivational system would result in behavioral activation and components of elicited species-specific behaviors in the operant response, and that the nigrostriatal self-stimulation should be characterized by stereotypy. Systematic observations of this kind do not yet exist. However, observations in a methodological study (Schiff, 1975) provide indirect support for these notions.

In Schiff's study it was found that lesions of the striatum had differential effects on operant responding for BSR in the MFB depending on the degree to which the operant response had components of behaviors elicited by the electrical stimulus. Responses that had significant elicited components were barely affected by the lesions. These responses were running back and forth in a tilt box, and also bar pressing on a bar that was relatively high off the ground. These bar pressing responses were characterized by "much activated biting and pawing of the lever." However, when the bar was close to the ground "biting of the bar was frustrated . . . and the rats acquired a discrete and well organized lever press response." In that case the same lesions interrupted bar pressing in all animals for an average of 7 days.

These two patterns of response are consistent with the characteristics ascribed to the two ascending systems. The effectiveness of the striatal lesions in interrupting only the more stereotyped response is likewise congruent with our speculations regarding the special properties of the two systems. Electrical stimulation of the MFB can likely activate both ascending systems. It is possible that the constraints of the operant situation biased one or the other for control over the operant behavior.

These described patterns of operant responding were also distinguished from each other by how they were acquired. The responses that had a significant elicited component were acquired very quickly in the first training session. The elicited behavior (biting the bar or locomotion) served to maintain the self-stimulation. The more stereotyped responding on the low bar "required more systematic and sustained shaping over a longer period of time." This is consistent with the finding that BSR derived from the substantia nigra is difficult to acquire (MacMillan, Simantirakis, & Shizgal, 1985).

These two patterns of response and response acquisition are evocative of some of the distinctions between "predisposed and constrained" learning described in Chapter 9 of this volume by Timberlake and Lucas. Therefore, the two ascending systems may be neural analogues to these two kinds of learning. Because the MFB has inputs into both systems the implication of this model is that the distinction between predisposed and constrained learning may be a matter of degree, depending on the relative activation of the two ascending systems.

II. ELICITED BEHAVIOR

Behaviors Elicited by Electrical Stimulation of BSR Sites

A variety of species-specific behaviors can be elicited by electrical stimulation of loci in the hypothalamus that will support BSR. This literature was reviewed by Glickman and Schiff (1967), and formed the basis of a consummatory response theory of reinforcement which stated that reinforcement represents the facilitation of activity in neurons which underly the expression of behaviors that are important for the survival of the organism.

Species-specific behaviors elicited from BSR sites include: feeding, drinking, exploration, sexual behavior, attack, shredding, hoarding and foot thumping (Glickman, 1973). The one behavioral pattern that is preeminently associated with reinforcing loci in the hypothalamus is locomotor approach (Christopher & Butter, 1968; Glickman, 1973), and is characterized by forward movement and sniffing and looks like exploration. This underlines the importance of approach behavior in positive reinforcement.

The generality of the phenomenon does not by itself indicate that the species-specific behaviors and BSR are mediated by the same neurons. In the light of the multitude of neurons present in the hypothalamus and passing through the MFB, the possibility that BSR and elicited behaviors were being driven by separate neurons in the vicinity of the electrode could not be eliminated.

More recent studies investigating the refractory period characteristics of neurons mediating BSR and stimulation-induced feeding or stimulation-induced exploration derived from the same MFB electrode site (Rompre & Miliaressis, 1980; Hawkins, Roll, Puerto, & Yeomans, 1983; Gratton & Wise, 1987a) have reported that the refractory periods for BSR neurons are very similar to those for stimulation-induced feeding and exploration. In addition, Gratton and Wise (1988b) have recently found that the conduction velocities and trajectories of the BSR neurons overlapped with those for stimulation-induced feeding. These findings indicate that neurons mediating reward and elicited behaviors (i.e., feeding and exploration) share similar anatomical and neurophysiological characteristics, and provide support to the suggestion of Glickman and Schiff (1967), that reinforcement represents the activation of neurons mediating the expression of species-specific approach behaviors. The directionality findings already discussed suggest that these neurons travel in a descending direction. Using a similar approach to Gratton and Wise (1988b), Durivage and Miliaressis (1987) have compared BSR and stimulation-induced activity derived from the MFB and VTA in the same animals. They found that collision between VTA and MFB was observed for either BSR or elicited activity, but not both. Thus, they suggest that MFB fibers mediating BSR and exploration can be dissociated. However, the measurement used for activity in the Durivage and Miliaressis (1987) study was based on movement detection, thus making it difficult to ascertain the extent to which the lack of collision observed for activity was associated with the expression of movements not related to locomotor or exploratory activity.

An important issue has been raised regarding the specificity of neural systems activated by BSR. Valenstein, Cox, and Kakolewski (1970) demonstrated that the behavior elicited by electrical stimulation of the hypothalamus can be switched to other behaviors with appropriate environmental and experimental manipulations. They concluded that hypothalamic stimulation produces a general state and does not activate specific neural systems underlying particular consummatory behaviors. This has been a controversial position (Hallonquist & Mrosovsky, 1986). It is worth pointing out that the demonstrations of switched behaviors were restricted to oral consummatory responses. It is perhaps not surprising that these behaviors are interchangeable because they are so in nature. For example, animals can regulate water intake by either eating or drinking. Block, Vallier, and Glickman, (1974) showed that chemical stimulation in brain loci that elicited drinking but not eating would induce rats to lick water sprouts or chew lettuce depending on what was available. It would be interesting to know if switching between electrically elicited behaviors were restricted to oral responses, or if animals could also be made to switch to functionally different responses such as copulation or attack.

If reinforcement is associated with the activation of neuronal systems involved in the expression of species-typical behaviors, then one would predict that pharmacological activation of reward-relevant DA neurons should also be capable of facilitating the expression of various species-typical behaviors. Indeed, as in the case of BSR sites, pharmacological activation of DA reward sites will also result in the activation of certain species-typical behaviors.

Behaviors Elicited by Chemical Stimulation of Ascending DA Systems

Locomotor Activity and Dopamine. In addition to mediating reward, activation of DA systems is also associated with general locomotor activation. That is, animals treated with low to moderate doses of drugs that increase DAergic transmission will show overall increases in activity which are characterized by increases in locomotion, sniffing and rearing (Fray, Sahakian, Robbins, Koob, & Iversen, 1980: Iversen & Iversen, 1981; Kelly, 1977; Swerdlow, Vaccarino, Amalric, & Koob, 1986). These behaviors resemble those manifested under conditions of high motivation or arousal (Iversen & Fray, 1975; Lyons & Robbins, 1975; Seiden, MacPhail, & Oglesby, 1975). Studies aimed at identifying the neural substrates of DA-sensitive locomotor activation indicate that, like DAergic reward, DA mediated locomotor activation requires the integrity of the mesolimbic DA system. This is supported by the following findings:

1. Locomotor activation induced by systemic injections of direct or indirect DA agonists can be blocked by DA antagonists (Maj, Swawinska, Kapturkie-

wicz, & Sarnek, 1972; Schlechter & Butcher, 1972; Roberts, Zis, & Fibiger, 1975; Vaccarino, Amalric, Swerdlow, & Koob, 1986).

2. Lesions of NA DA terminals attenuate the locomotor activation induced by systemic amphetamine treatment while lesions of the nigrostriatal system do not (Creese & Iversen, 1972, 1975; Joyce & Koob, 1981; Kelly, Seviour, & Iversen, 1975).

3. DA antagonists injected directly into the NA block amphetamine locomotion (Pijnenburg, Honig, & Van Rossum, 1975b).

4. Direct injections of DA agonists into the NA induce locomotor activation which is very similar to that induced by systemic amphetamine and which can be reversed with DA antagonist treatment (Anden & Jackson, 1975; Costall, Domeny, & Naylor, 1984; Costall, Fortune, Hui, & Naylor, 1980; Costall & Naylor, 1975; Jones, Mogenson, & Wu, 1981; Pijnenburg, Honig, Van der Heyden, & Van Rossum, 1976; Pijenenburg, Honig, & Van Rossum, 1975a; Pijnenburg & Van Rossum, 1973).

These results indicate that, as in the case of the rewarding properties, the locomotor activating properties of DAergic agonists require the integrity of DA systems, with the mesolimbic DA system being particularly important. Thus, DAergic activation of sites associated with reinforcement is also associated with activation of locomotor activity. The importance of this relationship has been stressed by Wise and Bozarth (1987).

Feeding Behavior and Dopamine.   Although systemic administration of amphetamine in moderate to high doses decreases food intake (Lewander, 1977), systemic administration in low doses increases food intake (Evans & Vaccarino, 1987; Winn, Williams, & Herberg, 1982). It has been further demonstrated that intracerebroventricular administration of amphetamine or the dopamine agonist, bromocriptine, in low doses can facilitate food intake in rats (Evans & Eikelboom, 1987; Morley, Levine, Grace, & Kneip, 1982). Thus, it appears that activation of DA systems can facilitate feeding behavior.

Studies aimed at identifying the central site of action for amphetamine-induced feeding have shown that microinjections of low doses of amphetamine into either the striatum or the NA produce stimulatory effects on food intake (Evans & Vaccarino, 1986; Winn et al., 1982). While both intra-NA and intrastriatal amphetamine microinjections produce an increase in feeding, these two sites appear to be functionally different. For example, intra-NA amphetamine can potentiate rat chow intake in food-deprived rats (Evans & Vaccarino, 1986) but not in nondeprived rats (Evans & Vaccarino, unpublished observation). In contrast, intrastriatal amphetamine microinjections can increase rat chow intake in nondeprived rats (Winn et al., 1982). In an effort to characterize the nature of amphetamine-induced feeding, Evans and Vaccarino (1988) have recently found that intra-NA amphetamine selectively increased palatable food intake in nondeprived rats. Thus, it appears that intra-NA amphetamine treatment is associated with increased feeding directed at the most rewarding food type. This is demonstrated by the fact that intra-NA amphetamine increased food intake following either deprivation of regular chow (thus making the regular chow more attractive) or introduction of an attractive food to a free-feeding rat. The selectivity of intra-NA amphetamine effects for the most attractive food type is demonstrated by the finding that when faced with a choice of different food types varying in sugar concentration, rats injected with intra-NA amphetamine will show a selective enhancement of the most attractive food. Striatal amphetamine-induced feeding appears to be a more generalized phenomenon as it is evident in chow intake in nondeprived rats (Winn et al., 1982) and also does not show the selectivity for palatable foods which is evident following NA injections. Although the mechanisms underlying the differences between striatal and NA-induced feeding are not understood, differences in NA and striatal involvement in reinforcement discussed earlier may help elucidate the basis for such differences.

Consistent with an excitatory role for DA in feeding are numerous studies demonstrating that interference with DAergic transmission inhibits feeding (Ungerstedt, 1971; Wise & Raptis, 1986; Wise, 1982). Wise and Raptis (1986) have found that pimozide, a DA antagonist, increases the latency and decreases the rate of feeding. Interestingly, pimozide's inhibitory effects on feeding appear to increase over repeated trials, much like reward termination is increasingly effective at extinguishing responding over repeated trials (i.e. extinction). Since pimozide treated animals are capable of responding at control levels and show a progressive decrease in their feeding behavior with repeated trials, the effects of pimozide on feeding have been taken to suggest that blockade of DA transmission causes a motivational deficit and that the progressive decrease in food intake is related to an attenuation of the reinforcing value of food reward (Wise & Colle, 1984; Wise & Raptis, 1986; Wise, 1982). Further evidence for the involvement of DA systems in food reward is the fact that DA antagonist treatment is more effective at decreasing intake of sweetened solutions than water (Sclafani, Aravich, & Xenakis, 1982). This latter result is consistent with the selective increases in sweetened food observed following amphetamine treatment.

As in the case for BSR derived from the MFB, stimulation-induced feeding derived from the MFB is also attenuated following treatment with a DA antagonist. Jenck, Gratton, and Wise (1986) found that pimozide blocked stimulation-induced feeding as evidenced by a dose-dependent increase in the frequency threshold required to produce feeding. These results parallel the BSR findings and indicate that MFB-derived feeding is also dependent on an intact ascending DA system.

Hoarding Behavior and Dopamine.   In addition to feeding and locomotion, hoarding behavior in rats has been found to be sensitive to manipulations of the mesolimbic DA system. Hoarding behavior can be observed in animals that are maintained on a food-deprivation schedule. Interference with mesolimbic DA transmission produces attenuation of hoarding which can be reversed by DA agonist treatment

(Alpert & Iversen, 1982; Kelley & Stinus, 1985). Although such a deficit might be due to motoric deficits, Kelley and Stinus (1985) have provided data which suggest that the hoarding deficit associated with mesolimbic DA interference is not due to motor, regulatory, or ingestive impairments. Kelley and Stinus (1985) further suggest the mesolimbic DA neurons are critical for the establishment of what Bindra called a "positive incentive motivational state." They viewed the mesolimbic system as being associated with activation of appetitive responses which facilitate the expression of species-typical behaviors. Thus, under normal conditions both external and internal stimuli driving a particular behavior (in this case, hoarding) are viewed as activating mesolimbic DA neurons, which function to facilitate the relevant response patterns.

Fighting Behavior and Dopamine.   Recently, the mesolimbic DA system has also been implicated in the expression of fighting behavior. Pucilowski and Valzelli (1986) found that destruction of DA terminals in the NA potentiated the expression of apomorphine-induced fighting in rats. Since apomorphine is a DA agonist and destruction of DA terminals produce supersensitivity of postsynaptic DA receptors, these results were taken to suggest that activation of NA DA receptors will facilitate the expression of fighting behavior given the appropriate external stimuli (Pucilowski & Valzelli, 1986).

Opiate Involvement in Ascending Reward System

The preceding sections suggest a response-oriented view of reinforcement systems by providing evidence that brain reward sites will elicit species-typical behaviors when activated. The evidence, thus far, has focused on phenomena associated (directly or indirectly) with DA activation. A further test for the generalizability of a response-oriented view of reinforcement would be to investigate the extent to which species-typical behaviors can be elicited by activation of reward sites which do not require DA function. Of interest here are studies examining the behavioral properties of opiate drugs such as morphine or heroin.

As in the case of DA agonists, animals will learn to self-administer opiate drugs and will develop a conditioned place preference for a place in which they have previously been exposed to such drugs (Koob, Pettit, Ettenberg, & Bloom, 1984; Mucha, et al., 1982; Weeks, 1962). These effects are centrally mediated (Bechara & van der Kooy, 1985; Koob et al., 1984; Vaccarino, Pettit, Bloom, & Koob, 1985), indicating that activation of opiate receptors in the brain can reinforce behavior. Intracranial self-administration studies aimed at identifying the critical brain regions mediating opiate reward have found that rats will self-administer opiates into the ventral tegmental area (VTA) (Bozarth & Wise, 1981b), lateral hypothalamus (Olds, 1979; Olds & Williams, 1980) and NA (Goeders, Lane, & Smith, 1984; Olds, 1982). Consistent with these results are conditioned place preference findings showing that microinjections of morphine into the VTA, NA, and lateral hypothalamus will produce a conditioned place preference (Phillips & LePiane, 1980, 1982; van der Kooy, Mucha, O'Shaughnessy, & Bucenieks,

1982). Further support for the involvement of these structures in opiate reward comes from studies demonstrating that blockade of opiate receptors in the VTA and NA attenuate heroin reward during intravenous (I.V.) self-administration (Britt & Wise, 1983; Vaccarino, Bloom, & Koob, 1985). Together, these findings indicate that activation of opiate receptors in the VTA, NA, and possibly the lateral hypothalamus, is sufficient to reinforce behavior.

In light of presence of DA cell bodies in the VTA, studies have addressed the possibility that opiate reward is dependent on the integrity of DA neurons. In support of this idea, it has been found that self-administration and conditioned place preference produced by intra-VTA opiate microinjections can be attenuated by blockade of mesolimbic DA transmission (Bozarth & Wise, 1981a; Phillips, LePiane, & Fibiger, 1983; Spyraki, Phillips, & Fibiger, 1983). While these results indicate that opiate reward is dependent on an intact DA system, other studies have suggested the presence of opiate reward, which is not dependent on DA transmission. Using the conditioned place preference and self-administration paradigms it has been found that blockade of DA receptors, in doses that significantly attenuated I.V. cocaine and amphetamine (indirect DA agonist) reward, did not attenuate systemic opiate reward (Ettenberg, Pettit, Bloom, & Koob, 1982; Mackey & van der Kooy, 1985). It has also been found that destruction of mesolimbic DA neurons markedly attenuated I.V. self-administration of cocaine but not opiate self-administration (Pettit, Ettenberg, Bloom, & Koob, 1984). The fact that activation of opiate receptors can continue to reinforce behavior following interference with DA transmission strongly suggests that in addition to a DA-dependent opiate reward site (i.e., the VTA), there are also other reward-relevant opiate sites.

Studies investigating the effects of VTA and NA opiate receptor blockade on I.V. opiate reward indicate that both NA and VTA opiate receptors contribute to opiate reward (Britt & Wise, 1983; Vaccarino, Bloom, & Koob, 1985). Of particular interest is the fact that while blockade of NA opiate receptors attenuates opiate reward, cocaine reward is not affected (Vaccarino, Bloom, & Koob, 1985), suggesting that NA opiate reward-relevant receptors are not directly associated with DA neurons. These results suggest that while the VTA is a site which mediates DA-dependent opiate reward, other non-DA dependent opiate receptors in the NA efferent to DA neurons, are also capable of reinforcing behavior. In light of the importance of the NA for opiate and DA reward and the probable independence of NA opiate reward from DA transmission, the NA appears to represent a site that has reward-relevant receptors associated with two independent sources (i.e., DA and opioid input). Thus, at the level of the NA, opiate receptor activation and DA receptor activation may represent two separate reward signals.

Locomotor Activity and Opiates.   As in the case of DA systems, examination of the neurochemical substrates mediating the locomotor activating effects of opiates reveals a striking parallel with the substrates underlying the rewarding properties of opiates. Like DAergic drugs, opiate drugs in low doses induce increased locomotor activity (at higher doses opiates induce a period of initial behavioral depression followed by a period of increased activity) (Babbini & Davis, 1972; Koob & Bloom, 1983). The finding that selective blockade of central opiate receptors attenuates the locomotor activation induced by systemic heroin (Amalric & Koob, 1985; Swerdlow, et al., 1986; Vaccarino & Corrigal, 1987) indicates that opiate receptors in the brain are important in mediating the locomotor activating effects of systemic opiates. Intracranial microinjection studies have found that activation of opiate receptors in the VTA and NA will produce behvioral activation (Broekkamp, Phillips, & Cools, 1979; Joyce & Iversen, 1979; Kalivas, Widerlow, Stanely, Breese, & Prange, 1983; Kelley, Stinus & Iversen, 1980; Pert & Sivit, 1977; Stinus, Koob, Ling, Bloom, & LeMoal, 1980; Vezina & Stewart, 1984; Vezina, Kalivas, & Stewart, 1987). Studies investigating the central substrates mediating the locomotor-activating properties of systemically administered opiate drugs are consistent with the latter studies and have found that blockade of opiate receptors in the VTA and NA results in an attenuation of the locomotor-activating effects of opiate drugs (Amalric & Koob, 1985; Koob, Vaccarino, Amalric, & Bloom, 1987; Koob, Vaccarino, Amalric, & Swerdlow, 1987; Vaccarino & Corrigal, 1987). Together, these findings indicate that, as in the case of opiate reward, the VTA and NA are sites associated with opiate-induced locomotion.

Studies examining the extent of DAergic involvement in opiate-induced locomotion also parallel the opiate reward findings. Intracranial microinjection studies have demonstrated that VTA-induced opiate locomotion is dependent on the integrity of the mesolimbic DA neurons while NA-induced opiate locomotion is not dependent on mesolimbic DA function (Kalivas et al., 1983; Pert & Sivit, 1977). Therefore, locomotor-relevant VTA opiate receptors induce locomotion via activation of mesolimbic DA neurons, but NA locomotor-relevant opiate receptors do not require the integrity of DA neurons. The importance of DA-independent mechanisms in opiate-induced locomotion is also supported by the finding that locomotion induced by systemic opiates is still present following interruption of mesolimbic DA transmission (Vaccarino et al., 1986). These findings indicate that opiate-induced locomotor function can occur either at the VTA (via the mesolimbic DA neurons) or directly in the NA (independent of DA transmission). Thus, it appears that non-DA rewarding stimulation is also associated with locomotor activation. Interestingly, the NA is important for both DA and non-DA (i.e., opiate) drug reward and locomotion.

Feeding Behavior and Opiates.   Systemic administration of opiate agonists, such as morphine, increases food intake, while administration of opiate antagonists decreases feeding in a variety of conditions (see Levine, Morley, Gosnell, Billington, & Bartness, 1985). Opiate antagonists also attenuate MFB stimulation-induced feeding (Jenck et al., 1986). Recently, studies have examined the extent to which sites associated with opiate reward are capable of stimulating food intake. Consistent with the feeding-reward parallel associated with DA systems, activation of both VTA and NA opiate receptors facilitates feeding (Cador, Kelly, LeMoal, & Stinus, 1986; Mucha & Iversen, 1986). Interestingly, the profile of increased food intake associated with NA opiate receptors appears to be different from that observed following DAergic activation. Unlike amphetamine's selective enhancement of palatable food intake, intra-NA opiate activation appears to produce a more generalized increase in intake. Animals faced with a choice of three different food types varying in attractiveness, will show an increase in intake of all the food types following intra-NA opiate activation (Evans & Vaccarino, in preparation). Thus, it appears that the role of NA opiate receptors facilitating feeding is different from the role of NA DA receptors. If we are to assume that the increased feeding observed following intra-NA opiate treatment is in some way linked to reinforcement functions, these data suggest that activation of NA opiate receptors increases the range of food stimuli found reinforcing to the animal. Consistent with this notion, Siviy, Calgagnetti, and Reid (1982) have provided evidence which indicates that the increased saccharine consumption observed following systemic opiate treatment is associated with a broadening of the range of saccharine concentrations which will be accepted by the animal. This is in contrast to the feeding effects of amphetamine which appear to be associated with a selective increase in intake of the food type normally found most palatable (Evans & Vaccarino, 1987).

III. DEVELOPING A MODEL[2]

The fundamental neural commonality between substrates of reinforcement and species-typical behaviors originally suggested by Glickman and Schiff (1967) is supported by the more recent data discussed here. Electrical stimulation studies have underlined the similarity between properties of neurons mediating BSR and those mediating species-typical behaviors derived from the MFB, and have supported the notion that these MFB neurons travel in a rostral-caudal direction.

However, it is clear that these MFB neurons not only project caudally to influence behavioral output but also send signals that diverge from this descending route and which may activate ascending pathways in the brain. The nigrostriatal system appears to be involved in the consolidation of memory, and the mesolimbic system appears to be critical for the reward properties of MFB stimulation. The mesolimbic system is also capable of facilitating the expression of the same class of species-specific approach behaviors that are elicited by MFB stimulation. Hoebel et al. (1982) have previously stressed the importance of descending MFB input to the ascending mesolimbic system for the expression of feeding and reward.

The particular behaviors facilitated by opiate or DAergic activation of the mesolimbic system appear to be determined by the external stimuli present, and

---

[2]The model developed in this section is summarized in Fig. 5.1.

by the internal state of the animal. The internal state of the animal and the relevant environmental cues (e.g., food and hunger) are also known to facilitate MFB BSR (Blundell & Herberg, 1968; Carey, Goodall, & Lorens, 1975; Goodall & Carey, 1975). Therefore, it is possible that mesolimbic activity feeds back to the hypothalamus, and it is the priming of hypothalamic pathways by the internal state of the animal and by the environmental cues, that determine the behavioral output of mesolimbic activation. In the absence of relevant environmental cues mesolimbic activation (just as with electrical stimulation of the MFB) expresses itself as an increase in locomotor activity.

Link Between the Mesolimbic Ascending System and the Descending System

The notion that mesolimbic signals influence MFB functions is supported by findings that show that opiate and DA treatments that activate the mesolimbic system have pronounced effects on the MFB substrates which mediate BSR and species-specific behaviors. DA antagonists and agonists have been found to increase and decrease, respectively, the stimulation thresholds for MFB BSR (Esposito, Faulkner, & Kornetsky, 1979; Fouriezos, Hanson, & Wise, 1978; Franklin, 1978; Gallistel, Boytim, Gomita, & Klebanoff, 1982; Gallistel & Karras, 1984; Goodall & Carey, 1975; Schaeffer & Michael, 1980; Stellar, Kelley, & Corbett, 1983; Wise, 1985; Wise & Stein, 1970; Zarevics & Settler, 1979). Also, Jenck et al. (1986) have found that DA blockade increases the stimulation frequency required for stimulation-induced feeding in the MFB. Similarly opiate antagonists have been shown to increase, while opiate agonists decrease the current and frequency thresholds for BSR and stimulation-induced feeding derived from the MFB (Esposito & Kornetsky, 1978; Jenck et al., 1986; West & Wise, 1986). Finally, it appears that the NA is a critical site for these effects (Broekkamp et al., 1975; Colle & Wise, 1986; West & Wise, 1986). Although the ascending signals are generally thought to express their behavioral effects post-synaptic to descending MFB substrates, it is also possible that the ascending signals described above exert a pre-synaptic influence on descending MFB substrates underlying BSR and species-typical behaviors.

There are recent data suggesting the route whereby this might occur. It has been found that an important first order NA output is the substantia innominata-lateral preoptic area (SI/LPOA) (Jones & Mogenson, 1980; Mogenson, Swanson, & Wu, 1983; Swanson & Cowan, 1975; Swanson, 1976; Williams, Crossman, & Slater, 1977; Zaborsky et al., 1982). Although studies have not investigated the extent to which this pathway is necessary for mesolimbic reward functions, it has been found to be critical for both opiate and DA induced locomotor activation (Swerdlow & Koob, 1984; Swerdlow, Swanson, & Koob, 1984a, 1984b; Swerdlow et al., 1986). Mogensen, Jones, and Yim (1980) have previously proposed that brain regions associated with the SI/LPOA are important for the interface between motivation and action. Furthermore, the LPOA region has also been suggested as a possible origin of MFB fibers critical for BSR (Yeomans, 1982; Stellar & Stellar, 1985). It is possible, then, that NA projections to the SI/LPOA represent the functional link between ascending mesolimbic and descending MFB signals involved in reward and species-specific behaviors.

Accordingly, we have anatomical and functional data that suggest a positive feedback system where mesolimbic activity produced by MFB stimulation serves to further maintain the activity in the MFB. In this contemporary formulation of a response theory of reinforcement it is activity in this system that is the neural basis of MFB reward. This is not to suggest that it acts in isolation from the rest of the brain. We know that other structures are involved in reward and memory (Collier & Routtenberg, 1984; Routtenberg, 1984). However, the neural events described in this model may be fundamental and necessary for the reinforcement process.

Caudal Projections of the MFB.   As already mentioned, the MFB must necessarily send information to posterior brainstem and spinal cord structures in order to produce motor activity. Recent anatomical findings may provide initial indications of what these pathways are.

A subcomponent of the midbrain reticular formation, the pedunculopontine nucleus, has been shown to receive projections which originate in both the SI/LPOA and medial preoptic area region of the hypothalamus (Swanson, Mogenson, Gerfen, & Robinson, 1984; Swanson, Mogenson, Simerly, & Wu, 1987). These neurons project downstream via the MFB on their way to the pedunculopontine nucleus (Swanson et al., 1984, 1987). They also (consistent with the proposed model) send projections to the VTA. Furthermore, behavioral studies have shown that the pedunculopontine nucleus is an important output for locomotor activity derived from the NA-SI/LPOA pathway (Brudzynski, Houghton, Brownlee, & Mogenson, 1986; Brudzynski & Mogenson, 1985; Mogenson, Swanson, & Wu, 1985; Mogenson & Wu, 1986). Thus, the pedunculopontine nucleus may represent an output for elicited behaviors derived from the MFB. Interestingly, the pedunculopontine nucleus has been found to send projections directly or indirectly to spinal cord structures involved in rhythmic movements (Grillner, 1976, 1985; Grillner & Shik, 1973).

IV. CONCLUDING THOUGHTS

Naturalistic Perspectives on Reinforcement

> *Even Psychologists who have watched hundreds of rats running a maze*
> *rarely realize that, strictly speaking, it is not the litter or the food the animal*
> *is striving towards, but the performance itself of the maternal activities*
> *or eating. (Tinbergen, 1951, p. 106)*

As Lehrman (1970) has observed, natural selection operates on behavioral outcomes. In view of this, it is not surprising that an ethologist such as Niko Tinbergen, working in an evolutionary framework, focused upon the actual performance of fitness-enhancing consummatory behaviors as the crucial reference point for understanding reinforcement. What was significant about reinforcing stimuli was their capacity to produce these consummatory behaviors at the optimum times in an animal's daily life. In addition, from an evolutionary vantage point, such stimuli might be expected to exert appropriate control over antecedent behaviors (e.g., foraging), whose performance was essential to completing the consummatory act (e.g., feeding).

Properties of Reinforcing Stimuli. Working backward in time, we might identify the following actions of the system facilitated by a reinforcing stimulus: (1) elicitation of the consummatory response, (2) maintenance of a suite of preparatory behaviors in the vicinity of the stimulus, (3) producing approach or withdrawal behaviors under the direct influence of the stimulus (a component of preferences and aversions), and (4) influencing approach or withdrawal to stimuli that predict the appearance of the reinforcing stimulus from a point spatially or temporarily removed from the reinforcing stimulus. In the case of a food-caching kangaroo rat (*Dipodomy's Microps*), the final consummatory behavior, eating, occurs in the burrow. It is preceded by selection from the food store and handling (e.g., husking), and these latter activities are presumably preceded by approach to the food store within the burrow system (Eisenberg, 1963; Kenagy, 1973). This cluster of activities is further dependent upon prior foraging sequences in which the rat left the borrow, locomoted to particular regions of the habitat, sifted through the sand for seeds with the nails on the forepaws, collected materials in the external, fur-lined cheek pouches (that characterize the family Heteromyidae), returned to the burrow system, and emptied the cheek pouches into the food store employing a set of stereotypic movements with the forepaws. The ultimate task of a comprehensive behavioral theory of reinforcement will be to specify the reinforcing events at each stage of this sequence, and to be able to predict their ability to facilitate the performance of different antecedent activities.

Some years ago, Carl Pfaffman (1969) noted that some reinforcers were much more effective than others at controlling behaviors spatially removed from the site of the reinforcing stimulus. Both food and weak concentrations of saline elicit consummatory (ingestive) behavior. Both food and saline solutions will produce approach to a visible stimulus and trigger the postural adjustments which prepare the consummatory responses. However, saline solutions fail to motivate behavior in a T-maze, while foods serve very efficiently in this regard.

Along similar lines, Glickman (1973) contrasted the controlling properties of stimuli facilitating three different consummatory systems in gerbils: feeding, shredding of nest materials, and scent-marking. Food pellets, cardboard or paper for shredding, and small blocks eliciting scent-marking, all reliably sustained consummatory activities. However, only the food and cardboard produced the kind of sustained approach and lingering in the vicinity of the stimulus that character-ize preference behaviors. Further, when bar-pressing was required to obtain ac-cess to food or nest materials, the food was much more effective. It seems possible that, in the gerbil's natural life situations, it is not required to leave the burrow system in order to scent mark, and probably forages for nest materials only when already in the vicinity of abundant sources. Thus, scent-marking and nest-material collection are relatively opportunistic behaviors, while foraging for food is ob-ligatory on a regular basis. In this view, the ability of reinforcing stimuli to con-trol behaviors antecedent to the consummatory response vary with the system that is activated in a manner that is ecologically reasonable.

The variations in the controlling properties of reinforcers noted above fit com-fortably with the limitations on response-reinforcer relationships described in the chapter by Timberlake and Lucas (this volume). The misbehavior of organisms described by Breland and Breland (1961) and the failures of particular reinforc-ers to control particular behaviors (Moore, 1973; Shettleworth, 1973; Sevenster, 1973) fit within a general framework that emphasizes the natural biological or-ganization of reinforcement systems.

Reinforcement, Physiology and Animal Behavior

It is clear that much that is central to the work of physiological psychologists is derived from problems originating within a behavioral framework. Research on the physiological substrates of memory, reinforcement and motivation has been driven by contemporary concerns of psychologists working at a purely behavioral level. It is also the case that input from the naturalistic-ethological perspective has occasionally been helpful to physiological workers in these areas, by influenc-ing the construction of test situations in which physiological manipulations are assayed (see, e.g., Schiff, Rusak, & Block, 1971). Unfortunately, these influences have been rather limited in the world of mammalian brain research. The field of neuroethology (e.g., Huber & Markl, 1983) has been dominated by research on nonmammalian forms.

The influence of events in physiological research on behavioral conceptions is frequently more difficult to discern, although some years ago, Hebb (1951), made a convincing case for the impact of physiological ideas on psychology, as exemplified by the influence of Sherrington's work on spinal reflexes on the de-velopment of the S–R models of behaviorism.

It is also the case that specific psychological views about reinforcement have been inhibited or facilitated by research in physiological psychology. The demise of drive-reduction notions of reinforcement was surely hastened by the publica-tion of Olds and Milner's (1954) research identifying positive reinforcement centers in the brain, apparently independent of any drives to be reduced. It also seems likely that the opportune convergence of physiological, psychological and ethological studies in the 1950s and 1960s, suggesting that there was significant correlation between stimuli that served as reinforcers and stimuli that elicited species-characteristic consummatory patterns, mutually facilitated the incorporation of such ideas.

Several new areas of convergence seem to be emerging from the independent studies of physiological and behavioral researchers during the past 15–20 years. For example, work reviewed in this chapter suggests a division of neurochemical/neuroanatomical reinforcement systems in the brain. One system (the mesolimbic) apparently has strong motivational properties and serves to facilitate a broad array of appetitive/searching behaviors. The second system may selectively facilitate memory formation, with limited access to particular subsets of highly stereotypic behavior sequences. Some common reinforcing stimuli (e.g., food) might be expected to activate both systems, while other natural reinforcing stimuli might activate one system much more powerfully than the other. Such an arrangement would be compatible with the behavioral discrepancies described above in the capacity of different reinforcement systems to control behaviors successively more remote from the final consummatory system.

Other physiological research presented in this chapter also has implications for behavioral conceptions of reinforcement, memory, and motivation. There is an interesting contrast between the relatively selective action of dopamine on feeding behavior and the broad facilitation produced by opiates. This kind of result could encourage psychological theorizing that utilizes general and specific modes of motivational activity. Finally, the recent convergence of behavioral and physiological studies on the "glue" functions of reinforcement should serve to promote exploration of a problem area in which research had been prematurely terminated. Psychological questions of reinforcement, memory, and motivation are both fundamental and difficult to answer. To the extent that the interplay of ethological, psychological, and physiological ideas provide insight and generate new research perspectives, such interaction should be valued.

ACKNOWLEDGMENT

We thank Dr. John Yeomans for helpful suggestions and comments on an earlier version of this chapter. Preparation of this chapter was supported in part by NSERC grant UO443 to FJV.

REFERENCES

Alpert, J. E., & Iversen, S. D. (1982). Feeding and food gathering following corticolimbic dopamine loss. *Neuroscience, 7 (suppl.)* S5.

Amalric, M., & Koob, G. (1985). Methyl-naloxonium in the nucleus accumbens blocks heroin locomotion in the rat. *Pharmacology, Biochemistry, and Behavior, 23*, 411–415.

Anden, N. E., & Jackson, D. M. (1975). Locomotor activity stimulation in rats produced by dopamine in the nucleus accumbens: Potentiation by caffeine. *Journal of Pharmaceutical Pharmacology, 27,* 666–670.

Babbini, M., & Davis, W. M. (1972). Time-dose relationships for locomotor activity effects of morphine after acute or repeated treatment. *British Journal of Pharmacology, 46,* 213–224.

Bechara, A., & van der Kooy, D. (1985). Opposite motivational effects of endogenous opioids in brain and periphery. *Nature, 314,* 533–534.

Beninger, R. J. (1983). The role of dopamine in locomotor activity and learning. *Brain Research Review, 6,* 173–196.

Berlyne, D. E. (1967). Arousal and reinforcement. In D. Levine (Ed.), *Nebraska Symposium on Motivation* (pp. 1–110). Lincoln: University of Nebraska Press.

Bielajew, C., & Shizgal, P. (1982). Behaviorally derived measures of conduction velocity in the substrate for rewarding medial forebrain bundle stimulation. *Brain Research, 237,* 107–119.

Bielajew, C., & Shizgal, P. (1986). Evidence implicating descending fibres in self-stimulation of the medial forebrain bundle. *The Journal of Neuroscience, 6,* 919–929.

Block, M. L., Vallier, G. H., & Glickman, S. E. (1974). Elicitation of water injestion in the mongolian gerbil (Meriones unguiculatus) by intracranial injections of Angiotensin II and L-Norephinephrine. *Pharmacology, Biochemistry, and Behavior, 2,* 235–242.

Blundell, J. E., & Herberg, L. M. (1968). Relative effects of nutritional deficit and deprivation period on rate of electrical stimulation of lateral hypothalamus. *Nature, 219,* 627–628.

Bozarth, M. A., & Wise, R. A. (1981a). Heroin reward is dependent on a dopaminergic substrate. *Life Science, 29,* 1881–1886.

Bozarth, M. A., & Wise, R. A. (1981b). Intracranial self-administration of morphine into the ventral tegmental area in rats. *Life Science, 28,* 551–555.

Bozarth, M. A., & Wise, R. A. (1983). Neural substrates of opiate reinforcement. *Progress in Neuropharmacology and Biological Psychiatry, 7,* 569–575.

Breland, K., & Breland, M. (1961). The misbehavior of organisms. *American Psychologist, 16,* 681–684.

Britt, M. D., & Wise, R. A. (1983). Ventral tegmental site of opiate reward: Antagonism by a hydrophilic opiate receptor blocker. *Brain Research, 258,* 105–108.

Broekkamp, C. L. E., Phillips, A. G., & Cools, A. R. (1979). Stimulant effects of enkephalin microinjection into the dopaminergic A10 area. *Nature, 278,* 560–562.

Broekkamp, C. L. E., Pijnenburg, A. J. J., Cools, A. R., & Van Rossum, J. M. (1975). The effect of microinjections of amphetamine into the neostriatum and the nucleus accumbens on self-stimulation behavior. *Psychopharmacology, 42,* 179–183.

Brogden, W. J. (1939). Sensory pre-conditioning. *Journal of Experimental Psychology, 25,* 323–332.

Brudzynski, S. M., Houghton, P. E., Brownlee, R. D., & Mogenson, G. J. (1986). Involvement of neuronal cell bodies of the mesencephalic locomotor region in the initiation of locomotor activity of freely behaving rats. *Brain Research Bulletin, 16,* 377–381.

Brudzynski, S. M., & Mogenson, G. J. (1985). Association of the mesencephalic locomotor region with locomotor activity induced by injections of amphetamine into the nucleus accumbens. *Brain Research, 334,* 77–84.

Cador, M., Kelley, A. E., LeMoal, M., & Stinus, L. (1986). Ventral tegmental area infusion of substance P, Neurotensin and enkephalin: Differential effects on feeding behavior. *Neuroscience, 18,* 659–669.

Carey, R. J., Goodall, E., & Lorens, S. A. (1975). Differential effects of amphetamine and food deprivation on self-stimulation of the lateral hypothalamus and medial frontal cortex. *Journal of Comparative and Physiological Psychology, 88,* 224–230.

Carr, G. D., & White, N. (1984). The relationship between stereotypy and memory improvement produced by amphetamine. *Psychopharmacology, 82,* 203–209.

Carr, G. D., & White, N. M. (1986). Anatomical dissociation of amphetamine's rewarding and aversive effects: An intra-cranial microinjection study. *Psychopharmacology, 39,* 340–346.

Christopher, S. M., & Butter, C. M. (1968). Consummatory behaviors and locomotion exploration evoked from self-stimulation sites in rats. *Journal of Comparative and Physiological Psychology, 66*, 335–339.

Colle, L. M., & Wise, R. A. (1986). Facilitation of lateral hypothalamic self-stimulation by amphetamine microinjections into nucleus accumbens. *Society for Neuroscience Abstracts, 12*, 930.

Collier, T. J., & Routtenberg, A. (1984). Electrical self-stimulation of dentate gyrus granule cells. *Behavioral and Neural Biology, 42*, 85–90.

Cooper, B. R., Cott, J. M., & Breese, G. R. (1976). Effects of catecholamine depleting drugs and amphetamines on self-stimulation of brain following various 6-hydroxydopamine treatments. *Psychopharmacology (Berlin), 37*, 235–248.

Corbett, D., Laferriere, A., & Milner, P. M. (1982). Plasticity of the medial prefrontal cortex: Facilitated acquisition of intracranial self-stimulation by pretraining stimulation. *Physiology and Behavior, 28*, 531–534.

Corbett, D., & Stellar, J. R. (1983). Neurological reactivity during medial prefrontal cortex stimulation: Effects of self-stimulation experience. *Physiology and Behavior, 31*, 771–776.

Corbett, D., & Wise, R. A. (1980). Intra-cranial self-stimulation in relation to the ascending dopaminergic systems of the midbrain: A moveable electrode mapping study. *Brain Research, 185*, 1–15.

Costall, B., Domeny, A. M., & Naylor, R. J. (1984). Locomotor hyperactivity caused by dopamine infusion into the nucleus accumbens of rat brain: Specificity of action. *Psychopharmacology, 82*, 174–180.

Costall, B., Fortune, D.H., Hui, S. C. G., & Naylor, R. J. (1980). Neuroleptic antagonism of motor inhibitory effects of apomorphine within the nucleus accumbens: Drug interaction at presynaptic receptors? *European Journal of Pharmacology, 63*, 347–358.

Costall, B., & Naylor, R. J. (1975). The behavioral effects of dopamine applied intracerebrally to areas of the mesolimbic system. *European Journal of Pharmacology, 32*, 87–92.

Coulombe, D., & White, N. (1982). The effect of post training hypothalamic self-stimulation on sensory preconditioning in rats. *Canadian Journal of Psychology, 36*, 57–66.

Creese, I., & Iversen, S. (1972). Amphetamine response in rats after dopamine neuron destruction. *Nature New Biology, 238*, 247–248.

Creese, I., & Iversen, S. D. (1975). The pharmacological and anatomical substrates of amphetamine response in the rat. *Brain Research, 83*, 419–436.

Durivage, A., & Miliaressis, E. (1987). Anatomical dissociation of the substrates of medial forebrain bundle self-stimulation and exploration. *Behavioral Neuroscience, 101*, 57–61.

Eisenberg, J. F. (1963). The behavior of heteromyid rodents. *University of California Publications in Zoology, 69*.

Esposito, R. U., Faulkner, W., & Kornetsky, C. (1979). Specific modulation of brain stimulation reward by haloperidol. *Pharmacology Biochemistry and Behavior, 10*, 937–940.

Esposito, R. U., & Kornetsky, C. (1978). Opioids and rewarding brain stimulation. *Neuroscience Biobehavioral Review, 2*, 115–122.

Ettenberg, A., Pettit, H. O., Bloom, F. E., & Koob, G. F. (1982). Heroin and cocaine intravenous self-administration in rats: Mediation by separate neural systems. *Psychopharmacology, 78*, 204–209.

Evans, K. R., & Eikelboom, R. E. (1987). Feeding induced by ventricular bromocriptine and amphetamine: A possible excitatory role for dopamine in eating behavior. *Behavioral Neuroscience, 101*, 591–593.

Evans, K. R., & Vaccarino, F. J. (1986). Intra-nucleus accumbens amphetamine: Dose-dependent effects on food intake. *Pharmacology, Biochemistry and Behavior, 25*, 1149–1151.

Evans, K. R., & Vaccarino, F. J. (1987). Effects of d- and l- amphetamine on food intake: Evidence for a Dopaminergic substrate. *Pharmacology Biochemistry and Behavior, 27*, 649–652.

Evans, K. R., & Vaccarino, F. J. (1988). *Effects of microinjections of amphetamine and morphine into the caudate and nucleus accumbens on feeding: Interactions with sweetness.* In preparation.

Fallon, J. H., & Moore, R. V. (1978). Catecholamine innervation of the basal forebrain, IV. Topography of the dopamine projection to the basal forebrain and neostriatum. *Journal of Comparative Neurology, 180,* 545-580.

Fibiger, H. C., & Phillips, A. C. (1976). Retrograde amnesia after electrical stimulation of the substantia nigra: Mediation by the dopaminergic nigrostriatal bundle. *Brain Research, 116,* 23-33.

Fouriezos, G., Hansson, P., & Wise, R. A. (1978). Neuroleptic-induced attenuation of brain stimulation reward. *Journal of Comparative Physiological Psychology, 92,* 659-669.

Fouriezos, G., & Wise, R. A. (1976). Pimozide-induced extinction of intra-cranial self-stimulation: Response patterns rule out motor or performance deficits. *Brain Research, 103,* 377-380.

Franklin, K. B. J. (1978). Catecholamines and self-stimulation: Reward and performance effects dissociated. *Pharmacology, Biochemistry and Behavior, 9,* 813-820.

Fray, P. J., Sahakian, B. J., Robbins, T. W., Koob, G. F., & Iversen, S. D. (1980). An observational method for quantifying the behavioural effects of dopamine agonists: Contrasting effects of d-Amphetamine and Apomorphine. *Psychopharmacology, 69,* 253-259.

Gallistel, C. R., Boytim, M., Gomita, Y., & Klebanoff, L. (1982). Does pimozide block the reinforcing effect of brain stimulation? *Pharmacology, Biochemistry and Behavior, 17,* 769-781.

Gallistel, C. R., & Karras, D. (1984). Pimozide and amphetamine have opposing effects on the reward summation function. *Pharmacology, Biochemistry and Behavior, 20,* 73-77.

Glickman, S. E. (1973). Responses and reinforcement. In R. A. Hinde & J. Stevenson-Hinde (Eds.), *Constraints on learning: Limitations and predispositions* (pp. 207-241). New York: Academic Press.

Glickman, S. E., & Schiff, B. B. (1967). A biological theory of reinforcement. *Psychological Review, 74,* 81-109.

Goeders, N. E., Lane, J. D., & Smith, J. E. (1984). Self-administration of methionine enkephalin into the nucleus accumbens. *Pharmacology, Biochemistry and Behavior, 20,* 451-455.

Goodall, E. B., & Carey, R. J. (1975). Effects of d-versus l-amphetamine, food deprivation, and current intensity on self-stimulation of the lateral hypothalamus, substantia nigra, and medial frontal cortex of the rat. *Journal of Comparative and Physiological Psychology, 89,* 1029-1045.

Gratton, A. P., & Wise, R. A. (1988a). Comparisons of refractory periods for medial forebrain bundle fibers subserving stimulation-induced feeding and brain stimulation reward: A psychophysical study. *Brain Research, 438,* 256-263.

Gratton, A. P., & Wise, R. A. (1988b). Comparisons of connectivity and conduction velocities for medial forebrain bundle fibers subserving stimulation-induced feeding and brain stimulation reward. *Brain Research, 438,* 264-270.

Grillner, S. (1976). Some aspects on the descending control of the spinal circuits generating locomotor movements. In R. M. Herman, S. Grillner, S. G. Stein, and D. G. Stuart (Eds.), *Neural control of locomotion* (pp. 351-375). New York: Plenum Press.

Grillner, S. (1985). Neurobiological bases of rhythmic motor acts in vertebrates. *Science, 228,* 143-149.

Grillner, S., & Shik, M. L. (1973). On the descending control of the lumbosacral spinal cord from the "mesencephalic locomotor region". *Acta. Physiologica Scandanavica, 87,* 320-333.

Hallonquist, J. D., & Mrosovsky, N. (1986). Electrically induced behavior and neural specificity in ground squirrels and dormice. *Physiology and Behavior, 38,* 387-397.

Hawkins, R. D., Roll, P. L., Puerto, A., & Yeomans, J. S. (1983). Refractory periods of neurons mediating stimulation-elicited eating and brain-stimulation reward: Interval scale measurement and tests of a model of integration. *Behavioral Neuroscience, 97,* 416-432.

Hebb, D. O. (1951). The role of neurological ideas in psychology. *Journal of Personality, 20,* 39-55.

Herberg, L. J., Stephens, D. N., & Franklin, K. B. J. (1976). Catecholamines and self-stimulation: Evidence suggesting a reinforcing role for noradrenaline and a motivating role for dopamine. *Pharmacology, Biochemistry and Behavior, 4,* 575-582.

Hoebel, B. G., Hernandez, L., McLean, S., Stanley, B., Aulissi, E., Glimcher, P., & Margolin, D. (1982). Catecholamine, enkephalin, and neurotensin in feeding and reward. In B. G. Hoebel & D. Novin (Eds.), *The neural basis of feeding and reward.* Brunswick, ME: Haer Institute.

Huber, F., & Markl, H. (Eds.). (1983). *Neuroethology and behavioral physiology: Routes and growing points.* New York: Springer-Verlag.

Hull, C. L. (1943). *Principles of behavior.* New York: Appleton.

Huston, J. P., Mondadori, C., & Waser, P. G. (1974). Facilitation of learning by reward of post-trial memory processes. *Experimentia, 30,* 1038–1040.

Iversen, S. D., & Fray, P. J. (1982). Brain catecholamines in relation to affect. In *Neural basis of behavior* (pp. 222–269). New York: Spectrum.

Iversen, S. D., & Iversen, L. (1981). *Behavioral Pharmacology,* (2nd Edition, pp. 149–169). Oxford, England: Oxford University Press.

Jenck, F., Gratton, A., & Wise, R. A. (1986). Effects of pimozide and naloxone on latency for hypothalamically induced eating. *Brain Research, 375,* 329–337.

Jones, D. L., & Mogenson, G. J. (1980). Nucleus accumbens to globus pallidus GABA projection subserving ambulatory activity. *American Journal of Physiology, 238,* R63–R69.

Jones, D. L., Mogenson, G. J., & Wu, M. (1981). Injections of dopaminergic, cholinergic, serotonergic and GABAergic drugs into the nucleus accumbens: Effects on locomotor activity in the rat. *Neuropharmacology, 20,* 29–37.

Joyce, E. M., & Iversen, S. D. (1979). The effect of morphine applied locally to mesencephalic dopamine cell bodies on spontaneous motor activity in the rat. *Neuroscience Letters, 14,* 207–212.

Joyce, E. M., & Koob, G. F. (1981). Amphetamine-, scopolamine- and caffeine-induced locomotor activity following 6-hydroxydopamine lesions of the mesolimbic dopamine systems. *Psychopharmacology (Berlin), 73,* 311–313.

Kalivas, P. W., Widerlov, E., Stanley, D., Breese, G., & Prange, A. J. (1983). Enkephalin action on the mesolimbic system: a dopamine-dependent and dopamine-independent increase in locomotor activity. *Journal of Pharmacology and Experimental Therapeutics, 227,* 229–237.

Kelley, A. E., & Stinus, L. (1985). Disappearance of hoarding behavior after 6-hydroxydopamine lesion of the mesolimbic dopamine neurons and its reinstatement with L-Dopa. *Behavioral Neuroscience, 99,* 531–545.

Kelley, A. E., Stinus, L., & Iversen, S. D. (1980). Interactions between D-ala-met-enkelphalin, A10 dopaminergic neurons, and spontaneous behavior in the rat. *Behavioral Brain Research, 1,* 3–24.

Kelly, P. H. (1977). Drug-induced motor behavior. In L. L. Iversen, S. D. Iversen, & S. H. Snyder (Eds.), *Handbook of psychopharmacology (Vol. 8).* New York: Plenum.

Kelly, P. H., Seviour, P. W., & Iversen, S. D. (1975). Amphetamine and apomorphine responses in the rat following 6-OHDA lesions of the nucleus accumbens septi and corpus striatum. *Brain Research, 94,* 507–522.

Kenagy, G. J. (1973). Daily seasonal pattern of activity and energetics in a heteromyid rodent community. *Ecology, 54,* 1201–1219.

Koob, G. F., & Bloom, F. E. (1983). Behavioral effects of opioid peptides. *British Medical Bulletin, 39,* 89–94.

Koob, G. F., Fray, P. J., & Iversen, S. D. (1978). Self-stimulation at the lateral hypothalamus and locus coeruleus after specific unilateral lesions of the dopamine system. *Brain Research, 146,* 123–140.

Koob, G. F., Pettit, H. O., Ettenberg, A., & Bloom, F. E. (1984). Effects of opiate antagonists and their quaternary derivatives on heroin self-administration in the rat. *Journal of Pharmacology and Experimental Therapeutics, 229,* 481–486.

Koob, G. F., Vaccarino, F. J., Amalric, M., & Bloom, F. E. (1987). Positive reinforcement properties of drugs: Search for neural substrates. In J. Engel, L. Oreland, D. H. Ingvar, B. Pernow, S. Rossner, & L. A. Pellborn (Eds.), *Brain reward systems and abuse* (pp. 35–50). New York: Raven Press.

Koob, G. F., Vaccarino, F. J., Amalric, M., & Swerdlow, (1987). Neural substrates for cocaine and opiate reinforcement. In S. Fisher, A. Raskin, & E. H. Uhlenhuth (Eds.), *Cocaine, clinical and behavioral aspects* (pp. 79–108). New York: Oxford University Press.

Lehrman, D. S. (1970). Semantic and conceptual issues in the nature-nurture problem. In L. Aaronson, E. Tobach, D. S. Lehrman, & J. S. Rosenblatt, (Eds.), *Development and evolution of behavior*: Essays in memory of T. C. Schneirla (pp. 17–74). San Francisco: W. H. Freeman.

Levine, A. S., Morley, J. E., Gosnell, B. A., Billington, C. J., & Bartness, T. J. (1985). Opioids and consummatory behavior. *Brain Research Bulletin, 14,* 663–672.

Lewander, T. (1977). Effects of amphetamine in animals. In W. R. Martin (Ed.), *Drug addiction II.* New York: Springer-Verlag.

Lyness, W. H., Friedle, N. M., & Moore, K. E. (1979). Destruction of dopaminergic nerve terminals in nucleus accumbens: Effect on d-amphetamine self administration. *Pharmacology, Biochemistry, and Behavior, 11,* 553–556.

Lyon, M., & Robbins, T. (1975). The action of central nervous system stimulant drugs: A general theory concerning amphetamine effects. In W. Essman & L. Valzelli (Eds.), *Current developments in psychopharmacology, Vol. 2* (pp. 80–163). New York: Spectrum.

Mackey, W. B., & van der Kooy, D. (1985). Neuroleptics block the positive reinforcing effects of amphetamine but not of morphine as measured by place conditioning. *Pharmacology, Biochemistry, and Behavior, 22,* 101–105.

MacMillan, C. J., Simantirakis, P., & Shizgal, P. (1985). Self-stimulation of the lateral hypothalamus and ventrolateral tegmentum: excitability characteristics of the directly stimulated substrates. *Physiology and Behavior, 35,* 711–723.

Maj. J., Sawinska, H., Kapturkiewicz, Z., & Sarnek, J. (1972). The effect of L-dopa and (D)-amphetamine on the locomotor activity after pimozide and phenoxybenzamine. *Journal of Pharmaceutical Pharmacology, 24,* 412–414.

Major, R., & White, N. (1978). Memory facilitation by self-stimulation reinforcement mediated by the nigro-striatal bundle. *Physiology and Behavior, 20,* 723–733.

McClelland, D. C., Atkinson, J. W., Clark, R. A., & Lowell, E. L. (1953). *The achievement motive,* New York: Appleton-Century-Crofts.

Meehl, P. E. (1950). On the circularity of the law of effect. *Psychological Bulletin, 47,* 52–75.

Mogenson, G. J., Jones, D. L., & Yim, C. Y. (1980). From motivation to action: Functional interface between limbic system and the motor system. *Progress in Neurobiology, 14–15,* 69–97.

Mogenson, G. J., Swanson, L. W., & Wu, M. (1983). Neural projections from the nucleus accumbens to globus pallidus, substantia innominata, and lateral preoptic-lateral hypothalamic area: An anatomical and electrophysiological investigation in the rat. *Journal of Neuroscience, 3,* 189–202.

Mogenson, G. J., Swanson, L. W., & Wu, M. (1985). Evidence that projections from substantia innominata to zona incerta and mesencephalic locomotor region contribute to locomotor activity. *Brain Research, 334,* 65–76.

Mogenson, G. J., & Wu, M. (1986). Subpallidal projections to mesencephalic locomotor region investigated with a combination of behavioral and electrophysiological recording techniques. *Brain Research Bulletin, 16,* 383–390.

Monaco, A. P., Hernandez, L., & Hoebel, B. G. (1981). Nucleus accumbens site of amphetamine self-injection: Comparison with lateral ventricle. In R. B. Chronister & J. F. DeFrance (Eds.), *The neurobiology of the nucleus accumbens.* Brunswick, ME: Haer Institute.

Mondadori, C., Ornstein, K., Waser, P. G., & Houston, J. P. (1976). Post-trial reinforcing hypothalamic stimulation can facilitate avoidance learning. *Neuroscience Letters, 2,* 183–187.

Moore, B. R. (1973). The role of directed Pavlovian reactions in simple instrumental learning in the pigeon. In R. A. Hinde & J. Stevenson-Hinde (Eds.), *Constraints on learning: Limitations and predispositions* (pp. 159–188). New York: Academic Press.

Morley, J. E., Levine, A. S., Grace, M., & Kneip, J. (1982). Dynorphin-(1,13), dopamine and feeding in rats. *Pharmacology, Biochemistry and Behavior, 16,* 701–705.

Mucha, R. F., & Iversen, S. D. (1986). Increased food intake after opioid microinjection into the nucleus accumbens and ventral tegmental area of rat. *Brain Research, 397,* 214–224.

Mucha, R. F., van der Kooy, D., O'Shaughnessy, M., & Bucenieks, P. (1982). Drug reinforcement studies by the use of place conditioning in rat. *Brain Research, 243,* 91–105.

Olds, J., & Milner, P. M. (1954). Positive reinforcement produced by electrical stimulation of septal area and other regions of rat brain. *Journal of Comparative and Physiological Psychology, 47,* 419–427.

Olds, M. E. (1979). Hypothalamic substrates for the positive reinforcing properties of morphine in the rat. *Brain Research*, *168*, 351–360.

Olds, M. E. (1982). Reinforcing effects of morphine in the nucleus accumbens. *Brain Research*, *237*, 429–440.

Olds, M. E., & Williams, K. N. (1980). Self-administration of D-ala-met-enkephalinamide at hypothalamic self-stimulation sites. *Brain Research*, *194*, 155–170.

Pert, A., & Sivit, C. (1977). Neuroanatomical focus for morphine and enkephalin-induced hypermotility. *Nature*, *265*, 645–647.

Pettit, H. O., Ettenberg, A., Bloom, F. E., & Koob, G. F. (1984). Destruction of the nucleus accumbens selectively attenuate cocaine but not heroin self-administration in rats. *Psychopharmacology*, *84*, 167–173.

Pfaffman, C. (1969). Taste preference and reinforcement. In J. Tapp. (Ed.), *Reinforcement and behavior* (pp. 215–241). New York: Academic Press.

Pffafman, C. (1960). The pleasure of sensation. *Psychological Review*, *67*, 253–268.

Phillips, A. G., Brooks, S. M., & Fibiger, H. C. (1975). Effects of amphetamine isomers and neuroleptics on self-stimulation from the nucleus accumbens and dorsal noradrenergic bundle. *Brain Research*, *85*, 13–22.

Phillips, A. G., & Fibiger, H. C. (1973). Dopaminergic and noradrenergic substrates of positive reinforcement. Differential effects of D- and L-amphetamine. *Science*, *79*, 575–577.

Phillips, A. G., & Fibiger, H. C. (1978). The role of dopamine in maintaining intra-cranial self-stimulation in the ventral tegmentum, nucleus accumbens, medial and sulcal prefrontal cortices. *Canadian Journal of Physiology*, *32*, 58–66.

Phillips, A. G., & LePiane, F. G. (1980). Reinforcing effects of morphine microinjections into the ventral tegmental area. *Pharmacology, Biochemistry and Behavior*, *12*, 965–968.

Phillips, A. G., Lepiane, F. G., & Fibiger, H. C. (1982). Effects of kainic acid lesions of the striatum on self-stimulation in the substantia nigra and ventral tegmental area. *Behavioral Brain Research*, *5*, 297–310.

Phillips, A. G., & LePiane, F. G. (1982). Reward produced by microinjection of (D-Ala), Met-enkephalinamide into the ventral tegmental area. *Behavioral Brain Research*, *5*, 225–229.

Phillips, A. G., LePiane, F. G., & Fibiger, H. C. (1983). Dopaminergic mediation of reward produced by direct injection of enkephalin into the ventral tegmental area of the rat. *Life Sciences*, *33*, 2505–2511.

Pijnenburg, A. J. J., Honig, W. M. M., Van der Heyden, J. A. M., & Van Rossum, J. M. (1976). Effects of chemical stimulation of the mesolimbic dopamine system upon locomotor activity. *European Journal of Pharmacology*, *35*, 45–58.

Pijnenburg, A. J. J., Honig, W. M. M., & Van Rossum, J. M. (1975a). Effects of antagonists upon locomotor stimulation induced by injection of dopamine and noradrenaline into the nucleus accumbens of nialamide-pretreated rats. *Psychopharmacology*, *41*, 175–180.

Pijnenburg, A. J. J., Honig, W. M. M., & Van Rossum, J. M. (1975b). Inhibition of D-amphetamine-induced locomotor activity by injection of haloperidol into the nucleus accumbens of the rat. *Psychopharmacology*, *41*, 87–95.

Pijnenburg, A. J. J., & Van Rossum, J. M. (1973). Stimulation of locomotor activity following injection of dopamine into the nucleus accumbens. *Journal of Pharmaceutical Pharmacology*, *25*, 1003–1005.

Porrino, L. J. (1987). Cerebral metabolic changes associated with activation of reward systems. In J. Engel, L. Oreland, D. H. Ingvar, B. Pernow, S. Rossner, & L. A. Pollborn (Eds.), *Brain reward systems & abuse* (pp. 51–60). New York: Oxford University Press.

Premack, D. (1965). Reinforcement theory. *Nebraska Symposium on Motivation* (pp. 123–180). In D. Levine (Ed.), Lincoln: University of Nebraska Press.

Pucilowski, O., & Valzelli, L. (1986). Chemical lesions of the nucleus accumbens septi in rats: Effects on muricide and apomorphine-induced aggression. *Behavioral Brain Research*, *19*, 171–178.

Redgrave, P. (1978). Modulation of intracranial self-stimulation by local perfusions of dopamine, noradrenaline and serotonin within the caudate nucleus and nucleus accumbens. *Brain Research*, *155*, 277–295.

Redgrave, P., & Mitchell, I. (1982). Functional validation of projection topography in the nigrostriatal dopamine system. *Neuroscience*, *7*, 885–894.

Roberts, D. C. S., Corcoran, M. E., & Fibiger, H. C. (1977). On the role of ascending catecholominergic systems in intravenous self-administration of cocaine. *Pharmacology, Biochemistry and Behavior*, *6*, 615–620.

Roberts, D. C. S., & Koob, G. F. (1982). Disruption of cocaine self-administration following 6-OHDA lesions of the VTA in rats. *Pharmacology, Biochemistry and Behavior*, *17*, 901–904.

Roberts, D. C. S., Zis, A. P., & Fibiger, H. C. (1975). Ascending catecholamine pathways and amphetamine induced locomotion: Importance of dopamine and apparent non-involvement of norepinephrine. *Brain Research*, *93*, 441–454.

Robertson, A., Laferriere, A., & Franklin, K. B. J. (1981). Amphetamine and increases in current modulate reward in the hypothalamus and substantia nigra but not in the prefrontal cortex. *Physiology and Behavior*, *26*, 809–813.

Rompre, P. P., & Miliaressis, E. (1980). A comparison of the excitability cycles of the hypothalamic fibres involved in self-stimulation and exploration. *Physiology and Behavior*, *24*, 995–998.

Routtenberg, A. (1984). The CA3 pyramidal cell in the hippocampus: site of intrinsic expression and extrinsic control of memory formation. In L. Squire & N. Butters (Eds.), *Neuropsychology of memory*. New York: Guilford.

Routtenberg, A., & Holzman, N. (1973). Memory disruption by electrical stimulation of substantia nigra, pars compacta. *Science*, *181*, 83–86.

Routtenberg, A., & Sloan, M. (1971). Self-stimulation in the frontal cortex of Rattus norvegicus, *Journal of Comparative and Physiological Psychology*, *75*, 269–276.

Schaefer, G. J., & Michael, R. P. (1980). Acute effects of neuroleptics on brain self-stimulation thresholds in rats. *Psychopharmacology*, *67*, 9–15.

Schenk, S., & Shizgal, P. (1982). The substrates for lateral hypothalamic and medial prefrontal cortex self-stimulation have different refractory periods and show poor spatial summation. *Physiology Behavior*, *28*, 133–138.

Schiff, B. B. (1975). Caudate lesions and self-stimulation: An argument for better behavioral methods in research on intracranial self-stimulation. In A. Wauquier & E. T. Rolls (Eds.), *Brain Stimulation Reward*. The Netherlands: North Holland.

Schiff, B. B., Rusak, B., & Block, R. (1971). The termination of reinforcing intracranial stimulation: An ecological approach. *Physiology and Behavior*, *7*, 215–220.

Schlechter, J. M., & Butcher, L. L. (1972). Blockade by pimozide of (D)-amphetamine-induced hyperkinesia in mice. *Journal of Pharmaceutical Pharmacology*, *24*, 408–409.

Sclafani, A., Aravich, P. F., & Xenakis, S. (1982). Dopaminergic and endorphinergic mediation of a sweet reward. In B. G. Hoebel & D. Novin (Eds.), *The neural basis of feeding and rewards* (pp. 507–515). Brunswick, ME: Haer Institute.

Seiden, L. S. R., MacPhail, R. C., & Oglesby, M. W. (1975). Catecholamines and drug behavior interactions. *Federation Proceedings*, *34*, 1823–1831.

Sevenster, P. (1973). Incompatibility of response and reward. In R. A. Hinde & J. Stevenson-Hinde (Eds.), *Constraints on learning: Limitations and predispositions* (pp. 265–283). New York: Academic Press.

Sheffield, F. D. (1966). A drive-induction theory of reinforcement. In R. N. Haber (Ed.), *Current Research in Motivation* (pp. 98–111). New York: Holt.

Shettleworth, S. (1973). Reinforcement and the organization of behavior in Golden Hamsters. In R. A. Hinde & J. Stevenson-Hinde (Eds.), *Constraints on learning: Limitations and predispositions* (pp. 243–264). New York: Academic Press.

Shizgal, P., Bielajew, C., Corbett, D., Skelton, R., & Yeomans, J. (1980). Behavioral methods for inferring anatomical linkage between rewarding brain stimulation sites. *Journal of Comparative and Physiological Psychology*, *94*, 227–237.

Siviy, S. M., Calcagnetti, D. J., & Reid, L. D. (1982). Opioids and palatability. In B. G. Hoebel & D. Novin (Eds.), *Neural basis of feeding and reward* (pp. 517–524). Brunswick, ME: Haer Institute.

Skinner, B. F. (1958). Reinforcement today. *American Psychologist, 13,* 94–99.

Spyraki, C., Fibiger, H. C., & Phillips, A. G. (1982). Dopaminergic substrates of amphetamine-induced place preference conditioning. *Brain Research, 253,* 185–193.

Spyraki, C., Fibiger, H. C., & Phillips, A. G. (1983). Attenuation of heroin reward in rats by disruption of the mesolimbic dopamine system. *Psychopharmacology, 79,* 278–283.

Stellar, J. R., Kelley, A. E., & Corbett, D. (1983). Effects of peripheral and central dopamine blockade on lateral hypothalamic self-stimulation: Evidence for both reward and motor deficits. *Pharmacology, Biochemistry and Behavior, 18,* 433–442.

Stellar, J. R., & Stellar, E. (1985). *The neurobiology of motivation and reward* (p. 142). New York: Springer-Verlag.

Stinus, L., Koob, G. F., Ling, N., Bloom, F. E., & Le Moal, M. (1980). Locomotor activation induced by infusion of endorphins into the ventral tegmental area: Evidence for opiate-dopamine interactions. *Proceedings of the National Academy of Sciences USA, 77,* 2323–2327.

Swanson, L. W. (1976). An autoradiographic study of the efferent connections of the preoptic region in the rat. *Journal of Comparative Neurology, 167,* 227–256.

Swanson, L. W., & Cowan, W. M. (1975). A note on the connections and development of the nucleus accumbens. *Brain Research, 92,* 324–330.

Swanson, L. W., Mogenson, G. J., Gerfen, C. R., & Robinson, P. (1984). Evidence for a projection from the lateral preoptic area and substantia innominata to the 'mesencephalic locomotor region' in the rat. *Brain Research, 295,* 161–178.

Swanson, L. W., Mogenson, G. J., Simerly, R. B., & Wu, M. (1987). Anatomical and electrophysiological evidence for a projection from the medial preoptic area to the 'mesencephalic and subthalamic locomotor regions' in the rat. *Brain Research, 405,* 108–122.

Swerdlow, N. R., & Koob, G. F. (1984). The neural substrates of apomorphine-stimulated locomotor activity following denervation of the nucleus accumbens. *Life Sciences, 35,* 2537–2544.

Swerdlow, N. R., Swanson, L. W., & Koob, G. F. (1984a). Electrolytic lesions of the substantia innominata and lateral preoptic area attenuate the 'supersensitive' locomotor response to apomorphine resulting from denervation of the nucleus accumbens. *Brain Research, 306,* 141–148.

Swerdlow, N. R., Swanson, L. W., & Koob, G. F. (1984b). Substantia innominata: Critical link in the behavioral expression of mesolimbic dopamine stimulation in the rat. *Neuroscience Letters, 50,* 19–24.

Swerdlow, N. R., Vaccarino, F. J., Amalric, M., & Koob, G. F. (1986). The neural substrates for the motor-activating properties of psychostimulants: A review of recent findings. *Pharmacology, Biochemistry and Behavior, 25,* 233–248.

Taylor, J. R., & Robbins, T. W. (1984). Enhanced behavioral control by conditioned reinforcers following microinjection of d-amphetamine into the nucleus accumbens. *Psychopharmacology, 84,* 405–412.

Taylor, J. R., & Robbins, T. W. (1986). 6-Hydroxydopamine lesions of the nucleus accumbens but not the caudate nucleus, attenuate enhanced responding with reward-related stimuli produced by intra-accumbens d-amphetamine. *Psychopharmacology, 90,* 390–397.

Thistlethwaite, D. (1951). A critical review of related experiments. *Psychological Bulletin, 48,* 97–129.

Tinbergen, N. (1951). *The study of instinct.* London: Oxford University Press.

Ungerstedt, U. (1971). Aphagia and adipsia after 6-hydroxydopamine induced degeneration of the nigrostriatal dopamine system. *Acta Physiologica Scandanavica, 367 (suppl),* 95–122.

Vaccarino, F. J., Amalric, M., Swerdlow, N., & Koob, G. F. (1986) Blockade of amphetamine but not opiate-induced locomotion following antagonism of dopamine function in the rat. *Pharmacology, Biochemistry and Behavior,* 61–65, 1986.

Vaccarino, F. J., Bloom. F. E., & Koob, G. F. (1985). Blockade of nucleus accumbens opiate receptors attenuates intravenous heroin reward in the rat. *Psychopharmacology, 86,* 37–42.

Vaccarino, F. J., & Corrigal, W. A. (1987). Effects of opiate antagonist treatment into either the periaqueductal grey or nucleus accumbens on heroin-induced locomotor activation. *Brain Research Bulletin, 19,* 545–549.

Vaccarino, F. J., Pettit, H. O., Bloom, F. E., & Koob, G. F. (1985). Effects of intracerebroventricular administration of methylnaloxone chloride on heroin self-administration in the rat. *Pharmacology, Biochemistry and Behavior, 23,* 495–498.

Valenstein, E. S., Cox, V. C., & Kakolweski, J. W. (1970). Re-examination of the role of the hypothalamus in motivation. *Psychological Review, 77,* 16–31.

Van der Kooy, D., Fibiger, H. C., & Phillips, A. G. (1977). Monoamine involvement: Hippocampal self-stimulation. *Brain Research, 136,* 119–130.

Van der Kooy, D., Mucha, R. F., O'Shaughnessy, M., & Bucenieks, P. (1982). Reinforcing effects of brain microinjections of morphine revealed by conditioned place preference. *Brain Research, 243,* 107–117.

Van der Kooy, D., Swerdlow, N. R., & Koob, G. F. (1983). Paradoxical reinforcing effects of apomorphine: Effects of nucleus accumbens and area postrema lesions. *Brain Research, 259,* 111–118.

Vezina, P., Kalivas, P. W., & Stewart, J. (1987). Sensitization occurs to the locomotor effects of morphine and the specific mu receptor agonist, DAGO, administered repeatedly to the ventral tegmental area but not to the nucleus accumbens. *Brain Research,* in press.

Vezina, P., & Stewart, J. (1984). Conditioning and place-specific sensitization of increases in activity induced by morphine in the VTA. *Pharmacology, Biochemistry and Behavior, 20,* 925–934.

Walker, E. L. (1969). Reinforcement—"The One Ring". In J. Tapp (Ed.), *Reinforcement and behavior.* New York: Academic Press.

Waxman, S. G. (1978). Variations in axonal morphology and their functional significance. In S. G. Waxman (Ed.), *Physiology and pathobiology of axons.* New York: Raven

Weeks, J. R. (1962). Experimental morphine addiction: Method for automatic intravenous injections in unrestrained rats. *Science, 138,* 143–144.

West, T. E. G., & Wise, R. A. (1986). Relative effects of naloxone on nucleus accumbens, lateral hypothalamic and ventral tegmental self-stimulation in the rat. *Society for Neuroscience Abstracts, 12,* 931.

Williams, D. J., Crossman, A. R., & Slater, P. (1977). The efferent projections of the nucleus accumbens in the rat. *Brain Research, 130,* 217–227.

Winn, P., Williams, S. F., & Herberg, L. J. (1982). Feeding stimulated by very low doses of d-amphetamine administered systemically or by microinjection into the striatum. *Psychopharmacology, 78,* 336–341.

Wise, R. A. (1978). Catecholamine theories of reward: A critical review. *Brain Res., 152,* 215–247.

Wise, R. A. (1981). Intracranial self-stimulation: mapping against the lateral boundaries of the dopaminergic cells of the substantia nigra. *Brain Res., 213,* 190–194.

Wise, R. A. (1982). Neuroleptics and operant behavior: The anhedonia hypothesis. *Behavioral and Brain Sciences, 5,* 39–87.

Wise, R. A. (1985). The anhedonia hypothesis: Mark III. *Behavioral and Brain Sciences, 8,* 178–186.

Wise, R. A., & Bozarth, M. A. (1987). A psychomotor stimulant theory of addiction. *Psychological Review, 94,* 469–492.

Wise, R. A., & Colle, L. M. (1984). Pimozide attenuates free feeding: Best scores analysis reveals a motivational deficit. *Psychopharmacol., 84,* 446–451.

Wise, R. A., & Raptis, L. (1986). Effects of naloxone and pimozide on initiation and maintenance measures of free feeding. *Brain Res., 368,* 62–68.

Wise, C. D., & Stein, L. (1970). Amphetamine: Facilitation of behavior by augmented release of norepinephrine from the medial forebrain bundle. In E. Costa & S. Garattini (Eds.), *Amphetamine and related compounds* (pp. 463–485). New York: Raven Press.

Yeomans, J. S. (1975). Quantitative measurement of neural post-stimulation excitability with behavioral methods. *Physiology and Behavior, 15,* 593–602.

Yeomans, J. S. (1979). The absolute refreactory periods of self-stimulation neurons. *Physiology and Behavior, 22,* 911–919.

Yeomans, J. S. (1982). The cells and axons mediating medial forebrain bundle reward. In B. B. Hoebel & D. Novin, (Eds.), *The neural basis of feeding and reward* (pp. 405-417). Brunswick, ME: Haer Institute.

Yeomans, J. S. (1988). Mechanisms of brain stimulation reward. In A. N. Epstein & A. Morrison (Eds.), *Progress in psychobiology and physiological psychology, 13,* (in press).

Young, P. T. (1959). The role of affective processes in learning and motivation. *Psychological Review, 66,* 104–125.

Zaborsky, L., Alheid, G. F., Alones, V. E., Oertel, W. H., Schmechel, D. E., & Heimer, L. (1982). Afferents of the ventral pallidum studied with a combined immunohistochemical-anterograde degeneration method. *Society for Neuroscience Abstracts, 8,* 218.

Zarevics, P., & Settler, P. (1979). Simultaneous rate-independent and rate-dependent assessment of intracranial self-stimulation: Evidence for the direct involvement of dopamine in brain reinforcement mechanisms. *Brain Research, 169,* 499–512.

III BIOLOGICAL CONSTRAINTS ON LEARNING

6
Selective Associations and Adaptive Specializations: Taste Aversions and Phobias

Vincent M. LoLordo
Anastasia Droungas
Dalhousie University

I. INTRODUCTION

One of the key concepts in the area of research associated with the label "constraints on learning" (e.g., Bolles, 1970; Rozin & Kalat, 1971; Shettleworth, 1972) is selective association. Selective association occurs whenever "connections between certain antecedent and consequent events (CS1–US1, CS2–US2) within a set of events (CS1, CS2, US1, US2) may be formed very easily, whereas connections between other antecedents and consequents (CS1–US2, CS2–US1) may not be formed at all, or only with great difficulty" (LoLordo, 1979, pp. 369–370; see, e.g., LoLordo & Jacobs, 1983; Schwartz, 1974 for discussions of the grounds for inferring selective association).

It now seems clear that selective associations, as defined above, do occur (see reviews by Domjan, 1982, 1983). The example that has attracted the most attention over the years is the one first described by Garcia and Koelling (1966). A flavor, rather than auditory and visual stimuli, was said to be selectively associated with illness, whereas the auditory and visual stimuli were said to be selectively associated with painful electric shock (a more complete description of this research can be found in Chapter 7 of this volume). A series of experiments from Domjan's laboratory (Domjan, 1982; Gemberling & Domjan, 1982; Miller, 1984) ruled out various alternatives to a selective associative account of this phenomenon, and indicated that the selective association requires very little early experience, since it is observed in very young animals.

Today most researchers would agree that the sheer fact of selective association does not compel us to abandon the belief that there are general laws of learning. In the case of food aversion learning, the status of another phenomenon called potentiation may determine whether we are obliged to conclude that the aversion is mediated by a behavior system which obeys laws of its own. Potentiation refers to the case where an odor, which would not itself become aversive because of its pairing with illness, does become aversive if it had been accompanied by a taste on that occasion. The primary focus of the next section of this essay is the question whether such potentiation, which is a result opposite the overshadowing typically seen after compound conditioning (e.g., Kamin, 1969), can be explained by current general principles of learning, or whether its explanation requires reference to some special property of the food aversion learning system.

II. POTENTIATION

Demonstrations of Potentiation

In a study by Rusiniak, Hankins, Garcia, and Brett (1979) rats failed to associate the odor of almond with lithium-induced toxicosis when the odor was presented alone. However, the same odor became strongly aversive after it was presented in compound with the taste of saccharine and was followed by lithium chloride poisoning. Aversion to the odor is said to be potentiated by taste.

In paradigms involving lithium chloride-induced toxicosis in the rat, taste has been used to mediate potentiated aversion to a number of different cues. In addition to taste-mediated potentiation of odor aversion (Bouton, Jones, McPhillips, & Swartzentruber, 1986; Coburn, Garcia, Kiefer, & Rusiniak, 1984; Durlach & Rescorla, 1980; Holder & Garcia, 1987; Holder, Leon, Yirmiya, & Garcia, 1987; Holland, 1983; Kiefer, Rusiniak, & Garcia, 1982; Lett, 1984; Palmerino, Rusiniak, & Garcia, 1980; Rusiniak, Palmerino, & Garcia, 1982; Rusiniak, Palmerino, Rice, Forthman, & Garcia, 1982; Westbrook, Homewood, Horn, & Clarke, 1983), there have also been demonstrations of potentiation of aversion to visual cues of food (Galef & Osborne, 1978), weaker tastes (Kucharski & Spear, 1985), auditory cues (Ellins & von Kluge, 1987; Holland, 1983), contextual cues (Best, Batson, Meachum, Brown, & Ringer, 1985; Best & Meachum, 1986; Miller, McCoy, Kelly, & Bardo, 1986). Potentiation has also been demonstrated in pigeons and quail (Clarke, Westbrook, & Irwin, 1979; Lett, 1984; Westbrook, Clarke, & Provost, 1980). In the pigeon lithium chloride-induced aversions are very readily formed with tastes. On the other hand, such aversions do not develop to visual stimuli when the latter are presented alone and followed by toxicosis. However, if visual stimuli are presented in compound with a taste the former become strongly aversive.

Theoretical Analysis of Potentiation

Although there are some studies in the literature that report failure to show potentiation in rats and quail (Bouton & Whiting, 1982; Mikulka, Pitts, & Philput, 1982; Wilcoxon, Dragoin, & Kral, 1971) successful demonstrations have predominated. Studies have ruled out nonassociative interpretations of the phenomenon (Best et al., 1985; Durlach & Rescorla, 1980; Rusiniak et al., 1982), such as generalized aversion between the two elements of the compound, enhancement of aversion due to unconditioned aversive properties of the potentiating stimulus, differential neophobia, and sensitization.

Theories of potentiation have either analyzed the phenomenon in terms of general principles governing the formation of associations in Pavlovian conditioning (Durlach & Rescorla, 1980), or in terms of specialized principles specific to the gastrointestinal defense system (Garcia, Forthman Quick, & White, 1984). One general principle of learning that might apply to potentiation is higher-order conditioning. Specifically, potentiation may reflect a secondary aversion similar to that produced through second-order conditioning or sensory preconditioning. A number of studies (Best et al., 1985; Galef & Osborne, 1978; Rusiniak et al., 1979; Westbrook et al., 1980) have examined whether potentiation can be reduced to sensory preconditioning or second-order conditioning. These studies have shown that such analyses of potentiation are not adequate.

Two additional theoretical accounts have been suggested. The "within-compound" learning analysis of potentiation (Clarke et al., 1979; Durlach & Rescorla, 1980) analyzes potentiation in terms of general principles of Pavlovian conditioning. The "sensory and-gate channelling" analysis (Garcia, Forthman Quick, & White, 1984; see also Galef & Osborne, 1978) advocates principles which are specific to the feeding system to account for the formation of associations in potentiation.

1. The "Within-Compound" Analysis of Potentiation. According to the "within-compound" analysis potentiation is another instance of within-compound conditioning (Rescorla & Cunningham, 1978), whereby each of the elements (S1 and S2) of a compound stimulus, in addition to forming an association with the US (S1–US and S2–US) also forms an association with the other (S1–S2). Consequently, upon presenting S1 there is twofold activation of the US representation. One path is through the direct association between S1 and the US, and the second is through the association between S1 and S2, whereby S1 activates the representation of S2, which in turn activates the representation of the US with which it is associated. The summation of the two activations of the US representation results in a larger conditioned response to an S1 which is conditioned in compound than to a stimulus conditioned alone (refer to Durlach, 1989 for a review of this approach).

According to this analysis potentiation of odor (S1) aversion is importantly dependent on the formation and maintenace of the taste-illness (S2–US) association, and the strength of the effect on odor should reflect the strength of the associations between odor and taste and also between taste and illness (Westbrook et al., 1983). Thus, postconditioning enhancement of the taste aversion should concomitantly enhance potentiation of the odor aversion, whereas postconditioning extinction of the taste aversion should eliminate potentiation of the odor aversion. Potentiation should also be diminished by manipulations that interfere with the formation of the association between odor and taste. For example, odor and taste may become dissociated before conditioning if either of the elements is presented alone, or both are presented, but separately. Alternatively, dissociation of odor and taste may occur during conditioning if the temporal or spatial contiguity between the two stimuli is eliminated.

2. The "sensory and-gate channelling" analysis of potentiation. According to the "sensory and-gate channelling" analysis potentiation is a phenomenon uniquely associated with the feeding system. Taste stimuli are said to "belong" to the internal or gut defense system in the sense that associations between taste cues and gastrointestinal malaise are very readily formed. On the other hand, exteroceptive cues, e.g., auditory and visual stimuli, "belong" to the external defense system in the sense that such stimuli readily form associations with pain- and fear-producing USs. Other stimuli, as for example odor, are relevant to both the internal and external defense systems, since odor is a property of both a poisonous food and an approaching predator. In the absence of taste cues odor is gated into the external defense system and exhibits properties similar to those exhibited by exteroceptive cues. Under such conditions odor becomes readily associated with fear- and pain-producing stimuli and competes for associative strength with concurrently present exteroceptive cues, as predicted by traditional Pavlovian conditioning theories (Rescorla & Wagner, 1972).

On the other hand, in the presence of feeding-related cues like tastes, odor is gated into the feeding system and exhibits properties similar to those exhibited by taste. For instance, odor becomes readily associated with gastrointestinal malaise and long delay aversion learning occurs with odors just as it does with tastes (Kucharski & Spear, 1985; Palmerino et al., 1980; however, see Westbrook et al., 1980 on taste-mediated potentiation of color aversion in the pigeon). Thus, in the internal defense system stronger cues potentiate weaker cues, whereas in the external defense system stronger cues overshadow weaker cues. According to the sensory and-gate channelling analysis the role of taste is to channel the odor into the feeding system and thus strengthen the odor-illness association. Based on the above, potentiation of an odor aversion by taste should not be critically dependent on the formation and maintenance of the taste aversion.

Does Potentiation Require Formation and Maintenance of an Association Between the Potentiating Stimulus and the US?

As mentioned earlier, the within-compound analysis of potentiation differs from the sensory and-gate analysis in that only the former predicts that potentiation of S1 (e.g., odor) by S2 (e.g., taste) critically depends on the formation and preservation of the association between S2 and the US. Evidence on whether formation of a taste aversion is necessary for potentiation has been obtained from studies that: (1) have varied the concentration of the taste and have thus affected the strength of the taste aversion; (2) have preexposed the taste and have thereby weakened or eliminated the taste aversion; and (3) have made lesions of the gustatory neocortex that eliminate the taste aversion. On the other hand, evidence on whether it is necessary to maintain the taste aversion, once it is formed, in order to demonstrate potentiation has been obtained from studies that have carried out postconditioning extinction of the taste aversion. These studies are reviewed in this section.

1. Elimination of taste aversion by manipulating taste concentration.   Rusiniak et al. (1979) have shown that a taste can still potentiate an odor aversion even when there is no aversion conditioned to the taste. Specifically, Rusiniak et al. (Experiment 3) examined potentiation of odor under different taste concentrations. Potentiation of odor aversion was found with taste concentrations that were too weak to support a conditioned taste aversion.

However, it could still be the case that there was a taste-illness association, but one that was too weak to be revealed in performance. For example, additional tests might have revealed that the weak tastes would mediate second-order conditioning or block acquisition of an aversion to a novel, stronger taste. Since these tests were not performed, the data from the experiment by Rusiniak et al. do not demonstrate unequivocally that potentiation can be obtained in the absence of a taste-illness association.

2. Elimination of taste aversion by preexposure to taste.   Best et al. (1985; Experiment 2) demonstrated that preconditioning exposure to the taste of saccharine, which prevented the taste aversion from being conditioned to saccharine, dramatically attenuated saccharine-mediated potentiation of the aversion to contextual cues. These data support the notion that the conditioning of a taste aversion is crucial for taste-mediated potentiation of the aversion to another cue. Similar results have been obtained by Best and Meachum (1986), who showed an attenuation of taste-mediated potentiation of the aversion to contextual cues resulting from preconditioning exposure to the taste cue, or to the taste in combination with the context cue. In both cases where the attenuation of potentiation was obtained, namely, following preexposure to taste, or to taste and context paired or unpaired, preconditioning exposure to the taste resulted in a substantial disruption of the conditioning of a taste aversion.

Holder et al. (1987) have recently reported that preconditioning exposure to taste attenuated the conditioning of a taste aversion, but did not disrupt the development of a taste-mediated odor aversion. Odor aversion following compound conditioning was equivalent in a group that had and a group that had not been preexposed to the taste. However, it is noteworthy that as a result of preexposure to the taste the odor aversion resulting from odor single element conditioning was much stronger than in the group that had not been preexposed to taste. Holder et al. suggested that it could be the case that preconditioning exposure to the taste does in fact disrupt taste-mediated potentiation of odor aversion. But since taste preexposure also facilitates single element conditioning of odor aversion the two effects might cancel each other, leaving the odor aversion equivalent in the compound cue group that had been preexposed to taste and the nonpreexposed group.

3. Elimination of taste aversion by gustatory neocortex lesions.   Kiefer et al. (1982) have argued that formation of a taste aversion is not critical for taste-mediated potentiation of odor aversion on the basis of the effects of lesioning the gustatory neocortex. Such a lesion is claimed to selectively eliminate taste aversions but to spare the detection of taste and the development of odor aversions. Kiefer et al. demonstrated potentiation of odor aversion when odor was conditioned in compound with taste in rats that had received such lesions. This odor potentiation was demonstrated when no taste aversion was discernible (Experiment 1B). Furthermore, odor potentiation was demonstrated when the lesioning occurred either before or after conditioning.

Thus, from these results it seems that the formation of a taste aversion may not be necessary for potentiation. However, it could also be the case, as already noted, that a taste-illness association had been established that was too weak to be manifested in performance. Such an association could be detected in a blocking procedure, or by use of a more sensitive indicator of an associatively mediated shift in the hedonic value of the taste, i.e., taste elicited oral-facial consummatory reactions (Grill & Norgren, 1978).

4. Postconditioning extinction of taste aversions.   In agreement with the within-compound analysis of potentiation, Durlach and Rescorla (1980; Experiment 4) have shown that the maintenance of the aversion to the taste used in compound conditioning with odor is crucial for potentiation of odor aversion. In rats, extinction of the taste aversion following a pairing of taste and odor with lithium chloride eliminated the taste-mediated potentiation of the odor aversion. Specifically, rats received preconditioning exposure to three different odorous solutions (O1, O2, O3) and two different tastes (S, N) for 11 days as follows: O1 was presented alone, while O2 and O3 were mixed together with S and N, respectively. Following this exposure, conditioning of each of the three solutions was carried out. Each solution was presented on one conditioning day, just as it was presented during the preconditioning exposure, that is, O1 was presented alone, but O2 was presented with S and O3 with N. On each of these days (days 3, 5, and 7) access to the given solution was followed by lithium chloride poisoning. On intervening days animals were given water. Following conditioning all animals were given 4 days of extinction during which they were presented with N, the taste that had been presented together with O3 during the conditioning phase. Subsequently, aversions to the three odors were assessed.

Data from the tests showed that there was a strong aversion to O2, the odor that had been conditioned together with the nonextinguished taste. The O2-odor aversion was stronger than the odor aversion to O1 that had been conditioned alone. This result illustrates taste-mediated potentiation of odor aversion. On the other hand, the odor aversion to O3, that had been conditioned together with the subsequently extinguished taste, was comparable to the odor aversion to O1. This result indicated that the taste-mediated potentiation of an odor aversion which arises by virtue of presenting the odor in compound with a taste during conditioning is eliminated if the aversion to the specific taste the odor had been conditioned with is extinguished.

Similar results have been provided by Best et al. (1985) with taste-mediated potentiation of aversion to contextual cues, Kucharski and Spear (1985) with the potentiation of the aversion to a weaker taste by a strong taste, Miller et al. (1986) with potentiation of morphine-based odor aversion by taste, and Westbrook et al. (1983; Experiments 3 and 4) with potentiation of odor aversion by taste. It is noteworthy that Westbrook et al. (Experiment 4) found that elimination of the taste-mediated potentiation of the odor aversion through extinction was not specific to the extinction of the aversion to the taste that had been conditioned together with the odor. Elimination of odor potentiation was also obtained when the aversion to another taste, which had been separately conditioned, was extinguished, contrary to Durlach and Rescorla's finding that the effect of extinction on taste-mediated odor potentiation was specific to the taste the odor had been conditioned with.

The nonspecific effect of extinction of the taste aversion on taste-mediated odor potentiation in the Westbrook et al. study was obtained using a within-subjects design (Experiment 4), and in that respect it parallels the study by Durlach and Rescorla. It may be that the nonspecific effect of extinction obtained in the experiment by Westbrook et al. is due to generalization between the taste that was used during compound conditioning with the odor and the separately conditioned taste. In a previous experiment in the same report (Westbrook et al.; Experiment 3) there was some evidence of generalization between the two tastes, since conditioning of one seemed to strengthen the aversion to the other. In the study by Durlach and Rescorla the lengthy preconditioning exposure to the different stimuli may have provided the rats the opportunity to discriminate between the two tastes and show little generalization between them. The other studies that replicated the extinction effect obtained by Durlach and Rescorla failed to include control groups to test the specificity of the extinction effect. In the absence of evidence for specificity the findings of these studies do not unequivocally support Durlach and Rescorla.

Contrary to the findings of Durlach and Rescorla, Lett (1984) has reported that extinction of the taste aversion did not result in the elimination of taste-mediated potentiation of odor aversions in rats or color aversions in pigeons. Lett has criticized the study by Durlach and Rescorla by suggesting that the long preconditioning exposure to the odor-taste compound may have facilitated the development of within-compound associations, which in turn permitted the demonstration of the extinction effect. As pointed out by Lett, the early demonstrations of potentiation (e.g. Clarke et al., 1979; Galef & Osborne, 1978; Rusiniak et al., 1979) did not involve such long preconditioning exposures to the compound CS. Thus, it is not clear whether the potentiation effect obtained by Durlach and Rescorla reflects the same phenomenon as was originally demonstrated.

It is the case however, that with the exception of Durlach and Rescorla, none of the studies (cited above) which showed that extinction of the taste aversion eliminated taste-mediated potentiation administered preconditioning exposure to the cues. Thus, it seems unlikely that the effect of extinction obtained by Durlach and Rescorla was solely due to preexposure to the cues before conditioning.

In an effort to further test predictions made by the within-compound analysis of potentiation, Westbrook et al. (1983; Experiment 5) have examined whether postconditioning enhancement of the taste aversion correspondingly produces an enhancement in the taste-mediated potentiation of an odor aversion. Specifically, following the pairing of taste and odor with lithium chloride the taste was further conditioned with a stronger dose of lithium. This manipulation was shown to enhance the odor aversion, compared to the condition where the taste aversion was not enhanced. However, this enhancement of the odor aversion was shown not to be specific to the enhancement of the aversion to the taste that had been presented together with the odor during conditioning; postconditioning enhancement of aversion to a taste that had been separately conditioned was as effective in enhancing the potentiated odor aversion. This finding was interpreted by the authors to signify that potentiated odor aversions can be modulated by manipulating the representation of the US. However, it could also be the case, as mentioned previously, that generalization between the tastes may have prevented the demonstration of specificity of enhancement.

In summary, the within-compound analysis and the sensory and-gate channelling analysis make opposite predictions concerning whether the formation and maintenance of an association between taste and illness are necessary in order for potentiation of odor aversion to be demonstrated. As noted above, the effects of gustatory neocortex lesions and the results of the taste concentration manipulation favor but do not unequivocally support the sensory and-gate channelling account's assertion that the formation of a taste-illness association is not necessary for potentiation. Subthreshold taste aversions that cannot be detected with consumption measures might still be mediating the potentiated odor aversions in these studies.

On the other hand, and against the sensory and-gate channeling analysis, the effects of preconditioning exposure to taste firmly support the notion that the development of a taste aversion is crucial for taste-mediated potentiation. In that respect, these data support the within-compound analysis. Furthermore, against the sensory and-gate channelling analysis, several studies, with the exception of Lett's, seem to demonstrate that it is crucial to maintain the taste aversion, once it is formed, in order to demonstrate potentiation of an odor aversion. However, these studies do not unequivocally support the within-compound analysis either, since it is not clear whether the attenuation and enhancement of odor potentiation by postconditioning extinction and strengthening of the taste aversion, respectively, are specific to the taste with which the odor was conditioned. Thus, the weight of the evidence is not preponderately on one side or the other.

Is Potentiation Uniquely Associated with the Feeding System?

The sensory and-gate channelling analysis sees potentiation as a property uniquely associated with the internal or gut defense system. Evidence that potentiation occurs in the gut defense system and overshadowing occurs in the external defense system when a weak and a strong cue are compounded during conditioning has been provided by Rusiniak et al. (1982). Conditioning of odor was examined with lithium chloride and shock as the USs. Taste-mediated potentiation of odor aversion was demonstrated by showing that rats presented with almond odor followed by lithium chloride poisoning learned an odor aversion only if the almond odor was presented in compound with saccharine taste. There was no aversion to almond odor if it was presented alone during conditioning. There was a strong saccharine taste aversion both when saccharine was conditioned as a single element and when it was conditioned in compound with the almond odor; the saccharine taste aversion, however, was weaker when saccharine taste was conditioned in compound.

On the other hand, rats presented with almond odor followed by shock learned an odor avoidance only if almond odor was presented as a single element during conditioning. Shock conditioned odor avoidance was disrupted if almond odor was presented in compound with saccharine taste during conditioning. There was a weak conditioned saccharine avoidance when saccharine was the only CS for shock; this avoidance was weaker when saccharine was conditioned in compound with almond odor. The latter finding showed that almond odor which is readily associated with shock when conditioned alone does not mediate potentiation of saccharine avoidance; instead it overshadows the weaker taste. Moreover, the overshadowing was mutual. These results were replicated with single and repeated trials, and also with weak and stronger poison and shock USs.

It might be especially informative to look for potentiation of odor aversion by taste with a US that is known to induce conditioned taste aversions but not to reduce the palatability of the taste, as measured by the pattern of oral-facial responses to infusion of the taste (e.g. Berridge & Grill, 1983; Grill & Norgren,

1978). Such USs include amphetamine and nicotine (Parker & Carvell, 1987), and lactose (Pelchat, Grill, Rozin, & Jacobs, 1983). An analysis of potentiation based on within-compound association would predict that such USs should induce as much potentiation as equally aversive doses of lithium chloride. On the other hand, if the sensory and-gate channelling analysis is taken to imply that only events which challenge the gut defense system will permit potentiation, then such stimuli should not induce potentiation, and might even lead to overshadowing.

Potentiation Versus Overshadowing in Food Aversion Learning

Within the gastrointestinal defense system, combining a taste cue with an odor cue does not always result in potentiation. Westbrook et al. (1983) have demonstrated overshadowing, instead of potentiation, of the odor cue by the taste cue when exposure to the reinforced compound was brief (2 min); with longer exposure (15 min) the authors demonstrated potentiation. Both overshadowing and potentiation were demonstrated in this study after a single conditioning trial. The strength of the odor aversion when odor was conditioned as a single element was also affected by the duration of exposure to the odor. The odor aversion resulting from single element conditioning was stronger with brief than with long exposure. The aversion conditioned to the taste was not measured in this study.

It is not clear how either of the two analyses of potentiation can account for these results. To salvage the within-compound analysis, one has to assume that:

1. Stimulus duration is an important parameter for the development of interelement associations, i.e., stimuli of short duration presented in a compound are less likely to form interelement associations than stimuli of longer duration;

2. When two stimuli are presented in compound, along with the development of interelement associations overshadowing between the two stimuli will also occur;

3. Interelement conditioning and overshadowing can occur on a single trial. If the interelement association is strong, the effect of overshadowing will be masked, whereas if the interelement association is weak the effect of overshadowing will be revealed.

There is some evidence favoring the last two of these assumptions. First, although Rescorla (1980) has not specifically addressed the issue of concurrent development of interelement associations and overshadowing, he has shown that interelement associations can develop in parallel with the development of blocking (pp. 58–59) and the development of conditioned inhibition (pp. 59–61). Second, Mackintosh and Reese (1979; Experiment 1) have demonstrated that overshadowing can in fact develop in a single conditioning trial when a target stimulus is presented in simultaneous compound with a more intense stimulus.

Finally, Rescorla and Durlach (1981) have shown that an interelement association can be detected after only one compound trial.

The sensory and-gate channelling analysis also has difficulty accounting for the finding that altering stimulus duration can reverse taste-mediated potentiation of odor to overshadowing of odor. Presumably, the presence of taste, regardless of stimulus duration, should be sufficient to channel the odor into the feeding system, and thus strengthen the odor-illness association. In defending their theoretical position Coburn et al. (1984) have criticized studies that have shown overshadowing of odor by taste by arguing that the overshadowing result is due to the mode of odor presentation. Specifically, they have argued that when the odor is mixed in with the drink it adds a taste component to the odorous drink. In cases where a taste is presented together with odor in the drink the former overshadows the weak taste of the odorant. The authors noted that their argument is supported by the fact that in cases where taste is shown to overshadow odor there is a strong odor aversion that develops as a result of single element odor conditioning. According to Coburn et al. this strong odor aversion reflects an aversion to the taste of the odorant.

The criticism advanced by Coburn et al. does not apply to the demonstration of overshadowing in the Westbrook et al. study, because in that study the odor was not presented in the drink. Instead, the odor was pumped into the conditioning apparatus in air streams. Thus, it cannot be claimed that the overshadowing demonstrated by Westbrook et al. reflects overshadowing between two tastes. Instead it reflects overshadowing of odor by taste.

Bouton et al. (1986) found that taste potentiated odor aversion if the odor was presented in a separate cup surrounding the drinking spout, but taste overshadowed odor if the odor was mixed in the drink with the taste. When odor was conditioned as a single element, odor aversion was stronger when odor was mixed in the water than when odor was presented in the cup surrounding the spout. These results, along with those of Westbrook et al., suggest that conditionability of odor may be a factor that determines whether compound conditioning will result in overshadowing or potentiation.

When an odor presented in the drink was diluted to such an extent that aversion to odor conditioned alone was substantially weakened, taste-mediated potentiation of the aversion to the proximal odor was in fact demonstrated (Experiment 4). Based on these results the authors argued that in order for a stimulus to become potentiated it should be weakly conditionable when presented alone. On the other hand, they suggested that strongly conditionable stimuli are overshadowed when presented in compound with taste.

The findings by Bouton et al., together with the findings by Westbrook et al., support the notion that odor conditionability may be an important factor in determining potentiation or overshadowing. Long duration or dilute odors that were weakly conditionable were potentiated by taste. On the other hand, brief or highly concentrated odors that were strongly conditionable were overshadowed by taste.

Neither the sensory and-gate chanelling analysis nor the within-compound analysis can explain this set of outcomes. The former would assert that when Bouton et al. placed odor cues in the drink, they were really studying the interaction of two tastes, in which realm competititon is the norm. This approach fails to account for two aspects of Bouton's results. First, a taste potentiated, rather than overshadowed, aversion to a weak odor in the drink. Second, a strong odor in the drink failed to potentiate aversion to a weak odor in the cup (Experiment 3). The within-compound analysis, which does not care whether the events are tastes or odors, fails because the two experiments are formally similar, yet produce divergent results.

Kucharski and Spear (1985) have shown that overshadowing, rather than potentiation, can occur if in compound conditioning the elements are presented successively instead of simultaneously. Specifically, when a weak taste was presented simultaneously with a strong taste the aversion to the weak taste was stronger than when it had been the only CS. However, if the weak taste preceded the strong taste potentiation was eliminated. Moreover, if the weak taste followed the strong taste there was overshadowing, and the aversion to the weak taste was even weaker than that resulting from single element conditioning. The strength of the aversion to the strong taste was also affected by whether compound conditioning was simultaneous or successive; it was stronger in simultaneous than in successive compound conditioning, regardless of order of presentation of the elements.

Coburn et al. (1984) also have obtained less potentiation of odor by taste with successive than with simultaneous compounds, although the taste aversion was equivalent in the two cases. The magnitude of the odor aversion was inversely related to the temporal gap interposed between the taste and odor. Moreover, a weaker odor aversion was obtained when taste was presented prior to odor in successive compound conditioning than when odor was presented first. It is not clear whether the weaker odor aversion obtained with taste-then-odor successive compound conditioning reflects overshadowing of odor by taste, since a group conditioned to odor alone was not included.

In a subsequent study which included appropriate controls Holder and Garcia (1987) found potentiation of odor aversion when odor and taste had been conditioned in a simultaneous compound. However, when odor and taste were presented successively, regardless of order of presentation the odor aversion was equivalent to that resulting from single element odor conditioning. The taste aversion was again not affected by the simultaneous vs. successive nature of compound conditioning.

This result showed elimination of taste-mediated odor potentiation with successive conditioning, but not overshadowing. These results are discrepant with those of Kucharski and Spear, who showed overshadowing in successive compound conditioning when the strong element preceded the weak element, and also showed attenuation of the aversion to the strong taste element with successive compound conditioning. Holder and Garcia have criticized the findings of Kucharski and Spear, claiming that they are specific to the combination of two tastes in compound conditioning. Alternatively, it is possible that there was overshadowing in the study by Holder and Garcia but that the one-bottle test of the odor aversion was relatively insensitive, and revealed such a weak odor aversion resulting from single element odor conditioning that overshadowing, i.e., an even weaker aversion in the compound conditioning group, could not be observed.

The finding that the sequential presentation of taste and odor results in an attenuation of potentiation is in agrement with the within-compound analysis. Rescorla (1980) has demonstrated that weaker within-compound associations between stimuli are formed in successive compared to simultaneous compound conditioning. Following up this result, Rescorla and Durlach (1981) briefly reported that aversion to an odor mixed in a drink was potentiated when saccharine was presented in the drink, but was overshadowed when saccharine was presented in the interval between odor and illness.

The sensory and-gate channelling analysis can also accommodate the finding of attenuation of potentiation resulting from sequential as opposed to simultaneous presentation of odor and taste. Based on the premises of this analysis, cues that are temporally and spatially proximal to taste are better channelled into the feeding system than cues that are temporally and spatially distal.

Although potentiation of odor aversion is eliminated when odor and taste are presented successively rather than simultaneously, the conditions under which such a manipulation leads to overshadowing of odor by taste are not well understood. Rescorla and Durlach observed overshadowing when odor in the drink preceded taste. Kucharski and Spear, on the other hand, failed to observe overshadowing when a weak taste preceded a strong one, but did obtain overshadowing when the strong taste came first. These results are compatible with the claim that the aversion to the weaker element is weakest when that element follows the stronger. Studies from Garcia's laboratory failed to obtain overshadowing with either order of presentation, though in one study the odor aversion was weaker when taste preceded odor than when the elements occurred in the reverse order. Of course in Garcia's studies groups conditioned to odor alone showed no aversion, so overshadowing could not be demonstrated. Garcia and his colleagues would deny the generality of the overshadowing result obtained by Kucharski and Spear and Rescorla and Durlach in sequential conditioning, claiming that overshadowing is specific to taste–taste interactions and would not occur when taste is conditioned with odor.

The within-compound analysis would attempt to explain the effect of order of stimulus presentation in these studies by assuming that any interelement associations are very weak, and that there is stronger overshadowing of odor by taste when taste precedes odor than when odor precedes taste, perhaps because of the greater informativeness of odor in the latter case. Mackintosh and Reese (1979; Experiment 2), have shown one-trial overshadowing of S1 by S2 when the two stimuli were presented sequentially in the order S1-then-S2, compared to simultaneous compound presentation, or single element S1 conditioning. Unfortunately, Mackintosh and Reese did not include an additional group that received S2-then-S1, allowing comparison of the magnitude of overshadowing under the two orders of presentation.

The within-compound analysis can also accommodate the results of Holder and Garcia. Because there is no odor aversion in the groups given single-element, odor conditioning, there can be no overshadowing, and the elimination of interelement associations through successive presentations of the two CSs can do no more than eliminate potentiation.

Conclusions

The outcomes of several studies, e.g., those concerning: (1) the effects of taste concentration and gustatory neocortex lesions upon taste-mediated potentiation of an odor aversion; and (2) direct comparisons of odor-taste compound conditioning with lithium chloride and shock USs, are problematic for a general process account, the within-compound analysis. Thus, despite its inability to predict that taste will overshadow odor when both are presented briefly prior to illness, and its difficulty explaining the attenuating effects of pre- and postconditioning presentations of the taste upon potentiation, the sensory and-gate channelling analysis remains a viable effort to account for the acquisition of aversions to various feeding-related cues in terms of an adaptively specialized mechanism.

III. HUMAN FEARS AND PHOBIAS

Another area where selective association has been thought to operate is in the development of human fears and phobias. In a 1971 paper Seligman asserted that Pavlovian conditioning was responsible for phobias, but that the associations established by such conditioning were prepared or selective. Specifically, he argued that because certain stimuli, e.g., snakes and spiders, were dangerous to pretechnological Man, modern Man is prepared or predisposed to learn to fear these stimuli. That is, only minimal input, e.g., one pairing with some aversive event, is required for these stimuli to evoke a fear response. Seligman suggested that such prepared fears are: (1) highly resistant to extinction, and (2) less affected by cognitive factors than other conditioned fears would be.

The preparedness model of human phobias was taken up by Öhman and his colleagues (e.g., Öhman, Dimberg, & Öst, 1985), who began by testing certain of the model's predictions about the results of human defensive conditioning experiments. In the 80s, Öhman's theorizing moved beyond application of the concept of preparedness in isolation to a "functional behavior systems approach" to fears and phobias (e.g., Bolles & Fanselow, 1980; Johnston, 1981; Timberlake, 1983, or Chapter 9 of this volume). Following Mayr (1974), Öhman suggested that behavior could be noncommunicative, or communicative within or between species. He further asserted that fear, which functions to protect the animal from actual or anticipated harm, could occur within any of these three realms (e.g., nature fears, animal fears, and social fears; Torgerson, 1979). Öhman's research and theorizing have focused on the two categories of communicative fears, animal and social phobias.

Öhman et al. (1985) suggested that it makes evolutionary sense for fear of a snake or some predator to depend on learning, rather than appearing on the first exposure to the predator, because the specificity required is so great that it would be inefficiently handled by the genes, and because predation pressure on a species may change rapidly over time, providing an adaptive advantage for learning. Of course the learning must be extremely efficient, or the organism wouldn't survive the conditioning episodes. But—a critic might reply—wouldn't even one pairing of the sight of a snake and snakebite be too many? Öhman would agree with the critic, but could respond on the basis of recent findings of Mineka and her colleagues (e.g., Mineka, Davidson, Cook, & Keir, 1984; Mineka, Keir, & Price, 1980), who observed that: (1) wild- but not laboratory-reared rhesus monkeys respond fearfully to a snake upon first seeing it in the laboratory, and (2) lab-reared rheses learn to fear snakes after relatively little exposure to another rhesus reacting fearfully to a snake.

In addition to predicting rapid learning of snake and other animal fears, Öhman's view predicts that such fears: (1) will be slow to extinguish; and (2) will include an atavistic, automatic affective component mediated by deep brain structures and independent of controlled processing routines. This response pattern will include activation of the sympathetic nervous system in preparation for flight.

Öhman's discussion of intraspecific, social fears focuses on the facial components of displays which have been used in agonistic encounters over the history of primates. Specifically Öhman, Dimberg, and Öst (1985) suggested that an angry facial expression, especially one directed at the observer, has over human history been correlated with aversive consequences for the observer. Thus, we should be predisposed to associate such an expression with aversive consequences. However, they asserted that unlike interspecific fears, intraspecific fears are "much more loosely and conditionally concocted, with a less prominent and reflexive role for active avoidance behavior" (p. 141). Although they agreed that inter- and intraspecific fears have in common an initial, automatic affective component, Öhman and his colleagues speculated that controlled processing plays a greater role in later components of intraspecific than of interspecific fear of responses. In the former case the initial affective response might be followed by any of a number of diverse responses, including gaze aversion, "submissive" vocalizations or remarks, or withdrawal from the scene of the encounter. Since, on the average, the need for sustained flight should be less in intraspecific fears than in interspecific ones, the metabolic consequences should be smaller in the former case, and an increase in heart rate should be less likely.

Thus, although Öhman's view incorporates the selective association feature of Seligman's preparedness account of phobias, it goes beyond preparedness to predict a number of differences in the patterns of responses to the two sorts of fear-evoking stimuli. In the sections that follow, some of the research on human conditioning that bears on Öhman's account of animal and social fears will be examined (also see McNally, 1987).

IV.   ANIMAL FEARS

Selective Association

Öhman, Dimberg, and Öst's (1985) view of animal fears implies that snakes and spiders are selectively associated with aversive stimuli. LoLordo (1979; also see Schwartz, 1974) described two experimental designs called the compound cue and single cue designs, which permit inferences about selective association. Only the single cue design has been applied to the case of animal fears. In this design four groups would receive factorial combinations of two CSs, say a snake and some control stimulus, e.g., a picture of a flower, and two USs, say weak electric shock and a nonaversive US. Rate of acquisition or asymptotic performance of some conditioned response would be assessed.

McNally (1987) has suggested that only one sort of outcome would support the selective association hypothesis, namely better conditioning to the snake CS than to the flower CS with the aversive US, along with the reverse effect with the control US. This may be too stringent a criterion; the possibility of selective association also should be taken seriously whenever there is the hypothesized difference between the two groups which receive the aversive US along with no difference between the two groups which receive the control US, so long as the group given flower-control US pairings acquires the conditioned response. If they do not, the experiment is not a fair test of the selective association hypothesis, because: (1) the control US might be ineffective, or (2) the flower CS might be ineffective. Neither of these possibilities implies selective association.

McNally (1987) has suggested that so few experiments using this design have been conducted because there has been no good basis for selecting a second US which would be more readily associated with the flower CS than with the snake CS. However, even if the demonstration of selective association did require that flower be better associated with the second US than snake, then an appetitive stimulus might be a good choice as the second US, on the intuition that a spider might be more poorly associated with some positive event than a flower would be. No experiments using an appetitive stimulus as the second US have been conducted. Instead, three other approaches to the problem have been taken.

1. Effects of Shock Versus the Imperative Stimulus in a Reaction Time

Task. Öhman, Fredrikson, Hugdahl, and Rimmö (1976) compared differential conditioning of the skin conductance response (SCR) in groups receiving pictures of snakes and spiders with conditioning in groups exposed to pictures of flowers and mushroooms. Uncomfortable but not painful electric shock was the US for half the people in each group, whereas the others were presented with a tone, which was the imperative stimulus for a simple reaction time task. This stimulus had been shown to produce differential conditioning of the SCR (Baer & Fuhrer, 1969), and thus its use allows the CR to be held constant across groups. During conditioning the electric shock or tone occurred at the end of CS+. Palmar skin conductance responses to CS+ and CS− were recorded, and the authors focused on differential SCRs occurring from 1–4 sec after onset of the CSs. These first-interval anticipatory responses (FARs) are thought to reflect conditioned changes in the meaning of the CS resulting from its contingent relation with some significant US (Öhman, 1983).

In acquisition there was strong, and equivalent, differential conditioning in the two groups that received shock. These data are incompatible with the hypothesis that snakes or spiders are selectively associated with aversive events. Failure of the two groups receiving the shock US to differ in acquisition is the modal result of the fifteen or so experiments that have this general form (see McNally, 1987, for a review of these experiments). Moreover, there was evidence of differential conditioning in the group that received pictures of flowers or mushrooms paired with the imperative stimulus only if the first extinction trial of each kind was considered a test trial, and no evidence of differential conditioning in the group that received snakes or spiders paired with the imperative stimulus even then. In a series of extinction trials which followed conditioning, differential SCRs persisted only for the group which had received snakes or spiders paired with shock.

This study provides weak evidence at best for the proposition that the imperative stimulus produced differential conditioning to flowers and mushrooms. In the absence of such evidence comparison of resistance to extinction in the four groups does not constitute a fair test of the selective association hypothesis (the same criticism applies to a replication by Öhman, Fredrickson, and Hugdahl, 1978).

2. The Effect of Shock Versus Safety. A second experimental approach to the study of selective association in fear conditioning has been to consider safety as a second US, and to ask whether stimuli that are easily associated with danger will not be easily associated with safety and vice versa (Jacobs & LoLordo, 1977, 1980; LoLordo & Jacobs, 1983). The logic of these experiments can be applied to the case of animal fears.

McNally & Reiss (1982, 1984) did not directly compare the relative effectiveness of pictures of snakes and spiders vs. flowers and mushrooms as both signals for shock and safety. Instead, they conducted only the safety signal half of the experiment. In their first experiment (McNally & Reiss, 1982) they instructed subjects about the contingency, and then administered 12 blocks of conditioning trials. Each block contained a trial on which a compound of tone and a picture of a mushroom was followed by shock, one in which application of vibration to the forearm was followed by shock, one on which a compound of tone and a picture of a flower was not reinforced, and one on which a compound of tone and a picture of a snake was not reinforced. One feature of this procedure departs from the standard Pavlovian conditioned inhibition of A+, AX− procedure: Tone was reinforced in compound with a picture of a mushroom, instead of by itself, so that subjects wouldn't infer that single stimuli were reinforced, and compounds nonreinforced. Following conditioning there was a summation test for inhibition (LoLordo & Fairless, 1985; Rescorla, 1969), in which the vibratory CS was presented in compound with snake, flower, or a novel picture of a triangle. CS duration and CS–US interval were 5 sec, and SCRs that occurred 1–6 sec after CS onset were called conditioned responses.

Twenty-one of 28 subjects had larger responses to the reinforced compound than to the two nonreinforced ones; only their test data were scored. In test, the measure of inhibition was the percentage change in SCR magnitude, re the response to the vibratory CS alone at the end of conditioning. At first all three compounds evoked larger responses than had the vibratory CS alone, but as testing progressed flower and snake suppressed responding to vibration more than triangle did. However, there was no difference between the suppressive effects of flower and snake, and thus no evidence supporting the hypothesis that people are predisposed not to associate paictures of snakes with safety. On the other hand, the data do not strongly disconfirm the hypothesis, since in the absence of test presentations of vibration alone there is no direct evidence that either flower or snake was a conditioned inhibitor. The results of a second experiment (McNally & Reiss, 1984) warrant similar conclusions.

3. The Effect of Shock Versus Loud Noise.   This line of research arose from Cook, Hodes, and Lang's (1986) failure to replicate the consistent finding from Ohman's laboratory of greater resistance to extinction of differential SCRs to snakes vs. spiders than to houses vs. household objects. The major differences between the studies from the Wisconsin laboratory and those from Öhman's laboratory was that the former used loud noise as the US, whereas the latter used electric shock. Hodes (1981; described by Cook et al., 1986) suggested that the noise might have been ineffective because it was not a tactile stimulus. Perhaps snakes and spiders are especially easily associated with aversive stimuli that, like electric shock, have a tactile component because over the history of the species the aversive stimulus with which those stimuli have been paired was painful stimulation of the skin.

This hypothesis was tested in an experiment that compared cardiac and electrodermal conditioning to pictures of snakes and spiders vs. houses and household objects in groups receiving the loud noise US or the uncomfortable electric shock US. An analysis of differential FAR magnitude in extinction yielded no significant effects. However, when probability, rather than magnitude, of the FAR was analyzed, the tendency for the response to be more probable in CS+ than CS− in extinction was greater for the snakes vs. spiders group that received shock than for the houses vs. household objects group that received shock. This difference was not found for the groups that received the noise US; if anything the differentiation persisted better in the group that saw houses vs. household objects.

Unfortunately, conditioned heart rate, which was recorded throughout this experiment, did not support a selective association hypothesis based on the importance of a tactile, aversive US. There was larger cardioacceleration to CS+ than to CS− during the differential conditioning phase of the experiment for the group that saw snakes and spiders, and no differential cardiac conditioning in the group that saw houses and household objects. These data indicate that defensive conditioning was better with snakes and spiders than with houses and household objects. However, there was no effect of type of US upon cardiac conditioning.

At the very least, this outcome implies that the pattern of SCRs in extinction should not be taken as evidence for selective association of fear, since cardiac acceleration is considered a defensive response (Graham, 1979), and thus a component of fear, whereas SCRs may be more related to attention or altered significance of the CS than to fear (Öhman, 1983; Öhman et al., 1985). Alternatively, Cook et al. (1986) suggested that fear conditioning may entail two processes: (1) conditioned mobilization for avoidance, as reflected in increased heart rate in the presence of the signal when the aversive stimulus is imminent (on acquisition trials), and (2) conditioning of stimulus significance, as reflected in the FAR. On this account, selective association occurred only for the second component.

Extension to Conditioned Responses Other than SCRs

Öhman (1983) has suggested that although the skin conductance FAR that has been used as the dependent variable in most of his research probably has a role in the initiation of emotions, it is doubtful that it is an index of fear. Thus, changes in skin conductance need to be supplemented with data from response systems with a more straightforward relation to fear. One such response is heart rate, which seems to accelerate as part of a defensive response pattern, but decelerates during orienting. Several papers have examined changes in heart rate along with skin conductance responses during aversive conditioning to fear-relevant and neutral stimuli.

Fredrikson and Öhman (1979) conducted a differential conditioning experiment in which subjects in one group saw pictures of snakes and spiders, whereas the CSs for the other group were pictures of flowers and mushrooms. Electric shock was the US. In extinction, heart rate revealed no differentiation, but the skin conductance response and finger pulse volume (FPV) showed the typical pattern of maintained differentiation only in the group that saw pictures of snakes and spiders.

The authors argued that the similar patterns of electrodermal and FPV responses indicate that the effect of CS content was upon general activation of the sympathetic nervous system, and that different patterns of heart rate responding would have been observed in the two groups if more trials had been given during conditioning. Fredrikson (1981) provided some support for this contention; at the end of a longer series of conditioning trials a fear-relevant CS+, but not a fear-relevant CS−, evoked an increase in heart rate. Unfortunately, there was no control group differentially conditioned with fear-irrelevant CSs.

Öhman et al. (1985) have briefly reported the results of several additional studies that measured heart rate. Öhman and Dimberg administered over 30 CS+ and 30 CS− trials to subjects in Snake/Spider and Flower/Mushroom groups. The fear-irrelevant group showed the typical pattern of greater deceleration to CS+ than to CS−, the difference being largest just before the US was due. The fear-relevant group, on the other hand, showed less deceleration to CS+ than to CS−, and the difference between the two groups was largest in the middle of the interstimulus interval. Comparable results have been obtained by Cook et al. (1986).

These results are provocative because they suggest, in a way that the skin conductance data do not, that snakes and spiders and neutral stimuli evoke different patterns of behavior during aversive conditioning. Moreover, the pattern evoked by snakes and spiders looks more like defensive responding than does the pattern evoked by fear-irrelevant stimuli. However, these studies provide no evidence that the relative effectiveness of snakes and spiders vs. neutral stimuli changes when USs other than shock are used.

Are Animal Fears Under Cognitive Control?

Following Seligman's (1970) suggestion that prepared associations are not under cognitive control, Ohman and his colleagues have proposed that fears of snakes and spiders, once acquired, do not require attention or cognition for their performance. This proposition was taken to imply that CRs to these stimuli would not be affected by conscious intentions as manipulated through verbal instructions. Hugdahl and Öhman (1977) tested this hypothesis, using a differential conditioning procedure in which individuals experienced two fear-relevant CSs, or two fear-irrelevant ones. This experimental design has the advantage of relying upon sensitive within-subject comparisons. Moreover, it provides a better measure of the associative effect of the treatment because the CS+ and CS− evoke comparable orienting SCRs on the initial trials. Subjects in the SN/SP group saw pictures of snakes and spiders, whereas controls saw pictures of circles and triangles. After acquisition half the people in each group had the shock electrodes removed, and were told that no more shocks would occur, whereas the others simply had the electrodes checked. Then 14 nonreinforced presentations of each CS occurred.

In acquisition the two groups showed significant differential conditioning, and did not differ in that respect, although the overall level of responding was greater in Group SN/SP. In extinction, there was a very clear effect of instructions in the control group; the differentiation survived in the uninstructed subgroup, but immediately extinguished in the instructed subgroup. However, the differentiation persisted in both subgroups of Group SN/SP; the experimenter's revelation that there would be no more shock had no effect upon differential responding to the two CSs. Hugdahl (1978) and Hygge and Öhman (1978) obtained similar results from instructed groups, but included no uninstructed ones.

In several other experiments instructions have had a powerful effect on responding to fear-relevant CSs in extinction. Öhman, Alme, and Mykleburst (cited in Ohman et al., 1985) conducted a differential conditioning experiment in which the probability of shock on a CS+ trial decreased gradually over trials, reaching zero 20 trials prior to disconnection of the electrodes and instructions that there would be no more shocks. The differentiation was maintained prior to the instructions, but disappeared soon after they were given, even in a group that saw fear-relevant CSs (see also Cook et al., 1986; McNally, 1981). Perhaps this happened because the 20 extinction trials prior to the instructions made the subjects believe those instructions, so that they stopped expecting shock.

Dawson, Schell, and Banis (1986) have conducted the most ambitious experiment concerning the question whether the differential SCR to fear-relevant CSs reflects a cognitive process. They looked for dissociations between cognitive processes and autonomic CRs to both fear-relevant and neutral CSs. In a 2 × 2 design one independent variable was CS type, and the other was presence/absence of prior information about extinction. Prior to the beginning of the conditioning session half the subjects were told that the shock would be completely turned off during the latter part of the experiment and that there would be no more shock. The other subjects were given no instructions.

Subjects were given a task designed to mask the differential conditioning enough to delay awareness of the CS-US contingencies. Each trial began with a slide displaying the integers 1, 2, 3, and 4 in some order. Three–four sec later four picture slides were presented sequentially, for 8 sec each, with 3–5 sec between them. Subjects saw either pictures of a spider, a mushroom, a cat, and a lake in random order, or pictures of a snake, a flower, a dog, and a mountain in random order. A few seconds after the last picture slide on each trial the subjects had to name the pictures in an order corresponding to the order of the digits at the start of the trial. They were told that a shock would occasionally occur during the sequence of slides, and that the shock was programmed in a predictable way. They were asked to report their expectancy of shock, from "absolutely certain no shock" to "absolutely certain shock," by repeatedly pressing one of 7 buttons as the trial progressed.

There were 16 differential conditioning trials, each of which contained either CS+ or CS−. For the fear-relevant CS groups snakes and spiders were CS+ and CS−; for the fear-irrelevant groups mushrooms and flowers were the CSs. The electric shock US occurred at the end of each CS+. Following conditioning, subjects received a large number of extinction trials, half with each CS. Subjects were considered aware of the contingency when they first reported that they expected shock because the CS+ was present. Roughly half the subjects became aware of the contingency, and regardless of group, awareness of the contingency was necessary for conditioning.

There was greater resistance to extinction of the differential FARs in the groups receiving the fear-relevant CSs, confirming Öhman's results. However, contrary to the data from Öhman's lab, this difference between fear-relevant and fear-irrelevant CS groups was far smaller in the instructed groups. Significantly, the bottom-press measure of expectancy of shock revealed the same pattern. Moreover, if the point of cognitive (expectancy) extinction is taken as the trial on which each person began indicating that he or she was absolutely certain there would be no shock, then the magnitude of the differential FAR was greater before this point than after it, but in both cases was the same for the fear-relevant and irrelevant groups. Thus, there is no evidence that conditioning involving fear-relevant CSs is any less cognitive than conditioning involving neutral CSs. Furthermore, given these results, what needs to be explained is why, in the absence of extinction instructions, the expectancy of shock was more persistent in the case of fear-relevant as opposed to neutral CSs.

In summary, the early results from Öhman's laboratory, which suggested that differential SCRs to pictures of snakes and spiders are immune to extinction instructions, are discrepant with other relevant data. The discrepancy would be resolved if the instructions had the right sorts of effects upon the expectancy of shock in the various experiments, but we do not know that. Lacking a resolution, there is not enough evidence to warrant the conclusion that differential skin conductance responses to snakes and spiders are less dependent on differential expectations of shock in the presence of the two stimuli than are comparable responses to neutral stimuli.

V. SOCIAL FEARS

Öhman and his colleagues (e.g., Öhman et al., 1985) have suggested that during the evolution of Man the occurrence of certain facial expressions, e.g., angry and fearful ones, has been positively correlated with aversive consequences to those who observed the expressions. Specifically, Öhman et al. asserted that there has been a positive correlation between the occurrence of an angry expression and subsequent aversive stimulation of the person towards whom the expression was directed. They further argued that the ability to learn this positive correlation, and thereby react appropriately to threat, has been adaptive in the strict sense, i.e., has conferred fitness upon its possessors. Thus, today's humans should be predisposed to acquire a fear response to an angry expression directed at them, if that expression precedes some aversive consequence.

This view implies selective association between an angry expression directed at the observer and an aversive consequence experienced by that observer, and thus implies that in a single-cue, 2 × 2 design in which four groups receive either angry or neutral faces (CSs) paired with either aversive or non-aversive consequences (USs) the group observing the angry face paired with the aversive US will acquire the fear CR sooner than the group observing the neutral face, whereas the two facial expressions will be equally readily associated with the nonaversive US.

There is more to this view of social fears than predictions about selective association. It also implies that the initial, affective response to an angry face will not automatically be channelled into flight, since in the history of our species aversion of the gaze or some submissive gesture may have been a more adaptive response to such confrontation than headlong flight. Thus, Öhman et al. predict that the autonomic CRs evoked by an angry face that has preceded an aversive event will be different from those evoked by a picture of a snake or spider that has been paired with the same event. The initial skin conductance response (SCR) should be the same, but the cardioacceleration conditionally evoked by the snake as part of the preparation for flight should not be evoked by the angry face (see Öhman, 1986; Öhman et al., 1985 for other predicted differences between social and animal fears). In what follows, we critically review the empirical studies that bear on this view.

Is There Evidence for Selective Associations?

There are no published experiments on fear of facial expressions that use the 2 × 2 design necessary for the demonstration of selective association of an angry or fearful facial expression with some aversive event. The studies that have been published include only half the complete design, comparing conditioning to an angry or fearful face and some control expression when each is paired with an aversive event in a between-groups design. Thus, it can still be asked whether the outcomes of those experiments are compatible with selective association. However, in the absence of additional experimental manipulations an outcome that is compatible with selective association is also compatible with the claim that an angry face is more salient than the control.

In a series of experiments Öhman and Dimberg (Dimberg, 1983, 1986a, 1987; Dimberg & Öhman, 1983; Öhman & Dimberg, 1978) have compared aversive classical conditioning of skin conductance responses (SCRs) to various facial expressions, using electric shock or loud noise as the US. The modal experimental design used in these experiments includes habituation to two facial expressions, followed by differential aversive conditioning. Finally, the two CSs are presented repeatedly in the absence of the US, and resistance to extinction of any conditioned responses is assessed.

Öhman and Dimberg (1978) compared the conditionability of angry, neutral and happy faces for college student subjects. For Group Angry +/Angry'— a photograph of a person with an angry expression directed at the observer preceded electric shock, whereas CS — was a photo of a different person, also expressing anger. One face was of a male, the other of a female. Group Neutral +/Neutral'— saw two neutral faces, and Group Happy +/Happy'—, two happy ones. On the basis of their earlier experiments on SCR conditioning to pictures of snakes and spiders Öhman and Dimberg expected the experimental manipulation to have differential effects primarily upon resistance to extinction of the early component (FAR) of the SCR to the CSs.

The experiment had three phases: habituation; conditioning, in which eight pairings of CS + and an uncomfortable electric shock were intermixed with eight nonreinforced presentations of CS —; and extinction. SCRs measured in the interval 1–4 sec after CS onset revealed a decline in responding to both CSs during habituation. All groups exhibited differential conditioning, showing larger SCRs to CS + than CS —. In extinction, the differentiation between CS + and CS — was maintained only in Group Angry +/Angry'—, and this effect was strong. Öhman and Dimberg concluded that the outcome of this experiment was compatible with selective association of angry faces and aversive events.

Dimberg & Öhman (1983) suggested that since the orientation of a face indicates whether the observer is the object of attention, the functional significance of an angry face might depend on whether the gaze is directed at the observer or elsewhere. They conducted an experiment in which one group was similiar to Group Angry +/Angry'—, but the CSs were photos of two different men with angry faces. Both had their face and eyes directed towards the observer. Group Angry away +/Angry' away — differed from the first group in one respect; the angry looks were directed about 30° to the left of the observer.

Responses during the habituation and conditioning phases were as in the previous experiment. Subjects who had the facial expressions directed at them retained the differential SCR throughout extinction, while subjects who saw averted angry expressions lost the differentiation almost immediately. There are two plausible accounts of this result: (1) that it reflected differential acquisition in the two groups, which was somehow manifested in performance only in extinction; and (2) that it was a result of the differential treatment of the two groups during extinction, and thus was a performance effect.

A second experiment was designed to tease apart these two possibilities. Two groups were treated like those of the previous experiment during the habituation and conditioning phases, but each was switched to the other gaze direction condition during extinction. Again performance of the two groups did not differ during conditioning; both showed clear differential skin conductance responding to the two CSs. However, differentiation was maintained in extinction only for the group that was switched from an averted angry face to an angry face looking at them. Analysis of the extinction data from the two experiments combined revealed that differential SCRs were maintained only when the angry face was directed at the subject during extinction, and gaze direction during conditioning had no effect. Thus, the direction of the angry expression had an effect on performance, but not on learning.

Dimberg and Öhman offered the plausible interpretation that subjects acquired a fear response to the angry face paired with shock whether it was directed at or away from them, but the learning was manifested in performance, i.e., continued differentiation in extinction, only when the angry face was directed at them during extinction. This account is compatible with the assumption that angry faces, but not the direction of their gaze, are selectively associated with aversive events. Further, it would have to be assumed that the shift in extinction to an angry face directed away immediately suppresses the conditioned fear, since the response to CS+ on the first extinction trial in the group that experienced that shift was so much smaller than the response at the end of conditioning that the differentiation was lost.

Dimberg (1986a) carried on the experimental analysis of aversive conditioning to facial expressions. In one experiment he asked whether the SCR could be aversively conditioned to a person's face regardless of its emotional expression, so that when the same face expressing anger was directed at the subject during extinction it would continue to evoke an elevated SCR. Group Angry+/Angry'− to Happy/Happy' saw two different people expressing anger during habituation and conditioning, but saw those people expressing happiness during extinction. Group Happy+/Happy'− to Angry/Angry' experienced the reverse shift.

Both groups showed reliable differential conditioning. In extinction, only the Happy to Angry group showed persistent differential responding. This outcome indicates that the SCR can be conditioned to a person's happy expression paired with shock, and implies that the conditioning will be manifested in strong resistance to extinction only if the CS+ person's expression is angry during extinction. Because an Angry to Angry group was not included in this experiment, we cannot know whether the happy face was as effective a CS as an angry face. Such an outcome would have been incompatible with the selective association hypothesis.

Dimberg repeated this experiment, substituting neutral faces for happy ones. Again both groups showed strong and equivalent differential conditioning. Both groups also exhibited a higher probability of an SCR during CS+ than CS− during extinction, but the effect was significantly greater in the Neutral to Angry group. The resistance to extinction shown by Group Angry to Neutral is the first instance of the differentiation persisting even though the stimulus persons' expressions during extinction were not angry. Again, this experiment would have had more bearing on the selective association hypothesis if an Angry to Angry group had been included, permitting comparison of the extinction performance of that group and Group Neutral to Angry.

In a final experiment, Dimberg (1986a) compared differential aversive conditioning to two happy faces directed towards the subject with differential conditioning to two happy faces directed away. Both groups exhibited differential SCRs to CS+ and CS− during acquisition. In extinction subjects in both groups saw the same persons they had observed during conditioning, but their expressions were angry and directed towards the subject. Differential SCRs persisted in both groups during extinction, but the effect was substantially larger in the group that had seen happy faces directed away during conditioning.

Dimberg argued that this outcome supports the hypothesis that happy faces directed at the subject have an inhibitory effect upon aversive classical conditioning. By "inhibitory" we assume he means something like Seligman's (1971) "contraprepared," i.e., that there would be less excitatory conditioning to happy faces than to neutral faces directed towards the observer or to other neutral stimuli, even though SCRs measured during conditioning might not reveal such a difference. A comparison of resistance to extinction in Neutral to Angry and Happy to Angry groups like those of the previous two experiments could provide evidence supporting this plausible claim, but no statistical analysis of the two experiments combined was performed. Moreover, a graphical comparison of the extinction data of the two groups suggests that the difference between them is small at best.

To sum up all these results, there is no firm evidence that the relative conditionability of various facial expressions paired with electric shock is ordered as Öhman and his colleagues predicted. Moreover, they have not systematically made the experimental comparisons that would best test their hypothesis, comparisons of resistance to extinction of differential SCRs in groups switched from angry, happy, or neutral CS+ and CS− faces directed at the subject in acquisition to angry faces directed at him in extinction. Furthermore, in one of the two experiments which has included this sort of comparison, that between angry faces directed towards vs. away from the subject in acquisition, the absence of an effect of direction of gaze in acquisition upon subsequent resistance to extinction tends to contradict Ohman's hypothesis.

In an independent line of research Lanzetta and Orr (Lanzetta & Orr, 1980, 1981; Orr & Lanzetta, 1980, 1984) have also studied aversive classical conditioning to facial expressions. They hypothesized that "well established codes relating facial expressive responses to particular classes of outcomes exist in long-term memory and that newly presented contingencies involving facial-expressive cues are readily learned and stored when they conform to this coding" (Orr & Lanzetta, 1980; p. 282). Moreover, they suggested that when the contingencies presented in an experiment are incompatible with the stored codes, learning will be retarded, re an appropriate control. This view is compatible with Ohman's but since it is stated very briefly it is difficult to decide whether it predicts that a subject is predisposed to become emotionally aroused in the presence of a fearful face that has preceded electric shock because of preexperimental learning or because the code has been inherited.

Orr and Lanzetta (1980) tested their hypothesis in a differential conditioning experiment in which Group Fearful+/Happy'− received an electric shock after each presentation of a fearful face, whereas a happy face was CS−. Group Happy+/Fearful'− received the reversed assignment of consequences to CSs. In experiments from Lanzetta's laboratory a subject saw fearful faces of several people, and happy faces of several (with the two sets partially overlapping), instead of just one of each presented by Öhman. Skin conductance was measured each second, and the CR was defined as the maximum response amplitude for sec 2–8 of the 8-sec CS minus the baseline value, which was the mean of the amplitudes at sec 0 and 1.

During conditioning Group Fearful+/Happy'− had significantly larger SCRs to CS+ than CS−. However, the SCR to the fearful faces was greater ("marginally significantly," in the authors' words) than the SCR to the happy faces even before conditioning. Thus, the effect observed during conditioning may reflect the tendency of electric shock which follows a fearful face to prevent the already large SCR to that face from habituating. Group Happy+ failed to exhibit differential conditioning, whereas Öhman and Dimberg obtained differentiation in a similar experiment.

The results of this experiment differed from those of comparable experiments by Öhman and Dimberg in another respect. Group Fearful+ showed little resistance to extinction of the differentiation, whereas Öhman and Dimberg found strong resistance to extinction. Whether the discrepancy stems from the use of fearful vs. angry facial expressions is unclear.

An ecologically based view would very likely predict that some parameters would affect aversive conditioning to angry and fearful expressions differently. For example, people have been most likely to suffer aversive consequences of angry expressions when those expressions were directed at them. This has probably not been the case for fearful expressions, which most often would have been directed at the fear-evoking stimulus. Consequently, the large effect of direction of an angry expression upon performance found by Dimberg and Öhman (1983) should not be found for direction of a fearful face during extinction.

Lanzetta and Orr (1981) compared the conditionability of fearful, neutral, and happy facial expressions with the conditionability of a presumably neutral tone CS, when electric shock followed the tone in compound with a facial expression. Three groups, one for each kind of facial expression, received conditioning trials on which the facial expression was presented 1 sec before the tone, and both stimuli terminated 3 sec later. Shock occurred at the end of 6 of the 9 conditioning trials. Then subjects received several nonreinforced presentations of each element of the compound.

SCRs did not differ among the groups during conditioning. On the extinction test trials the group exposed to fearful faces responded more to those faces than to the tone, replicating an earlier result (Lanzetta & Orr, 1980). The group exposed to happy faces tended to respond more to the tone than to the faces, but the effect was not statistically significant (p = .058). Nor was that effect significant in an earlier, similar experiment. The group exposed to neutral faces responded equally to the tone and faces.

Lanzetta and Orr asserted that their results are compatible with the hypothesis that people are prepared to associate fearful facial expressions with aversive events. Such fearful expressions thus overshadow (Pavlov, 1927) neutral stimuli when the two are used as a compound signal for electric shock. Recently, Orr and Lanzetta (1984) proposed two additional accounts of the overshadowing of tone by fearful facial expressions. The first is that fearful faces evoke conditioned arousal at the start of the experiment because of preexperimental pairings with aversive events. Thus, the fearful faces block conditioning of arousal to the tone when the compound is paired with shock, and tone subsequently evokes weaker SCRs than fearful faces. This argument assumes that blocking (Kamin, 1969) can occur even when qualitatively different aversive events occur in the first two phases of the experiment, since the subjects presumably had not experienced electric shocks prior to the experiment. Such an effect has been shown for fear conditioning in rats, using shock and loud noise as USs (Bakal, Johnson, & Rescorla, 1974). The second alternative to selective association is that fearful facial expressions are more salient than tone, and thus should overshadow tone whatever the US used.

Orr and Lanzetta tested these hypotheses by recording SCRs on a series of extinction trials on which a previously aversively conditioned tone CS was compounded with fearful, neutral, or happy facial expressions in three groups, and was presented by itself in a control group. If fearful faces are excitatory conditioned stimuli for adult humans, then the SCRs should be larger in the group receiving fearful faces plus tone than in the group receiving tone alone or neutral faces plus tone. On the other hand, Orr and Lanzetta maintained that the salience account would predict less responding to tone plus fearful faces than to tone alone or tone plus neutral faces, because the fearful faces would attract attention, essentially acting as Pavlovian external inhibitors (Pavlov, 1927) of the SCR to tone. It should be noted that "salience" as ability to externally inhibit CRs is not necessarily the same as "salience" as associability or conditionability; in their argument, Orr and Lanzetta have moved from one meaning to the other. An account of the previous overshadowing result in terms of salience in the latter sense or in terms of selective association predicts no difference in responding to tone alone, tone plus neutral faces, and tone plus fearful faces in the present experiment.

Baseline skin conductance scores grew over test trials for the group receiving tone plus fearful faces, and were significantly higher than the scores for the other groups, which declined across test trials. This result complicates interpretation of the phasic SCRs to the stimuli, which were measured as differences from baseline values. Although phasic SCRs showed no main effect of groups, the groups by trials interaction for the tone plus neutral faces and tone plus fearful faces groups was significant, indicating that phasic SCRs were higher for the latter group on at least some trials. Because of the higher baseline in the latter group, the obtained difference scores may underestimate the true difference between the groups. These results seem most compatible with the suggestion that at the start of the experiments fearful faces already are excitatory conditioned stimuli. The alternative accounts, including the selective association hypothesis, do not predict the outcome of this experiment.

Social Fears, SCRs, and Other Conditioned Responses

Although the aforementioned research on conditioning to facial expressions arose from an interest in social fears, the papers that have been discussed thus far have measured only SCRs. As noted earlier, Ohman et al. (1985) have recognized that skin conductance responses do not reflect a specific emotion, fear, but instead reflect diffuse emotional arousal. Thus, much stronger tests of a selective associative account of fear conditioning to facial expressions could be made if other components of emotional responses, e.g., expressive and experiential ones, were recorded along with autonomic responses.

Dimberg (1987) recorded facial EMG activity as a measure of expressive, emotional responses. It has been shown that activity in the zygomatic muscle, which normally elevates the cheeks to a smile, is increased when a person thinks pleasant thoughts (Schwartz, Brown, & Ahern, 1980) or looks at a happy face (Dimberg, 1982). Conversely, activity in the corrugator muscle, the muscle used in frowning, increases in response to unpleasant thoughts (Schwartz et al., 1980), the sight of an angry face (Dimberg, 1982), or ''fear-relevant'' stimuli such as slides of snakes (Dimberg, 1986b). EMG activity in both zygomatic and corrugator muscles was recorded in this experiment. Autonomic measures included the SCR measure used in the earlier experiments, heart rate, and the time it took the SCR to recover to half its peak amplitude. Relatively fast recovery is thought to characterize orienting responses (ORs), and relatively slow recovery, defensive CRs (Grings & Dawson, 1978).

The differential conditioning procedure of the earlier studies was used, but a few changes were made. The US was a 100-dB, 1-sec noise instead of electric shock. Second, only half as many trials were administered in each phase of the experiment as in the earlier experiments. Two groups were included. Group Angry+/Angry'– saw pictures of two different males directing angry expressions at them throughout the experiment, whereas Group Happy+/Happy'– saw two males with happy expressions.

None of the facial response or autonomic measures revealed differential conditioning during the conditioning phase. The failure to replicate the differential SCRs observed in the earlier experiments may be a result of the weaker US and fewer conditioning trials used in this experiment. In extinction the SCR data did replicate earlier findings; the differentiation was maintained only in the group that saw the angry faces. Of course this result may reflect only a performance effect, and thus may tell us nothing about associative learning. Facial EMGs,

SCR recovery time, and heart rate also revealed group differences in extinction. Only the group exposed to the angry faces differentiated between the two CSs, and only with the corrugator muscle. The SCR to CS+ recovered more slowly on extinction trials in the group that saw angry faces than in the one that saw happy ones. Furthermore, only the group exposed to angry faces exhibited differential cardiac responding; their heart rate decelerated during CS− but not during CS+. Moreover, it accelerated following termination of CS+, but not after CS−.

These outcomes are all compatible with the assertion that there was greater differential fear conditioning to the angry faces. Their coherence is impressive, and testifies to the value of recording several dependent variables. However, in the absence of any direct evidence of conditioning, all these data are in the same logical position as the SCR data; they may reflect a performance effect, rather than an effect on learning. Clearly, what is needed is an experiment with a design that permits conclusions about the relative conditionability of various facial CSs, records all these dependent variables, and uses parameters that result in differential SCRs, and perhaps the other responses as well, during acquisition. Only when such an experiment is conducted will we know whether people are predisposed to associate angry faces with aversive events, and react fearfully to the former.

The Role of Awareness in Experimental Analogues of Social Fears

It can only be speculated that, like fear conditioning to pictures of snakes (Dawson, Schell, & Banis, 1986), conditioning fear, or at least an SCR, to a picture of a man with an angry expression does require awareness. But does performance of the response, once it has been conditioned, require the person's awareness of the angry expression? Öhman (1986) asserted that once angry faces, snakes, and other fear relevant stimuli have been paired with an aversive event, they become especially effective in engaging automatic processing mechanisms. Thus, such stimuli should evoke fear even though the person is unaware that she has been exposed to them.

Öhman and Dimberg (cited in Öhman, 1986) have conducted preliminary tests of this hypothesis, using a backward masking procedure (Marcel, 1983). Subjects received differential aversive conditioning, with CS+ being an angry expression, and CS− a different person's happy expression. On subsequent extinction trials CS presentations were only 30 msec long, and were immediately followed by a 30-msec masking stimulus, a neutral face. With these parameters subjects may be unaware that any stimulus precedes the mask. If they are told there was a face, and forced to guess "happy" or "angry," they perform no better than chance. Nevertheless, the masked CS+ evoked significantly larger SCRs than the masked CS− throughout extinction, suggesting that the angry face evokes a conditioned arousal response after preattentive, automatic processing. This result is striking, and will be even more impressive if a neutral stimulus that has been paired with shock and would evoke an SCR in extinction fails to do so when it is followed by a mask. In that case there would be further reason to concede angry faces have some special status in the control of performance. Further research might then compare the effects of angry facial expressions and pictures of snakes and spiders in this backward masking paradigm. As noted earlier, Öhman and his colleagues would expect the two sorts of fear-relevant stimuli to have similar effects on SCRs, but different effects upon cardiac responding.

Conclusions

Beginning with Seligman's suggestion that phobias reflect prepared associations and some additional ideas about human evolution, Öhman and his colleagues have generated a wealth of predictions about our acquisition of social fears. Experiments in which SCRs were measured have provided little evidence supporting Öhman's fundamental assertion that angry faces are selectively associated with painful events. However, the measurement of multiple responses, including responses of the muscles controlling facial expressions, has recently been introduced into the conditioning experiments. Analysis of response patterns, rather than a single dependent variable, will do better justice to the concept of fear, and may yet provide evidence for selective effects. In any case, these experiments and others applying current methodology from the area of human information processing to questions about fear have enriched our understanding of fears and phobias.

REFERENCES

Baer, P. E., & Fuhrer, M. J. (1969). Cognitive factors in differential conditioning of the GSR: Use of a reaction time task as the UCS with normals and schizophrenics. *Journal of Abnormal Psychology, 74*, 544–552.

Bakal, C. W., Johnson, R. D., & Rescorla, R. A. (1974). The effect of change in US quality on the blocking effect. *Pavlovian Journal of Biological Psychology, 9*, 97–103.

Berridge, K. C., & Grill, H. J. (1983). Alternating ingestive and aversive consummatory responses suggests a two-dimensional analysis of palatability in rats. *Behavioral Neuroscience, 97*, 563–573.

Best, M. R., Batson, J. D., Meachum, C. L., Brown, E. R., & Ringer, M. (1985). Characteristics of taste-mediated environmental potentiation in rats. *Learning and Motivation, 16*, 190–209.

Best, M. R., & Meachum, C. L. (1986). The effect of stimulus preexposure on taste-mediated environmental conditioning: Potentiation and overshadowing. *Animal Learning and Behavior, 14*, 1–5.

Bolles, R. C. (1970). Species-specific defense reactions and avoidance learning. *Psychological Review, 77*, 32–48.

Bolles, R. C., & Fanselow, M. S. (1980). A perceptual-defensive-recuperative model of fear and pain. *The Behavioral and Brain Sciences, 3*, 121–131.

Bouton, M. E., Jones, D. L., McPhillips, S. A., & Swartzentruber, D. (1986). Potentiation and overshadowing in odor-aversion learning: Role of method of odor presentation, the distal-proximal cue distinction, and the conditionability of odor. *Learning and Motivation, 17*, 115–138.

Bouton, M. E., & Whiting, M. R. (1982). Simultaneous odor-taste and taste-taste compounds in poison-avoidance learning. *Learning and Motivation*, *13*, 472–494.

Clarke, J. C., Westbrook, R. F., & Irwin, J. (1979). Potentiation instead of overshadowing in the pigeon. *Behavioral and Neural Biology*, *25*, 18–29.

Coburn, K. L., Garcia, J., Kiefer, S. W., & Rusiniak, K. W. (1984). Taste potentiation of poisoned odor by temporal contiguity. *Behavioral Neuroscience*, *98*, 813–819.

Cook, E. W., III, Hodes, R. L., & Lang, P. J. (1986). Preparedness and phobia: Effects of stimulus content on human visceral conditioning. *Journal of Abnormal Psychology*, *95*, 195–207.

Dawson, M. E., Schell, A. M., & Banis, H. T. (1986). Greater resistance to extinction of electrodermal responses conditioned to potentially phobic CSs: A noncognitive process? *Psychophysiology*, *23*, 552–561.

Dimberg, U. (1982). Facial reactions to facial expression. *Psychophysiology*, *19*, 643–647.

Dimberg, U. (1983). Emotional conditioning to facial stimuli: A psychobiological analysis. *Acta Universitatis Upsaliensis, Abstracts of Upsala Dissertations from the Faculty of Social Sciences*, *29*, Uppsala, Sweden: Almquist and Wiksell.

Dimberg, U. (1986a). Facial expressions as excitatory and inhibitory stimuli for conditioned autonomic responses. *Biological Psychology*, *22*, 37–57.

Dimberg, U. (1986b). Facial reactions to fear-relevant and fear-irrelevant stimuli. *Biological Psychology*, *23*, 153–161.

Dimberg, U. (1987). Facial reactions, autonomic activity and experienced emotion: A three component model of emotional conditioning. *Biological Psychology*, *24*, 105–122.

Dimberg, U., & Ohman, A. (1983). The effects of directional facial cues on electrodermal conditioning to facial stimuli. *Psychophysiology*, *20*, 160–167.

Domjan, M. (1982). Selective associations in aversion learning. In M. L. Commons, R. J. Herrnstein, & A. R. Wagner (Eds.), *Quantitative analysis of behavior: III. Acquisition* (pp. 257–272). Cambridge, MA: Ballinger.

Domjan, M. (1983). Biological constraints on instrumental and classical conditioning 10 years later: Implications for general process theory. In G. Bower (Ed.), *Psychology of learning and motivation*. (Vol. 17). New York: Academic Press.

Durlach, P. (1989). Learning and performance in Pavlovian conditioning: Are failures of contiguity failures of learning or performance? In S. B. Klein & R. R. Mowrer (Eds.), *Contemporary learning theories: Pavlovian conditioning and the status of traditional learning theory*. Hillsdale, NJ: Lawrence Erlbaum Associates.

Durlach, P. J., & Rescorla, R. A. (1980). Potentiation rather than overshadowing in flavor-aversion learning: An analysis in terms of within-compound associations. *Journal of Experimental Psychology: Animal Behavior Processes*, *6*, 175–187.

Ellins, S. R., & von Kluge, S. (1987). Preexposure and extinction effects of lithium chloride induced taste-potentiated aversions for spatially contiguous auditory food cues in rats. *Behavioral Neuroscience*, *101*, 164–169.

Fredrikson, M. (1981). Orienting and defensive reactions to phobic and conditioned fear stimuli in phobics and normals. *Psychophysiology*, *18*, 456–465.

Fredrickson, M., & Öhman, A. (1979). Cardiovascular and electrodermal responses conditioned to fear-relevant stimuli. *Psychophysiology*, *16*, 1–7.

Galef, B. G., Jr., & Osborne, B. (1978). Novel taste facilitation of the association of visual cues with toxicosis in rats. *Journal of Comparative and Physiological Psychology*, *92*, 907–916.

Garcia, J., Forthman Quick, D., & White, B. (1984). Conditioned disgust and fear from mollusk to monkey. In D. L. Alkon & J. Farley (Eds.), *Primary neural substrates of learning and behavior change* (pp. 47–61). Cambridge, England: Cambridge University Press.

Garcia, J., & Koelling, R. A. (1966). Relation of cue to consequence in avoidance learning. *Psychonomic Science*, *4*, 123–124.

Gemberling, G. A., & Domjan, M. (1982). Selective associations in one-day old rats: Taste-toxicosis and texture-shock aversion learning. *Journal of Comparative and Physiological Psychology, 96*, 105–113.

Graham, F. K. (1979). Distinguishing among orienting, defense, and startle reflexes. In H. D. Kimmel, E. H. van Olst, & J. F. Orlebeke (Eds.), *The orienting reflex in humans* (pp. 137–167). Hillsdale, NJ: Lawrence Erlbaum Associates.

Grill, H. J., & Norgren, R. (1978). The taste reactivity test: I. Mimetic responses to gustatory stimuli in neurologically normal rats. *Brain Research, 143*, 263–269.

Grings, W. W., & Dawson, M. E. (1978). *Emotions and bodily responses: A psychophysiological approach.* New York: Academic Press.

Hodes, R. L. (1981). *A psychophysiological investigation of the classical conditioning model of fears and phobias.* Unpublished doctoral dissertation, University of Wisconsin, Madison.

Holder, M. D., & Garcia, J. (1987). Role of temporal order and odor intensity in taste-potentiated odor aversions. *Behavioral Neuroscience, 101*, 158–163.

Holder, M. D., Leon, M., Yirmiya, R., & Garcia, J. (1987). Effect of taste preexposure on taste and odor aversions. *Animal Learning and Behavior, 15*, 55–61.

Holland, P. C. (1983). Representation-mediated overshadowing and potentiation of conditioned aversions. *Journal of Experimental Psychology: Animal Behavior Processes, 9*, 1–13.

Hugdahl, K. (1978). Electrodermal conditioning to potentially phobic stimuli: Effects of instructed extinction. *Behaviour Research and Therapy, 6*, 315–321.

Hugdahl, K., & Öhman, A. (1977). Effects of instruction on acquisition and extinction of electrodermal responses to fear-relevant stimuli. *Journal of Experimental Psychology: Human Learning and Memory, 3*, 608–618.

Hygge, S., & Öhman, A. (1978). Modeling processes in the acquisition of fears: Vicarious electrodermal conditioning to fear-relevant stimuli. *Journal of Personality and Social Psychology, 36*, 271–279.

Jacobs, W. J., & LoLordo, V. M. (1977). The sensory basis of avoidance responding in the rat. *Learning and Motivation, 8*, 446–466.

Jacobs, W. J., & LoLordo, V. M. (1980). Constraints on Pavlovian aversive conditioning: Implications for avoidance learning in the rat. *Learning and Motivation, 11*, 427–455.

Johnston, T. D. (1981). Contrasting approaches to a theory of learning. *The Behavioral and Brain Sciences, 4*, 125–139.

Kamin, L. J. (1969). Selective association and conditioning. In N. J. Mackintosh & W. K. Honig (Eds.), *Fundamental issues in associative learning* (pp. 42–64). Halifax, Canada: Dalhousie University Press.

Kiefer, S. W., Rusiniak, K. W., & Garcia, J. (1982). Flavor-illness aversions: Gustatory neocortex ablations disrupt taste but not taste-potentiated odor cues. *Journal of Comparative and Physiological Psychology, 96*, 540–548.

Kucharski, D., & Spear, N. E. (1985). Potentiation and overshadowing in preweanling and adult rats. *Journal of Experimental Psychology: Animal Behavior Processes, 11*, 15–34.

Lanzetta, J. T., & Orr, S. P. (1980). The influence of facial expressions on the classical conditioning of fear. *Journal of Personality and Social Psychology, 39*, 1081–1087.

Lanzetta, J. T., & Orr, S. P. (1981). Stimulus properties of facial expressions and their influence on the classical conditioning of fear. *Motivation and Emotion, 5*, 225–234.

Lett, B. T. (1984). Extinction of taste aversion does not eliminate taste potentiation of odor aversion in rats or color aversion in pigeons. *Animal Learning and Behavior, 12*, 414–420.

LoLordo, V. M. (1979). Selective associations: In A. Dickinson & R. A. Boakes (Eds.), *Mechanisms of learning and motivation: A memorial to Jerzy Konorski* (pp. 367–398). Hillsdale, NJ: Lawrence Erlbaum Associates.

LoLordo, V. M., & Fairless, J. L. (1985). Pavlovian conditioned inhibition: The literature since 1969. In R. R. Miller & N. E. Spear (Eds.), *Information processing in animals: Conditioned inhibition.* Hillsdale, NJ: Lawrence Erlbaum Associates.

LoLordo, V. M., & Jacobs, W. J. (1983). Constraints on aversive conditioning in the rat. Some theoretical accounts. In M. D. Zeiler & P. Harzem (Eds.), *Advances in analysis of behavior (Vol. 3)*. Chichester, England: Wiley.

Mackintosh, N. J., & Reese, B. (1979). One-trial overshadowing. *Quarterly Journal of Experimental Psychology, 31*, 519–526.

Marcel, A. (1983). Conscious and unconscious perception: An approach to the relations between phenomenological experience and perceptual process. *Cognitive Psychology, 15*, 238–300.

Mayr, E. (1974). Behavior programs and evolutionary strategies. *American Scientist, 62*, 650–659.

McNally, R. J. (1981). Phobias and preparedness: Instructional reversal of electrodermal conditioning to fear-relevant stimuli. *Psychological Reports, 48*, 175–180.

McNally, R. J. (1987). Preparedness and phobias: A review. *Psychological Bulletin, 101*, 283–303.

McNally, R. J., & Reiss, S. (1982). The preparedness theory of phobias and human safety-signal conditioning. *Behavior Research and Therapy, 20*, 153–159.

McNally, R. J., & Reiss, S. (1984). The preparedness theory of phobias: The effects of initial fear level on safety-signal conditioning to fear-relevant stimuli. *Psychophysiology, 21*, 647–652.

Mikulka, P. J., Pitts, E., & Philput, C. (1982). Overshadowing and potentiation in taste aversion learning. *Bulletin of the Psychonomic Society, 20*, 101–104.

Miller, J. S., McCoy, D. F., Kelly, K. S., & Bardo, M. T. (1986). A within-event analysis of taste-potentiated odor and contextual aversions. *Animal Learning and Behavior, 14*, 15–21.

Miller, V. (1984). Selective association learning in the rat: Generality of response system. *Learning and Motivation, 15*, 58–84.

Mineka, S., Davidson, M., Cook, M., & Keir, R. (1984). Observational conditioning of snake fear in rhesus monkeys. *Journal of Abnormal Psychology, 93*, 355–372.

Mineka, S., Keir, R., & Price, V. (1980). Fear of snakes in wild- and lab-reared rhesus monkeys. *Animal Learning and Behavior, 8*, 653–663.

Öhman, A. (1983). The orienting response during Pavlovian conditioning. In D. Siddle (Ed.), *Orienting and habituation: Perspectives in human research*. Chichester, England: Wiley.

Öhman, A. (1986). Face the beast and fear the face: Animal and social fears as prototypes for evolutionary analysis of emotion. *Psychophysiology, 23*, 123–145.

Öhman, A., & Dimberg, U. (1978). Facial expressions as conditioned stimuli for electrodermal responses: A case of "preparedness"? *Journal of Personality and Social Psychology, 36*, 1251–1258.

Öhman, A., Dimberg, U., & Öst, L. -G. (1985). Animal and social phobias: Biological constraints on learned fear responses. In S. Reiss & R. R. Bootzin (Eds.), *Theoretical issues in behavior therapy* (pp. 123–175). New York: Academic Press.

Öhman, A., Fredrikson, M., & Hugdahl, K. (1978). Orienting and defensive responding in the electrodermal system: Palmar-dorsal differences and recovery rate during conditioning to potentially phobic stimuli. *Psychophysiology, 15*, 93–101.

Öhman, A., Fredrikson, M., Hugdahl, K., & Rimmö, P. -A. (1976). The premise of equipotentiality in human classical conditioning: Conditioned electrodermal responses to potentially phobic stimuli. *Journal of Experimental Psychology: General, 105*, 313–337.

Orr, S. P., & Lanzetta, J. T. (1980). Facial expressions of emotion as conditioned stimuli for human autonomic responses. *Journal of Personality and Social Psychology, 36*, 1251–1258.

Orr, S. P., & Lanzetta, J. T. (1984). Extinction of an emotional response in the presence of facial expression of emotion. *Motivation and Emotion, 8*, 55–66.

Palmerino, C. C., Rusiniak, K. W., & Garcia, J. (1980). Flavor-illness aversions: The peculiar roles of odor and taste in memory for poison. *Science, 208*, 753–755.

Parker, L. A., & Carvell, T. (1987). Orofacial and somatic responses elicited by lithium-, nicotine- and amphetamine-paired sucrose solution. *Pharmacology, Biochemistry, and Behavior, 24*, 883–887.

Pavlov, I. P. (1927). *Conditioned reflexes*. Oxford, England: Oxford University Press.

Pelchat, M. L., Grill, H. J., Rozin, P., & Jacobs, J. (1983). Quality of acquired responses to tastes by *Rattus norvegicus* depends on type of associated discomfort. *Journal of Comparative Psychology, 197*, 140–153.

Rescorla, R. A. (1969). Pavlovian conditioned inhibition. *Psychological Bulletin, 72*, 77–94.

Rescorla, R. A. (1980). Simultaneous and successive associations in sensory preconditioning. *Journal of Experimental Psychology: Animal Behavior Processes, 6*, 207–216.

Rescorla, R. A., & Cunningham, C. L. (1978). Within compound flavor associations. *Journal of Experimental Psychology: Animal Behavior Processes, 4*, 267–275.

Rescorla, R. A., & Durlach, P. J. (1981). Within-event learning in Pavlovian conditioning. In N. E. Spear & R. R. Miller (Eds.), *Information processing in animals: Memory mechanisms* (pp. 81–112). Hillsdale, NJ: Lawrence Erlbaum Associates.

Rescorla, R. A., & Wagner, A. R. (1972). A theory of Pavlovian conditioning: Variations in the effectiveness of reinforcement and nonreinforcement. In A. H. Black & W. F. Prokasy (Eds.), *Classical conditioning II: Current research and theory* (pp. 64–99). New York: Appleton-Century-Crofts.

Rozin, P., & Kalat, J. W. (1971). Specific hungers and poison avoidance as adaptive specializations of learning. *Psychological Review, 78*, 459–486.

Rusiniak, K. W., Hankins, W. G., Garcia, J., & Brett, L. P. (1979). Flavor-illness aversions: Potentiation of odor by taste in rats. *Behavioral and Neural Biology, 25*, 1–17.

Rusiniak, K. W., Palmerino, C. C., & Garcia, J. (1982). Potentiation of odor by taste in rats: Tests of some nonassociative factors. *Journal of Comparative and Physiological Psychology, 96*, 775–780.

Rusiniak, K. W., Palminero, C. C., Rice, A. G., Forthman, D. L., & Garcia, J. (1982). Flavor-illness aversions: Potentiation of odor by taste with toxin but not shock in rats. *Journal of Comparative and Physiological Psychology, 96*, 527–539.

Schwartz, B. (1974). On going back to nature: A review of Seligman and Hager's "Biological boundaries of learning". *Journal of the Experimental Analysis of Behavior, 21*, 183–198.

Schwartz, G. E., Brown, S. L., & Ahern, G. L. (1980). Facial muscle patterning and subjective experience during affective imagery: Sex differences. *Psychophysiology, 17*, 75–82.

Seligman, M. E. P. (1970). On the generality of the laws of learning. *Psychological Review, 77*, 406–418.

Seligman, M. E. P. (1971). Phobias and preparedness. *Behavior Therapy, 2*, 307–320.

Shettleworth, S. J. (1972). Constraints on learning. *Advances in the study of behavior, 4*, 1–68.

Timberlake, W. (1983). The functional organization of appetitive behavior: Behavior systems and learning. In M. D. Zeiler & P. Harzem (Eds.), *Advances in analysis of behavior (Vol. 3): Biological factors in learning*. Chichester, England: Wiley.

Torgerson, S. (1979). The nature and origin of common phobic fears. *British Journal of Psychiatry, 134*, 343–351.

Westbrook, R. F., Clarke, J. C., & Provost, S. (1980). Long-delay learning in the pigeon: Flavor, color, and flavor-mediated color aversions. *Behavioral and Neural Biology, 28*, 398–407.

Westbrook, R. F., Homewood, J., Horn, K., & Clarke, J. C. (1983). Flavor-odor compound conditioning: Odor-potentiation and flavor-attenuation. *Quarterly Journal of Experimental Psychology, 35B*, 13–33.

Wilcoxon, H. C., Dragoin, W. B., & Kral, P. A. (1971). Illness-induced aversions in rat and quail: Relative salience of visual and gustatory cues. *Science, 171*, 826–828.

7 Limits of Darwinian Conditioning

John Garcia
University of California, Los Angeles

Linda Phillips Brett
Syntex Laboratories, Inc.
Palo Alto, California

Kenneth W. Rusiniak
Eastern Michigan University

I. INTRODUCTION TO DARWINIAN CONDITIONING PRINCIPLES

The principles of Darwinian food conditioning were clearly described by Poulton (1887) in a remarkable 83-page paper entitled ''The Experimental Proof of the Protective Value of Color and Marking in Insects in Reference to Their Vertebrate Enemies,'' published in the proceedings of the Zoological Society of London. When considering the adaptive value of cryptic coloration for caterpillars, Darwin was disturbed by blatant exceptions to his rule of camouflage; some tender larval insects marked by brilliant color patterns openly display themselves on bare twigs and stems. A. R. Wallace supplied a working hypothesis: such insects are advertising their bitter taste and toxic property (Darwin, 1871).

Poulton (1887) reviewed some 20 years of observations and experiments supporting Wallace's contention. Showy larval insects often possess an emetic toxin with a distinctive bitter taste. Their vertebrate predators eat one or two insects, become ill, and thereafter reject similar specimens at a distance. Darwinian research focused on the insect population and the effect of coloration and toxicity upon the natural selection and survival of members of the prey species.

Modern conditioned food aversion (CFA) research focuses on the predator that eats the poisonous plant or animal and the mechanisms by which the predator learns to avoid poison and select safe food. Garcia and Hankins (1977) discussed Poulton's seminal paper in the light of CFA and entitled their review ''On the Origin of Food Aversion Paradigms'' in an obvious reference to Darwin's

181

(1859) major work. They listed ten general propositions; we have revised and reordered that list, dropping some, adding a few, and modifying others on the basis of CFA research during the last decade. The revised list follows:

1. Food aversion learning.   Acceptable food becomes aversive when followed by *emetic* illness. We emphasize emetic because the illness must be *nausea* referred to the stomach. Any psychological stimulation or physiological disturbance that excites the emetic system will produce an aversion. The following discomforts are not adequate for CFA unless they also produce nausea: allergic reactions, lower bowel bloating, pain of any region other than the stomach. Poisons that do not cause nausea and vomiting at certain doses will not produce aversions (Coil, Rogers, Garcia, & Novin, 1978; Garcia, Lasiter, Bermudez-Rattoni, & Deems, 1985; Pelchat, Grill, Rozin, & Jacobs, 1983).

2. Food preference learning.   Food becomes more palatable for hungry animals if it is followed by repletion of caloric hunger (Cabanac, 1979; Deems, Oetting, Sherman, & Garcia, 1986; Garcia, Hankins, & Rusiniak, 1974; Sherman, Hickis, Rice, Rusiniak, & Garcia, 1983).

3. Flavor-recuperation learning.   When a flavor is presented to a thiamine-deficient animal and followed by an injection of thiamine, the animal will acquire a preference for that flavor (Garcia, Ervin, Yorke, & Koelling, 1967; Harris, Clay, Hargreaves, & Ward, 1933). In similar fashion, a flavor followed by recuperation from emetic illness will become more palatable. This "medicine effect" is symmetrical with, but opposite to, the "poison" effect induced when the same flavor is followed by an emetic malaise of the same degree (Green & Garcia, 1971).

4. Taste primacy in CFA.   Taste is the primary arbiter of what is fit to eat. Lesser aversions may be acquired to other stimuli in a diminishing hierarchy of effectiveness. After taste, odor apparently comes next (Garcia & Koelling, 1967), closely followed by food cues that impinge on the mouth, such as moisture, temperature, or tactile cues, which may also stimulate the taste receptors (Garcia, Hankins, Robinson, & Vogt, 1972; Nachman, Rauschenberger, & Ashe, 1977). A distinctive place defined by albedo, texture and acoustics will become aversive when paired with nausea in repeated trials (Best, Best, & Henggeler, 1977; Garcia, Kimeldorf, & Hunt, 1956).

5. Taste potentiation of distal cues.   Other weak cues for CFA (odor, color, place, noise), when accompanied by taste and followed by nausea, become strongly aversive when tested alone in extinction. For example, odor alone is a weak cue for poison while taste alone is a strong cue under the same circumstance; however, when odor and taste are combined into a compound cue, taste potentiates the weak odor cue so that it is powerfully aversive when tested alone in extinction (Palmerino, Rusiniak, & Garcia, 1980; Rusiniak, Hankins, Garcia, & Brett, 1979). For another example, red-tailed hawks cannot discriminate black mice paired with nausea from safe white mice; however, when a distinctive taste is added to the coat of the black mice, hawks will reject black mice at a distance, after a single black mouse-poison trial (Brett, Hankins, & Garcia, 1976). Similar potentiation effects were obtained with blue water in pigeons (Clarke, Westbrook, & Irwin, 1979), colored capsules of food in rats (Galef & Osborne, 1978), and auditory cues with food in rats (Ellins, Cramer, & Whitmore, 1985; Ellins & Von Kluge, 1987).

6. Taste is not a conditioned stimulus (CS).   In all these potentiation cases discussed above, the taste stimulus is not acting like a strong CS component, because it does not block or overshadow conditioning to the weaker CS components, such as odor, color, or noise (Kamin, 1969). Taste is acting like an unconditioned stimulus (US), as it is potentiating neutral feeding stimuli such as mild odors, colors, and noises immediately preceding the taste of food in the mouth. The function of a US is to potentiate any neutral stimulus that precedes it. After all, taste was Pavlov's original US (Garcia, 1988; Garcia & Holder, 1985).

7. Nausea is not a US.   Nausea does not meet the requirements for Pavlov's (1927) US. The Pavlovian US should excite an observable unconditioned response (UR) at its onset; US intensity at onset is more important than US duration for rapid conditioning. The duration of both the CS and US, and their interstimulus interval, are measured in seconds, or fractions thereof, if conditioning is to occur within a few trials. In contrast, durations of flavor and nausea stimuli and their interstimulus intervals are often measured in hours. Intensity at the onset of the nauseating treatment is not very important in CFA; accumulated dose is much more important. For example, an exposure of hours to low-intensity X-ray is as effective as a brief high-intensity exposure of minutes if the total dose is equivalent. Furthermore, control rats drinking water when exposed to X-ray, or when injected with toxin, will not necessarily exhibit an unconditional depression in water consumption, yet experimental animals given a taste cue in the water will exhibit a CFA towards the end of the session or on the next session (Buchwald, Garcia, Feder, & Bach-y-Rita, 1964; Garcia, McGowan, & Green, 1972).

8. Incentive modification.   Taste aversions result from a nausea-induced feedback (FB) process which adjusts the hedonic value of a peripheral US commensurate with the latter's internal homeostatic utility. FB adjustment of taste works in both directions as indicated in propositions 2 and 3 above. FB hedonic adjustment operates in other homeostatic systems such as temperature regulation. When the core (FB) temperature is too high, a warm US contacting the skin is unpleasant and the animal seeks a cool place. This system also works in both directions (Cabanac, 1979; Garcia, Hankins, & Rusiniak, 1974).

9. Unconscious affective CFA processing.   Neither an appreciation of nausea

FB nor an awareness of its association with a taste US is necessary for CFA; a simple disgust is the only essential psychological requirement. For example, if an animal is given an attractive flavor and rendered unconscious before and during the nauseating treatment, it will display a strong aversion when tested with the flavor in the waking state several days later. A variety of agents used to produce anesthesia, tranquility, or cortical inactivation during the nausea treatment have no effect upon CFA. In fact, the acquired aversion is often stronger than in awake controls (Bermudez-Rattoni, Forthman Quick, Sanchez, Perez, & Garcia, in press; Burešová & Bureš, 1973; Roll & Smith, 1972.).

10. Prolonged cumulative CFA effects. The role of temporal and intensity parameters in successful flavor-nausea conditioning cannot be subsumed under traditional learning theories. It is as if we reduced a buzzer CS so low that it did not elicit the dog's attention, and diluted the vinegar US so much that the dog did not salivate. Yet, when we continued the paired treatments day after day, the dog began to salivate and gradually salivation became more and more copious (Garcia, 1988; Garcia & Holder, 1985). Aversions are acquired for long-term familiar diets paired with chronic conditions where no orientation to the onset of the taste US and no UR to the onset of malaise FB are manifested. When an animal is subjected to thiamine deficiency or to a low-grade toxin, it may be days or weeks before a depression in consumption of the diet appears (Harris et al., 1933; Richter, 1943). Similar prolonged-duration learning is observed when a diet is paired with cancer growth over days or weeks (Bernstein, 1985).

11. The CS-US-FB paradigm unites Pavlovian and Darwinian conditioning. In Pavlovian conditioning, for example, an auditory CS catches an animal's attention and a food US induces it to eat. In the process, the animal acquires a "cognitive map" of the locus of CS and US in the spatiotemporal context of the experiment. Then Darwinian conditioning takes over. For example, the animal might go to sleep and digest the food, providing feedback (FB) which, if positive, maintains or enhances the palatability of the food. If instead gastric malaise ensues, the food will become aversive, but the animal will not discover its aversion until the food is encountered again.

Experimental evidence for this curious CFA without awareness has been gathered in a paradigm called "instrumental responding for devaluated reinforcers" (Dickerson, Nicholas, & Adams, 1983). Animals trained to work at an instrumental task to obtain a sweet reinforcer, then given a sweet-nausea treatment in another place, will continue to work unabated although they will reject the sweet reinforcer when it is offered (Garcia, Kovner, & Green, 1970; Holman, 1975). Others have reported some depression in instrumental responding after the reinforcer has been devaluated; however, a much greater depression is observed in consummatory responding, i.e., drinking the sweet fluid (Colwill & Rescorla, 1985a; 1985b). A caveat: If the nausea treatment provides taste-potentiation of any cue present in the subsequent testing situation, then a CFA elicited by that cue will depress instrumental responding (Wilson, Sherman, & Holman, 1981).

II. IN DEFENSE OF GUT AND SKIN

We can learn much about the psyche, mind, behavioral repertoire, or whatever you choose to call this ephemeral aspect of animal life we study, by examining the ecological pressures in the niches on this earth where animals are found. No matter whether you take the position that psychological functions cannot be reduced to anatomical structures or whether you believe that function and structure are simply two descriptions of the same phenomena, the behavior of an animal can be categorized, like the structures of its brain and body, into discrete systems designed by natural selection to meet the specific contingencies found in its ecological niche.

It is generally agreed that food is the primary requirement of our animal subjects and that food supply sets the ultimate limits on animal populations. Thus, it is reasonable to suppose that the gut and its associated structures represent an important primary functional system in vertebrates like ourselves. It is not surprising that both Pavlov and Thorndike, as well as Poulton, made food in the mouth the central event of their respective conditioning paradigms. All three theorists were cognizant of the entire feeding sequence, but each focused on a different link in the instrumental-consummatory chain.

The differences among these three theorists and their findings are due, in part, to the divided structure of the vertebrate mouth and the duality of its neural projections to the medulla oblongata. Duality in structure reflects duality of function. The mouth is the point of transition where the instrumental phase of food capture ends and the consummatory phase of food digestion begins (Finger & Morita, 1985; Garcia, 1988; Hamilton & Norgren, 1984; Herrick, 1948).

The front of the mouth, lined with ectodermal tissue, is fitted with receptors that project via the facial nerve to the rostral tip of the nucleus solitarius. This is the beginning of a brain subsystem, the outflow of which guides the instrumental motor patterns leading to food capture. This peripheral system by which the animal contacts the external world attracted the attention of experimental psychologists. Pavlov (1927) studied distal (CS) signals paired with reflexive (US) responses to food contacting the mouth and noted the acquisition of anticipatory feeding reactions to distal stimuli. Thorndike observed the effect of food in the mouth upon prior instrumental motor patterns and found that food increased the frequency of some patterns more readily than others (see Seligman & Hager, 1972).

In contrast, the back of the mouth, lined with endodermal tissue, is fitted with receptors that project via the glossopharyngeal nerve to a more medial area of the solitary nucleus immediately adjacent to the areas that receive feedback from food absorption in the gut via the vagus nerve. The area postrema, which provides feedback from food products circulating in the blood, also impinges upon this area of the solitary nucleus. This is the beginning of a brain subsystem which guides the consummatory phase of feeding. This internal system attracted the attention of evolutionary biologists. Poulton (1887) was concerned with the effects of subsequent food absorption upon the palatability of food in the mouths of predators and the spread of that effect to distal cues emanating from the prey species. Recent research, archival as well as experimental, has revealed a form of gut learning where internal states hold sway and temporal parameters of associative learning are increased a hundredfold and, in many cases, a thousandfold or more. As we have discussed in our introduction, the primary function of this internal FB is to adjust adaptively the hedonic valence of the food US.

These two buccal subsystems display a functional "wisdom of the body" coordinated and supported by selective learning mechanisms. For example, sweet receptors predominate in the anterior buccal cavity providing positive reinforcement for successful hunting strategies of hungry vertebrates. Sweet is the universal sign for calories in vertebrate feeding niches. Bitter receptors predominate in the posterior buccal cavity, providing the ultimate test for toxins before food is swallowed. Bitter is the universal sign for toxins. Vertebrates often seize food in the anterior region, then reject it when the food contacts the posterior region, attesting to independent evaluation by these two subsystems. Though sweet is a naturally positive sign, it can be made negative by a few sweet-nausea trials. And the native bitter signal can be made positive by a few pairings of bitter and repletion of internal needs or recuperation from illness. Learning about food and its effects represents the plastic component of instinctive feeding patterns (Garcia & Hankins, 1975).

The bodies of the large vertebrates that we are concerned with here, like those of all other organisms, are a rich supply of food for others, so a skin defense system must have evolved soon after the gut system. There is considerable overlap between this skin-defense system and the anterior buccal subsystem. Both skin and the anterior buccal region are of ectodermal origin. The distal receptors and the motor mechanisms used to track down food are the same ones used to avoid and escape predators. Keen analysis of distal signs and speedy reactions are obviously advantageous in obtaining food or avoiding attacks. Accordingly, when Pavlovians and Thorndikians studied the effects of electrocutaneous shock upon the adaptive behavior of their subjects, the signals and the spatiotemporal parameters derived from feeding paradigms conformed quite nicely to those obtained with the new electric-shock avoidance techniques, giving rise to the notion that universal laws of attention and contiguity were under observation.

However, within the skin-defense system there is a vast difference between the external, or peripheral, CS–US pain functions and the internal US–FB functions, just as we have seen in the external-internal divisions of the gut-defense system. Following a pain US there are a number of FB mechanisms which "feed back'' to modulate pain. For example, an endogenous analgesia increases pain threshold. This FB has prolonged cumulative effects and it operates effectively in anesthetized rats; thus, it displays some features discussed in propositions 8, 9, and 10 (Garcia, 1988; Terman, Shavit, Lewis, Cannon, & Liebeskind, 1984).

The skin-defense system is illustrated in Fig. 7.1, above the gut-defense system. Figure 7.1 is, of course, a grossly simplified schema emphasizing the broad similarity of function in the two systems which is outweighed by the unique internal properties of each system. On the left side of the figure, environmental stimuli make contact with the receptors of the animal. Distal signals (CSs) such as sights, sounds, and odors can be utilized by either system through the operation of sensory gates which we discuss below. As already mentioned, the temporal parameters for utilization of these signals are specified in the Pavlovian and Thorndikian paradigms.

The very real differences between systems follow the impact of the US upon the ectodermal surface of the animal. As two examples in Fig. 7.1, we have shown (1) a predatory attack (US) upon the skin-defense system, evoking an internal analgesia to reduce the intensity of the painful US, and (2) a toxic food (US) in the mouth evoking a nauseating FB which renders the food taste (US) aversive. These internal FB receptors operate in a bath of bodily fluids sensing concentrations of endogenous and absorbed substances; thus, internal receptors can detect the cumulative effects of prolonged US exposure as we pointed out in proposition 10. Each internal FB has an indirect effect upon behavior through the modulation of its own particular US; therefore, the parameters for conditioning are prolonged and the learning is selective. Furthermore, because the hedonic value of the peripheral US is modulated by the homeostatic FB reflecting the internal needs of the animal, US–FB conditioning results in a motivational change that

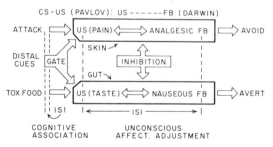

FIG. 7.1. Schematic diagram of the skin-defense system evolved to defend vertebrates against predators and the gut-defense system evolved to defend them against poisoned food. Inputs are shown on the left, outputs on the right. Sensory gates channel distal cues into the appropriate system depending upon the readiness state of the animal. Skin and gut excitation are mutually inhibitory. CS–US associations result in a cognitive map (on the left) according to Pavlov (or Thorndike). The affective value of the US is adjusted by homeostatic feedback (FB; on the right) with reference to survival needs according to Darwin.

can operate in the absence of cognitive awareness of the internal causes leading to that change. These hedonic effects can spread to distal CSs paired with the US (left side of Fig. 7.1) altering the subsequent instrumental patterns of behavior (right side of Fig. 7.1). As indicated at the center of Fig. 7.1, the skin and gut systems are separated by reciprocal inhibition. Depending upon both the demands of the external situation and its internal state, the animal allocates its energy and attention to one or the other. If the animal is fearful for its skin, its appetite is suppressed and gastric motility is reduced as it engages its motor system for flight. But if the animal has consumed a large meal in the comfort of its territory, digestion proceeds, postprandial sleep waves sweep over its cortex, and the motor system relaxes.

Distal signals are also gated into either the skin system or the gut system depending upon the internal state of the organism and the stimuli that impinge upon it. For example, if a rat encounters a novel odor as it approaches the water spout in its habitual drinking place, that odor will be gated into the gut system if the water contains a novel taste US. There it will be available for integration with nausea but not shock. But if the odor is not followed by a novel taste US, then it will be gated into the skin system where it is available for association with shock but not available for integration with nausea (Rusiniak, Palmerino, Rice, Forthman, & Garcia, 1982). But even the gate is not a neutral, symmetrical process. The gate operates in biased ways depending on the cue; odor appears to have equal access to either the skin-defense system or the gut-defense system, but noise, on the other hand, seems to have much easier access to the skin-defense system, reflecting its evolutionary and ontogenetic relations to the skin pressure sense (Garcia, 1988).

III. LIMIT: CONDITIONED AVERSIONS
FOR INDISCRIMINATIVE TASTES

One limit of Darwinian conditioning is set by the reflexive neurophysiological US–FB coupling of the gustatory and visceral afferents within the gut system. In the absence of any distinctive novel taste cue, animals afflicted with nausea will seek to "pin" their aversions on familiar food and water, even in the face of a wealth of environmental stimuli perfectly correlated with repeated bouts of nausea. Such aversions to indiscriminative tastes might be termed "vacuum learning" in that they resemble the discharge of fixed action patterns in the absence of appropriate releasing stimuli by animals under high drive. Lorenz (1937) described such "vacuum behavior" in a captive startling long deprived of the opportunity to exercise the insect-hunting pattern of its species. The starling would fly into the air, execute its capture maneuver, return to its perch, and perform its killing and eating behavior in the absence of insect targets. Rusiniak (1976) found vacuum learning in his analysis of the day-by-day drinking and feeding records of animals repeatedly exposed to X-rays by Garcia and his associates. Recalling "pseudoconditioning," Rusiniak refers to the transient depressions as "pseudoaversions" because they appear after nausea in the absence of conditional pairing of a taste stimulus with nausea. The intensity and duration of these pseudoaversions seem to be an index of the salience of the cues paired with nausea.

In the first experiment, shown in Fig. 7.2A, Garcia and Koelling (1967) habituated their rats to drink their daily ration of water in the same plastic box at the same time each day. Then, on every third day, the animals were stimulated by various cues. The cues were first presented alone as a pretest. On the next three trials the cues were paired with X-rays at a dose (54r) calculated to induce nausea. On the last three trials, the cues were presented alone in extinction. Water was presented as usual on the 2 days between test days. The cue was a distinctive environment marked by lighting, floor texture, and noise differences. The water, spout, and bottle were the same throughout the 26 days, so there were no discriminative taste or other oral cues in the distinctive environment.

The data are presented in Fig. 7.2A, where the pseudoaversions are indicated with asterisks. Depressed intake appears on the first water day after each nausea treatment; water intake on the day before and the day after is relatively higher. Thus, the pseudoaversion is characterized by a V-shaped nadir centering on the first intervening water day; since no nausea follows drinking, water intake rebounds on the second intervening day. There are no "true aversions" depicted in Fig. 7.2A. In a "true aversion" the intake nadirs would center upon days marked by the cues paired with X-rays.

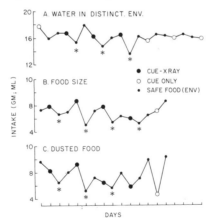

FIG. 7.2.   Daily intake records for animals exposed to X-rays every third day in conjunction with a variety of cues. Asterisks indicate pseudoaversions to plain food and water which occur in the absence of discriminative taste cues. A. X-rays were paired with distinctive environmental cues (adapted from Garcia & Koelling, 1967). B. Size of the food pellet was the cue paired with X-ray. C. Dust on the surface of the pellet was a weak taste cue paired with X-ray. Adapted from Garcia, McGowan, Ervin, & Koelling (1968).

A suspicious depression appears after the pretest, but this may be due to another cause. Drinking is high when the novel environmental cues are first presented and rats are known to exhibit polydipsia under mild stress and arousal. On the next day, the rats may compensate by drinking a little less. This is a weak effect which does not appear in any of the subsequent tests for pseudoaversions.

The graphs for two other groups tested by Garcia and Koelling (1967) do not appear here but can be seen in their report. Those daily intake records are revealing. When vinegar-water instead of the distinctive environment served as the cue, a progressive true aversion to the taste developed; all the nadirs in the record centering on the vinegar-water days. When a weak odor cue was used, pseudoaversions appeared in the first part of the record and were replaced by true aversions to the odor later on in the record.

In another experiment, shown in Figs. 7.2B and 7.2C, Garcia, McGowan, Ervin, and Koelling (1968) pitted two cues, either pellet size or pellet taste, against two forms of punishment, either X-rays or foot shock. Because we are concerned here with the daily food intake of the two X-ray groups, which were run on the same schedule as the Fig. 7.2A group, the shock results are not displayed; but in summary it can be said that the size of the pellet was an effective cue for foot shock while the taste was not.

When pellet size was the cue paired with X-ray (Fig. 7.2B), transient pseudoaversions (indicated by asterisks) appear on each day after the animals were exposed to the nauseating X-rays, although the taste of food is constant across all days. True aversions for the size cue paired with X-ray never appear, yet the rats can discriminate the size difference quite easily, as indicated by the performance of the size-shock group.

When a taste was added to the pellets, a different pattern occurred, which is best understood by considering how the taste was presented (see Fig. 7.2C). The taste cue was formed by rolling small chunks of Purina chow in either flour or powdered sugar. The pellets, all the same size and dusted in white powder, looked the same but tasted different on the surface. The central bulk of the pellets tasted the same, so the taste cue was superficial and weak. The data reflect this weak discriminability. The first part of the daily record reveals a series of pseudoaversions (marked by asterisks) with the nadirs on the days after the first three X-ray exposures when the animals are eating the safe-tasting food. Paradoxically, consumption of the food taste paired with X-ray is relatively high. True aversions to the taste paired with X-ray appear on the last acquisition day and on the extinction test, flanked by high consumption of the safe food. Again, when weak cues are used in repeated trials, pseudoaversions are replaced by true aversions.

It might be tempting to conclude that X-ray exposure produces a transient anorexia on the next day, since postirradiation anorexia is often reported. However, the same effect is observed in water intake (Fig. 7.2A) and postirradiation adipsia is rarely reported (Kimeldorf & Hunt, 1965). Furthermore, postirradiation depression disappears after the true aversion develops. It is more likely that the putative postirradiation anorexia is caused by a transient pseudoaversion than the other way around.

Similar shifts from pseudoaversions to true aversions in the daily drinking record can be observed when weak odor cues are paired with lithium chloride. Rusiniak (1976) used an almond-scented (2%) water in a pretest, then paired the solution with lithium chloride treatment calculated to produce moderate nausea on four acquisition trials followed by a posttest with the scented solution alone. Again, tests and trials were separated by two water days. A second group was treated in identical fashion except that the lithium treatment was delayed 30 min.

The results are shown in Figs. 7.3A and 7.3B, respectively. In the first part of both records, nadirs in intake occur on the first water day after the first and second lithium treatments. These pseudoaversions are not marked by asterisks. Again, water intake increases on the second water day, indicating the transient nature of the pseudoaversions. Intake of almond-scented water is high on the first two acquisition trials, indicating that a true aversion has not yet developed. On the last two acquisition days and the final extinction test, true aversion for almond-scented water appears with nadirs centered on the test days; water consumption is high on the intervening days, indicating the elimination of the pseudoaversion. In both Figs. 7.3A and 7.3B, the path of the nadirs across days is continuous from pseudoaversion to true aversion as if the animals merely displace their aversion for plain (safe) water to the almond-scented (nausea) water.

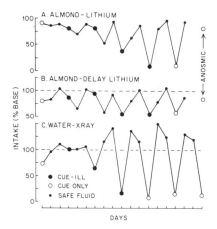

FIG. 7.3. Daily water intake records for animals treated with nauseating agents every third day. (There are no asterisks indicating the pseudoaversions to plain water without the discriminative cue.) Note that pseudoaversions disappear as true aversions to odor appear. A. Almond-scented water was followed by a lithium injection. B. The same cue followed by delayed lithium. Animals lost the aversion when they were rendered anosmic (adapted from Rusiniak, 1976). C. Familiar plain water served as the cue paired with X-ray. Saccharin-water was available on the intervening days. Adapted from Garcia and Koelling (1967).

After the extinction test, the rats were rendered anosmic by zinc sulfate treatment to the nasal mucosa. Another test with almond-scented water indicates that the aversion is primarily olfactory (see right side of Figs. 7.3A and 7.3B). Rusiniak (1976) reports on two other groups treated much the same as those in Figs. 7.3A and 7.3B. The effects are similar, attesting to the reliability of this pattern of pseudoaversion shifting into true aversion.

Aversions, whether psuedo or true, to plain familiar water may seem dubious in view of the facilitatory effect of novelty in CFA (Revusky & Bedarf, 1967). Actually, water aversions are quite easy to establish if water is discriminative, i.e., if the alternative (safe) fluid tastes different. Garcia and Koelling (1967) raised 40 rats on either plain-water or saccharin-water since infancy. Half of each rearing group had saccharin-water paired with X-ray and plain-water on the intervening (safe) days and the other half received the converse pairing. All four groups acquired true aversions to the fluid paired with X-rays. Only the water-reared, water-tested group is shown here in Fig. 7.3C. The true aversion to familiar plain-water paired with X-ray develops progressively in the absence of any pseudoaversion and persists through three extinction tests, demonstrating that the taste of water, despite its familiarity, is a potent cue when paired with nausea, provided that the taste of saccharin on safe trials offers a distinctive discrimination.

Almond-scented water has a potential taste component since the almond flavor was mixed directly in the drinking water. In order to test for pseudoaversions in the absence of this potential water taste, Rusiniak (1976) used amyl acetate (banana odor) in the air of the chamber as a cue paired with lithium. Half of the animals were rendered anosmic by zinc sulfate treatment and the remainder were given a sham anosmia (saline) treatment. Two acquisition trials and one extinction test were employed on the same 3-day cycle. The animals drank water

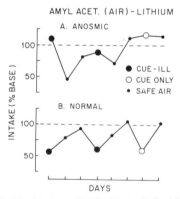

FIG. 7.4.   Daily drinking records of rats treated with lithium every third day. Amyl acetate in the air of the drinking chamber served as the cue paired with lithium. A. Note the anosmic rats' pseudoaversions to plain water following the cue-ill trials. B. Normal rats display true aversions to the odor cue. Adapted from Rusiniak (1976).

in a scrubbed-out compartment on the intervening days. The data are presented in Fig. 7.4. The anosmic animals display pseudoaversions with nadirs on the first water day after both banana-lithium days. In contrast, the intact animals exhibit their nadirs on every banana day, presumably indicating neophobia, i.e., depressed consumption due to the presence of the novel pungent banana odor on the first day, followed by odor aversions induced by lithium on the two succeeding test days. In any case, the diametrically opposed behavior in the two groups demonstrates that pseudoaversions develop in the absence of water taste cues and that they cannot be attributed to any postlithium adipsia.

IV. LIMIT: SIMULTANEOUS CONDITIONING OF OPPOSING REACTIONS TO TASTE

Another limit of Darwinian conditioning is set by the neurophysiological separation of the skin and gut systems. Recall that when food enters the mouth it impinges on the anterior buccal subsystem, which is part of the skin, and then moves on to stimulate the posterior buccal subsystem, which is part of the gut. We have called taste a US because that is how it is defined in Pavlovian experimental paradigms; but in truth, taste is simply a stimulus and as such it can be used as a signal or a CS for a shock US for a thirsty animal. This sets up a dilemma. Taste followed by thirst-reduction FB should be positive, while taste followed by pain should be negative. The question is, what will the animal do? A preliminary study using a two-way instrumental avoidance task indicated that simultaneous conditioning in both paradigms was possible (Garcia & Hankins, 1977).

Brett (1977) conducted an extensive multigroup experiment utilizing various distal stimuli as well as taste in a conditioned emotional response (CER) paradigm. Essentially, she trained her rats to drink their daily ration of water in an elongated box with a drinking spout at one end. The daily drinking session was divided into ten 60-sec trials timed from the first lick. Between trials, each rat was returned to its individual home cage. After 2 weeks, the rats were accustomed to the schedule and so the acquisition training began.

On five 60-sec drinking trials, rats were given a distinctive taste to drink paired with a single (0.5 sec) foot shock at the midpoint of the 60-sec period. The shock intensity was adjusted for each rat so as to momentarily interrupt its drinking. On the other five trials the rats were given water as usual without shock. Shock trials and nonshock trials were presented unsystematically so that taste was the only cue for shock. Odor was not a cue because the animals were rendered anosmic by intranasal perfusion of zinc sulfate 3 days prior to acquisition training.

The foot shock at the midpoint of each taste-shock trial effectively divided the trial into a period from 0 to 30 sec when taste "warned" the rat that shock was coming and a period from 31 to 60 sec when it was "safe" to drink. "Taste as a CS for a shock US" was free to exert a negative effect on drinking during the warning period and "taste as a US for a thirst-reduction FB" was free to exert a positive effect on drinking during the safe period. So that she might see the greatest possible changes in hedonic responses to taste as a US, Brett selected flavor stimuli initially unpleasing to the rat's palate: a discernibly bitter quinine-water (0.15 g/L) solution and a strongly sweet saccharin-water (10 g/L) mixture. In order to observe changes in drinking of these unpalatable solutions in the absence of pain, two parallel groups were run under exactly the same conditions with shock deleted.

The results for the taste groups and their nonshocked controls are illustrated in Fig. 7.5. Mean drinking during the five taste trials each day is plotted along with the water trials for Day 1 and Day 10. First, consider the two lower graphs generated by nonshocked groups drinking either strong saccharin or bitter quinine. Both groups display a dislike for the two tastes on Day 1, as shown by a declining slope of licking; this effect is especially evident in those drinking quinine water, suggesting that the bitter taste is somewhat more aversive than the

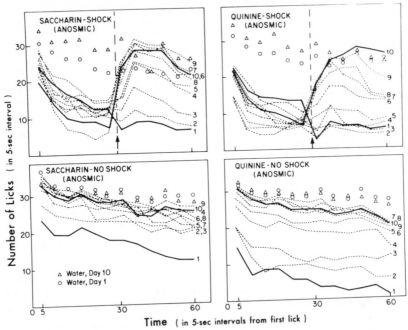

FIG. 7.5.   Mean number of licks per 5-sec interval for daily blocks of five acquisition trials are marked in solid bold lines for Days 1 and 10. Days 2 through 9 are marked with dashed lines. A single pulse of shock delivered at the midpoint of the 60-sec interval was paired with the cues indicated at the upper left of each quadrant. Five acquisition trials and five nonshock water trials were presented in unsystematic order each day. Only the water scores for Day 1 (open triangle) and Day 10 (open squares) are shown. Adapted from Brett (1977).

strongly sweet taste. By Day 10, drinking patterns of both groups indicate that the initially repugnant tastes had become as preferred as, or only slightly less preferred than, plain water. This is a simple example of US–FB conditioning, with reduction of thirst serving the FB role.

Now consider the two groups at the top of Fig. 7.5., which had strong saccharin and quinine paired with a single shock at the midpoint of the 60-sec drinking period. On Day 1, both groups exhibit a downward slope of drinking in the 0- to 30-sec (warning) period, with the nadir coming in the 5-sec interval after the shock. On Day 10, both groups exhibit greater suppression with the nadir coming in the 5-sec interval prior to shock in the anticipatory manner of Pavlovian conditioning. Immediately after the shock, drinking rebounds to water baseline levels in the final (safe) 31- to 60-sec Interval, creating an X-shape pattern at the cross-over of Days 1 and 10. This latter rise is due to Darwinian US–FB modulation of the "naturally" aversive taste. Drinking in the latter 30-sec interval over the ten trials exhibits an orderly increase, somewhat retarded in comparison to the nonshocked controls, indicating that shock has a rather small disruptive effect on US–FB *performance*; in all probability, shock has no real effect upon the *hedonic shift* itself.

In order to observe the behavior of other rats under these rather bizarre conditions where taste in the mouth signaled a pain in the foot, Brett trained four other groups in the same apparatus with different stimuli. In a prior experiment, Garcia and Koelling (1966) reported that a bright-noisy stimulus was a more effective cue for foot shock than taste. Therefore, for two groups of rats (one anosmic, one sham-anosmic), each lick at a water spout on acquisition trials produced a "bright-noisy" CS provided by a 2.0 watt light bulb located 1.5 cm below the spout and by an abrupt increase (from 62 db to 90 db) in the level of white noise in the experimental room; the duration of the bright-noisy stimulus was the same as the duration of the lick so that this distal CS could be compared with the taste CS. In sham-anosmia treatment, physiological saline was substituted for zinc sulfate, making the handling of the rat similar but the treatment benign as far as olfaction is concerned.

The upper left of Fig. 7.6 shows the record of anosmic animals that had the bright-noisy signal contingent upon licking the water spout. In general, their performance is not as adaptive to the shock contingency as the anosmic animals of the saccharin and quinine groups in Fig. 7.5. Conditioned suppression is weaker on Day 10 than on Day 1. In addition, the nadir of suppression is in the 5-sec interval after the shock on most trials; as a result there is no X-shaped cross-over pattern between the first and last day's performance. The sham-anosmic animals (Fig. 7.6, lower left) exhibited a similar ragged performance. Though the conditioned suppression in the warning period (0–30 sec) is equivalent on Day 1 and Day 10, suppression is greater on the early sessions (Days 2–5) than on the later sessions (Days 6–9). The nadir of suppression never *anticipates* the shock; thus, Pavlovian conditioning is absent or very weak compared to the taste-shock groups in Fig. 7.5.

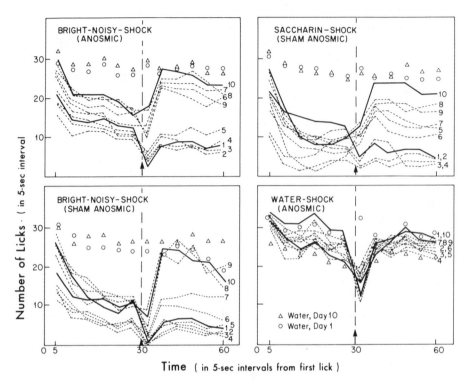

FIG. 7.6. Please refer to the caption under Figure 5. The bright-noisy signal pulse was contingent on the lick of the rat on the water spout. Adapted from Brett (1977).

Thus, in comparison with the earlier selective association experiment by Garcia and Koelling (1966), where the bright-noisy stimulus contingent on licking as a signal for shock was far superior to the taste stimulus, these data indicate that taste may be superior. These diametrically opposed results indicate that there are no simple answers in the psychology of animal learning. Whether a bright-noisy signal is better than taste as a signal for foot shock depends on the entire learning situation. Prolonged training in simple situations may cause the animal to abandon simple habits acquired in a few trials. The damnable thing is that the rat is extremely adaptive; placed in one situation designed to demonstrate selective cue-consequence learning it will do just that. Then, placed in another situation designed to demonstrate another hunch of the experimenter, it may *undo* selective learning, forcing the experimenter to retreat to a *post hoc* explanation such as the one that follows.

There are a number of critical differences between the Garcia and Koelling and Brett (1977) experiments. First, in the former, shock was applied 0.5 sec after the onset of licking, whereas in the latter, shock was applied 30 sec later.

Contiguity of CS–US pairs from onset to onset facilitates Pavlovian conditioning. Second, the former study consisted of four trials a day for 4 days, while the latter employed ten trials a day for 10 days. It is a well-established fact, but perhaps not a well-known one, that shock-avoidance behavior tends to be replaced by shock-escape behavior during prolonged training. Rats give up anticipatory avoidance responses to an auditory CS and revert to "freezing" behavior until shock is delivered (Anderson & Nakamura, 1964; Coons, Anderson, & Myers, 1960). No doubt noise-shock contingencies engage the skin defenses, eliciting "flight-freeze" reactions in the rat, and with repeated trials "flight" awaits the impact of the US for some, as yet undefined, reason. Finally, in the Brett study, the thirsty animals in the saccharin and quinine groups had very strong taste stimuli calculated to enhance the action of thirst reduction FB on the nonpreferred taste US. The animals in the bright-noisy groups were just as thirsty but they had *no discriminative taste* calling for FB facilitation.

The saccharin-shock (sham-anosmic) group shown in the upper right of Fig. 7.6 exhibits a pattern similar to that of the saccharin-shock group (anosmic group) shown in the upper left of Fig. 7.5. However, on Day 10, the performance of the anosmic animals is visibly superior to that of the sham anosmic group; i.e., the anosmic rats exhibit greater suppression during the warning period (0–30 sec) and greater consumption during the safe period (31–60 sec) than the animals that can smell the saccharin (Hankins, Rusiniak, & Garcia, 1976). Odor, like noise, is an excellent signal for skin insults. Adding a distal odor CS to the saccharin taste seems to have pushed performance of these sham-anosmic animals in the direction of the bright-noisy (sham-anosmic) group (lower left, Fig. 7.6). Note that both groups give up the strong suppression prior to shock displayed in the early trials.

Finally, the water-shock (anosmic) group exhibits some adaptation to shock; the nadir created by shock on Day 10 is slightly less than on Day 1, and drinking is weakly suppressed during the 0- to 30-sec period. On the water trials (open triangles) of Day 10, rats suppressed drinking during the entire 0- to 60-sec period, indicating that the midpoint timing yielded weak "safety" information in absence of the shock stimulus itself.

V. THE "DRIFT" FROM LEARNING TO INSTINCT

Like nausea, nutritious FB is locked onto taste, and via taste potentiation, onto distal feeding cues in accordance with propositions 2 and 5 in our introduction. Furthermore, the build-up of palatability of food cues can be as gradual and prolonged as the build-up of an aversion for a diet with a low-grade toxin or thiamine deficiency as we stated in proposition 10. The resultant behavior can seem quite bizarre on occasion. Take the well-known phenomenon Breland and Breland (1961) called "instinctive drift." They aptly titled their paper "Misbehavior of

Organisms," a sly reference to B. F. Skinner's volume "Behavior Of Organisms" (refer to Chapter 9 of this volume by Timberlake and Lucas). Instinctive drift was a breakdown in the performance expected by the Brelands and presented them with much the same problem we had in explaining the reversal of selective learning seen in Figs. 7.5 and 7.6.

The Brelands were engaged in *applied* learning; they were manufacturing entertaining behavioral displays for commercial advertising, and along the way they discovered some basic scientific facts. For example, they describe how a pig was "shaped" by operant techniques to take a token in its mouth and deposit it in a toy bank to receive an immediate food reward. For a while, the pig performed the instrumental routine flawlessly, but as time went by, its performance deteriorated. The pig ran eagerly to pick up each dollar but it became reluctant to go to the bank and deposit it cleanly and promptly. Instead the pig dallied, dropped the coin, and repeatedly mouthed it and rooted it around the floor. Finally the pig took as much as 10 min to travel 6 feet and deposit the coin. This problem behavior developed in training successive pigs. Increasing the pig's deprivation made the "pig-headed" misbehavior worse. The advertising exhibit was ruined.

The Brelands described similar behavioral changes in other mammals and birds, explaining that with repeated trials instrumentally trained behavior "drifted" towards instinctive species-specific behavior. For example, a raccoon was first rewarded with food for picking up coins. This preliminary phase went well enough. Next, a container was introduced and the raccoon was required to drop the coin into the container in exchange for food. Then the trouble began. The raccoon seemed unable to let go of the coin. He would rub it against the side of the container, put it in, and pull it out again. However, he would finally release it and receive food. In the final training phase he was given two coins to deposit in the container and operant behavior went completely awry. The raccoon rubbed the two coins together, dipped them into the container, pulled them out, and again rubbed them together. The rubbing behavior delayed food reinforcement and became progressively worse, so that the planned commercial exhibit was finally abandoned. In nature, raccoons rub their food clean, often dipping it in water. Children often toss sugar cubes to wild raccoons near brooks and watch with great glee as the sugar cubes dissolve under this rubbing and dipping behavior.

Gallinaceous birds exhibited similar behaviors. When reinforced with food for pecking at capsules sliding down a ramp, 20% of the chickens trained by the Brelands grabbed the capsules and pounded them on the floor of the cage, as if they were nuts to be cracked. As a result, there was no food reinforcement. Another chicken was required to operate an electric bat to hit a tiny baseball past some toy players to the fence in order to activate the feeder. In the first training phase, a screen was placed between the chicken and the baseball field. All went well initially; the chicken repeatedly batted the ball until she hit the fence, heard the feeder click, and proceeded to eat. The trouble came when the screen was removed to photograph the baseball-playing chicken in action. Instead of going to the food hopper to eat, the chicken became wildly excited, leaped onto the playing field, and pecked at the baseball as if it were a food item attempting to escape. Any farmer's child, familiar with chickens and grasshoppers, would recognize the behavior at once.

The Brelands quickly took advantage of this species-specific behavior. Hungry dabbling ducks that swung their bills from side to side while seining food became "piano players." Hungry chickens that scratch for food became "dancers." A reversal of roles would be too costly in terms of time and effort, though perhaps not impossible. The problem of reinforcing species-specific behavioral patterns with food was classically described by Thorndike (Seligman & Hager, 1972). When reinforced for scratching its jaw with its hind paw in the feline fashion, the stereotypic pattern drifted into a perfunctory wave in the direction of the jaw as the cat focused on the distal stimulus of food rather than on a peripheral itch. There is little doubt that a clever and patient behavioral engineer can train a cat with food reinforcement to deliver a chin-scratch pattern that looks just like one elicited by an itchy jaw. The conceptual crux of the problem is whether a food-reinforced scratch pattern should ever be considered the same as an itch-reduction scratch pattern. We think not: The two behavioral patterns serve different functional ends for the cat no matter how similar they may appear to human observers, and that motivational difference is essential for a complete description of the behavior.

Instinctive drift of operant habits towards species-specific patterns is an incomplete explanation. We do not dispute the Brelands' account; we merely suggest a mechanism for "instinctive drift" from the perspective of the CS–US–FB paradigm. Take the case of the pig, for example. The nutritious FB from the food delivered by the toy bank raises the palatability of the taste US of the token carried in the pig's mouth to the bank slot. Through taste-potentiation, the odor, texture, and aspect of the token become food cues and the hungry pig tries to eat the token rather than drop it down the slot. The animal becomes "addicted" to the token, and the hungrier it becomes the stronger becomes its "token food habit." For raccoons, the value of the coin US in the mouth was enhanced by contingent food reinforcement until it elicited the species-specific feeding pattern and interfered with the operant pattern desired by the Brelands. For chickens, capsules and balls by virtue of the operant connection with food, because food objects in their own right and elicited the gallinaceous feeding patterns directly, thus disrupting the instrumental trip to the food hopper.

Similar "misbehavior" was reported in experimental laboratories dedicated to "pure" science. Hungry pigeons "eat" the key activating the feeder as if the key were grain. But thirsty pigeons try to "drink" the key delivering water (Jenkins & Moore, 1973). Hungry rats will gnaw the lever that delivers the food pellet, particularly during extinction. Moore (1973) pointed out that these reactions resemble Pavlovian conditioned responses rather than Skinnerian "free" operants. But in all these cases, the influence of Darwinian FB upon the hedonic value of taste, distal food cues, and taste-potentiated distal cues, demonstrated by the introductory propositions 2, 4, and 5, respectively, will cause the animals' behavior to drift from an instrumental mode to a consummatory mode with respect to the experimental manipulanda.

It must be pointed out that instrumental responses *do not always* drift in the direction of instinctive patterns. The current often goes the other way. With increased practice and proper training, instinctive fears and reactions diminish and instrumental skills are sharpened, as we all know. Prey and predators can be trained to work together. Instrumental skills honed by the "law of least effort" can also spoil entertaining displays. For example, a trained male goat gave up butting the rear of a fake farmer bending over its pen. The goat gently pushed the dummy with its horns, just far enough to activate the feeder, then at the click of the relay turned and walked across the yard to the feeder.

In one sense, the difference between instrumental behavior and consummation is illusory. There are many ways to obtain food, but there is only one way to eat it. Thus, the former seems plastic and the latter seems fixed. But on closer examination, each instrumental routine proves to be rather fixed, as "selective learning" studies show. The confusion stems from a tendency to view behavior as either learned or instinctive. This distinction is completely spurious; you cannot have one without the other. Recently, Gould and Marler (1987) related how bees and birds gain their marvelous species repertoires through "learning by instinct." Learning itself may be the primary instinct. A voluminous literature on curiosity, exploration, habituation, and play reveals that animals must acquire a "cognitive map" of their territory, or the experimental set-up, before they engage in any other behavior. A neonatal mammal, including a human baby, knows enough at birth to instinctively reject bitter and accept sweet, but it can also learn the opposite reaction in a trial or two. Learning and instinct are two sides of the same behavioral coin.

ACKNOWLEDGMENT

This research was supported by the following grants: USPHS NIH NS11618 and HDO5958. Send requests for reprints to John Garcia, 1950A Chilberg Rd., Mt. Vernon, WA, 98273.

REFERENCES

Anderson, N. H., & Nakamura, C. Y. (1964). Avoidance decrement in avoidance conditioning. *Journal of Comparative and Physiological Psychology, 57,* 196–204.

Bermudez-Rattoni, F., Forthman Quick, D. L., Sanchez, M. A., Perez, J. L., & Garcia, J. (in press). Odor and taste aversions conditioned in anesthetized rats. *Behavioral Neuroscience.*

Bernstein, I. L. (1985). Learned food aversions in the progression of cancer and its treatment. *Annals of the New York Academy of Sciences*, *443*, 365–380.

Best, P. J., Best, M. R., & Henggeler, S. (1977). The contribution of environmental non-ingestive cues in conditioning with aversive internal consequences. In L. M. Barker, M. R. Best, & M. Domjan (Eds.), *Learning mechanisms in food selection* (pp. 371–393). Waco, TX: Baylor University Press.

Breland, K., & Breland, M. (1961). The misbehavior of organisms. *American Psychologist*, *16*, 681–684.

Brett, L. P. (1977). *Experimental extensions of the cue-consequence aversive conditioning paradigm.* Unpublished doctoral dissertation, University of California, Los Angeles.

Brett, L. P., Hankins, W. G., & Garcia, J. (1976). Prey-lithium aversions. III. Buteo hawks. *Behavioral Biology*, *17*, 87–98.

Buchwald, N. A., Garcia, J., Feder, B. H., & Bach-y-Rita, G. (1964). Ionizing radiation as a perceptual and aversive stimulus. II. Electrophysiological studies. In T. J. Haley, & R. S. Snyder (Eds.), *The second international symposium on the responses of the nervous system to ionizing radiation* (pp. 688–699). Boston, MA: Little, Brown.

Burešová, O., & Bureš, J. (1973). Cortical and subcortical components of the conditioned saccharin aversion. *Physiology and Behavior*, *11*, 435–439.

Cabanac, M. (1979). Sensory pleasure. *Quarterly Review of Biology*, *54*, 1–29.

Clarke, J. C., Westbrook, R. F., & Irwin, J. (1979). Potentiation instead of overshadowing in the pigeon. *Behavioral and Neural Biology*, *25*, 18–29.

Coil, J. D., Rogers, R. C., Garcia, J., & Novin, D. (1978). Conditioned taste aversions: Vagal and circulatory mediation of the toxic unconditioned stimulus. *Behavioral Biology*, *24*, 509–519.

Colwill, R. M., & Rescorla, R. A. (1985a). Postconditioning devaluation of a reinforcer affects instrumental responding. *Journal of Experimental Psychology: Animal Behavior Processes*, *11*, 120–132.

Colwill, R. M., & Rescorla, R. A. (1985b). Instrumental responding remains sensitive to reinforcer devaluation after extensive training. *Journal of Experimental Psychology: Animal Behavior Processes*, *11*, 520–536.

Coons, E. E., Anderson, N. H., & Myers, A. K. (1960). Disappearance of avoidance responding during continued training. *Journal of Comparative and Physiological Psychology*, *53*, 290–292.

Darwin, C. (1859). *The origin of species by means of natural selection: Or, the preservation of favored races in the struggle for life.* Reprinted, 1936. New York: The Modern Library.

Darwin, C. (1871). *The descent of man and selection in relation to sex.* Reprinted, 1936. New York: The Modern Library.

Deems, D. A., Oetting, R. L., Sherman, J. E., & Garcia, J. (1986). Hungry, but not thirsty, rats prefer flavors paired with ethanol. *Physiology and Behavior*, *36*, 141–144.

Dickerson, A., Nicholas, D. J., & Adams, C. D. (1983). The effect of the instrumental training contingency on susceptibility to reinforcer devaluation. *Quarterly Journal of Experimental Psychology*, *35B*, 35–51.

Ellins, S. R., Cramer, R. E., & Whitmore, C. (1985). Taste potentiation of auditory aversions in rats: A case for spatial contiguity. *Journal of Comparative Psychology*, *99*, 108–111.

Ellins, S. R., & Von Kluge, S. (1987). Pre-exposure and extinction effects of lithium chloride induced taste-potentiated aversions for spatially contiguous auditory food cues in rats. *Behavioral Neuroscience*, *101*, 164–169.

Finger, T. E., & Morita, Y. (1985). Two gustatory systems: Facial and vagal gustatory nuclei have different brainstem connections. *Science*, *227*, 776–778.

Galef, B. G., & Osborne, B. (1978). Novel taste facilitation of the association of visual cues with toxicosis in rats. *Journal of Comparative and Physiological Psychology*, *92*, 907–916.

Garcia, J. (1988). Food for Tolman: Cognitions and cathexes in concert. In T. Archer, & L. G. Nilsson (Eds.), *Aversion, avoidance and anxiety: Perspectives on aversively motivated behavior*. Hillsdale, NJ: Lawrence Erlbaum Associates.

Garcia, J., Ervin, F. R., Yorke, G. H., & Koelling, R. A. (1967). Conditioning with delayed vitamin injections. *Science, 155*, 716–718.

Garcia, J., & Hankins, W. G. (1975). The evolution of bitter and the acquisition of toxiphobia. In D. Denton, & J. Coghlan (Eds.), *Olfaction and taste* (Vol. 5, pp. 39–41). New York: Academic Press.

Garcia, J., & Hankins, W. G. (1977). On the origin of food aversion paradigms. In L. Barker, M. Domjan, & M. Best (Eds.), *Learning mechanisms in food selection* (pp. 3–19). Waco, TX: Baylor University Press.

Garcia, J., Hankins, W. G., & Rusiniak, K. W. (1974). Behavioral regulation of the milieu interne in man and rat. *Science, 185*, 824–831.

Garcia, J., Hankins, W. G., Robinson, J. H., & Vogt, J. L. (1972). Baitshyness: Tests of CS–US mediation. *Physiology and Behavior, 3*, 807–810.

Garcia, J., & Holder, M. D. (1985). Time, space and value. *Human Neurobiology, 4*, 81–89.

Garcia, J., Kimeldorf, D. J., & Hunt, E. L. (1956). Spatial avoidance behavior in the rat as a result of exposure to ionizing radiation. *British Journal of Radiation Research, 5*, 79–87.

Garcia, J., & Koelling, R. A. (1966). The relation of cue to consequence in avoidance learning. *Psychonomic Science, 5*, 123–124.

Garcia, J., & Koelling, R. A. (1967). A comparison of aversions induced by X-rays, drugs, and toxins. *Radiation Research Supplement, 7*, 439–450.

Garcia, J., Kovner, R., & Green, K. F. (1970). Cue properties vs. palatability of flavors in avoidance learning. *Psychonomic Science, 20*, 313–314.

Garcia, J., Lasiter, P. S., Bermudez-Rattoni, F., & Deems, D. A. (1985). A general theory of aversion learning. *Annals of the New York Academy of Sciences, 443*, 8–21.

Garcia, J., McGowan, B. K., & Green, K. F. (1972). Biological constraints on conditioning. In A. H. Black, & W. F. Prokasy (Eds.), *Classical conditioning II: Current research and theory*, (pp. 3–27). New York: Appleton-Century-Crofts.

Garcia, J., McGowan, B. K., Ervin, F. R., & Koelling, R. A. (1968). Cues: Their relative effectiveness as a function of the reinforcer. *Science, 160*, 794–795.

Gould, J. L., & Marler, P. (1987). Learning by instinct. *Scientific American, 256*, 74–85.

Green, K. F., & Garcia, J. (1971). Recuperation from illness: Flavor enhancement in rats. *Science, 173*, 749–751.

Hamilton, R. B., & Norgren, R. (1984). Central projections of gustatory nerves in the rat. *Journal of Comparative Neurology, 222*, 560–577.

Hankins, W. G., Rusiniak, K. W., & Garcia, J. (1976). Dissociation of odor and taste in shock-avoidance learning. *Behavioral Biology, 18*, 345–358.

Harris, L. J., Clay, J., Hargreaves, F. J., & Ward, A. (1933). Appetite and choice of diet. The ability of the vitamin B deficient rat to discriminate between diets containing and lacking the vitamin. *Proceedings of the Royal Society of London, 63*, 161–190.

Herrick, C. J. (1948). *The brain of the tiger salamander.* Illinois: University of Chicago Press.

Holman, E. W. (1975). Some conditions for the dissociation of consummatory and instrumental behavior in rats. *Learning and Motivation, 6*, 358–366.

Jenkins, H. M., & Moore, B. R. (1973). The form of the auto-shaped response with food or water reinforcers. *Journal of the Experimental Analysis of Behavior, 20*, 163–181.

Kamin, L. J. (1969). Predictability, surprise, attention and conditioning. In B. Campbell, & R. M. Church (Eds.), *Punishment and aversive behavior* (pp. 279–296). New York: Appleton-Century-Crofts.

Kimeldorf, D. J., & Hunt, E. L. (1965). *Ionizing radiation: Neural function and behavior.* New York: Academic Press.

Lorenz, K. (1937). Uber die bildung des instinktbegriffes. *Naturwiss, 25*, 289–331.

Moore, B. R. (1973). The role of directed Pavlovian reactions in simple instrumental learning in the pigeon. In R. A. Hinde, & J. Stevenson-Hinde (Eds.), *Constraints on learning: Limitations and predispositions* (pp. 159–188). New York: Academic Press.

Nachman, M., Rauschenberger, J., & Ashe, J. (1977). Studies of learned aversions using non-gustatory stimuli. In L. M. Barker, M. R. Best, & M. Domjan (Eds.), *Learning mechanisms in food selection* (pp. 395–417). Waco, TX: Baylor University Press.

Palmerino, C. C., Rusiniak, K. W., & Garcia, J. (1980). Flavor-illness aversions: The peculiar roles of odor and taste in memory for poison. *Science, 208*, 753–755.

Pavlov, I. P. (1927). *Conditioned reflexes*. Oxford, England: Oxford University Press.

Pelchat, M. L., Grill, H. J., Rozin, P., & Jacobs, J. (1983). Quality of acquired responses to taste by Rattus norvegicus depends on type of associated discomfort. *Journal of Comparative Psychology, 97*, 140–153.

Poulton, E. B. (1887). The experimental proof of the protective value of color and marking in insects in reference to their vertebrate enemies. *Proceedings of the Zoological Society of London*, pp. 191–274.

Revusky, S. H., & Bedarf, E. W. (1967). Association of illness with the prior consumption of novel foods. *Science, 155*, 219–220.

Richter, C. P. (1943). Total self-regulatory functions in animals and human beings. *Harvey Lecture Series, 38*, 63–103.

Roll, D. L., & Smith, J. C. (1972). Conditioned taste aversion in anesthetized rats. In M. E. P. Seligman, & J. L. Hager (Eds.), *Biological boundaries of learning* (pp. 98–102). New York: Appleton-Century-Crofts.

Rusiniak, K. W. (1976). *Roles of olfaction and taste in appetitive and consummatory behavior during illness aversion conditioning*. Unpublished doctoral dissertation, University of California, Los Angeles.

Rusiniak, K. W., Hankins, W. G., Garcia, J., & Brett, L. P. (1979). Flavor-illness aversions: Potentiation of odor by taste in rats. *Behavioral and Neural Biology, 25*, 1–17.

Rusiniak, K. W., Palmerino, C. C., Rice, A. G., Forthman, D. L., & Garcia, J. (1982). Flavor-illness aversions: Potentiation of odor by taste with toxin but not shock in rats. *Journal of Comparative and Physiological Psychology, 96*, 527–539.

Seligman, M. E. P., & Hager, J. L. (1972). *Biological boundaries of learning*. New York: Appleton-Century-Crofts.

Sherman, J. E., Hickis, D. F., Rice, A. G., Rusiniak, K. W., & Garcia, J. (1983). Preferences and aversions for stimuli paired with ethanol in hungry rats. *Animal Learning and Behavior, 11*, 101–106.

Terman, G. W., Shavit, Y., Lewis, J. W., Cannon, J. T., & Liebeskind, J. C. (1984). Intrinsic mechanisms of pain inhibition: Activation by stress. *Science, 226*, 1270–1277.

Wilson, C. J., Sherman, J. E., & Holman, E. W. (1981). Aversion to the reinforcer differentially affects conditioned reinforcement and instrumental responding. *Journal of Experimental Psychology: Animal Behavior Processes, 7*, 165–174.

8 Schedule-Induced Polydipsia: Is the Rat a Small Furry Human? (An Analysis of an Animal Model of Human Alcoholism)

Anthony L. Riley
The American University

Cora Lee Wetherington
University of North Carolina at Charlotte

I.   INTRODUCTION

Despite concerns regarding the use of animal models of human pathology (Bond, 1984; Dole, 1986; Keehn, 1979, 1986; Kuker-Reines, 1982), a wide range of human conditions find an analogue in animal research (Bond, 1984; Gross, 1973; Keehn, 1979; 1986; Maser & Seligman, 1977). From depression (Seligman, 1975), schizophrenia (Lyon & Nielsen, 1979), toxicology (Riley & Tuck, 1985a), anxiety (Treit, 1985), obesity (Storlein, 1984) and drug addiction (Singer & Wallace, 1984), the search for an encompassing animal model has occupied considerable research efforts, primarily because similar research using human subjects cannot be conducted under adequate control conditions or is simply too intrusive to be considered ethical (Bond, 1984; Colotla, 1981). In few places has this effort to establish an animal model been as extensive as in the specific pathology of alcoholism (Colotla, 1981; Eriksson, Sinclair, & Kiianmaa, 1980; Forsander & Eriksson, 1972; Gilbert, 1978; Mello, 1973, 1985).

With respect to alcoholism, animal models have been utilized to examine a range of issues surrounding alcohol use and abuse. Animals have been used to ascertain the physiological effects and pharmacological consequences of alcohol, alcohol dependence and withdrawal, tolerance and drug interactions. Animals have also been used in an attempt to illuminate the behavioral concommitants and causes of alcoholism. These pharmacological and behavioral questions have generated a wide range of specific models. In these models, animals receive the alcohol through a variety of procedures, e.g., by forced inhalation and gastric intubation, through a sustained ethanol release tube (SERT), as part of general fluid intake, through liquid diets and by oral, intragastric and intravenous self-administration (Gilbert, 1978; Mello, 1985; Pohorecky, 1981; Samson, 1987).

II. CRITERIA FOR ANIMAL MODELS OF HUMAN ALCOHOLISM

In an attempt to evaluate the efficacy of these various paradigms as animals models of alcoholism, a number of criteria have been offered (Cicero, 1980; Dole, 1986; Falk, 1982; Falk & Samson, 1976; Falk, Samson, & Winger, 1972; Gilbert, 1978; Lester & Freed, 1972, 1973; Mello, 1985; Pororecky, 1981). Although the specific components of any list of criteria varies, some components are common to all (or most). Specifically, within the putative model:

1. Animals should orally ingest alcohol excessively and chronically.

2. The amount consumed should be sufficient to produce blood alcohol levels (BAL) analogous to those seen in an alcoholic. Imbedded in this criterion is the requirement that the elevated blood levels should be maintained for a large portion of the day, i.e., the increases should not reflect a transient increase in BAL.

3. The amount of alcohol consumed should have intoxicating effects, i.e., nontrivial amounts should be consumed.

4. Alcohol should be preferred to water or other solutions of equal value and palatability.

5. Alcohol should be reinforcing, i.e., as evidenced by responding or working for alcohol.

6. There should be unequivocal evidence of physical dependence following chronic exposure to the alcohol.

7. Tolerance (both pharmacokinetic and pharmacodynamic) should develop.

8. Food and alcohol should be separate and concurrently available such that alcohol consumption cannot be construed as due to nutritional need.

9. There should be clear biomedical complications resulting from alcohol exposure.

10. The experimental procedure underlying the animal model should have an elective aspect, i.e., alcohol intake should be voluntary. Events such as shock avoidance or food delivery should not be contingent on alcohol consumption.

Similar to any list of criteria by which a phenomenon is being evaluated, few if any of the animal models of alcoholism satisfy all the stated criteria. Some models generate high BALs, insure physical dependence, produce tolerance, and generate alcohol intake independent of hunger, but are neither oral nor elective in nature (e.g., forced inhalation, gastric intubation, and SERT). Others are oral in nature, produce clear evidence of the reinforcing nature of alcohol and insure physical dependence and tolerance, yet involve supplying the alcohol in the food supply, making consumption of alcohol necessary for nutrients and thereby nonelective (e.g., adulterated or liquid diet models; though, see Gill, France, & Amit, 1986; Samson, 1987). Others appear elective in nature, generate high levels of consumption, produce high BALs and insure dependence and tolerance, but bypass the oral route, the route by which humans intake alcohol (e.g., intragastric and intravenous self administration; though see Mello, 1985 for a criticism of this criterion).

III. SCHEDULE-INDUCED POLYDIPSIA

Although each of the aforementioned models satisfies some of the noted criteria, it appears that none of the models addresses all of them. In fact, most of the models fail to satisfy two specific criteria, that is, oral consumption and elective (or voluntary) intake. Although insisting that a model satisfy all or most of a list of criteria may be inappropriately demanding, a paradigm introduced by Falk seemingly satisfies each of the criteria of an animal model and specifically provides an oral, elective baseline (Falk, 1961, 1964, 1969, 1971, 1977). This model is termed schedule-induced polydipsia (SIP) and refers to the fact that mildly food-deprived animals given free access to water while receiving food deliveries on a spaced feeding schedule drink voluminous amounts of water during experimental sessions, typically in the period immediately following each pellet delivery (see Christian, Schaeffer, & King, 1977; Freed, Zec, & Mendelson, 1977). These characteristics of SIP are shown in Fig. 8.1. As illustrated, the amount of water consumed under the spaced feeding schedule far exceeds that consumed when animals are given the same number of pellets in a single massed meal, i.e., non-spaced (left-hand panel), and drinking appears primarily restricted to the first half of the interpellet interval and highest in the 5–10 sec period immediately following pellet delivery (right-hand panel).

In the first reported occurrence of SIP (Falk, 1961), food deprived rats were given food for bar pressing on a variable-interval 1-min schedule. During the schedule, water was continuously available. Although the animals were not water-deprived and fluid consumption had no programmed consequences, subjects drank from 3-4 times the amount of water during the 3.14-hour session than they nor-

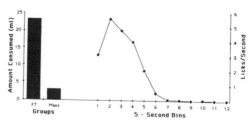

FIG. 8.1.   Mean consumption (ml) of water for subjects receiving spaced (Group FT) and massed (Group Mass) food deliveries (left panel). The post-pellet temporal distribution of licking (licks/sec) for subjects receiving spaced food deliveries (right panel). All data are from the 15th day of exposure to the feeding condition, i.e., at asymptote.

mally drank in a 24-hour period when given free access to food and water. Since this original demonstration, it has been reported that schedule-induced polydipsia can be affected by a range of manipulations, e.g., the specific schedule of food delivery (Falk, 1966a; Riley, Wetherington, Delamater, Peele, & Dacanay, 1985; Roper, 1980; Wetherington, 1979), concurrent availability of other behaviors such as wheel running (Roper, 1978; Segal, 1969; Staddon & Ayres, 1975; Wetherington & Riley, 1986), size, number and nutritional constituents of the delivered pellets (Christian, 1976; Couch, 1974; Flory, 1971), available fluid such as quinine or saccharin (Falk, 1966b; Segal & Deadwyler, 1965; Valenstein, Cox, & Kakolewski, 1967), degree of food deprivation (Falk, 1969; Freed & Hymowitz, 1972), period of the interpellet interval in which fluid is available (Gilbert, 1974), physiological and pharmacological intervention (Chapman & Richardson, 1974; Falk, 1964; Kulkosky, Moe, Woods, & Riley, 1975; Riley & Wetherington, 1987; Wayner & Greenberg, 1972; Yoburn & Glusman, 1982), and subject examined (Shanab & Peterson, 1969). The theoretical interpretations for this drinking behavior are as numerous as these parametric manipulations (see Christian et al., 1977; Falk, 1969; Staddon, 1977; Wetherington, 1982). For example, SIP has been described as being elicited by periods associated with the absence of food (Lashley & Rosellini, 1980; Shurtleff, Delamater, & Riley, 1983), operantly reinforced by its contiguous relationship to food (Clark, 1962), maintained by removing the animal from a period negatively correlated with food (Keehn & Colotla, 1971; Staddon, 1977), elicited by a dry mouth accompanying food consumption (Stein, 1964), a displacement activity occurring when eating is blocked by the unavailability of food (Falk, 1971) and as a food-related behavior sensitized by repeated food presentations (Wetherington, 1982; Wetherington & Riley, 1986). Independent of the effects of the parametric manipulations or the theoretical underpinnings of SIP, one fact remains, specifically, animals drink voluminous amounts of water when given spaced presentations of food.

More importantly, they will also drink alcohol under similar conditions (Holman & Myers, 1968; Lester, 1961; Mello & Mendelson, 1971; Senter & Sinclair, 1967). For example, Lester (1961) reported that if alcohol was made available in place of water during spaced food deliveries, animals would consume alcohol. Further, Falk and his colleagues (Falk, Samson & Winger, 1972) demonstrated that not only would alcohol be consumed, but like water it would be consumed to excess (e.g., up to 8–14 g/kg) and in amounts that generated BALs as high as 300 mg/dl (average 100 mg/dl). Since these original investigations, the induction of alcohol consumption by scheduled food deliveries has been replicated and extended (Colotla, 1981; Falk & Samson, 1976; Falk, Samson, & Tang, 1973; Gilbert, 1978; Hawkins, Schrot, Githens, & Everett, 1972; McMillan, Leander, Ellis, Lucot, & Frye, 1976; Meisch & Thompson, 1972; Mello & Mendelson, 1971; Ogata, Ogata, Mendelson, & Mello, 1972a, 1972b; Samson & Falk, 1974, 1975; Tang & Falk, 1977). These findings are important for the potential use of this procedure as an animal model of alcoholism. As described, animals drink alcohol under spaced food deliveries, i.e., the animal orally self-administers alcohol. This intake is in excess and produces intoxication. Falk and Samson (1976) have demonstrated clear evidence that as a result of spaced feedings animals shift their preference to alcohol (in relation to specific concentrations of sucrose). Meisch and colleagues (Meisch, 1975; Meisch & Thompson, 1972, 1974) have noted that spaced feedings increase the reinforcing value of alcohol (see also Falk, 1982). Further, rats maintained under a schedule sufficient to generate SIP develop tolerance to alcohol (Samson & Falk, 1974) and display clear evidence of withdrawal signs, e.g., audiogenic seizures (Falk & Samson, 1976; Falk et al., 1972; McMillan et al., 1976; Samson & Falk, 1974, 1975; Tang & Falk, 1979; though see Heintzelman, Best, & Senter, 1976). Finally, intake is elective (Falk & Samson, 1976). Animals self-administer alcohol when there is no clear fluid deficiency and when there are no reinforcers such as the presentation of food or the removal of shock contingent upon the consumption of alcohol.

IV. THE ELECTIVE NATURE OF SIP

Although SIP does appear to meet the requirements of an animal model of alcoholism, one issue remains puzzling, i.e., the elective nature of SIP. As noted by others, SIP is elective in nature with animals voluntarily choosing and consuming the intoxicating amounts of alcohol. That animals voluntarily consume alcohol during SIP is in contrast to other procedures in which animals are given free access to alcohol. In other free-choice situations, alcohol intake is limited and often avoided such that animals do not consume intoxicating amounts of al-

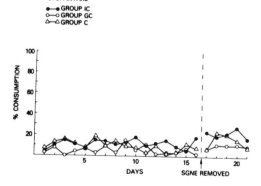

FIG. 8.2.   The mean percentage of total intake as alcohol (10%) for Groups IC (individually caged), GC (Group caged) and C (colonially caged) given a concurrent choice of water, alcohol and a sweetened alcohol mixture (SGNE). On Day 17, the SGNE mixture was removed. From Kulkosky et al. (1980). Reprinted by permission of the Psychonomic Society.

cohol and do not become physically dependent (Deutsch & Eisner, 1977; Mello, 1985; Myers, 1966; Myers & Veale, 1972; Pohorecky, 1981; Samson, 1987; Wilson, 1972). This general avoidance of alcohol under free-feeding conditions is illustrated in Fig. 8.2, which depicts the percentage of alcohol consumed by individually (Group IC), grouped (Group GC) and colonially (Group C) caged rats given a concurrent choice of water, ethanol (10%) and a solution of saccharin/glucose/NaCl/ethanol (SGNE) (Kulkosky, Zellner, Hyson, & Riley, 1980). Under none of the three housing conditions was alcohol preferred (average alcohol preference approximately 10%). Although it might be expected that little alcohol would be consumed because of the concurrent availability of the sweetened mixture, i.e., SGNE; as illustrated there was little change in alcohol preference when the sweetened solution was removed.

Such avoidance of alcohol outside the SIP paradigm may be based on a number of factors:

1. *Aversive taste*—As noted by Myers (1966) and Myers and Veale (1972), animals do not generally prefer the taste of alcohol, an unconditioned aversion presumably based on the aversive sensory properties of alcohol and one sufficient to limit alcohol intake. The fact that in Fig. 8.2 alcohol is avoided by all groups on its initial exposure to the subjects (i.e., on Day 1) is consistent with such an unconditioned aversion.

2. *Postingestional metabolic consequences*—Another explanation for the rat's failure to consume alcohol under free-choice conditions stems from the fact that the postingestional consequences of alcohol may be aversive. That is, even if alcohol is consumed on an initial exposure, the postingestional effects of alcohol could be sufficiently aversive to condition an aversion to the taste of alcohol (Garcia & Ervin, 1968; Revusky & Garcia, 1970; Riley & Tuck, 1985b; Rozin & Kalat, 1971). Evidence for this possibility comes from two sources. In unpublished work from our lab (see lower panels, Fig. 8.3), we have noted that if rats drink limited quantities on their first exposure to alcohol (presumably due to its aversive taste), they will increase its consumption on subsequent exposures (possibly due to habituation to the taste cues or an acquired preference). On the other hand, if consumption on the initial exposure is substantial, e.g., greater than 10 ml, these animals will decrease consumption on subsequent exposures (see upper panels, Fig. 8.3), suggesting that when alcohol is drunk at levels possibly exceeding metabolic capacity (Deutsch, Walton, & Thiel, 1978; Kulkosky, 1978, 1979; Kulkosky & Cornell, 1979; Pohorecky, 1981), the aversive postingestional consequences of alcohol condition an aversion. It is interesting in this context that subjects who drink little alcohol on its initial exposure and increase alcohol intake on subsequent exposures eventually decrease consumption. Again, it is as if when some maximal level of alcohol is exceeded, the aversive postingestional consequences affect subsequent choice. More direct evidence for the aversiveness of alcohol

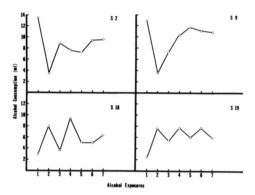

FIG. 8.3.   Mean consumption (ml) of alcohol for four water-deprived subjects given 20-min access to alcohol (7%) every fourth day for seven consecutive alcohol exposures.

(and for the possible role of the postingestional consequences in conditioning aversions to the taste of alcohol) is provided by the work on the ability of exogenous-
ly administered alcohol to condition an aversion in water-deprived rats (Baker
& Cannon, 1982; Cappell, LeBlanc, & Endrenyi, 1973; Davison & House, 1975;
Eckardt, Skurdal & Brown, 1974; Lester, Nachman, & LeMagnen, 1970). As
illustrated in Fig. 8.4, doses of alcohol ranging from 2 to 5 g/kg were all effective in conditioning an aversion to saccharin when saccharin consumption was
followed 15 min later by an injection of alcohol. In fact, the aversions induced
by the two higher doses of alcohol were similar in strength and the rate of acquisition as the aversions induced by the emetic LiCl (Kulkosky, Sickel, & Riley,
1980).

Thus, whether the taste of alcohol is aversive or whether the postingestional
consequences of alcohol are sufficiently aversive to condition an aversion, a number of factors appear to be acting to limit alcohol ingestion under free-choice conditions (Baker & Cannon, 1982). In this context, therefore, it is surprising that
alcohol is so readily and excessively consumed under another elective, voluntary
procedure, i.e., SIP. Rats' avoidance of alcohol consumption under free-choice
conditions raises the question of whether SIP is truly elective.

V.   THE INTERACTION OF SIP AND CONDITIONED
TASTE AVERSIONS

Early work from our lab addressed this question directly by examining the effects of conditioned taste aversion training on the schedule-induced consumption
of saccharin (Riley, Lotter, & Kulkosky, 1979). Taste aversion conditioning, i.e.,
pairing a taste with toxicosis, generally reduces acceptance of the taste. If animals

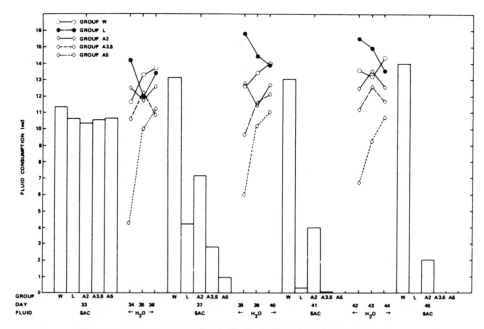

FIG. 8.4.   Mean consumption (ml) of saccharin (SAC) over repeated conditioning trials and of water (H2O) over repeated water-recovery sessions for rats receiving injections of distilled water (Group W), LiCl (Group L) or alcohol at 2 g/kg (Group A2), 3.5 g/kg (Group A3.5) and 5 g/kg (Group A5). From Kulkosky et al. (1980). Reprinted by permission of Pergamon Press.

continue to consume a poison-associated solution under the SIP procedure, this would argue against the view that SIP was voluntary. There is no logical bases for assuming that animals would voluntarily choose to drink such tastes. In a direct test of this, animals were given saccharin in place of water during spaced food sessions in which they received food pellets independently of their behavior on a fixed-time 60-sec schedule. Immediately following the session, animals were given an injection of either the emetic LiCl (1.8 mEq, .15M LiCl) or the saline vehicle. Prior to presenting the saccharin solution, all animals were displaying high levels of SIP, drinking on average approximately 25 ml of water. When saccharin initially replaced water, animals continued to display high levels of SIP (see Day 14, Fig. 8.5). On the following exposure to saccharin on the SIP baseline, SIP was markedly affected in subjects that had received the LiCl injection following saccharin consumption, reducing to approximately 20% of the water baseline and 30% of the amount of saccharin consumed by subjects that had not received the prior pairing of saccharin and LiCl, i.e., nonpoisoned controls. Although clearly affected by aversion conditioning, recovery of schedule-induced drinking when LiCl no longer followed saccharin consumption was very rapid.

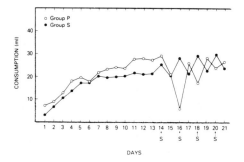

FIG. 8.5. Mean consumption (ml) during polydipsia acquisition (water only) and subsequent alternating saccharin (S) or water presentations. Subjects in Group P were injected with LiCl following saccharin consumption on Day 14. Subjects in Group S were injected with physiological saline on this day. From Riley et al. (1979). Reprinted by permission of the Psychonomic Society.

That is, when saccharin was presented again on Day 18 consumption had already recovered to water baseline, and by the third postconditioning saccharin exposure consumption was at nonpoisoned control levels. This rapid recovery of drinking a poison-associated taste is in marked contrast to the generally slow recovery of drinking poison-associated tastes under water deprivation or under ad libitum, feeding and drinking conditions (Barnett, 1963; Colby & Smith, 1977; Elkins, 1973; Grote & Brown, 1973; Rzoska, 1953). For example, Grote and Brown (1973) have reported that under water deprivation 14 daily exposures to saccharin were necessary before saccharin consumption had recovered to its prepoisoned baseline. Under nondeprived drinking conditions, aversions were still evident after 27 nonpoisoned saccharin exposures. In comparison to these examples, the rapid recovery of drinking poison-associated solutions under SIP suggests that the procedure of spaced feedings induces drinking in a manner sufficient to override or mask the display of the aversion to saccharin when saccharin is no longer being paired with LiCl.

Although drinking poison-associated solutions do appear to recover faster under schedules of spaced food deliveries (as compared to water-deprived and non water-deprived drinking), procedural differences between the various studies examining the effects of taste aversions on drinking make it difficult to conclude that the differential effects are a function of the spaced food deliveries under the SIP baseline. For example, the various studies differ in taste solutions, aversive agent, and number of conditioning trials, factors all of which could affect the level of aversion conditioning and, consequently, the effects of aversions on drinking. When direct comparisons of the effects of taste aversions on SIP were made to the effects of taste aversions on drinking under water deprivation (Riley, Hyson, Baker, & Kulkosky, 1980), the insensitivity of SIP to conditioned taste aversions was still apparent. Specifically, following the acquisition of drinking under

SIP and under water deprivation, saccharin was substituted for water during the session; that is, animals were given saccharin in place of water during either the spaced feedings sessions (Group SIP) or the daily 20-min fluid access period (i.e., under water deprivation; Group WD). Immediately following the session, subjects were injected with LiCl or the saline vehicle. This conditioning procedure was repeated every other day until five conditioning trials had been administered. As illustrated in Fig. 8.6, when compared to the effects of taste aversions on drinking under water deprivation, consumption of the poison-associated taste under spaced feedings was less affected during acquisition of the aversion and recovered significantly faster when its consumption was no longer associated with LiCl. It is interesting in this context that this insensitivity was still present when the effects of taste aversions on drinking during spaced feedings and massed feedings were compared (see Riley et al., 1980). Specifically, animals were given a single food pellet once a minute for 60 min (i.e., Group SIP) or all their pellets in a single massed meal (i.e., a prandial drinking condition; Group PD). Once drinking had stabilized under the two feeding conditions, saccharin was substituted for water and the animals were injected with LiCl immediately following the session. As illustrated in Fig. 8.7, similar to the comparison to drinking under water deprivation SIP was less affected during acquisition of aversions and faster to recover once conditioning was terminated than drinking under the prandial feeding condition. These data suggest that the relative insensitivity of SIP in relation to water deprivation was not a function of food deprivation or the presence of food (factors also present in the prandial feeding condition). Such a comparison further suggests that the relative insensitivity of SIP to taste aversions is a function of the strong tendency to drink following pellet delivery, again a tendency sufficient to override taste aversions and a tendency which argues against an elective interpretation of SIP.

This tendency to drink is inferred from the fact that animals continue to consume poison-associated tastes and that if SIP is suppressed by conditioning its recovery is significantly faster than under other drinking paradigms. This tendency is reflected in other ways as well. For example, animals given repeated pairings of saccharin and LiCl under spaced feedings eventually decrease consumption of that solution although the probability of initiating licking following the delivery of a pellet (i.e., bout probability) remains functionally unaffected and high. Further, licking immediately following pellet delivery is maintained at or near prepoisoned levels even when overall saccharin consumption has been dramatically reduced by repeated conditioning trials (Riley, Wetherington, Wachsman, Fishman, & Kautz, 1988). Such weak effects of conditioned taste aversions on components of elicited behaviors have been noted by others (see Brett, Hankins, & Garcia, 1976; Gay, Leaf, & Arble, 1975; Gustavson, Garcia, Hankins, & Rusiniak, 1974; Johnston, Zahorik, Immler, & Zakon, 1978; Langley, 1981; Peters, 1983; Reidinger & Mason, 1986).

Throughout the discussion of the relative insensitivity of SIP to taste aversions, it has been assumed that aversions were in fact being acquired on the SIP

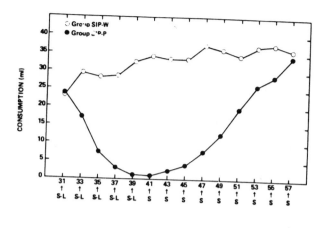

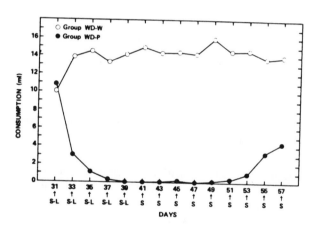

FIG. 8.6. Mean consumption (ml) of saccharin under schedule-induced polydipsia (Groups SIP-P and SIP-W; top graph) and water deprivation (Groups WD-P and WD-W; bottom graph) during conditioning (S-L) and extinction (S). Subjects were either injected with LiCl during conditioning (P) or were given the saline vehicle (W). From Riley et al. (1980). Reprinted by permission of the Psychonomic Society.

baseline, but that the tendency to drink induced by the spaced pellet deliveries masked or overrode the display of the aversion. Another interpretation for the relatively weaker aversions under SIP is that for some as yet undetermined reason aversions are only weakly acquired under such a schedule of food delivery (possibly due to the initially large amounts of fluid consumed under SIP, a factor known to affect aversion conditioning, see Archer & Sjoden, 1979; Braveman & Crane, 1977; Deutsch, 1978). Accordingly, the weaker taste aversions under SIP would not be due to a failure of the aversion to be displayed because of the strong tendency to drink elicited by pellet delivery. This interpretation then would

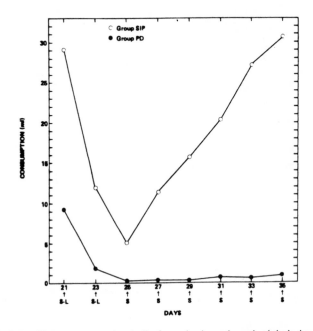

FIG. 8.7.   Mean consumption (ml) of saccharin under schedule-induced polydipsia (Groups SIP) and massed feeding (prandial drinking; Group PD) during conditioning (S-L) and extinction (S). All subjects were injected with LiCl during conditioning. From Hyson et al. (1981). Reprinted by permission of the Psychonomic Society.

not necessitate any conclusions regarding the voluntary or elective nature of SIP. In a test of whether aversions are masked under SIP or simply not acquired as strongly as under other drinking paradigms, Hyson, Sickel, Kulkosky, and Riley (1981) examined the effects of aversion established off the SIP baseline (e.g., under water deprivation) on SIP and compared these effects to those on prandial drinking. If the relative insensitivity of SIP to taste aversions reflects the acquisition of weak aversions under SIP, aversions established off baseline should markedly affect SIP and in a manner similar to the effects of taste aversions on prandial drinking. On the other hand, if the insensitivity of SIP is a function of the overriding tendency to drink, SIP and prandial drinking should be differentially affected by off-baseline aversion conditioning. In their report, aversions to saccharin were first established in water-deprived animals receiving either one, two, or four pairings of saccharin and LiCl. Once aversions were established, the subjects were adapted to a spaced (SIP) or massed (PD) feeding baseline. Under SIP, animals were given one pellet once a minute for 60 min. Under the prandial feeding condition, animals were given all 60 pellets at once in a single massed meal. Once drinking had stabilized, the poison-associated saccharin solution was substituted for water under the two feeding conditions. As illustrated in Fig. 8.8, consumption was clearly affected under both conditions with subjects in all groups reducing consumption on both feeding baselines (compare consumption on the first extinction trial to the amount of water consumed during water baseline under both spaced and massed feedings). The degree of suppression, however, was different under SIP and PD. Specifically, subjects receiving saccharin under SIP displayed weaker aversions on the first trial (for subjects having received only one conditioning trial, i.e., SIP-1 vs. PD-1). Also, recovery of drinking under the SIP baseline when saccharin was no longer associated with LiCl was significantly faster than under the PD condition for all groups. It is important to note that these differential effects of aversions on the two baselines could not reflect the differential acquisition of aversions in that all aversions were established under identical conditions (i.e., in the home cage under

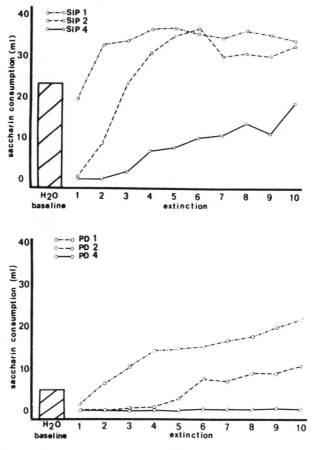

FIG. 8.8   Mean consumption (ml) of saccharin for Groups SIP-1, SIP-2 and SIP-4 (top graph) and for Groups PD-1, PD-2 and PD-4 (bottom graph) over the multiple extinction trials following off-baseline conditioning during water deprivation. From Hyson et al. (1981). Reprinted by permission of The Psychonomic Society.

water deprivation). That aversions continued to affect drinking under spaced feedings relatively less than under massed feeding further supports the view that it is the inducing properties of SIP that render it less sensitive and not the acquisition of weaker aversions under SIP.

If aversions are acquired under SIP but are not displayed because of the elicited tendency to drink, aversions established under SIP should be evident if the inducing properties of SIP are removed or lessened. This was tested by Hyson et al. (1981) who examined the effects of taste aversions established under an SIP baseline on drinking in water-deprived animals. As already noted, taste aversions readily suppress consumption under water deprivation. Following the acquisition of drinking water under spaced (Group SIP) and massed (Group PD) feeding, animals were given saccharin in place of water during the feeding sessions. Immediately following the session, different groups of animals were injected with either LiCl or the saline vehicle. All subjects were then water deprived and given restricted access to water until drinking stabilized. At this point, saccharin was given in place of water during the daily drinking period. As illustrated in Fig. 8.9, independent of whether aversions were established under spaced or massed feeding conditions, consumption of the poison-associated taste was suppressed under water deprivation. Further, this suppression was identical for the two baseline feeding conditions. Thus, when the inducing agent is removed aversions conditioned under spaced feedings can be expressed. This was also addressed in a related study from our lab in which following the recovery of drinking a poison-associated taste under spaced feedings, animals were given the same taste in the home cage under water deprivation. Although there was no evidence of an aversion on the SIP baseline following the unpoisoned presentations of saccharin, i.e., subjects were drinking at or near control levels, when these same

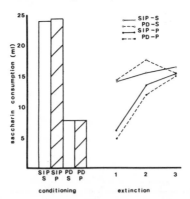

FIG. 8.9 Mean consumption (ml) of saccharin for Groups SIP and PD during conditioning on the spaced or massed feeding baselines, respectively (left panel) and during extinction under water deprivation (right panel). Groups were either injected with LiCl (P) during conditioning or the saline vehicle (S). From Hyson et al. (1981). Reprinted by permission of the Psychonomic Society.

subjects were tested under water deprivation in the home cage, saccharin was avoided. That is, after the apparent recovery of drinking a poison-associated taste under SIP, consumption of that taste was still relatively suppressed under water deprivation. It is clear that although the taste was consumed under SIP, an aversion to the taste was still intact. It was simply masked by the tendency to drink induced by pellet delivery and only evident when the tendency to drink induced by pellet delivery was removed.

Manipulations known to reduce the general tendency to lick under spaced feedings should also reduce the overriding effects SIP has on the display of taste aversions. That is, under conditions in which the tendency to lick under the SIP baseline is reduced, SIP should be affected by aversion learning. One such condition is the acquisition or development of SIP (Keehn & Stoyanov, 1986; King & Schaeffer, 1973; Schaeffer & Salzberg, 1973). During the development of SIP, the tendency to lick, i.e., to initiate a drinking bout, following pellet delivery is low. Accordingly, it might be expected that taste aversions would dramatically affect the acquisition of SIP. In a test of this, Riley et al. (1979) examined the effects of previously acquired taste aversions on the acquisition of SIP. Specifically, animals were first given taste aversion conditioning in the home cage under water deprivation. Following a single pairing of saccharin with LiCl (Groups P and SW) or the saline vehicle (Group SS), SIP training was initiated. Animals were given free food deliveries once a min independent of their behavior. For one group of rats previously given a poisoned exposure to saccharin in the home cage (Group SW), water was available during the free food deliveries. For two additional groups, saccharin was the available solution. As described, for

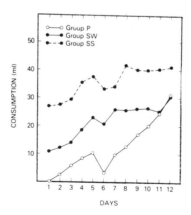

FIG. 8.10.   Mean consumption (ml) of saccharin (Groups P and SS) and water (Group SW) during the acquisition of schedule-induced drinking. All subjects had previous exposure to saccharin in the home cage under water deprivation. Subjects in Groups P and SW had been injected with LiCl following the home cage saccharin exposure. Subjects in Group SS had been given an injection of the saline vehicle. From Riley et al. (1979). Reprinted by permission of the Psychonomic Society.

one of these groups (Group P), saccharin had been previously associated with LiCl. For the second group (Group SS), saccharin had been associated with a control injection of saline. As illustrated in Fig. 8.10, when the poison-associated taste was given during the acquisition of SIP, drinking was markedly affected. Further, SIP was reduced for the duration of the study, not reaching saccharin control levels even after 12 nonpoisoned exposures to saccharin on the SIP baseline (compare Group P to Group SS). It is interesting in this context that other manipulations reported to have little effect on established SIP markedly affect its acquisition (Corfield-Sumner & Bond, 1978; Porter, McDonough, & Young, 1982; Porter, Young, & Moeschil, 1978; Riley & Wetherington, 1987; Yoburn & Glusman, 1982).

Another way to reduce the general tendency to lick following spaced food deliveries is to provide the opportunity to engage in alternative behaviors in addition to drinking during spaced feedings (Roper, 1978; Staddon & Ayres, 1975). One such behavior is wheel running (Levitsky & Collier, 1968; Penney & Schull, 1977; Riley, Peele, Richard, & Kulkosky, 1981; Riley et al., 1985; Segal, 1969; Wetherington & Riley, 1986). As illustrated in Figs. 8.11 and 8.12, the availability of wheel running under a schedule of spaced feedings reduces the overall level of consumption of water as well as affects the temporal distribution of post-pellet licking (an index of lick tendency) (see Riley et al., 1981; Wetherington & Riley, 1986). In a test of the effects of conditioned taste aversions on SIP when the opportunity to run and drink were concurrently available (Riley et al., 1981), animals were given a poison-associated taste to drink during spaced feeding sessions. For one group of subjects (Group SC), a running wheel was available, but locked. For a second group (Group SO), the wheel was available and unlocked. For both groups, the poison-associated taste suppressed SIP. For subjects for which the wheel was locked, recovery of SIP was rapid and at water baseline levels within three sessions. For subjects for which the wheel was un-

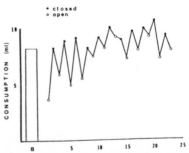

FIG. 8.11. Mean consumption (ml) of water under spaced feedings for subjects with concurrent access to either an unlocked (open circles) or locked (closed circles) running wheel. B refers to the amount of water consumed during the SIP baseline prior to the introduction of the alternating wheel open and wheel closed sessions. From Riley et al. (1981). Reprinted by permission of the Psychonomic Society.

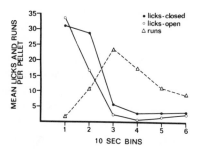

FIG. 8.12. Mean number of licks and runs in the six successive 10-sec intervals following pellet delivery under a spaced feeding schedule. The licks-open condition (open circles) refers to sessions during which subjects had access to both a drinking tube and an unlocked wheel. The licks-closed condition (closed circles) refers to sessions during which subjects had access to a drinking tube and a locked wheel. Runs in the licks-open condition are indicated by the open triangles. After Wetherington & Riley (1986).

locked, recovery was slower, not reaching water-baseline levels even after seven exposures to saccharin and never approaching the levels of the subjects in the wheel closed condition (see Fig. 8.13). It appears, therefore, that animals given the choice to either drink a poison-associated taste or run, sometimes choose to run, thereby lowering the tendency to drink (Roper, 1978). That SIP can be affected by taste aversion training under such conditions suggests that the fast recovery of SIP under conditions in which only drinking is made available is due to the elicited nature of SIP, a response induced by pellet delivery and nonelective.

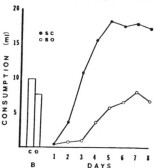

FIG. 8.13. Mean consumption (ml) of saccharin under SIP for subjects when a poison-associated taste (saccharin) was substituted for water during the spaced feeding sessions. Groups SO had concurrent access to an unlocked running wheel. Group SC had access only to the saccharin solution, i.e., the running wheel was locked and running unavailable. B refers to the amount of water consumed by Groups SO and SC during spaced feedings prior to the introduction of the poison-associated saccharin solution. From Riley et al. (1981). Reprinted by permission of the Psychonomic Society.

As illustrated, when this tendency is reduced by concurrently available behaviors, SIP no longer overrides the display of taste aversions. This is further illustrated by an examination of the effects of taste aversions on SIP when the animal is given a choice to drink either the poison-associated taste or water during spaced feeding sessions (Riley et al., 1979). Previous research on the schedule-induced consumption of alcohol has shown that the concurrent availability of alcohol and an alternative solution (e.g., water, sucrose) reduces alcohol polydipsia (Falk & Samson, 1976; Tang & Falk, 1986). In the Riley et al. (1979) report, following the acquisition of SIP saccharin replaced water during the spaced feeding session. Subjects were either injected with LiCl or the saline vehicle immediately following the session. On subsequent SIP sessions, all subjects were given access to both saccharin and water. Unlike the case when only saccharin was available, animals displayed a marked aversion to saccharin which recovered slowly (see Fig. 8.14). Further, when an analysis was made of the position of the saccharin and water tubes in relation to the food hopper, even more dramatic effects were revealed. That is, when the poison-associated saccharin taste was in a position most removed from the hopper (in relation to the position of water), saccharin SIP was almost totally suppressed, a suppression still evident after three nonpoisoned exposures to saccharin. When saccharin was adjacent to the hopper, suppression was minimal and drinking had fully recovered by the third nonpoisoned saccharin exposure. Animals with no prior aversion to saccharin were only minimally, and inconsistently, affected by the relative positions of the saccharin and water (see Fig. 8.15). The fact that SIP can be suppressed by conditioned taste aversions when the tendency to lick is generally reduced (e.g., during acquisition of SIP and when choices are given such as the concurrent availability

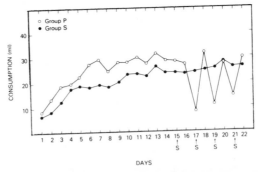

FIG. 8.14.   Mean consumption (ml) during polydipsia acquisition (water only) and subsequent alternating saccharin (S) and water presentations. Subjects in Group P were injected with LiCl following saccharin consumption on Day 15. Subjects in Group S received the saline vehicle at this time. On subsequent saccharin presentations (i.e., Days 17, 19, and 21), both water and saccharin were available during the spaced feeding sessions. From Riley et al. (1979). Reprinted by permission of the Psychonomic Society.

of a running wheel or water) suggests that under general conditions of spaced food deliveries, SIP is elicited by the spaced pellet deliveries. This elicited drinking is nonelective and nonvoluntary, and apparently of sufficient strength to override the display of a conditioned taste aversion.

VI. EVALUATION OF SIP AS AN ANIMAL MODEL OF ALCOHOLISM

Such conclusions have implications for SIP as an animal model of alcoholism. As described earlier, there are a range of animal models, each of which satisfies to varying degrees the multiple criteria used in evaluating animal analogs. Several advantages of SIP as an animal model are the facts that alcohol is orally consumed under SIP and the drinking appears elective. Given that these two criteria presumably reflect characteristics of human alcoholism, SIP seems a reasonable model to assess both pharmacological and behavioral (etiology) issues. As noted, however, it is not clear that SIP is elective. Although rats seldom drink alcohol in free-choice situations, they readily drink alcohol under conditions of spaced feeding. This discrepancy can possibly be explained by the fact that not only do animals drink alcohol under such conditions, but they also drink poison-associated tastes. That such consumption occurs despite the fact that the solution is aversive and that the solution is avoided in other contexts (as well as the fact that the solution is avoided during spaced feedings when the tendency to drink following pellet delivery is reduced) suggest that SIP engenders drinking that is forced and induced and in no way voluntary.

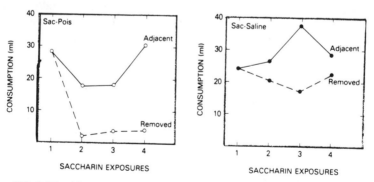

FIG. 8.15.   Mean consumption (ml) of saccharin during the initial exposure to saccharin (the exposure followed by either LiCl or saline) and the multiple two-bottle (saccharin and water) extinction trials on the polydipsia baseline. Adjacent and removed refer to the positions of saccharin in relation to the food hopper. Sac-Pois and Sac-Saline refer to whether subjects were injected with LiCl or saline following saccharin consumption on the conditioning trial. From Riley et al. (1979). Reprinted by permission of the Psychonomic Society.

What this has to say about its use as an animal model can be examined in two ways:

1. Because SIP does not meet the criterion of being an elective animal model, it should be reevaluated as such a model. As a nonelective animal model, it appears no better than other nonelective models. For example, forced inhalation, SERT and intragastric intubation can all produce high BALs, tolerance, dependence and biomedial consequences. In fact, because of the time and equipment needed to produce the schedule-induced consumption of alcohol the SIP model actually appears less time and cost-efficient than some of the other nonelective models (Pohorecky, 1981). In this regard, SIP does not appear to be an unusually useful animal model.

2. A more dramatic decision, however, would be to note that it is possible that our criteria are wrong and that instead of discounting SIP as a model we should instead be revising our criteria. This conclusion necessitates taking a different view of human alcoholism.

VII. INDUCED DRINKING: A REEVALUATION OF HUMAN ALCOHOLISM

Such a view has been discussed for several years (see Falk & Samson, 1976; Gilbert, 1978) and was most recently described in a report by Falk in which he questioned traditional accounts of drug taking behvior as well as drug dependence (Falk, 1982; see also Cantor, 1981). Instead of accepting that drug use and drug dependence reflect some intrinsic property of the drug (e.g., naturally addicting) or of the individual (e.g., addicitive personalities), Falk (1982) discussed factors independent of the drug and "outside of the skin" (p. 85). Falk discussed at length environmental factors which affect the response to a drug, both in terms of a short term effect or dependence liability (see also Ader, 1985; Eikelboom & Stewart, 1982; Siegel, 1979). For example, the fact that the heroin addiction rates among Vietnam veterans decreased upon return to the U.S. (from 20% to 1%) attests to the situation specificity of heroin use and addiction. It is not clear whether the failure of heroin use and addiction among Vietnam veterans to continue at high rates upon their return to the U.S. was a function of the lack of social reinforcement for drug use in the changed environment, the absence of the obvious boredom of inactivity or stress of war or the actual changes in the environmental stimuli associated with drug taking. Independent of which of these factors (if not all) were operating, the role of the environment in our response to a drug is clear. Drug taking is not simply a property of the drug or the individual; the environment is important, if not crucial.

In the aforementioned accounts, the environment has acted in such a manner to reinforce drug taking or mediate and modulate a drug's effects. In other cases, the environment can be seen as actually inducing drug taking itself, an issue which has important implications for the use of schedule-induced polydipsia as an animal model of alcoholism. Falk (1982) noted that similar to the experimental conditions which induce excessive behavior (including drug taking) in animals, i.e., spaced feeding, rewards in humans are also intermittently administered. Although these rewards are not necessarily food as in the induction procedure of animals, the rewards nonetheless are not always available. These intermittent rewards, like in the animal case, induce behavior. In the research with animals, SIP is most typically studied. As others have shown, however, other behaviors may also occur and be induced by spaced food deliveries, e.g., aggression (see Roper, 1981 for a critical analysis of the issue of induced behaviors). In the case with humans, we are all subject to spaced rewards and the induction embedded in such schedules. Many behaviors may be induced by such schedules, the specific ones occurring being affected or directed in part by the available alternatives. As Falk (1982) described,

> Life could be described as a scramble for commodities and activities, which are only intermittently attained: food, territory, money, sexual and social intercourse. The particular excessive behavior induced by these natural generator schedules depends upon what behavioral opportunities are available in life's situations, and whether the individual is prepared to exploit these opportunities. Drugs offer quick and powerful behavioral alternatives when they occur in an impoverished environment upon which generator schedules are imposed. (p. 390)

From this perspective of drug taking in humans, schedule-induced polydipsia seems a clear animal analog of the human pathology. The schedule-induced consumption of alcohol in animals is a nonelective, involuntary behavior. Alcohol intake in humans may reflect in part a similar nonelective, induction base. Although this interpretation of human drug taking is consistent with the position of the important role of the environment in drug use and abuse, it is certainly a difficult position to test. Unlike the animal case in which one has control of the extraneous conditions which could affect drug taking, e.g., hunger, genetic variations, stress, behavioral choices, reinforcers, such control is not available in the human case (Sanger, 1986). For example, under normal living conditions not only does one not have control of the exact reinforcers for humans, it is not clear that one could adequately define what the reinforcers were for any specific individual or the schedule under which they were being delivered. All this makes the argument that human alcoholism is schedule-induced difficult (if not impossible) to test directly.

It can, however, be addressed indirectly in the laboratory. That is, if human alcohol intake and alcoholism are in any way induced by the intermittent delivery of rewards, humans should display schedule-induced behavior under controlled laboratory conditions in which scheduled rewards are presented to the subject. In the first attempt at demonstrating schedule-induced behavior in humans,

Kachanoff, Leveille, McLelland, and Wayner (1973) reinforced schizophrenic inpatients with pennies for pulling a cord. The schedule by which they were reinforced ranged from an FI 30 sec to an FI 150 sec. In addition to recording the operant response of cord-pulling, Kachanoff et al. monitored activity and drinking from a water fountain. Interestingly, three subjects did increase the amount of drinking and pacing during the scheduled rewards above the level displayed prior to the introduction to the schedule and during extinction when cord pulling was no longer reinforced. Given that reinforcement was not contingent on either of these behaviors and that they each occurred at a greater level during the spaced rewards than during the baseline and extinction conditions, the position that behaviors could be induced in humans under schedules of intermittent reinforcement was supported.

Since this initial investigation, schedule-induced behaviors in humans have been examined in a number of different studies scheduling a wide variety of rewards and measuring a range of schedule-induced behaviors (Cantor, 1981; Cantor, Smith, & Bryan, 1982; Cherek, 1982; Cherek & Brauchi, 1981; Clarke, Gannon, Hughes, Singer, & Wallace, 1977; Fallon, Allen, & Butler, 1979; Frederiksen & Peterson, 1977; Lasiter, 1979; Muller, Crow, & Cheney, 1979; Porter, Brown, & Goldsmith, 1982; Sanger, 1986; Wallace & Oei, 1981; Wallace, Sanson, & Singer, 1978; Wallace & Singer, 1976; Wallace, Singer, Wayner, & Cook, 1975). For example, Porter and his colleagues (Porter et al., 1982) examined schedule-induced drinking, vocalizations and movement in children. In this study, children were given candy reinforcers on one of three schedules, i.e., FR 1 (in which each response produced an M&M), an FI 30 and an FI 60. The FR 1 schedule was regarded as a massed baseline and served as the control condition for nonscheduled reward. Movement, vocalizations and drinking were all affected by the scheduled candy. Specifically, three of the four subjects under the FI 30 and two of the four under the FI 60 increased drinking above the FR 1 baseline. Similarly, three of the four subjects under both FI 30 and FI 60 increased in movement. Finally, two of the four subjects under the FI 30 and three of the four under the FI 60 increased vocalizations. Overall, the effect was clear. Scheduled rewards appeared to induce a range of behaviors.

In a further examination of schedule-induced behavior in humans, Cherek (1982) scheduled the delivery of money on one of four fixed interval schedules of reinforcement, specifically, FI 30, FI 60, FI 120, and FI 240. Normal volunteers in this study were given money reinforcement for pressing a button. In addition to button pressing, smoking (number of cigarettes smoked, puffs per cigarette, puffs per cigarette per hour and puff duration) was recorded. Although there was no effect of variations in the interpellet interval (IPI) on the number of cigarettes smoked or puff duration, the measures of puffs per hour and number of puffs per cigarette were affected. Specifically, puffs per hour and number of puffs per cigarette displayed a clear inverted U-shaped function with increases in the IPI, i.e., these two measures were highest under the FI 120 conditions, with lower levels at the intervals shorter and longer than the FI 120. The variations of schedule-induced behaviors (in this case puffs per hour and puffs per cigarette) with increases in the IPI is an effect well established in the literature on SIP (Falk, 1966a; Riley et al. 1985; Roper, 1980; Wetherington, 1979). Further, for the number of puffs per cigarette measure the behavior appeared to be displayed highest in the first third of the interpellet interval, i.e., the period typically associated with the highest rate of SIP (Shurtleff et al., 1983; Staddon, 1977).

Muller et al. (1979) extended the range of rewards used in the attempts at inducing behavior in humans by reinforcing normal college students under an FI 120 for plunger pulling by tokens which could subsequently be exchanged for money. In addition to recording the operant, locomotor activity was continuously monitored. In relation to a baseline condition in which no scheduled events occurred, activity increased during the scheduled rewards. Not only did the FI 120 schedule increase locomotor activity, but this activity was generally highest in the first quarter of the interpellet interval, again an effect consistent with the temporal distribution of SIP in animals. In a second study using moderately retarded adolescent inpatients, Muller et al. demonstrated similar increases in locomotor activity above a baseline condition in which no events were scheduled. An interesting point about this replication was that in this experiment although rewards were scheduled, they were not contingent on responding, i.e., the tokens were delivered according to a fixed time schedule. SIP has also been reported to occur under both response-dependent and independent schedules (Segal, Oden, & Deadwyler, 1965). Finally, in the second study the specific schedule varied across sessions (FI 16, FI 80, and FI 140). Similar to research with SIP, the rate of locomotor activity was highest under the shortest FI (i.e., FI 16) (Killeen, 1975; Wetherington, 1979).

Utilizing a somewhat different paradigm, Wallace et al. (1975) examined schedule-induced behaviors in college students through a computer-simulated gambling game. According to a specific schedule, responses on the keyboard produced a video display indicating a card sequence and the amount of money won. This display was presented on an FI 60 schedule. As a control baseline, subjects either listened to a tape while not playing the computer game or played the game on an FI 5 schedule (these two conditions were used as the baseline comparisons). For all seven subjects, the indices of schedule-induced behaviors (i.e., playing and moving) increased under the FI 60 schedule in relation to either not playing or playing the game under the FI 5. Wallace et al. (1975) described a range of induced behaviors under the FI 60,

> although there was no consistent polydipsia or hyperphagia induced by the present fixed interval schedules, occasionally copious drinking occurred and large amounts of food were consumed. Several instances of other bizarre behaviors were observed such as blending Cheezels and Coca Cola and drinking the mixture, tearing scrap paper into hundreds of pieces and arranging them in symmetrical patterns, pressing the space bar with a bare foot, tossing Cheezels into a paper cup, vocalization and play acting. (p. 653)

The preceding examples of schedule-induced behavior utilized different rewards, e.g., food, candy, money, or tokens, but they were all discrete rewards contingent upon responding. Cantor et al. (1982) demonstrated that rewards scheduled in other ways can also generate or induce behavior. In their design, 28 male undergraduates were run on a pursuit rotor task in which the aim of the subject was to track a target. Alternating with periods in which the pursuit rotor task was in effect (Task Periods) were periods in which the pursuit rotor task was off (Control Periods). Groups differed in terms of the rate at which they tracked, i.e., 55 revolutions/min (Fast Group) or 7 revolutions/min (Slow Group). The logic of Cantor et al. in this manipulation was that the faster the speed of the rotor, the lower the subject's time on the target (reinforcer). Given that schedule-induced behaviors occur in periods that are associated with the absence of reinforcers, it was expected that more behaviors would be induced under the condition of the fast revolutions than under the slow. The schedule-induced behaviors measured in this study were eating, drinking, grooming, and miscellaneous activity ("fiddles"). As predicted, each of these behaviors was observed with greater frequency under the pursuit rotor task than under the control condition. Further, the behaviors occurred at a higher frequency in the Fast Group, consistent with the position that schedule-induced behaviors are associated with periods of low reinforcer frequency.

These examples of schedule-induced behaviors illustrate that intermittent rewards can induce behavior in humans. In each of the described studies (as well as a range of others), some degree of schedule-induction was evident (for a concise and thorough review of these studies, see Sanger, 1986). Although there is clearly evidence of induced behavior in humans, there are a number of problems and inconsistencies in the aforementioned research that should be noted. First, schedule-induced behavior in humans was often weak and variable, sometimes being evident for only some of the measured behaviors in some of the individuals measured. Second, unlike SIP the schedule-induced behaviors in humans did not always vary with changes in the rate of the delivery of the reward. Third, in most of the findings the induced behaviors were evident on the first exposure to the schedule, i.e., not displaying the slow, gradual development typical of SIP (Keehn & Stoyanov, 1986; Shurtleff et al., 1983). Fourth, in most of the research no appropriate baseline condition was run to compare the effects of scheduled rewards. Typically, only a no manipulation or irrelevant manipulation baseline was used for comparison (though see Fallon et al., 1979; Porter et al., 1982). As noted by Roper (1981), the most appropriate baseline with which to compare behaviors occurring under a schedule condition is a baseline in which the subjects are given the same rewards, but not spaced or scheduled (though see Cohen & Looney, 1984; Wetherington & Riley, 1985, 1986). A final issue concerns the fact that in all of the research on schedule induction in humans specific rewards were administered on schedules with short intervals, i.e., between 5 and 240 sec. It simply is not clear to what extent these conditions can generalize to the more complex conditions of humans. With these reservations noted, it is still clear that under many conditions there are parallels between SIP in animals and schedule-induced behaviors in humans, e.g., excessiveness, schedule variations, temporal distribution.

VIII.   IS THE RAT A SMALL FURRY HUMAN?

The issues in this review have come full circle. The chapter began as a critical evaluation of SIP as an animal model of human alcoholism. Because SIP did not appear elective, its utility as an animal model which assumed the elective nature of human alcoholism seemed limited. With that as a beginning premise, it seems somewhat odd that the chapter ends with the position that SIP may be useful as a model after all. Revising our thinking on SIP necessitated a revision of our view on alcoholism, acknowledging that the environment plays a nontrivial role in the initiation of drug use and abuse. Viewing alcoholism as having some induced property allowed for a reconsideration of our criteria for animal models of alcoholism and, further, a reevaluation of SIP. In an analysis of the rat as a model of human toxicological evaluation, Oser (1981) concluded that "Man is not a big rat." In this vein, we would have to agree that "The rat is not a small furry human." If, however, approaching a human pathology from a basic animal analog gives insight into some of the controlling (or inducing) factors in the pathology and gives some possibilities for ways to redirect behavior into less damaging and more acceptable paths (Bond, 1984; Falk, 1982; Mello, 1985), the semantic mistake may be tolerable.

ACKNOWLEDGMENT

The research on which this chapter is based as well as the preparation of this chapter were supported in part from funds from the Mellon Foundation and National Science Foundation Grant No. BNS-8406445. Cora Lee Wetherington is currently at the National Institute on Drug Abuse, 5600 Fishers Lane, Rockville, Maryland 20005. Requests for reprints can be sent to either author.

REFERENCES

Ader, R. (1985). Conditioned taste aversions and immunopharmacology. *Annals of the New York Academy of Sciences*, *443*, 293–307.

Archer, T., & Sjoden, P. O. (1979). Positive correlation between pre- and postconditioning saccharin intake in taste-aversion learning. *Animal Learning & Behavior*, *7*, 144–148.

Baker, T. B., & Cannon, D. S. (1982). Alcohol and taste-mediated learning. *Addictive Behaviors*, *7*, 221–230.

Barnett, S. A. (1963). *The rat: A study in behavior*. Chicago: Aldine Press.

Bond, N. W. (1984). *Animal models in psychopathology*. New York: Academic Press.

Braveman, N. S., & Crane, J. (1977). Amount consumed and the formation of conditioned taste aversions. *Behavioral Biology, 21,* 470–477.

Brett, L. P., Hankins, W. G., & Garcia, J. (1976). Prey-lithium aversions. III: Buteo hawks. *Behavioral Biology, 17,* 87–98.

Cantor, M. B. (1981). Bad habits: Models of induced ingestion in satiated rats and people. In S. Miller (Ed.), *Behavior and nutrition.* New York: Franklin Institute Press.

Cantor, M. B., Smith, S. E., & Bryan, B. R. (1982). Induced bad habits: Adjunctive ingestion and grooming in human subjects. *Appetite: Journal for Intake Research, 3,* 1–12.

Cappell, H., LeBlanc, A. E., & Endrenyi, L. (1973). Aversive conditioning by psychoactive drugs: Effects of morphine, alcohol and chlordiazepoxide. *Psychopharmacologia, 29,* 239–246.

Chapman, H. W., & Richardson, H. M. (1974). The role of systemic hydration in the acquisition of schedule-induced polydipsia by rats. *Behavioral Biology, 12,* 501–508.

Cherek, D. R. (1982). Schedule-induced cigarette self-administration. *Pharmacology, Biochemistry and Behavior, 17,* 523–527.

Cherek, D. R., & Brauchi, J. T. (1981). Schedule-induced cigarette smoking behavior during fixed-interval monetary reinforced responding. In C. M. Bradshaw, E. Szabadi, & C. F. Lowe (Eds.), *Quantification of steady-state behavior.* Amsterdam: Elsevier.

Christian, W. P. (1976). Control of schedule-induced polydipsia: Sugar content of the dry food reinforcer. *The Psychological Record, 26,* 41–47.

Christian, W. P., Schaeffer, R. W., & King, G. D. (1977). *Schedule-induced behavior: Research and theory.* Montreal: Eden Press.

Cicero, T. J. (1980). Animal models of alcoholism. In E. Erikkson, J. D. Sinclair, & K. Kiianmaa (Eds.), *Animal models in alcohol research.* New York: Academic Press.

Clark, F. C. (1962). Some observations on the adventitious reinforcement of drinking under food reinforcement. *Journal of the Experimental Analysis of Behavior, 5,* 61–63.

Clarke, J., Gannon, M., Hughes, I., Singer, G., & Wallace, M. (1977). Adjunctive behavior in humans in a group gambling situation. *Physiology & Behavior, 18,* 159–161.

Cohen, P. S., & Looney, T. A. (1984). Induction by reinforcer schedules. *Journal of the Experimental Analysis of Behavior, 41,* 345–353.

Colby, J. J., & Smith, N. F. (1977). The effect of three procedures for eliminating a conditioned taste aversion in the rat. *Learning and Motivation, 8,* 404–413.

Colotla, V. A. (1981). Adjunctive polydipsia as a model of alcoholism. *Neuroscience & Biobehavioral Reviews, 5,* 335–342.

Corfield-Sumner, P. K., & Bond, N. W. (1978). Effects of preloading on the acquisition and maintenance of schedule-induced polydipsia. *Behavioral Biology, 23,* 238–242.

Couch, J. V. (1974). Reinforcement magnitude and schedule-induced polydipsia: A reexamination. *Psychological Record, 24,* 559–562.

Davison, C. S., & House, W. J. (1975). Alcohol as the aversive stimulus in conditioned taste aversion. *Bulletin of the Psychonomic Society, 6,* 49–50.

Deutsch, J. A., & Eisner, A. (1977). Ethanol self-administration in the rat induced by forced drinking of ethanol. *Behavioral Biology, 20,* 81–90.

Deutsch, J. A., Walton, N. Y., & Thiel, T. R. (1978). The importance of postingestional factors in limiting alcohol consumption in the rat. *Behavioral Biology, 22,* 128–131.

Deutsch, R. (1978). Effects of CS amount on conditioned taste aversions at different CS–US intervals. *Animal Learning & Behavior, 6,* 258–260.

Dole, V. P. (1986). On the relevance of animal models to alcoholism in humans. *Alcoholism: Clinical and Experimental Research, 10,* 361–363.

Eckhardt, M. J., Skurdal, A. J., & Brown, J. S. (1974). Conditioned taste aversion produced by low doses of alcohol. *Physiological Psychology, 2,* 89–92.

Eikelboom, R., & Stewart, J. (1982). Conditioning of drug-induced physiological responses. *Psychological Review, 89,* 507–528.

Elkins, R. L. (1973). Individual differences in baitshyness: Effects of drug dose and measurement technique. *The Psychological Record, 23,* 349–358.

Eriksson, K., Sinclair, J. D., & Kiianmaa, K. (Eds.). (1980). *Animal models in alcohol research.* New York: Academic Press.

Falk, J. L. (1961). Production of polydipsia in normal rats by an intermittent food schedule. *Science, 133,* 195–196.

Falk, J. L. (1964). Studies on schedule-induced polydipsia. In M. J. Wayner (Ed.), *Thirst.* New York: Macmillan.

Falk, J. L. (1966a). Schedule-induced polydipsia as a function of fixed interval length. *Journal of the Experimental Analysis of Behavior, 9,* 37–39.

Falk, J. L. (1966b). Analysis of the water and sodium chloride solution acceptance by schedule induced polydipsia. *Journal of the Experimental Analysis of Behavior, 9,* 111–114.

Falk, J. L. (1969). Conditions producing psychogenic polydipsia in animals. *Annals of the New York Academy of Science, 157,* 569–593.

Falk, J. L. (1971). The nature and determinants of adjunctive behavior. *Physiology & Behavior, 6,* 577–588.

Falk, J. L. (1977). The origin and functions of adjunctive behavior. *Animal Learning & Behavior, 5,* 325–335.

Falk, J. L. (1982). Drug dependence: Myth or motive? *Pharmacology, Biochemistry and Behavior, 19,* 385–391.

Falk, J. L., & Samson, H. H. (1976). Schedule-induced physical dependence on ethanol. *Pharmacological Reviews, 27,* 449–464.

Falk, J. L., Samson, H. H., & Tang, M. (1973). Chronic ingestion techniques for the production of physical dependence on ethanol. In M. Gross (Ed.), *Alcohol intoxication and withdrawal: Experimental studies.* New York: Plenum Press.

Falk, J. L., Samson, H. H., & Winger, G. (1972). Behavioral maintenance of high concentrations of blood ethanol and physical dependence in the rat. *Science, 177,* 811–813.

Fallon, J. H., Allen, J. D., & Butler, J. A. (1979). Assessment of adjunctive behaviors in humans using a stringent control procedure. *Physiology & Behavior, 22,* 1089–1092.

Flory, R. K. (1971). The control of schedule-induced polydipsia: Frequency and magnitude of reinforcement. *Learning and Motivation, 2,* 215–227.

Forsander, O., & Eriksson, K. (Eds.). (1972). *Biological aspects of alcohol consumption: Vol. 20.* Helsinki: The Finnish Foundation for Alcohol Studies.

Frederiksen, L. W., & Peterson, G. L. (1977). Schedule-induced aggression in humans and animals: A comparative parametric review. *Aggressive Behavior, 3,* 57–75.

Freed, E. X., & Hymowitz, N. (1972). Effects of schedule, percent body weight and magnitude of reinforcer on acquisition of schedule-induced polydipsia. *Psychological Reports, 31,* 95–101.

Freed, W. J., Zec, R. F., & Mendelson, J. (1977). Schedule-induced polydipsia: The role of orolinqual factors and a new hypothesis. In J. A. W. M. Weijnen & J. Mendelson (Eds.), *Drinking behavior: Oral stimulation, reinforcement, and preference.* New York: Plenum Press.

Garcia, J., & Ervin, F. R. (1968). Gustatory-visceral and telereceptor-cutaneous conditioning: Adaptations in internal and external milieus. *Communications in Behavioral Biology, 1,* 389–415.

Gay, P. E., Leaf, R. C., & Arble, F. B. (1975). Inhibitory effects of pre- and posttest drugs on mouse-killing by rats. *Pharmacology, Biochemistry and Behavior, 3,* 33–45.

Gilbert, R. M. (1974). Ubiquity of schedule-induced polydipsia. *Journal of the Experimental Analysis of Behavior, 21,* 277–284.

Gilbert, R. M. (1978). Schedule-induced self-administration of drugs, In D. E. Blackman & D. J. Sanger (Eds.), *Contemporary research in behavioral pharmacology.* New York: Plenum Press.

Gill, K., France, C., & Amit, Z. (1986). Voluntary ethanol consumption in rats: An examination of blood/brain ethanol levels and behavior. *Alcoholism: Clinical and Experimental Research, 10,* 457–462.

Gross, M. (Ed.). (1973). *Alcohol intoxication and withdrawal: Experimental studies.* New York: Plenum Press.

Grote, F. W., Jr., & Brown, R. T. (1973). Deprivation level affects extinction of a conditioned taste aversion. *Learning and Motivation, 4,* 314–319.

Gustavson, C. R., Garcia, J., Hankins, W. G., & Rusiniak, K. W. (1974). Coyote predation control by aversive conditioning. *Science*, *184*, 581–583.

Hawkins, T. D., Schrot, J. F., Githens, S. H., & Everett, P. B. (1972). Schedule-induced polydipsia: An analysis of water and alcohol ingestion. In R. M. Gilbert & J. D. Keehn (Eds.), *Schedule effects: Drugs, drinking, and aggression.* Toronto: University of Toronto Press.

Heintzelman, M. E., Best, J., & Senter, R. J. (1976). Polydipsia-induced alcohol dependency in rats: A reexamination. *Science*, *191*, 482–483.

Holman, R. B., & Myers, R. D. (1968). Ethanol consumption under conditions of psychogenic polydipsia. *Physiology & Behavior*, *3*, 369–371.

Hyson, R. L., Sickel, J. L., Kulkosky, P. J., & Riley, A. L. (1981). The insensitivity of schedule-induced polydipsia to conditioned taste aversions: Effect of amount consumed during conditioning. *Animal Learning & Behavior*, *9*, 281–286.

Johnston, R. E., Zahorik, D. M., Immler, K., & Zakon, H. (1978). Alterations of male sexual behavior by learned aversions to hamster vaginal secretion. *Journal of Comparative and Physiological Psychology*, *92*, 85–93.

Kachanoff, R., Leveille, R., McLelland, J. P., & Wayner, M. J. (1973). Schedule-induced behavior in humans. *Physiology & Behavior*, *11*, 395–398.

Keehn, J. D. (1979). *Psychopathology in animals: Research and treatment implications.* New York: Academic Press.

Keehn, J. D. (1986). *Animal models for psychiatry.* Boston: Routledge & Kegan Paul.

Keehn, J. D., & Colotla, V. A. (1971). Stimulus and subject control of schedule-induced drinking. *Journal of the Experimental Analysis of Behavior*, *16*, 257–262.

Keehn, J. D., & Stoyanov, E. (1986). The development of adjunctive drinking by rats: Conditioned and unconditioned components. *Animal Learning & Behavior*, *14*, 411–415.

Killeen, P. (1975). On the temporal control of behavior. *Psychological Review*, *82*, 89–115.

King, G. D., & Schaeffer, R. W. (1973). Developmental analysis of schedule-induced polydipsia. *Psychological Reports*, *32*, 1087–1095.

Kuker-Reines, B. (1982). *Psychology experiments on animals: A critique of animal models of human psychopathology.* Boston: New England Anti-vivisection Society.

Kulkosky, P. J. (1978). Free-selection ethanol intake of the golden hamster *(Mesocricetus auratus)*. *Physiological Psychology*, *6*, 505–509.

Kulkosky, P. J. (1979). Effect of addition of ethanol and NaCl on saccharin + glucose polydipsia. *Pharmacology, Biochemistry and Behavior*, *10*, 277–283.

Kulkosky, P. J., & Cornell, N. W. (1979). Free-choice ethanol intake and ethanol metabolism in the hamster and rat. *Pharmacology, Biochemistry and Behavior*, *11*, 439–444.

Kulkosky, P. J., Moe, K., Woods, S. C., & Riley, A. L. (1975). Effect of ventromedial hypothalamic lesions on schedule-induced polydipsia. *Physiological Psychology*, *3*, 172–174.

Kulkosky, P. J., Sickel, J. L., & Riley, A. L. (1980). Total avoidance of saccharin consumption by rats after repeatedly paired injections of ethanol or LiCl. *Pharmacology, Biochemistry and Behavior*, *13*, 77–80.

Kulkosky, P. J., Zellner, D. A., Hyson, R. L., & Riley, A. L. (1980). Ethanol consumption of rats in individual, group, and colonial housing conditions. *Physiological Psychology*, *8*, 56–60.

Langley, W. (1981). Failure of food-aversion conditioning to suppress predatory attack of the grasshopper mouse, *Onychomys leucogaster*. *Behavioral and Neural Biology*, *33*, 317–333.

Lashley, R. L., & Rosellini, R. A. (1980). Modulation of schedule-induced polydipsia by Pavlovian conditioned states. *Physiology & Behavior*, *24*, 411–414.

Lasiter, P. S. (1979). Influence of contingent responding on schedule-induced activity in human subjects. *Physiology & Behavior*, *22*, 239–244.

Lester, D. (1961). Self-maintenance of intoxication in the rat. *Quarterly Journal of Studies on Alcohol*, *22*, 223–231.

Lester, D., & Freed, E. X. (1972). The rat views alcohol—Nutrition or nirvana? In O. Forsander & K. Eriksson (Eds.), *Biological aspects of alcohol consumption: Vol. 20.* Helsinki: The Finnish Foundation for Alcohol Studies.

Lester, D., & Freed, E. X. (1973). Criteria for an animal model of alcoholism. *Pharmacology, Biochemistry and Behavior, 1,* 103–107.

Lester, D., Nachman, M., & LeMagnen, J. (1970). Aversive conditioning by ethanol in the rat. *Journal of Studies on Alcohol, 31,* 578–586.

Levitsky, D. A., & Collier, G. (1968). Schedule-induced wheel running. *Physiology & Behavior, 3,* 571–573.

Lyon, M. & Nielsen, E. B. (1979). Psychosis and drug-induced stereotypies. In J. D. Keehn (Ed.), *Psychopathology in animals: Research and treatment implications.* New York: Academic Press.

Maser, J. D., & Seligman, M. E. P. (Eds.). (1977). *Psychopathology: Experimental models.* San Francisco: Freeman.

McMillan, D. E., Leander, J. D., Ellis, F. W., Lucot, J. B., & Frye, G. D. (1976). Characteristics of ethanol drinking patterns under schedule-induced polydipsia. *Psychopharmacology, 49,* 49–55.

Meisch, R. A. (1975). The function of schedule-induced polydipsia in establishing ethanol as a positive reinforcer. *Pharmacological Reviews, 27,* 465–473.

Meisch, R. A., & Thompson, T. (1972). Ethanol intake during schedule-induced polydipsia. *Physiology & Behavior, 8,* 472–475.

Meisch, R. A., & Thompson, T. (1974). Rapid establishment of ethanol as a reinforcer for rats. *Pscyhopharmacologia, 37,* 311–321.

Mello, N. K. (1973). A review of methods to induce alcohol addiction in animals. In T. Thompson & P. B. Dews (Eds.), *Advances in behavioral pharmacology.* New York: Academic Press.

Mello, N. K. (1985). Animal models of alcoholism: Contributions of behavioral pharmacology. In L. S. Seiden & R. L. Balster (Eds.), *Behavioral pharmacology: The current status.* New York: Alan R. Liss.

Mello, N. K., & Mendelson, J. H. (1971). Evaluation of a polydipsia technique to induce alcohol consumption in monkeys. *Physiology & Behavior, 7,* 827–836.

Muller, P. G., Crow, R. E., & Cheney, C. D. (1979). Schedule-induced locomotor activity in humans. *Journal of the Experimental Analysis of Behavior, 31,* 83–90.

Myers, R. D. (1966). Voluntary alcohol consumption in animals: Peripheral and intra-cerebral factors. *Psychosomatic Medicine, 28,* 484–497.

Myers, R. D., & Veale, W. L. (1972). The determinants of alcohol preference in animals. In B. Kissin & H. Begleiter (Eds.), *The biology of alcoholism: Vol. 2. Physiology and behavior.* New York: Plenum Press.

Ogata, H., Ogata, F., Mendelson, J. H., & Mello, N. K. (1972a). Evaluation of a technique to induce alcohol dependence and tolerance in the mouse by the use of schedule-induced polydipsia. *Japanese Journal of Studies of Alcohol, 7,* 27–35.

Ogata, H., Ogata, F., Mendelson, J. H., & Mello, N. K. (1972b). A comparison of techniques to induce alcohol dependence and tolerance in the mouse. *Journal of Pharmacology and Experimental Therapeutics, 180,* 216–230.

Oser, B. L. (1981). The rat as a model for human toxicological evaluation. *Journal of Toxicology and Environmental Health, 8,* 521–542.

Penney, J., & Schull, J. (1977). Functional differentiation of adjunctive drinking and wheel running in rats. *Animal Learning & Behavior, 5,* 272–280.

Peters, R. H. (1983). Learned aversions to copulatory behaviors in male rats. *Behavioral Neuroscience, 97,* 140–145.

Pohorecky, L. A. (1981). Animal analog of alcohol dependence. *Federation Proceedings, 40,* 2056–2064.

Porter, J. H., Brown, R. T., & Goldsmith, P. A. (1982). Adjunctive behavior in children on fixed interval food reinforcement schedules. *Physiology & Behavior, 28,* 609–612.

Porter, J. H., McDonough, J. J., & Young, R. (1982). Intraperitoneal preloads of water, but not isotonic saline, suppress schedule-induced polydipsia in rats. *Physiology & Behavior, 29,* 795–801.

Porter, J. H., Young, R., & Moeschil, T. P. (1978). Effects of water and saline preloads on schedule-induced polydipsia in the rat. *Physiology & Behavior, 21,* 333–338.

Reidinger, R. F., Jr., & Mason, J. R. (1986). Effects of learned flavor avoidance on grooming in rats. *Physiology & Behavior, 37,* 925–931.

Revusky, S., & Garcia, J. (1970). Learned associations over long delays. In G. Bower & J. Spence (Eds.), *Psychology of learning and motivation: Advances in research and theory: Vol. 4.* New York: Academic Press.

Riley, A. L., Hyson, R. L., Baker, C. S., & Kulkosky, P. J. (1980). The interaction of conditioned taste aversions and schedule-induced polydipsia: Effects of repeated conditioning trials. *Animal Learning & Behavior, 8,* 211–217.

Riley, A. L., Lotter, E. C., & Kulkosky, P. J. (1979). The effects of conditioned taste aversions on the acquisition and maintenance of schedule-induced polydipsia. *Animal Learning & Behavior, 7,* 3–12.

Riley, A. L., Peele, D. B., Richard, K. D., & Kulkosky, P. J. (1981). The interaction of conditioned taste aversions and schedule-induced polydipsia: Availability of alternative behaviors. *Animal Learning & Behavior, 9,* 287–290.

Riley, A. L., Tuck, D. L. (1985a). Conditioned taste aversions: A behavioral index of toxicity. *Annals of the New York Academy of Sciences, 443,* 272–292

Riley, A. L., & Tuck, D. L. (1985b). Conditioned food aversions: A bibliography. *Annals of the New York Academy of Sciences, 443,* 381–437.

Riley, A. L., Wetherington, C. L., Wachsman, A. M., Fishman, H. S., & Kautz, M. A. (1988). The effects of conditioned taste aversions on schedule-induced polydipsia: An analysis of the initiation and post-pellet temporal distribution of licking. *Animal Learning & Behavior, 16,* 292–298.

Riley, A. L., & Wetherington, C. L. (1987). The differential effects of naloxone hydrochloride on the acquisition and maintenance of schedule-induced polydipsia. *Pharmacology, Biochemistry and Behavior, 26,* 677–681.

Riley, A. L., Wetherington, C. L., Delamater, A. R., Peele, D. B., & Dacanay, R. J. (1985). The effects of variations in the interpellet interval on wheel running in the rat. *Animal Learning & Behavior, 13,* 201–206.

Roper, T. J. (1978). Diversity and substitutability of adjunctive activities under fixed-interval schedules of reinforcement. *Journal of the Experimental Analysis of Behavior, 30,* 83–96.

Roper, T. J. (1980). Changes in rate of schedule-induced behavior in rats as a function of fixed-interval schedule. *Quarterly Journal of Experimental Psychology, 32,* 159–170.

Roper, T. J. (1981). What is meant by the term "schedule-induced," and how general is schedule-induction? *Animal Learning & Behavior, 9,* 433–440.

Rozin, P., & Kalat, J. W. (1971). Specific hungers and poison avoidance as adaptive specializations of learning. *Psychological Review, 78,* 459–486.

Rzoska, J. (1953). Bait shyness, a study in rat behaviour. *The British Journal of Animal Behaviour, 1,* 128–135.

Samson, H. H. (1987). Initiation of ethanol-maintained behavior: A comparison of animals models and their application to human drinking. In T. Thompson, P. Dews, & J. Barret (Eds.), *Advances in behavioral pharmacology: Vol. 6.* Hillsdale, New Jersey: Lawrence Erlbaum Associates.

Samson, H. H., & Falk, J. L. (1974). Alteration of fluid preference in ethanol-dependent animals. *Journal of Pharmacology and Experimental Therapeutics, 190,* 365–376.

Samson, H. H., & Falk, J. L. (1975). Pattern of daily blood ethanol elevation and the development of physical dependence. *Pharamcology, Biochemistry and Behavior, 3,* 1119–1123.

Sanger, D. J. (1986). Drug taking as adjunctive behavior. In S. R. Goldberg & I. P. Stolerman (Eds.), *Behavioral analysis of drug dependence*. New York: Academic Press.

Schaeffer, R. W., & Salzberg, C. (1973). Licking response distributions associated with the acquisition of schedule-induced polydipsia. *Bulletin of the Psychonomic Society*, *2*, 205–207.

Segal, E. F. (1969). The interaction of psychogenic polydipsia with wheel running in rats. *Psychonomic Science*, *14*, 141–144.

Segal, E. F., & Deadwyler, S. A. (1965). Determinants of polydipsia: VI. Taste of drinking solution on DRL. *Psychonomic Science*, *3*, 101–102.

Segal, E. F., Oden, D. L., & Deadwyler, S. A. (1965). Determinants of polydipsia: IV. Free reinforcement schedules. *Psychonomic Science*, *3*, 11–12.

Seligman, M. E. P. (1975). *Helplessness*. San Francisco: Freeman.

Senter, R. J., & Sinclair, J. D. (1967). Self-maintenance of intoxication in the rat: A modified replication. *Psychonomic Science*, *9*, 291–292.

Shanab, M. E., & Peterson, J. L. (1969). Polydipsia in the pigeon. *Psychonomic Science*, *15*, 51–52.

Shurtleff, D., Delamater, A. R., & Riley, A. L. (1983). A reevaluation of the CS- hypothesis for schedule-induced polydipsia under intermittent schedules of pellet delivery. *Animal Learning & Behavior*, *11*, 247–254.

Siegel, S. (1979). The role of conditioning in drug tolerance and addiction. In J. D. Keehn (Ed.), *Psychopathology in animals: Research and treatment implications*. New York: Academic Press.

Singer, G., & Wallace, M. (1984). Schedule-induced self-injection of drugs: An animal model of addiction. In N. W. Bond (Ed.), *Animal models in psychopathology*. New York: Academic Press.

Staddon, J. E. R. (1977). Schedule-induced behavior. In W. K. Honig & J. E. R. Staddon (Eds.), *Handbook of operant behavior*. Englewood Cliffs, NJ: Prentice Hall.

Staddon, J. E. R., & Ayres, S. L. (1975). Sequential and temporal properties of behavior induced by a schedule of periodic food delivery. *Behaviour*, *54*, 26–49.

Stein, L. (1964). Excessive drinking in the rat: Superstition or thirst? *Journal of Comparative and Physiological Psychology*, *58*, 237–242.

Storlien, L. H. (1984). Animal models of obesity. In N. W. Bond (Ed.), *Animal models in psychopathology*. New York: Academic Press.

Tang, M., & Falk, J. L. (1977). Ethanol dependence as a determinant of fluid preference. *Pharmacology, Biochemistry and Behavior*, *7*, 471–474.

Tang, M., & Falk, J. L. (1979). Ethanol withdrawal and disriminative motor control: Effect of chronic intake level. *Pharmacology, Biochemistry and Behavior*, *11*, 581–584.

Tang, M., & Falk, J. L. (1986). Ethanol polydipsic choice: Effects of alternative fluid polydipsic history. *Alcohol*, *3*, 361–365.

Treit, D. (1985). Animal models for the study of anti-anxiety agents: A review. *Neuroscience & Biobehavioral Reviews*, *9*, 203–222.

Valenstein, E. S., Cox, V. C., & Kakolewski, J. W. (1967). Polydipsia elicited by the synergistic of a saccharin and glucose solution. *Science*, *157*, 552–554.

Wallace, M., & Oei, T. P. (1981). Differences in schedule induced behavior as a function of reinforcer in humans. *Physiology & Behavior*, *27*, 1027–1030.

Wallace, M., Sanson, A., & Singer, G. (1978). Adjunctive behavior in humans on a food delivery action schedule. *Physiology & Behavior*, *20*, 203–206.

Wallace, M., & Singer, G. (1976). Adjunctive behavior and smoking induced by a maze solving schedule in humans. *Physiology & Behavior*, *17*, 849–852.

Wallace, M., Singer, G., Wayner, M. J., & Cook, P. (1975). Adjunctive behavior in humans during game playing. *Physiology & Behavior*, *14*, 651–654.

Wayner, M. J., & Greenberg, I. (1972). Effects of septal lesions on palatability modulation and schedule-induced polydipsia. *Physiology & Behavior*, *9*, 663–665.

Wetherington, C. L. (1979). Schedule-induced drinking: Rate of food delivery and Herrnstein's equation. *Journal of the Experimental Analysis of Behavior*, *32*, 323–333.

Wetherington, C. L. (1982). Is adjunctive behavior a third class of behavior? *Neuroscience & Biobehavioral Reviews*, *6*, 329–350.

Wetherington, C. L., & Riley, A. L. (1985). Differences in food consumption under intermittent and continuous reinforcement schedules of water delivery: Some implications for schedule-induced behavior. *Animal Learning & Behavior*, *13*, 331–337.

Wetherington, C. L., & Riley, A. L. (1986). Schedule-induced polydipsia: Interactions with wheel running. *Animal Learning & Behavior*, *14*, 416–420.

Wilson, C. W. M. (1972). The limiting factors in alcohol consumption. In O. Forsander & K. Eriksson (Eds.), *Biological aspects of alcohol consumption: Vol. 20.* Helsinki: The Finnish Foundation for Alcohol Studies.

Yoburn, B. C., & Glusman, M. (1982). Effects of chronic d-amphetamine on the maintenance and acquisition of schedule-induced polydipsia in rats. *Physiology & Behavior*, *28*, 807–818.

9 Behavior Systems and Learning: From Misbehavior to General Principles

William Timberlake
Gary A. Lucas
Indiana University

Traditional learning research frequently treated organisms as unorganized bundles of reflexes and random responses. Organized behavior was attributed to the selective strengthening of particular responses by the temporally contiguous presentation of unique events called reinforcers. According to Lloyd Morgan (1896), "Just as a sculptor carves a statue out of a block of marble, so does acquisition carve an activity out of a mass of random movements" (p. 23). Hull (1943) added, "An ideally adequate theory . . . ought to begin with colorless movement and mere receptor impulses . . . and from these build up step by step both adaptive and maladaptive behavior" (p. 25). Skinner (1953) reiterated, "Learned behavior is constructed by a continual process of differential reinforcement from undifferentiated behavior" (p. 92).

Because learning was viewed as the fundamental mechanism organizing reflexes and random responses into larger functional units, it has been treated as the primary determinant of behavior. Theorists have assumed that research on learning was research into the basis of all organized behavior. Further, because aspects of learning appeared general across species, research on one species (e.g., rats or pigeons) has been assumed to apply to the behavior of all species (e.g., humans). To promote this level of generalization researchers developed standard experimental paradigms and focused on the use of presumably species-independent stimuli and responses (Galef, 1984; Schwartz, 1978; Timberlake, 1983b).

We present here an alternative *behavior system* approach in which an organism is viewed as a set of organized and interrelated regulatory systems that precede, support, and constrain learning (Timberlake, 1983a, 1983b, 1984). In this view learning evolved within the context of an already functioning system, such as feeding, or defense (e.g., Mayr, 1974), rather than as an autonomous general process suitable for constructing behavior from random movement. Specific instances of learning result from the interaction of system structures and processes with the stimulus support and contingent organization of the environment. Common aspects of learning across species imply common ontogenetic and phylogenetic selection pressures, though not necessarily common mechanisms. A major emphasis of our view is captured by the words of Garcia and Garcia Y Robertson (1985), "All organisms . . . possess the basic behavioral patterns that enable them to survive in their niches, but learning provides the fine tuning necessary for successful adaptation."

In the first half of this chapter we review briefly the traditional view of learned behavior, emphasizing its scientific heritage of isolation and abstraction, and some disadvantages of its dependence on methodology to define the nature of learning. We then develop the behavior system approach which conceptualizes learning in terms of the modification of functional systems. The second half of the chapter applies the behavior system approach to research in animal learning, beginning with predispositions in and constraints on learning and ending with a consideration of some traditional general principles.

I. THE TRADITIONAL APPROACH

Philosophical and Scientific Heritage

The philosophy of associationism has exerted a powerful influence on the traditional study of animal learning. Associationism was concerned with the relations among mental elements. Learning research translated these unobservable elements into overt and controllable stimuli and responses, thus distinguishing the study of learning from introspection and the collection of anecdotes. However, this fledgling science continued the associationist emphasis that learning consisted of new associations imposed on a nearly blank slate.

The sciences most influencing learning research have been reflex physiology and physics. Reflex physiology provided a prototypical unit of behavior, the stimulus-response combination. It also provided an emphasis on abstraction and isolation of the phenomena under study. Just as nerve conduction was studied in an isolated frog's leg using nonspecific mechanical or electrical stimulation, learning was studied in a rat or pigeon isolated in a simplified environment using arbitrary stimuli, such as lights or tones.

A desire to emulate physics also contributed to the abstract treatment of learning. Classical physical laws, such as the law of falling bodies, do not depend on external or differentiated characteristics of the entities involved, such as their shape or composition. These laws depend on summary characteristics of an entity, such as its location or speed. Following a similar style of abstraction in learning led to the development of laws in which animals were treated not unlike billiard balls with memories, undifferentiated entities acted on by external forces (e.g., reinforcers), which altered some general quality of the organism (e.g., its direction or rate of movement).

Thus, the formal concepts of learning were isolated from its particulars of occurrence much as laws of falling bodies or nerve conduction were isolated from the specific entities and circumstances of their study. Thorndike (1911) in his original work on learning claimed, "Formally the crab, fish, turtle, dog, cat, monkey, and baby have very similar intellects and characters. All are systems of connections subject to change by the laws of exercise and effect." Skinner (1956) followed up with, "Of course . . . species have behavioral repertoires which are as different as their anatomies. But once you have allowed for differences in the ways in which they make contact with the environment, and in the ways which they act upon the environment, what remains of their behavior shows astonishingly similar properties" (p. 230).

The Importance of Methodology

Because animals differ markedly in how they contact and act upon the environment, researchers have depended on apparatus and procedures to isolate the common principles of learning from the contribution of species-typical structure. To this end, rats are most often studied in dimly lit, low-roofed chambers of modest size containing a small movable object to manipulate. Pigeons are studied in larger, well-lit chambers with punctate stimuli to peck.

A result of using methodology to isolate learning is that the nature of learning has come to be defined implicitly in terms of the apparatus and explicitly in terms of experimental paradigms, primarily operant and Pavlovian conditioning. There has been a tendency to treat the process of learning as isomorphic with the manipulations used to investigate it. Thus, if the experimenter controls the relation of a stimulus and a reinforcer (a Pavlovian paradigm), learning is most frequently attributed to S–S associations. If the experimenter controls the relation of a response and a reinforcer (an operant paradigm), learning is attributed to R–S associations. Recent theorists have questioned the restrictiveness of this procedure to the extent of suggesting that similar connections may occur in all paradigms (e.g., Colwill & Rescorla, 1986; Hearst, 1975).

A limitation of using experimental paradigms to define learning is the difficulty of dealing with naturally occurring learning in which an analysis in terms of Pavlovian or operant conditioning is difficult or incomplete. For example, it has been awkward to deal with bird song learning or language development, in part because it is difficult to identify and control a presumed reinforcer. Further, the acquisition and production of such learning appears heavily dependent on preorganized structures that lack representation in the traditional paradigms (see Shettleworth, 1972, 1984, for many other examples of complex natural learning).

Perhaps the most telling point is the importance of "tuning" presumably arbitrary apparatus and procedures to produce an expected outcome. Small, seemingly innocuous changes may alter radically the form and regularity of the result. For example, Breland and Breland (1961) noted that small changes in the timing of reward in an operant chain could produce the sudden emergence of extensive "misbehavior" that was incompatible with the operant chain. Similarly, any experimenter constructing a lever which rats are required to press for food discovers that unless the lever has the thick, stubby, rounded end found in most commercial levers, rats frequently will bite, shake, push under with their nose, and gnaw it rather then press it.

In a classic case of tuning Skinner (personal communication, 1977) had difficulty teaching Pliny (a rat) to deposit a marble down a small chimney to obtain food. The rat would not release the marble cleanly, but would fidget and fumble it, almost releasing and then retrieving it repeatedly. Skinner solved the problem by making the chimney taller so that the rat could not see or retrieve the marble after it had been released.

The danger of the tuning process is that it assumes the appropriateness of the traditional abstract model of learning. The goal of tuning has become to select a combination of stimulus features that eliminate or reduce the intrusion of obvious species-typical responses (e.g., biting or shaking a lever by a rat), while maintaining reliable and orderly output. Presumably tuning produces a less differentiated set of stimulus reactions and motor responses and, thus, allows examination of the essence of learning unobscured by species-typical qualities. However, the importance of tuning for successful research argues *for* the importance of species-typical elements in learning. Tuning frequently involves detuning—changing the environment enough to obscure the contribution of the species-typical organization underlying behavior so it need not be recognized, while still taking advantage of it. At the least, the importance of tuning indicates the existence of coherent determinants of learned behavior that are not addressed in traditional theory.

In short, the analysis of learning has been divided into two parts, the principles of learning stated in textbooks, and the species-typical qualities of learning addressed in the design of the apparatus and procedures. We think that this dichotomy has hindered severely the further development of learning theory, and interfered with the application of laboratory principles to the study of learning in natural and applied settings. We believe that what is needed is an organism-centered theory of learned behavior that combines the information present in both the abstract principles *and* the methodology of traditional learning.

II. A BEHAVIOR SYSTEM APPROACH

Philosophical and Scientific Heritage

The philosophical heritage of the behavior system approach is partly in functionalism and nativism. The organism is assumed to begin with considerably more than a blank slate; learning is defined by changes in existing perceptual and response structures and the motivational processes of a functioning organism. Though largely ignored (Timberlake, 1983b), the importance of the animal's organization for its learning was emphasized by early investigators such as Kline (1898), Small (1900), and even John Broadus Watson (1914), who noted:

> Before beginning upon the simplest problem in learning, it is necessary . . . to have some knowledge at least of the instinctive modes of response of the animal and of the receptors to which we are making appeal. In behavior up to the present time, we have largely put the cart before the horse. In entire ignorance of instinctive capacity and sense organ functions, we have plunged in medias res and attempted to do satisfactory work on learning. (p.45)

The scientific heritage of the behavior system approach is primarily in evolutionary and organismic biology. The emphasis is on ecologically relevant regulation and structure. As a result the behavior system approach is more compatible with classic chemistry than physics in that it emphasizes structures and interregulation (equilibria) of entities rather than their undifferentiated causal properties. Traditional learning models appear sophisticated from the viewpoint of classical physics, but from the viewpoint of biology or chemistry they are incomplete because they fail to model organismic structures and processes related to learning.

In the next several sections, we outline a behavior system approach that attempts to account for both the functional organization of the organism and its relation to learning. This approach is compatible with and owes a debt to a number of prior theorists who are not adequately acknowledged including Bindra (1976), Bolles (1970), Davey (in press), Garcia, McGowan, and Green (1972), Hogan (in press), Holland (1984), Hollis (1982), Johnston (1981), Kamil and Yoerg (1982), Rozin and Kalat (1971), Rozin and Schull (1987), Seligman (1970), Shettleworth (1972), Staddon (1975, 1983), and Williams (1981).

The Nature of Behavior Systems

A behavior system is a complex control structure related to a particular function or need of the organism, such as feeding (Timberlake, 1983b), reproduction (Baerends & Drent, 1982), defense (Bolles 1970; Bolles & Fanselow, 1980), or body care (Fentress, 1973). The critical features of a behavior system are: (1) motivational processes that prime other structures and help organize and maintain the sequence of their expression, and (2) perceptual-motor structures (modules) that relate specific stimulus sensitivities to particular response components. The response components in a module are often sequentially and temporally related, and they are readily elicited, initiated, controlled, and terminated by stimuli resembling effective stimuli in natural settings.

Figure 9.1 shows a first attempt by Timberlake (1983b) to describe a behavior

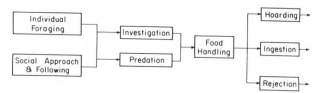

FIG. 9.1.   A schematic representation of some components of the feeding system in the rat. From Timberlake (1983b).

system analysis of feeding in the rat. This organization was derived from reports by Barnett (1975), Ewer (1971), Galef and Clark (1972), Steiniger (1950), Telle (1966), and from personal observation. The feeding system is divided into relatively independent functional groupings of stimulus sensitivities and associated response components (perceptual-motor modules) including searching, investigating, predating, and food handling. These modules are loosely organized in several sequences that lead from searching for food to handling and consuming food.

A Control Structure.   Figure 9.2 shows a more comprehensive representation of the same feeding system (see Davey, in press, for an even more complex account). Several concepts implicit in Fig. 9.1 have been made explicit here by using four hierarchically arranged levels of control: systems, subsystems, modes, and perceptual-motor modules. The four levels serve to select and coordinate the expression of individual responses (action patterns). The figure shows only the static structure of what are actually levels of ongoing processes.

The overall structure resembles the top-half of the hierarchical motivation model of Tinbergen (1951). The higher levels (shown on the left of this diagram) are concerned with motivation and global organization, while the lower levels (to the right of the diagram) are primarily concerned with local organization and form of expression. Despite similarities, the present conception differs from Tinbergen's (1951) model in several important ways. First, as becomes apparent in the next section, the system structures and processes are not seen as fixed, but as a framework that supports and is altered by learning. We are as interested in the flexibility and *incompleteness* of these structures as in their invariance. Second, the structure of appetitive behavior (Craig, 1918) is represented along with the structure of presumably more stereotyped consummatory behavior. Third, sequencing of responses is explicitly dealt with by the addition of the concept of modes. In our example, the modes range from general search to handling and consuming food, and depend on the probability of food and the nature of other cues present. Fourth, the hierarchical organization is represented as a lattice hierarchy to emphasize that the same component may be controlled by different higher order states within and even across systems (e.g., Gallistel, 1980).

It is important to note that the "levels" of organization proposed here are functional concepts that designate characteristic combinations of determinants and class-

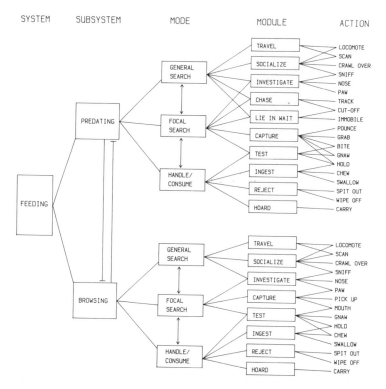

FIG. 9.2.   A more detailed representation of the control hierarchy underlying the feeding system in the rat. Vertical lines with flat ends represent
an inhibitory relation. For other information see text.

es of outcome, not specific neural locations. Continued research will clarify the
number, hierarchy, and independence of control levels required to account for
particular instances of behavior (e.g., Fentress, 1983). In addition, as these concepts are mapped on to neural and hormonal mechanisms (e.g., Davis, 1984;
Thompson, 1986), we anticipate that their operation will be uniquely constrained
by the architecture of the nervous system in ways we cannot now predict. In the
long run, this separation between function and physiology provides the possibility of using behavioral and physiological analyses as limiters and guides for each
other. For the present, the structures shown in Figs. 9.1 and 9.2 are best viewed
as working hypotheses about the functional organization with which a rat con-
fronts foraging for food.

The highest level of control, the *system*, accounts for the tendency of behavior
to be organized around important functions. Feeding, drinking, mating, body care,
social bonding, care of young, defense, and territoriality are functions that have
been assumed to comprise partially independent systems of behavior in most mammalian species (Scott, 1958; Tinbergen, 1951). Systems can be viewed as gener-

al motivational states (actually processes) that prime a set of underlying substates and modules related to a particular function. For example, the feeding system is a collection of perceptual-motor modules, modes, and subsystems related to obtaining and ingesting food. Different systems, such as feeding and drinking, may overlap in terms of control, instigation, and expression. Phenomena such as displacement behavior and polydipsia probably depend on such overlap (e.g., Lucas, Timberlake, & Gawley, 1988).

Subsystems, the next lower level of motivational control, refer to coherent strategies that serve the general function of the system. The activation of a subsystem should sensitize the animal to particular types of stimuli and potentiate particular subsets of modes and modules and their expression in coherent sets of action patterns. In the feeding systems of the rat different subsystems are presumed to control behavior related to markedly different food types. For example the predatory subsystem organizes motivational and stimulus-response structures relevant to locating and capturing moving prey. Thus, when the animal is "in" the predatory subsystem, small moving stimuli should be more salient and likely to trigger behaviors such as chasing. In contrast, a "browsing" subsystem is related to procuring stationary food items and has different stimulus sensitivities and response components.

The next level of control is *modes*. Modes are motivational substates related to the sequential and temporal organization of action patterns with respect to terminal stimuli in the system. In the feeding system modes are based in part on the local probability of finding food. For example, a feeding sequence typically begins in a general search mode, characterized by attention to novelty and search for food-related cues. When cues highly predictive of immediate food are encountered, the animal enters a focal search mode, in which action patterns are more focused and related to the immediate procurement of food. When food is certain, the animal enters a handling/consuming mode in which action patterns are focused on dealing with the food item. As the certainty of food declines following ingestion, the animal first reenters the focal search mode looking for more food. If this postfood focal search proves unsuccessful, then the probability of finding food locally declines further, and the animal re-enters a general search mode.

Thus, in foraging for scattered food the rat's behavior will reflect repeated cycles of food-related modes that mirror the local distribution of food. This cycling will continue until quiescence or interruption. Note that the relation between modes and probability of food and the differential priming of modules related to the current mode will produce a sequence of action patterns with purposive character. To the extent that successive modes and modules can be instigated with little or no specific experience with the controlling stimuli, "innate" strings of behavior will occur. Such a succession of modes helps explain the rapid organization of apparently purposive sequences of behavior, like rat-killing in inexperienced cats, or caring for newborn pups by inexperienced mother rats. It can also explain variations in prey behavior (e.g., avoidance, freezing, and attack) as a function of distance from predatory strike (Fanselow & Lester, 1987). We consider it possible that modes from different subsystems and systems share some common characteristics related to a general "arousal" (e.g., Killeen, 1982, though see Bolles & Fanselow, 1980).

Modes can be viewed as subdivisions of the appetitive-consummatory dimension of behavior proposed by Craig (1918). The general search mode represents the appetitive end of this dimension, whereas focal search and handling/consuming modes reflect more the consummatory end of the dimension. Note that the appetitive-consummatory sequence is sometimes characterized as a sequence of variable to stereotyped behavior. This occurs largely because general search components are frequently less focused and more influenced by a variety of stimuli. However, we suggest that stereotypy is not the critical factor distinguishing appetitive and consummatory action patterns. Some appetitive patterns such as stalking or searching can be very stereotyped, while consummatory patterns have variable aspects (e.g., ingesting different types of food by pigeons—Zweers, 1982). The more important distinction is the extent to which action patterns are controlled by a final set of goal related stimuli.

The lowest level of control consists of *perceptual-motor modules* (see Davey, in press; Hogan, in press), predispositions to respond to particular stimuli with particular response components. It is worth reiterating that modules, like other behavior system concepts, are functional not physiological. At a neural level motor control is not localized in a specific brain area, and distribution of input processing is, if anything, even more diffuse.

The stimulus sensitivities in a module can be treated as sensory filters that gate or sharpen particular stimulus dimensions or configurations (Baerends & Kruijt, 1973). In classical ethological literature, the sensitivity of gull chicks to contrasting spots on long thin objects held vertically and moved horizontally is typically attributed to such filters (Tinbergen & Perdeck, 1950). As Hailman (1967) has clearly shown, such filtering often begins with relatively broad tuning that is narrowed with experience and maturation. Thus, gull chicks initially peck at a variety of contrasting punctate stimuli independently of the configural stimuli around them. With experience they focus more on the source of food and the resemblance of the configural stimuli to their actual parents. We take this as a prototype of the stimulus tuning that occurs in many instances of learning.

The motor organization in a module is treated as resulting from motor "programs" that are related to particular stimulus sensitivities and to other motor programs. The importance of motor organization in behavior has become increasingly clear as research has progressed from observation to physiological analysis (e.g., Camhi, 1982; Gallistel, 1980). In human research, researchers as early as Lashley (1951) pointed out that highly skilled finger movements like those found in piano playing frequently occur with such speed that the ordering of the sequence by feedback circuitry in the nervous system was not possible.

Functional Aspects of Responses and Stimuli.   The concepts of systems, sub-systems, modes, and modules contact the environment through stimuli and responses. The basic *unit of output* is termed here an *action pattern*. The most salient aspect of action patterns is that they are typically recognizable as coherent, relatively stereotyped movement topographies, although fine-grained analysis often reveals a range of variability (e.g., Barlow, 1977). The environment is involved in the definition of an action pattern, but so are limb and body position, and temporal patterning.

Action patterns vary in strength of coupling with particular modules. Some action patterns may be controlled by different modules, and frequently more than one recognizable action pattern can be controlled by the same module. For this reason, measurements are frequently referenced to functional categories more appropriate to the level of the module (or higher) than to the topography of a single action pattern. Anyone who has watched a rat digging (a set of behaviors we assume to be controlled by input to a single module) will note that several action patterns work together to produce the digging unit. For example, the fore-feet are alternated in a scraping motion to loosen the substrate (one action pattern) while the rear feet are regularly brought forward together to shovel the loosened material behind (a second action pattern). The critical point in measurement is to maintain access to the underlying structure and processes.

Another important characteristic of action patterns is that though coherent and relatively stereotyped they are not permanently fixed in number or form. Modules that underlie action patterns can be refined, combined and even reassembled as part of learning. However, once such alterations have taken place the result will be an action pattern that like others is coherent, relatively stereotyped, and usually functional.

The basic *input functions* to a behavior system are the effects of external stimuli. Stimuli have multiple effects both at the higher and lower levels of the system. First, external stimuli serve to increase or decrease the strength, extent, or perseverance of motivational processes ranging from the system down to the mode. The increasing function we will term *instigation*, the decreasing function we will term *reduction*. In general the influence of external stimuli will vary with the functional level. At the system level, the strength of the motivational processes typically will be more related to internal rather than external stimuli, while at the lower levels the contribution of external stimuli will be greater.

External stimuli also elicit, initiate, entrain, and control behavior at the level of modules. *Elicitation* refers to the ability of a stimulus to produce a relative short latency and short duration action pattern, the basis of a reflex. *Initiation* refers to the ability of a stimulus to produce a longer duration organized sequence of action patterns. This effect of stimuli has been termed a trigger or releasing function (Davey, in press; Tinbergen, 1951). *Entrainment* refers to the ability of a stimulus to coordinate a complex set of temporally organized action patterns preceding (and following) its occurrence. Thus, the periodic availability of food can entrain a complex and coordinated set of rhythmic action patterns around it (e.g., Bolles & Moot, 1973; Lucas et al., 1988). Finally, *control* refers to the dual functions of local guidance and support of action patterns as they occur. For example, when a rat runs in a running wheel the movement of the wheel and its feedback serve to sustain running, and the side walls of the wheel provide orientation for running.

Behavior Systems and Learning

Having provided the conceptual context of a functioning organism, we can turn now to learning. Perhaps the most salient characteristic of learning in the behavior system approach is its complexity and diversity. Both attributes follow from the view that learning evolved as a modifier of an already functioning system (e.g., Nottebohm, 1972). Learning emerged where there was a *loosening* of the structures and processes involved in a system to provide a particular kind of *window* or *template* for the environment to influence the final form and control of behavior (e.g., Mayr, 1974).

Because of the complexities of a functioning system of behavior there are a remarkable number of ways in which learning can occur. For example, learning can occur as changes in the integration, differentiation, tuning, instigation, elicitation, and linkage within and across entities in the system. Most modifications take place within and between modules, but similar effects may occur at higher system levels, particularly, it appears, in development (Hogan, in press). Subsystems and systems may be integrated, differentiated, linked, and their instigation tuned with certain forms of experience (e.g., Alberts & Gubernick, 1984; Fentress, 1983; Hogan, 1984).

Rather than learning being restricted to one or two fundamental paradigms, the procedural conditions for learning include simple motor repetition, stimulus exposure and withdrawal, as well as response or stimulus contingent, noncontingent, and independent delivery of a reinforcer. Thus, from a behavior system view, the answer to Tolman's (1932) classic question, "Is there more than one kind of learning?," is a resounding yes. There are as many potential kinds of learning as there are ways evolved to modify the functioning of a system through experience.

This potential complexity of learning may appear overwhelming and unnecessary in a research area still dominated by questions about stimulus-stimulus versus stimulus-response control of keypecking in pigeons. But researchers have long known that current models are not a complete account of the necessary and sufficient conditions for learning; such models can be used only because agreed upon apparatus and procedures have been used to constrain their application. These agreements have been sustained by orderly data, the appealing view of learning as connection or response strengthening, and the belief that learning as studied in traditional paradigms forms the basis of all behavior. Though these agreements have begun to fail, there seems every reason to keep the traditional goal of integrating learning and behavior. In the long run a theory of behavior that incorporates learning is more powerful than a theory of learning or behavior alone.

The behavior system approach reopens the issue of how learning occurs by asking how it fits within the structure and processes of the organism. For example, the stimulus-stimulus connections presumably formed in a Pavlovian paradigm are, at the least, connections between modules rather than between stimuli. The outcome is also likely to depend on relations between modes and even systems. Further, connections between modules are not unique to Pavlovian procedures, nor do they represent adequately all the forms of learning that occur. The presence of food activates the entire feeding system; the quality and density of food activate particular subsystems and modes. Repetition of stimuli will tune filters, integrate and link modules, and instigate motivational substates. This level of complexity is important for understanding learning in the context of evolution, physiology, and behavior.

A final important question about behavior systems concerns their origin and development. A behavior system has a developmental history that can be modified (e.g., Alberts & Gubernick, 1984; Hogan, 1984, Tierney, 1986). For our purposes the critical issue is the nature of the system structures and processes at a particular time, and how that is modified. Thus, we refer to the system as preorganized, emphasizing that the organism always enters a learning circumstance with considerable structure already present.

It should be clear that preorganized systems do not mean that structures are either innate or learned. Genes and environment are coevolved. As John Emlen (1973) noted, "No animal learns without genetic guidance. To do so would be to change phenotype without regard to its consequences for fitness." To which we would add, "Similarly, no genetic guidance evolves without an assumed environment, for this would require that a genotype evolve and be expressed without regard to its means of expression, and, thus, also without regard for its fitness."

Experimental Paradigms and Behavior Systems

Once it is understood that learning occurs as changes in the functioning of a behavior system, the distinction between types of learning no longer depends primarily on methodology (apparatus and procedures). Instead, learning is determined by how the apparatus and procedures interact with the available motivational states, stimulus sensitivities, and response components. This realization has several far-reaching advantages.

The initial advantage is that this reconceptualization provides a framework for opening the analysis of learning to a concern with ecological requirements and phylogenetic resources. It is no longer necessary to fit learning into the standard laboratory paradigms of operant or Pavlovian conditioning in order to study or model it in common terms. For example, bird song learning can be studied (as it has been) without identifying a putative reinforcer. Such studies suggest that song learning in many species depends on the presence of auditory templates that link the species song with production templates that guide singing. In some species the auditory template can be altered most readily in early life, while in others the species song is insensitive to early experience, but can be modified later (King & West, 1984; Logan, 1983; Marler & Peters, 1982; Nottebohm, 1972). Many other cases of learning in natural environments (see Shettleworth, 1972, 1984), are also amenable to study in a behavior system framework.

A second advantage is the realization that current learning paradigms can be very useful in the continued analysis of learning. Though no longer the end-points of investigation, learning paradigms are relatively standardized tools that can be used to contact and explore the components of functional systems of behavior. For example, Pavlovian conditioning can provide information about the nature of stimulus filters and the opportunity to study the response organization available in a particular module. Operant conditioning provides a means for differentiating structures within a module and linking structures from different modules.

A third advantage of separating the conceptualization of learning from its paradigms of study is that a behavior system can be used as a common framework for analyzing and extending the accumulated results of traditional learning research. From the behavior system view regular data are likely to be based on contact with a functional system. What is missing is a specific understanding of how laboratory procedures and apparatus design contact elements of the relevant system. In general, the more closely an experimental circumstance copies the stimulus conditions of an animal's selection environment, the more accurately will a conditioning procedure entrain naturally occurring episodes of behavior (e.g., Jenkins, Barrera, Ireland, & Woodside, 1978).

A final issue in analyzing and extending laboratory results is how to treat the typical distinction between learning and performance. Without question a primary focus of the behavior system approach is on behavior (performance). This is an appropriate focus for an evolution-based theory because ultimately it is behavior that determines survival. Nonetheless, the behavior system approach is an account of behavior including learning, rather than an account of behavior alone. Thus, it is quite appropriate to use current criteria for separating learning from performance, though as our understanding of learning becomes more integrated and complex present distinctions and control groups may well change.

The remainder of this chapter examines several phenomena of traditional laboratory learning to show how a behavior system analysis can account for these phenomena and contribute to their further development. This endeavor provides an opportunity to show that the behavior system approach, provided moderate knowledge of the species, readily generates specific explanations and predictions. The next section focuses on several instances of predispositions and constraints in learning. The final section attempts to interpret and clarify examples of general learning principles.

III. PREDISPOSITIONS AND CONSTRAINTS
IN LEARNING

Because learning is presumed to occur within the preorganized structures and processes of a behavior system, it follows that learning should show considerable variation in ease, stimulus responsiveness, and response content. Marked examples of this variation traditionally have been categorized as predispositions and constraints on learning (see Chapter 6 by LoLordo & Droungas of this volume). *Predispositions* refer to instances in which the organism learns more rapidly or in a different form than expected. *Constraints* refer to those cases in which the organism learns less rapidly or less completely than expected. Predispositions and constraints, though seemingly causal entities, are in reality only descriptions of outcomes.

In the behavior system approach predispositions and constraints have content because they are based on behavior system structures and processes. But one cannot specify a predisposition or constraint only in terms of particular structures and processes. It is necessary to consider the contribution of the environment as well. Predispositions occur when the environmental circumstances fit well with the structures and processes the animal brings to the situation. Constraints occur when the circumstances do not fit the structures and processes of the animal. Thus, predispositions and constraints do not exist within the organism, but in the combination of the behavior system with the environment. We review several examples of predispositions and constraints and show how the contribution of a behavior system can be tested and its organization explored.

Predispositions

In traditional learning research it is difficult to appreciate the importance of the appetitive structure of the animal because it is incorporated into the design of the apparatus and procedures. This has allowed researchers to focus on stimulus manipulations as causal. Thus, when keypecking develops to a lighted key as a function of contingent presentation of a food hopper, many researchers conclude that the response contingency did all the important work. However, we review here several phenomena that question this view, including autoshaped keypecking, unrewarded maze learning, misbehavior, and *superstition*. In each of these cases complex behavior emerges either without an explicit reward or without an appropriate response contingency. These phenomena are difficult to explain in traditional learning terms, but their persistence and robustness underscores the importance of preorganized appetitive structures and processes in determining responding.

Autoshaping.   Brown and Jenkins (1968) surprised most operant learning researchers by showing that keypecking in hungry pigeons could be reliably produced simply by illuminating the response key for 8 sec before the aperiodic delivery of food (see Tomie, Brooks, & Zito, 1989 for a review of this literature). The procedure was termed "autoshaping" because keypecking was *automatically* shaped (elicited or initiated) by the pairing of keylight and food. Though autoshaping has become a fixture of current learning research, its occurrence was unexpected: first, because a Pavlovian procedure produced positive conditioning of a directed skeletal (voluntary) response; and second, because the particular skeletal responses conditioned were those that previously had been carefully (and often laboriously) shaped as arbitrary operants.

Though a surprise in the context of traditional models of learning, autoshaped keypecking fits well within a behavior system approach. The pigeon, a visually guided feeder, is presented with a highly salient punctate visual stimulus that is a reliable predictor of food. In many cases the keylight also shares with the food hopper the common feature of being brightly illuminated. These qualities of the keylight should be adequate initially to engage specific modules related to search and exploratory pecking. The interval between the keylight and food is made sufficiently short that the certainty of food availability coupled with the characteristics of the keylight will support pecking related to focal search and handling-consuming modes. But the interval is kept long enough and the hopper left dark to prevent domination of responding by focal search activity directed to the hopper.

As noted before, the autoshaping paradigm can be a very useful tool for investigating the structure of a behavior system. The animal is free to show any form of response and the CS and US can be readily manipulated. For example, by choosing different USs it should be possible to compare the nature of pecking modules in different systems. In the pigeon a keylight paired with imminent food produces forceful, open-beak pecks much as though the animal were attempting to grasp a piece of grain from the key (although the pecks are usually too forceful to be successful—Timberlake & Lucas, 1985). In contrast, a keylight paired with water produces mumbling and bowing to the key similar to the responses pigeons use in obtaining water (Jenkins & Moore, 1973; Woodruff & Williams, 1976).

Similarly, by choosing different CSs and different species and using food reward one should be able to engage other modules appropriate to the food system for a particular species. An illustration of these effects was provided by Timberlake (1983b) in analyzing the social-feeding structures of rats. Based on data from Ewer (1971) and Galef and Clark (1972) it was hypothesized that a set of social modules should exist in the feeding system of rats. Rats are social feeders. They follow each other to food sources; they investigate and steal food items from the mouths of other rats (Whishaw & Tomie, 1987); and they also learn to distinguish appropriate foods based on the feeding location and odors of other rats. We assumed that a rat CS predicting food would engage a social-feeding module and, thus, produce enhanced social behaviors.

Timberlake and Grant (1975) supported this hypothesis by showing that a rat predicting food elicited a variety of social behaviors including orienting, approaching, sniffing the mouth and ano-genital area, and contacting, including pawing, grooming and crawling over the stimulus rat. As seen in Fig. 9.3 these action patterns increased rapidly when a rat predicted food (panel A), but not so when the rat appeared alone (B), or was randomly paired with food (C). When a rat-size wood block predicted food (D) rats oriented toward the block but rarely approached or contacted it. Timberlake (1983b) summarizes a variety of other experiments testing predictions contrasting the treatment of social predictive stimuli by rats and hamsters.

Maze Running.   Small (1900) selected maze running as an instrumental behavior because in his estimation it "conformed to the psychobiological character of the rat." If he was right, the rat should have a well organized appetitive structure

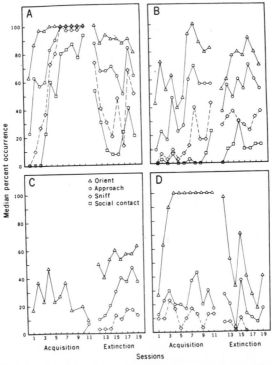

FIG. 9.3.   Median percent trials with orients, approaches, sniffs, and social contacts to stimulus rats by four groups of subject rats. In Group Paired (A) the stimulus rat predicted food. In Group Social (B) the stimulus rat was presented alone. In Group Random (C) the stimulus rat and food were randomly presented. In Group Wood Block (D) a rat-sized wood block predicted food. From Timberlake & Grant (1975).

for maze running appropriate to finding its way rapidly around burrows and above-ground paths (Calhoun, 1962). Classic latent learning studies support this view in showing that rats learn about the maze in the absence of food reward (Blodgett, 1929; Tolman & Honzig, 1930). More recent research has analyzed some of the nature of the appetitive structure underlying maze running.

Following the lead of a number of investigators, Timberlake (1983a) showed that improvements in straight-alley running developed in the absence of explicit reward for completing the alley. In addition, he found that the acquisition of alley running was retarded by bright lights, by the presence of novel odors in the alley, by short alleys or open spaces with few vertical walls, by delaying release from the start box, and by removing the rat from the alley immediately after it completed the run. Alley running was facilitated by darkness, unusual stimuli at the end of the tunnel, long alleys, and allowing the rat to roam the alley after traversing it. Timberlake (1983a) argued that alley running was a released behavior, initiated and controlled by vertical edges, facilitated by the presence of long uninterrupted paths, and improved by habituation of exploratory and fear reactions to local alley cues.

Figure 9.4 compares run and start times in rats given 0, 1, or 10 pellets of food. It is clear that food had an effect, particularly in reducing start times. However, improved alley running emerged more in parallel in the groups. As Timberlake (1983a) noted, "Alley running was for many years a key instrumental response in the development of general, context-free theories of learning. The present results suggest we did not adequately understand it. Reward in the goal box of an alley is not the only or even the primary determinant of alley running in rats" (p. 214).

These results are not limited to straight alleys or rats. Brant and Kavanau (1965) showed rapid and marked acquisition of running speed and error reduction in canyon mice exposed to a 75 x 75 foot complex maze attached to their home environment. Such findings together with the straight-alley research raise the possibility that latent learning occurs largely because rats and mice are predisposed to identify and traverse long uninterrupted pathways in their environment.

Misbehavior. Like autoshaped pecking and unrewarded maze running, misbehavior emerges without an appropriate response-reward contingency (refer to Chapter 7 of this volume by Garcia, Brett, and Rusiniak). But more strikingly its occurrence represents the failure of an explicit response contingency to control behavior (Breland & Breland, 1961). In the two most frequently cited examples, pigs and raccoons were first trained to pick up, transport, and deposit a token in a container to obtain reward. When the number of tokens to be transported and deposited prior to reward was increased, organized interfering responses began to emerge. The raccoon instead of releasing the tokens into the container ". . . spent seconds, even minutes rubbing them together . . . and dipping them into the container." The pig ". . . instead of carrying the dollar and

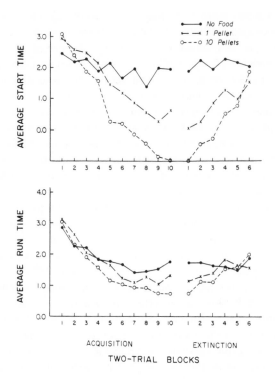

FIG. 9.4.   Average Log n start times and run times (in seconds) for three groups of rats running in an alley for 0, 1, or 10 food pellets. Note that the primary effect of food was to reduce the start times. Run times decreased roughly in parallel for all groups. Adapted from Timberlake (1983a).

depositing it simply and cleanly, . . . would repeatedly drop it, root it, drop it again, root it along the way, pick it up, toss it up in the air, drop it, root it some more, and so on.'' As Breland and Breland (1961) remarked, ''These egregious failures came as a rather considerable shock to us . . . the animal simply did not do what it had been conditioned to do.''

These effects appear straight-forward from a behavior system view. The feeding system was activated by the presence of food. As training of the instrumental response progressed, regular pairings were produced between the token and food. The hard small token when paired with food apparently fit stimulus filters connected with components of food-related action patterns, rooting responses for the pig, and crustacean washing for the raccoon. It appears to be important that the token-food interval in these pairings was relatively long, because the misbehavior did not emerge until an increase in the instrumental requirement lengthened this interval. Such an outcome would follow if the imminent delivery of food produced a focal search mode related to immediate feeding that blocked acquisition or expression of search patterns more related to discovering and capturing food. When the delay between food items became longer, more complex search patterns emerged directed toward the predictive tokens.

Several predictions about misbehavior follow from a behavior system account. First, if misbehavior occurs because of the pairing between appropriate stimuli and reward, then it should emerge without an operant requirement, simply as the result of pairing an appropriate stimulus and food. Second, most forms of misbehavior should be much less likely under short CS–US intervals because focal search responses directed to the food location will supercede responses directed to the predictive stimulus. Finally, differences in misbehavior should occur to the same predictive stimulus as a function of the system engaged because different modules should be involved.

All these predictions were tested using a rolling ball bearing as a predictor of food (or water) for rats. Because rats prey on insects and small vertebrates, a small moving object should fit stimulus filters for modules related to prey capture. Figure 9.5 shows that rats exposed to a rolling ball bearing followed by food readily increased orient, approach, and contact to the bearing compared to a group of rats receiving random pairings of the ball bearing and food. The modal pattern of interaction with the bearing involved the predatory responses of digging it out of the entrance hole, seizing it in the mouth and paws, carrying it to a corner of the apparatus, and alternately chewing, releasing, and retrieving it.

As to the effects of CS–US interval, Figure 9.6 shows that the percentage of trials with a bearing contact varied directly with the length of the interval. When food was presented at a short interval (approximately 1.6 sec after the bearing entered the chamber—group Before-Exit), very little bearing-directed behavior occurred; instead the animal went to the food tray. When food delivery was delayed until the bearing exited the chamber (group Actual-Exit) or until 2.5 sec after an unimpeded bearing would have exited (group After-Exit), considerably more behavior was directed to the bearing.

The third study in this group (Timberlake, 1983c) examined the prediction that handling modules related to food should produce more extensive and complex interaction with a bearing than handling modules related to water. Figure 9.7 shows that the duration of contact was significantly longer and more complex (measured by carrying and chewing) to bearings predicting food than to bearings predicting water. It's worth noting that these results do not support the stimulus substitution view in Pavlovian conditioning because the rats were never observed to lick the bearing predicting water (cf. Davey & Cleland, 1982).

Superstition. The classical superstition paradigm is a short fixed-time (FT) schedule of food delivery (Skinner, 1948). The action patterns that result are of interest because they represent behavior in the absence of either response contingencies or specific predictive cues. Therefore, in a behavior system view, resultant action patterns should be related to modes and modules activated by the

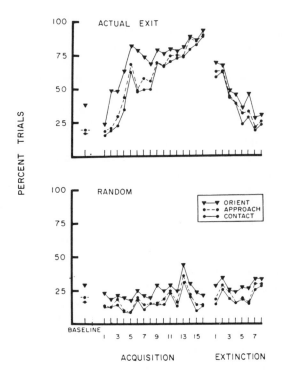

FIG. 9.5. The mean percentage of trials with orients, approaches, and contacts to a moving ball bearing by two groups of rats. In Group Actual-Exit food was presented when the ball bearing exited the test chamber. In Group Random the ball bearing and food were presented randomly. Adapted from Timberlake, Wahl, & King (1982).

stimulus circumstances and the inter-food interval, and, thus, should be recognizably species-typical.

In apparent contrast to this expectation Skinner (1948) reported that pigeons exposed to a short FT schedule developed unpredictable (superstitious) responses presumably based on repeated accidental pairings of that response with food. However, later research has not supported Skinner's interpretation. Staddon and Simmelhag (1971) reported that most of their birds showed the same final behavior under a fixed-time schedule, namely pecking the magazine wall just prior to food delivery. Timberlake and Lucas (1985) and Innis, Simmelhag, and Staddon (1983) reported a related pattern of wall-directed behavior (without pecking) for most of their birds (see also Reberg, Innis, Mann, & Eizenga, 1978).

Timberlake and Lucas (1985) further tested the accidental response contingency explanation by explicitly pretraining pecking or turning. Birds were trained to either peck or turn on a short interval schedule for 3 days before receiving response-independent food. Because of their high probability, pecking and turn-

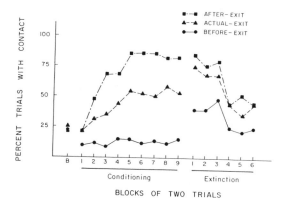

FIG. 9.6.   The mean percentage of trials with contacts to a moving ball bearing by three groups of rats. In Group Before-Exit food was presented 1.6 sec after the ball bearing entered the chamber. In Group Actual-Exit food was presented when the ball bearing actually left the chamber. If the bearing was delayed in the chamber, so was the delivery of food. In Group After-Exit food was presented 2.5 sec after an unimpeded ball-bearing would have exited the test chamber (approximately 5.6 sec after it first entered the chamber). Adapted from Timberlake, Wahl, & King (1982).

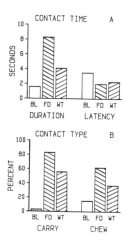

FIG. 9.7.   Panel A shows the mean duration of contact and mean latency to contact a moving ball bearing presented alone in baseline (BL), or after pairing with either food (FD) or water (WT). Panel B shows the percentage of total contact trials in which carrying or chewing of the ball bearing occurred as a function of these same training conditions. Adapted from Timberlake (1983c).

ing should have been very likely to be rewarded by chance during the FT schedules. However, as shown in Fig. 9.8, though turning and pecking were increased in initial probability by pretraining, they rapidly dropped out in favor of wall-directed and "stand away" behavior under the FT schedule.

From a behavior system view *superstitious* behaviors should reflect aspects of food-search behavior supported by the interfood interval and the physical characteristics of the chamber. The interpretation is straight-forward for floor or wall pecking, but more difficult for wall-directed bumping and stepping. Timberlake and Lucas (1985) offered the possibility that the wall directed behavior was related to food begging behavior in mobile squab. In fact, observations of 14–20 day-old squab begging show that they step back and forth in front of a newly encountered parent, frequently pressing their breast against them, and moving their head repeatedly near the parent's beak.

Constraints

In the behavior system view constraints on learning are formally the same as predispositions. They both reflect a combination of system structures and processes

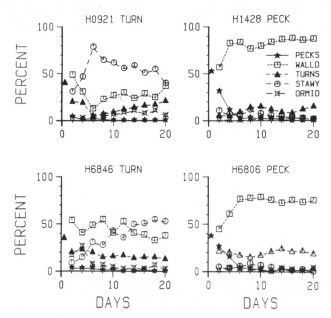

FIG. 9.8. The percentage of behavior categories recorded across 2-day blocks for 4 pigeons when grain was presented at 15 second intervals (FT 15 sec). The solid point to the left of each graph indicates the percentage occurrence of the behavior category (Peck or Turn) that was trained prior to the beginning of the FT 15 sec schedule. From Timberlake & Lucas (1985).

with a particular environment. Thus, by changing the stimulus circumstances to either facilitate or oppose the expression of the structures engaged by the environment, predispositions become constraints, and vice versa. For example, if a lighted key is paired with food for a pigeon, there is ample evidence of a predisposition to learn to peck, but if a response contingency is added that omits food if the keylight is pecked, a constraint on learning not to peck will be shown (Williams & Williams, 1969). Similarly, signaling illness with a gustatory cue produces ready learning to avoid that cue, but signaling shock with the same gustatory cue does not produce such ready learning (Garcia & Koelling, 1966).

At a mode level, constraints can be shown by entraining mode-appropriate action patterns to a situation and then presenting stimuli or requiring responses typical of a different mode. For example, Timberlake (1986) conditioned focal search patterns to the food tray by frequent periodic presentation of food to hungry rats. This focal search mode interfered with the emergence of more general search responses to a moving bearing predicting food.

At a system level constraints can be produced by imposing a contingency relation between the expression of modules from different systems. A classic example of this type of constraint is Sevenster's (1973) attempt to train a stickleback (a small territorial fish) to swim through a ring or bite a rod in order to court a female or aggressively display to a rival. In the stickleback's natural repertoire swimming through a ring resembles swimming through a nest, a well organized response sequence in courtship that entices the female to deposit eggs in the nest. On the other hand, biting and tugging a rod are behaviors related to aggression toward rivals. The expression of courtship and aggression systems are mutually incompatible. In fact one function of courtship appears to be to decrease aggression toward an *invading* female.

Based on these system differences, it should be easy to produce biting of an intruding glass rod for access to a rival, and to produce swimming through a ring for access to a female. It should be more difficult to bite a glass rod that predicts courtship because courtship inhibits aggressive behavior.

Similar structures exist within a defensive system (Bolles, 1970; Bolles & Fanselow, 1980; Fanselow & Lester, 1988). Bolles noted that animals have special repertoires of species-specific defense reactions (SSDRs) related to running, freezing, and defensive threat. Fanselow and Lester (1987) argued that these action patterns could be controlled by the distance to the *strike* by the predator (an idea corresponding to our notion that modes in the feeding system control responding as a function of distance from food).

The ease of escape and avoidance learning depends on whether the environmental contingencies and stimuli promote or compete with the expression of the structures and processes of the defensive system. For example, it is easy to train a rat to jump out of a box to avoid shock, but not so easy to train the same jumping topography when it does not permit escape. In contrast it is easy to get a rat to press (manipulate) a lever to obtain food, but more difficult to train the animal to repeatedly press a lever to turn off shock. Frequently the best that can be obtained is freezing on the lever.

Summary

Predispositions and constraints are outcomes, not causes. They represent the interaction of behavior system structures and processes with the stimulus circumstances and response linkages imposed by the environment. In other words, the same system can produce either predispositions or constraints, depending on the environment. It follows from this view that there is not a simple causal dimension of preparedness underlying learning (Seligman, 1970). For example, it is not instructive to argue that jumping is a more prepared avoidance response than barpressing when the relative speed of learning these responses can be reversed by small changes in the contingency or the environment. What is of most interest in examples of predispositions and constraints is that they provide evidence that behavior system structures and processes are critical determinants of behavior under typical learning paradigms.

IV. BEHAVIOR SYSTEMS AND GENERAL PRINCIPLES OF LEARNING

The data reviewed above strongly support the importance of species-typical behavior systems in determining learning. However, the relevance of these data to more typical laboratory learning may be unclear. Many investigators assume that predispositions and constraints are simply biological boundary conditions for the operation of general learning laws. Within these boundaries lies a large territory where unconstrained and unpredisposed learning is the rule. Other researchers have argued that general learning principles extend even to boundary phenomena. Predispositions and constraints simply require the use of different constants in a prototypical equation describing learning (e.g., Logue, 1979). Thus, it has been argued that taste aversion learning, despite its unique time course and stimulus relations, follows the same laws as any other form of learning but with longer time constants.

In the behavior system view all learning occurs as modification of the structures and processes of the relevant behavior system(s). The stimulus conditions and constraints imposed by the experimenter or the environment are critical in determining how a system is modified, but there is no unconstrained learning based only on the experimenter's operations. To be sure, there are circumstances under which learning appears to follow the classic reinforcement model–the reinforcer-based differentiation of responding from undifferentiated behavior. However, close inspection of such circumstances should reveal a systematic elimination of support for response tendencies that might compete with experimenter-designated learning, and increased support for structures and processes relevant to the desired action patterns.

This section examines several traditional principles and processes in laboratory learning for the potential contribution of specific behavior systems. Our interest is not in disproving general learning principles, but rather in placing them in an appropriate organismic context. A general principle that is not related to an animal's evolution and ecology is only half a principle. The rest of it is embedded in the apparatus and procedures. The issues we consider include acquisition and extinction, response form, temporal contiguity, and US predictability. These are by no means an exhaustive list of issues, but we feel they are representative and important. In briefly discussing each we try to show how the behavior system approach can account for the known effects as well as suggest exceptions and extensions.

Acquisition and Extinction

In the most common view, acquisition is produced by the selective strengthening (probability increasing) action of an unconditioned stimulus contingent on a stimulus or response. The contiguity and predictability of the unconditioned stimulus (US) determine the degree of strengthening. In the behavior system view acquisition is determined by the fit between the structures and processes of the organism and the environment. The physical characteristics of the environment and the predictive stimuli are critically important through their roles in producing motivation and eliciting and initiating the expression of particular modules. Contiguity and predictability of the US are also important but for the same reasons. The use of *arbitrary* stimuli probably means that the stimuli produce a weak fit across several modules. In effect, the use of *arbitrary* stimuli reduces the contribution of their physical characteristics and emphasizes the effects of contiguity and predictability in selecting a module.

Basic issues in acquisition can be illustrated by considering the procedure of shaping a rat to press a lever through the "principle of successive approximation." This principle refers to the procedure of making successive rewards contingent on action patterns closer and closer to the desired response. Anyone who has taught undergraduates to shape rats soon discovers that the process is not simple. There are important *tricks*. Depending on how adept they are at such tricks, some students are exceptional shapers, many are not. This spread in ability occurs even in professional scientists. Few can match Skinner's talent in training animals. Such variation suggests that concern with the response-reward contingency must be tempered by an awareness of the structures and processes of relevant behavior systems.

A behavior system analysis of shaping a rat to leverpress suggests three general steps: (1) Allow a hungry rat to find and eat food in the experimental chamber. (2) Present food at a high enough density that the rat shows focused exploration in the area of the food tray, but not so densely as to restrict search to the food tray alone. (3) Present food contingent on investigatory and handling activities that contact and move the lever.

We can minimize step 2 by withholding the lever until the animal has found the food and is engaged in postfood search. We can also provide intermediate steps such as the discriminative training of a feeder click that predicts delivery of food. This step is most useful when the lever is not very close to the feeder. However, in a carefully designed and "tuned" experimental chamber, the size, location, and movement of the lever do most of the work in bridging the gap between steps 1 and 3.

This account of shaping has little to do with a strict view of successive approximation, but careful observation of shaping suggests that shapers don't control the timing of reward delivery with sufficient accuracy to follow this rule in any precise way. Like predisposed and constrained learning, shaping appears based on a combination of the experimenter's manipulations with the rat's particular stimulus sensitivities, response components, and motivational processes. In behavior system terms, shaping activates the food system, instigates a combination of general and focal search modes primarily focused on the area of the food tray, and links modules related to food capture or handling to the movement of the lever.

As would be anticipated from this view, lever pressing does not have to be shaped by response-contingent reward; it can be produced in a Pavlovian procedure by pairing insertion of the lever with the delivery of food. Food entrains focal search responses to the area of the food tray. Insertion of the lever elicits investigation. The response-dependent movement of the lever supports the linking and expression of handling or capture modules, provided food is coming at a slow enough rate to "time-out" postfood search focused on the food tray.

The present focus on the system context of learning may clarify a classic disagreement among traditional theories of learning, whether animals learn by eliminating inappropriate behaviors or by strengthening new, appropriate behaviors (Harlow, 1949; Staddon, 1983). The obvious answer is that learning occurs in both ways. Consider the cats in Thorndike's (1911) puzzle box. Their original actions involved inappropriate squeezing and clawing directed to the bars of the box. Only after these escape reactions dropped out did the cat move on to components of search and manipulation related to food that produced elements of the response which the experimenter had picked to study.

Finally, consideration of the structures and processes of a behavior system also has ramifications for the concept of extinction, a process that classically has been viewed as the reverse of acquisition. In a behavior system extinction can occur in several forms, ranging from a decrease in the instigation of motivational states to the explicit unlinking of different modules. Timberlake (1986) has argued that many of the behavioral effects of extinction are due to shifts in modes from focal search/food handling back to more general search and finally to quiescence as the instigation of the underlying motivational processes decreases.

Thus, behaviors under simple extinction may not be so much unlearned as made less accessible by mode shifts. If the appropriate mode is reinstated through priming or delay, the extinguished behavior may reappear almost immediately (spontaneous recovery). Such a mechanism makes sense for an animal foraging in limited but renewable patches. After failing to find more food, it should not unlearn the position of the patch or the locations within it, but only learn that the patch is now depleted. Extinction should not prevent it from returning at a later point. Extinction of a different sort might be expected where the modules themselves are disrupted and incorporated in new learning. Such extinction would be slower, more permanent, and would more likely show interference effects than spontaneous recovery.

Response Form

Pavlovian Conditioning.   The predominant model of response form in Pavlovian conditioning is based on the concept of stimulus substitution (Mackintosh, 1974). In simplest form this model argues that through repeated pairings the CS comes not only to predict but to substitute for the US in eliciting the UR. Thus, the conditioned response (CR) should be highly similar, if not identical, to the unconditioned response (UR) in both its form and orientation. For example, salivation that was initially produced by the presentation of meat powder in a dog's mouth comes to be elicited by a bell that has been paired with the meat powder.

In the behavior system view instances of apparent substitution should occur only under a restricted set of circumstances. The effect of the Pavlovian paradigm is to attach one or more food-system modules to the CS. Which modules are attached and the specificity of their expression will depend on the match of their stimulus filters to the physical characteristics of the CS and the timing, predictability, and type of food delivery. With the typical conditions of a very short CS-US interval, a highly predictable food US, and a presumably neutral CS, we would expect to produce behaviors closely related to handling and consuming food. Thus, salivation should occur because the high probability of contact with a particular food item places the animal in a consummatory mode and primes appropriate contact and ingestion modules thereby producing salivation.

Using longer CS–US intervals, lower predictability, or physical characteristics of the CS that fit filters for more search related modules, we would expect more general appetitive behaviors that are tied less closely to the UR. These circumstances are more typical of the autoshaping paradigm (Hearst & Jenkins, 1974), and can produce remarkably complex and flexible behavior. For example, Jenkins et al., (1978) describe a procedure with dogs in which they replicated the traditional Pavlovian stimulus procedure of pairing a head-high auditory-visual stimulus with food; but they also allowed the dogs to move about freely and initiate their own trials. During conditioning the dogs treated the stimulus less as a substitute for food than as a social surrogate. Dogs approached, pranced, bowed, tail-wagged and barked at the CS, all behaviors related to greeting and begging food from another dog. Apparently what was conditioned were modules related to social-feeding. Jenkins et al. (1978) concluded ". . . the experimental CS–US episode mimics a naturally occurring episode for which preorganized behavior patterns exist. . . . We propose that the artificial signal substitutes for a natural signal, not for the object being signaled as in the Pavlovian concept of substitution."

In another example, Wasserman (1973) paired the illumination of a small response key with the presentation of a heat reward to week old domestic chicks placed in a cold environment. Chicks both pecked and "snuggled" (the CRs) against the lighted response key. However, their response to the heatlamp US was one of "twittering" and then sprawling to the chamber floor with wings extended in a "curtsy" (the URs). Hogan (1974) noted that pecking at the hen by chicks is a natural signal that encourages brooding (covering and warming of chicks) by the hen, and that snuggling into the feathers is a natural response of a cold chick to the brooding hen. That is, the behaviors directed to the keylight were selected from modules appropriate for the chick's interaction with a brooding hen.

The form of the UR to the heat lamp is equally interesting. The sprawling and wing extensions seen in these week-old chicks are typical of "sunning" postures in adult chickens, a behavior elicited by a bright source of heat, which presumably serves to expose feather parasites to the sun. Thus, while pairing the predictive keylight with warmth-activated search modules related to brooding, the intense light-heat of the heatlamp elicited a module related to sunning.

Instrumental (Operant) Conditioning.   The classic assumption in instrumental and operant conditioning is that the response form is determined *solely* by the response-reward contingency. Responses followed most closely by reward are strengthened the most, thereby selecting the final form by the cumulative effects of successive rewards (e.g., Hull, 1943). From the data we have reviewed, this is not a defensible view. Instead the form of instrumental responses appears to be highly dependent on preorganized modules.

Consider that the three major forms of laboratory instrumental behaviors, key-pecking in pigeons, lever pressing in rats, and maze running in rats, have been shown to develop without explicit response-reward contingencies. Even the possibility that accidental response-reward contingencies may have helped acquisition seems unimportant given their apparent lack of effect on superstitious behavior in pigeons (Timberlake & Lucas, 1985). Further, comparisons of the form of the same response produced by Pavlovian and operant responding can show great similarities. For example, the form of a rat's behavior to a ball bearing was similar whether the bearing was simply paired with food or the rat was required to contact the bearing to receive food (Timberlake, Wahl, & King, 1982).

In short, operant behavior appears to involve the expression of preorganized response components sensitive to elicitation, initiation, support, and control by particular environmental stimuli. A clear example of the importance of environmental stimuli was provided by Moore and Stuttard's (1979) analysis of the classic puzzle box conditioning studies of cats by Guthrie and Horton (1946). Guthrie and Horton (1946) found that the response of rubbing against a pole was readily acquired and attributed it to the contingent consequence of escape. However, Moore and Stuttard (1979) showed the stereotyped rubbing was related to the greeting rubs used by cats in social contexts and was initiated by the presence of human observers. Rubbing was not likely to emerge if the human observer could not be seen by the cat.

Despite this unpromising brief review of response-reward contingencies as a determinant of response form, there appear to be several ways in which such contingencies do directly and indirectly modify responding. Response contingencies can change the interval between important stimuli and food, thereby changing the degree of instigation of a particular module, as occurs in the development of misbehavior. Modules can be refined and organized in anticipation of response-contingent reward. Modules from different systems can be linked by a response contingency, and stimulus filtering and linkages to particular behavior can be affected using reward as feedback. Also, response contingencies may affect the persistence of action patterns under devaluation of the reinforcer (see Cleland & Davey, 1982).

Finally, despite their organized quality, behavior system structures do not inevitably produce fixed responding. Oscillation between several behaviors can be produced when a stimulus fits several filters, or the filters are connected with a variety of response components. For example, Muenzinger (1928) noted that lever related responding in guinea pigs slipped in and out of several distinct forms over long time periods. Novel responses can be produced by several means, including simultaneous activation of two semi-compatible modules. For example, if contact with a wall-mounted key is required for a pigeon to obtain water, the pigeon often assumes a modified bow with its neck arched up to press the key.

A more complex example of novel behavior is the case of the dolphins rewarded with food only when they produced a response noticeably unlike any previous response (Pryor, Haag, & O'Reilly, 1969). It might be argued that such novelty disputes that system structures always constrain learning. However, as far as we can judge, the novel behaviors appear to be constructed from a repertoire of response components all potentially related to pursuing prey items. It should be noted that when dolphins are trapped in nets during commercial tuna fishing they rarely display these creative jumping abilities in service of escape. Instead they are frequently trapped with the tuna because diving, their customary escape response, is not effective.

Temporal Contiguity

Temporal contiguity is one of the original conditions for association emphasized by philosophers. Though there is good evidence that temporal contiguity is not sufficient for reinforcement in either Pavlovian procedures (Rescorla, 1967) or operant procedures (Premack, 1965; Timberlake, 1980), it is still widely assumed that the strength of both Pavlovian and operant conditioning is positively related to the temporal contiguity of the reinforcer (Kaplan & Hearst, 1984). The argument we make here is that this association between response strength and temporal contiguity is mediated by the structures of the organism, not by the strengthening effect of the reinforcer. In this view the US acts as an entrainer of food modes, the expression of which depends on the constraints imposed by the stimuli presented and the responses required.

Pavlovian Conditioning (CS–US Interval).   For many years animal learning texts noted that the optimum interstimulus interval (ISI—the time from CS onset to US onset) for Pavlovian conditioning was around .5 sec. However, this value has been shown to be relatively specific to eyelid conditioning. For example, Ost and Lauer (1965) reported that the optimal ISI for salivary conditioning in dogs was 5–10 sec. Maximum misbehavior to a ball bearing appears to occur in a slightly longer range. Kamin (1965) reported little decrement in conditioned suppression to shock cues with ISIs in the 1 to 3 min range. The optimal ISI for conditioning of wheel running in anticipation of food access may well occur at intervals approaching the hour range.

The behavior system approach accounts readily for these diverse data because it argues that the optimal interval for conditioning should vary with the mode and modules involved. This prediction follows because modes (and, thus, modules) are arranged on an appetitive-consummatory dimension ranging from interaction with terminal stimuli at the consummatory end to general search at the appetitive end. In the feeding system, modules related to food handling and focal search should condition most readily at the shorter intervals, whereas modules related to more general search should condition most readily at longer CS-US intervals. Thus, modules related to salivation, food tray behavior, and keypecking (in different species) should condition more readily at intervals approaching 5 sec or less. In contrast, modules related to prey capture, systematic search, social approach, and restless activity should condition more readily at longer intervals.

There has been little systematic comparison of the optimum conditioning interval of different CSs, especially those that are likely to control different modules. An interesting test can be done using two concurrent CSs, a circumstance typically producing overshadowing of one stimulus by the other. When two stimuli are compounded at long intervals, the cue that best fits the physical filters for more general search behavior should be responded to the most. When the same two stimuli are compounded at shorter intervals, the cue that best fits the filters for more focal search should control more of the behavior.

In a specific test of this prediction in our laboratory, Shuming Cheng compared the responding in single element extinction tests of different groups of animals all receiving pairings of the stimulus compound of a flashing-light and a ball bearing with food, but trained at CS-US intervals of 2, 4, 12, or 24 sec. We hypothesized that at longer intervals a moving object (the ball bearing) would better fit stimulus filters related to predatory search and capture, while at shorter intervals the light would be a better fit for stimulus filters controlling focal search due to its location near the food tray. Figure 9.9 shows that the peak of responding to the ball bearing occurred at a CS-US interval of 12 sec whereas the peak of responding to the light occurred at 4 sec.

Instrumental (Operant) Conditioning.   The basic finding with delay of reinforcement in instrumental conditioning is that minimum delay is best (e.g., Mackintosh, 1974). However, it seems likely that this result may share some restrictions in common with the results for CS-US intervals. One would anticipate that this generalization would be most accurate for behaviors closely related to handling and consuming food, or for single choice responses where considerable interference with retention is likely and the reward serves an important feedback function. With behaviors related to continuous general search, more intense and extensive responding might be produced with longer delays. Certainly delaying reward for a particular keypeck on fixed-ratio or variable-interval schedule can increase keypecking rate and amount. One would expect even a stronger effect for wheel running or locomotor exploration in rats because they are more related to general search mode. Thus, the effects of temporal delay should depend on the type of response measured, the supporting stimuli available, and the quality of the stimuli that accompany the delivery of the US.

However, it is worth noting that the use of response contingencies adds some

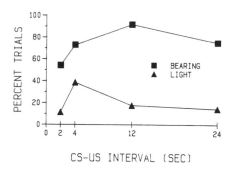

FIG. 9.9. The percentage of trials on which four groups of rats approached a ball bearing or a flashing-light stimulus presented alone during extinction tests. During training the four groups were trained with the Light-Ball bearing compound presented 2, 4, 12, or 24 sec prior to food delivery.

interesting complications to the interpretation of the effects of temporal delay. First, in operant conditioning the animal's behavior produces stimulus change in the environment. These new stimuli can fit filters for modules more closely related to obtaining food (as in the case of misbehavior). Thus, a delay may not result in increased vigor of a particular response, but in an increase in some alternative response. Second, adding a response contingency that enforces a particular delay between any examples of a particular response and reward (e.g., a DRO schedule) may increase the possibility of engaging alternative modules. The module that the schedule relates to reward is a good predictor but usually has inappropriate timing. Alternative modules are bad predictors, but with potentially better timing (given a basic rate of reward). The results should show considerable conflict between different modules.

In short, to the extent that it enhances the entrainment of a particular module, temporal contiguity is an important contributor to the emergence of learned responding in both instrumental and Pavlovian paradigms. But the key factor is the production of an appropriate interval rather than the strengthening of a particular response (Staddon, 1975). The distinction is seen in that different responses can emerge under different intervals of temporal contiguity.

Among the implications of such a view is that the juxtaposition of response and reward reflects the animal's contribution as much as the experimenter's. In other words temporal contiguity is in many respects a dependent variable. This is easiest to see when no particular response is required of the subject. For example, in the superstition study we reported earlier, we rewarded either wall pecking or turning to increase their probability, and then we released the pigeon into the condition of fixed-time delivery of food. Despite their high probabilities and resultant temporal proximity to rewards, turning and pecking were dropped in favor of temporal contiguity between an initially low probability wall-directed behavior and reward. In other words, neither pecking, turning, or wall-directed behavior followed the rules of response-contingent strengthening. Instead wall-directed behavior was organized and entrained by the periodic delivery of food.

Another example was provided by King and Timberlake (see Timberlake et al., 1982) when they set up a condition of random presentations of ball bearings and food. After a few days of exposure to this condition, several rats reliably came to seize the bearing, carry it to the food tray, and sit and chew it until the pellet arrived. The behavior of the rats at this point appeared as though it had been reinforced by the response-contingent delivery of food. But considering the developmental sequence it was clear that the appetitive structures of the rat interacting with the environment produced the final temporal ordering. Anticipated food delivery had entrained expression of the most strongly instigated feeding modules present resulting in chewing on the bearing in front of the food tray.

Predictability (Contingencies and Partial Reinforcement)

The importance of contingency relations between the CS and the US in determining responding has been a pivotal finding in learning theory (see Durlach, 1989 or Mackintosh, 1974; Rescorla, 1967). In behavior system terms, the issue of contingency translates into how behavior is entrained by responding to predictable and unpredictable rewards. In operant or instrumental conditioning the results of a decrease in the predictability of reward given the response is often an increase in the frequency, vigor, or persistence of responding during acquisition and extinction. In traditional Pavlovian conditioning the result is more often a decrease in the frequency, vigor, and persistence of the conditioned response (Mackintosh, 1974). However, autoshaped behaviors resemble operant behaviors in showing an increase in responding under partial reinforcement.

Such a mixture of results is understandable from a behavior system view using some of the same arguments applied to the effects of temporal delay. A decrease in reward predictability, like an increase in CS–US interval, should move the subject from a focal search/handling mode toward a more general search mode. To the extent that the measured behavior is related to more general search behaviors it should increase in amount or vigor; to the extent that the measured behavior is related to more focal search behaviors or food handling behaviors, it should decrease in amount and vigor.

In this view a difference in the response measured may partially account for the classic differences between the effects of partial reinforcement on responding in Pavlovian and instrumental appetitive paradigms (Mackintosh, 1974). In Pavlovian paradigms the response measured, such as salivation, is closely related to focal search/food handling. Thus, supporting a more general search mode by decreasing the predictability of reward will decrease the response. On the other hand, in instrumental paradigms the responding distant from reward is more related to general search mode. Decreasing reward predictability will increase the importance of these more reward-distant behaviors.

As might be anticipated from this analysis, partial reinforcement has been shown to increase running rate in the initial portions of a straight alley, but not near the goal box. Further support is offered by Boakes (1979) demonstration that when the appearance of a lever perfectly predicts food for hungry rats, they predominantly go to the food tray (a typical focal search response). But when food follows the lever only 50% of the time, the rats spend more time with the lever.

V. CONCLUSIONS

We have shown that the behavior system approach can be applied broadly to the current data and procedures of animal learning; it potentially encompasses both naturally occurring and laboratory learning. In the latter case it deals with anomalies, such as misbehavior, superstition, and constraints on learning, as well as with general principles. It argues that Pavlovian and operant paradigms are tools rather than reflections of basic learning processes, that response form is based on the motor components of the modules involved, and that traditional causal variables, such as temporal contiguity and predictiveness, can be as much derivative as productive of organized behavior. Further, phenomena such as overshadowing and blocking may be critically related to particular modules and motivational states rather than to general information processing rules (Timberlake, 1986).

In the behavior system view learning occurs as modification of the structures of a behavior system, and learned responding occurs as a function of the interaction of those structures with the contingencies and support of the environment. Though we have not emphasized it, a behavior system approach is compatible with many notions of recent cognitive theory while providing a larger framework that emphasizes regulation and responding. For example, the behavior system approach leans heavily on concepts of stimulus filtering, tuning, and linkage between stimuli in the context of their relation to particular response components and modes. There appear to be potential relations between concepts of automatic and controlled processing and how stimuli are involved in learning at the level of both modules and modes (e.g., Kaye & Pearce, 1984; Shiffrin & Schneider, 1977).

The behavior system approach is still in its infancy. The pictures we have drawn and the hypotheses we have advanced will not remain unchanged. Further, our exposition has concentrated disproportionately on the single system of feeding, and is much too incomplete to assimilate the entire sweep of traditional learning phenomena built up by concentrated effort over 90 years of research. The behavior system approach is not an attempt to deny the reliability and importance of previous learning research, but is an attempt to include the major generalizations, exceptions, and methodology in a more inclusive framework.

We feel confident that this approach has identified an important issue, the organism's contribution to learning. The adaptive structures and processes that the organism brings to the learning situation have been ignored inappropriately for historical reasons ranging from rejection of introspection and internal causation to an attempt to isolate learning from issues of instinct and performance (Timberlake, 1983b). Studying learning within a behavior system organization provides a framework which relates learning to the larger scope of the animal's behavior, including motivational changes and interactions, development and evolution, and physiological underpinnings.

ACKNOWLEDGMENTS

Preparation of this chapter was supported by NSF Grant GB 84–11445 and PHS grant MH 37892. We thank Graham Davey, Jerry Hogan, W. J. Jacobs, Connie Mueller, Sara Shettleworth, and Jeff Bitterman for their comments.

REFERENCES

Alberts, J. R., & Gubernick, D. J. (1984). Early learning as ontogenetic adaptation for ingestion by rats. *Learning and Motivation, 15,* 334–359.

Baerends, G. P., & Drent, R. H. (1982). The herring gull and its eggs. *Behaviour, 82,* 1–416.

Baerends, G. P., & Kruijt, J. P. (1973). Stimulus Selection. In R. A. Hinde & J. Stevenson-Hinde (Eds.), *Constraints on learning: Limitations and predispositions* (pp. 23–50). New York: Academic Press.

Barlow, C. W. (1977). Modal action patterns. In T. A. Sebeok (Ed.), *How animals communicate.* Bloomington: Indiana University Press.

Barnett, S. A. (1975). *The rat: A study in behavior.* Chicago: University of Chicago Press.

Bindra, D. (1976). *A theory of intelligent behavior.* New York: Wiley.

Blodgett, H. C. (1929). The effects of the introduction of reward upon the maze performance of rats. *University of California Publications in Psychology, 4,* 113–134.

Boakes, R. A. (1979). Interactions between type I and type II processes involving positive reinforcement. In A. Dickinson & R. A. Boakes (Eds.), *Mechanisms of learning and motivation: A memorial volume to Jerzy Konorski* (pp. 233–268). Hillsdale, NJ: Lawrence Erlbaum Associates.

Bolles, R. C. (1970). Species-specific defense reactions and avoidance learning. *Psychological Review, 77,* 32–48.

Bolles, R. C., & Fanselow, M. S. (1980). A perceptual-defensive-recuperative model of fear and pain. *The Behavioral and Brain Sciences, 3,* 291–301.

Bolles, R. C., & Moot, S. A. (1973). The rat's anticipation of two meals a day. *Journal of Comparative and Physiological Psychology, 83,* 510–514.

Brant, D. H., & Kavanau, J. L. (1965). "Unrewarded" exploration and learning of complex mazes by wild and domestic mice. *Nature, 204,* 267–269.

Breland, K., & Breland, M. (1961). The misbehavior of organisms. *American Psychologist, 16,* 681–684.

Brown, P. L., & Jenkins, H. M. (1968). Auto-shaping of the pigeon's key-peck. *Journal of the Experimental Analysis of Behavior, 11,* 1–8.

Calhoun, J. B. (1962). *The ecology and sociology of the norway rat.* Bethesda, MD: U. S. Department of Health, Education, and Welfare, Publication 1008.

Camhi, J. M. (1982). *Neuroethology: Nerve cells and the natural behavior of animals.* Sunderland, MA: Sinauer Associates.

Cleland, G. G., & Davey, G. L. (1982). The effects of satiation and reinforcer devaluation on signal-centered behavior in the rat. *Learning and Motivation, 13,* 343–360.

Colwill, R. M., & Rescorla, R. A. (1986). Associative structures in instrumental learning. In G. H. Bower (Ed.), *The psychology of learning and motivation* (Vol. 20, pp. 55–104). New York: Academic Press.

Craig, W. (1918). Appetites and aversions as constituents of instincts. *Biological Bulletin of the Marine Biological Laboratory, Woods Hole, MA., 34,* 91–107.

Davey, G. L. (in press). *Ecological learning theory.* London: Macmillan.

Davey, G. L., & Cleland, G. G. (1982). Topography of signal-centered behaviour in the rat: Effects of deprivation state and reinforcer type. *Journal of the Experimental Analysis of Behavior, 38,* 291–314.

Davis, W. J. (1984). Motivation and learning: Neurophysiological mechanisms in a "Model" system. *Learning and Motivation, 15,* 377–393.

Durlach, P. J. (1989). Learning and performance in Pavlovian conditioning: Are failures of contiguity failures of learning or performance. In S. B. Klein & R. R. Mowrer (Eds.), *Contemporary learning theories: Pavlovian conditioning and the status of traditional learning theory.* Hillsdale, NJ: Lawrence Erlbaum Associates.

Emlen, J. M. (1973). *Ecology: An evolutionary approach.* Reading, MA: Addison-Wesley.

Ewer, R. F. (1971). The biology and behavior of a free-living population of black rats (Rattus rattus). *Animal Behavior Monographs, 4*(3).

Fanselow, M. S., & Lester, L. S. (1988). A functional behavioristic approach to aversively motivated behavior: Predatory imminence as a determinant of the topography of defensive behavior. In R. C. Bolles & M. D. Beecher (Eds.), *Evolution and learning.* Hillsdale, NJ: Lawrence Erlbaum Associates.

Fentress, J. C. (1973). Specific and nonspecific factors in the causation of behavior. In P. P. G. Bateson & P. H. Klopfer (Eds.), *Perspectives in ethology* (Vol. 1). New York: Plenum Press.

Fentress, J. C. (1983). Ethological models of hierarchy and patterning of species-specific behavior. In P. Teitelbaum & E. Satinoff (Eds.), *Handbook of behavioral Neurobiology* (Vol. 6, pp. 185–234). New York: Plenum Press.

Galef, B. G., Jr. (1984). Reciprocal heuristics: A discussion of the relationship of the study of learned behavior in laboratory and field. *Learning and Motivation, 15,* 479–493.

Galef, B. G., Jr., & Clark, M. M. (1972). Mother's milk and adult presence: Two factors determining initial dietary selection by weanling rats. *Journal of Comparative and Physiological Psychology, 78,* 220–228.

Gallistel, C. R. (1980). *The organization of action: A new synthesis.* Hillsdale, NJ: Lawrence Erlbaum Associates.

Garcia, J., & Garcia Y Robertson, R. (1985). Evolution of learning mechanisms. In B. L. Hammonds (Ed.), *Psychology and learning.* Washington, D.C.: American Psychological Association.

Garcia, J., & Koelling, R. A. (1966). Relation of cue to consequence in avoidance learning. *Psychonomic Science, 4,* 123–124.

Garcia, J., McGowan, B. K., & Green, K. F. (1972). Biological constraints on conditioning. In A. H. Black & W. F. Prokasy (Eds.), *Classical conditioning II: Current research and theory* (pp. 3–27). New York: Appleton-Century-Crofts.

Guthrie, E. R., & Horton, G. P. (1946). *Cats in a puzzle box.* New York: Holt, Rinehart and Winston.

Hailman, J. P. (1967). The ontogeny of an instinct. *Behaviour Supplements, 15,* 1–159.

Harlow, H. F. (1949). The formation of learning sets. *Psychological Review, 56,* 51–65.

Hearst, E. (1975). The classical-instrumental distinction: Reflexes, voluntary behavior, and categories of associative learning. In W. K. Estes (Ed.), *Handbook of learning and cognitive processes, Vol. 2, Conditioning and behavior therapy* (pp. 181–223). Hillsdale, NJ: Lawrence Erlbaum Associates.

Hearst, E., & Jenkins, H. M. (1974). Sign tracking: The stimulus-reinforcer relation and directed action. *Monograph of the Psychonomic Society.* Austin, TX: The Pscyhonomic Society.

Hogan, J. A. (1974). Responses in Pavlovian conditioning studies. *Science, 186,* 156–157.

Hogan, J. A. (1984). Pecking and feeding in chicks. *Learning and Motivation, 15,* 360–376.

Hogan, J. A. (in press). Cause and function in the development of behavior systems. In E. M. Blass (Ed)., *Handbook of behavioral and neurobiology* (Vol. 9). New York: Plenum Press.

Holland, P. C. (1984). Origins of behavior in Pavlovian conditioning. In G. H. Bower (Ed.), *The Psychology of Learning and Motivation,* (Vol. 8, pp. 129–174). New York: Academic Press.

Hollis, K. L. (1982). Pavlovian conditioning of signal-centered action patterns and autonomic behavior: A biological analysis of function. In J. S. Rosenblatt, R. Hinde, C. Beer, & M.-C. Busnel (Eds.), *Advances in the study of behavior* (Vol. 12, pp. 1–64). New York: Academic Press.

Hull, C. L. (1943). *Principles of behavior.* New York: Appleton-Century-Crofts.

Innis, N. K., Simmelhag-Grant, V. L., & Staddon, J. E. R. (1983). Behavior induced by periodic food delivery: The effects of interfood interval. *Journal of the Experimental Analysis of Behavior, 39,* 309–322.

Jenkins, H. M., Barrera, F. J., Ireland, C., & Woodside, B. (1978). Signal-centered action patterns of dogs in appetitive classical conditioning. *Learning and Motivation, 9,* 272–296.

Jenkins, H. M., & Moore, B. R. (1973). The form of the auto-shaped response with food or water reinforcers. *Journal of the Experimental Analysis of Behavior, 20,* 163–181.

Johnston, T. D. (1981). Contrasting approaches to a theory of learning. *The Behavioral & Brain Sciences*, *4*, 125–139.

Kamil, A. C., & Yoerg, S. I. (1982). Learning and foraging behavior. In P. P. G. Bateson & P. H. Klopfer (Eds.), *Perspectives in ethology* (Vol. 5, pp. 325–364). New York: Plenum Press.

Kamin, L. J. (1965). Temporal and intensity characteristics of the conditioned stimulus. In W. F. Prokasy (Ed.), *Classical conditioning: A symposium* (pp.192–207). New York: Appleton-Century-Crofts.

Kaplan, P. S., & Hearst, E. (1984). Trace conditioning, contiguity, and context. In M. L. Commons, R. J. Herrnstein, & A. R. Wagner (Eds.), *Quantitative analyses of behavior. Vol. 3: Acquisition*. Cambridge, MA: Ballinger.

Kaye, H., & Pearce, J. M. (1984). The strength of the orienting response during Pavlovian conditioning. *Journal of Experimental Psychology: Animal Behavior Processes*, *10*, 90–109.

Killeen, P. R. (1982). Incentive theory. In D. J. Bernstein (Ed.), *Nebraska symposium on motivation (1981): Response Structure and Organization*. Lincoln: University of Nebraska Press.

King, A. P., & West, M. J. (1984). Social metrics of song learning. *Learning and Motivation*, *15*, 441–458.

Kline, L. W. (1898). Suggestions toward a laboratory course in comparative psychology. *American Journal of Psychology*, *10*, 399–430.

Lashley, K. S. (1951). The problem of serial order in behavior. In L. A. Jeffress (Ed.), *Cerebral mechanisms in behavior*. New York: Wiley.

Logan, C. A. (1983). Biological diversity in avian vocal learning. In M.D. Zeiler & P. Harzem (Eds.), *Advances in analysis of behavior: Vol. 3. Biological factors in learning* (pp. 43–176). Chichester, England: Wiley.

Logue, A. W. (1979). Taste aversion and the generality of the laws of learning. *Psychological Bulletin*, *86*, 276–296.

Lucas, G. A., Timberlake, W., & Gawley, D. J. (1988). Adjunctive behavior of the rat under periodic food delivery in a 24-hr environment. *Animal Learning & Behavior*, *16*, 19–30.

Mackintosh, N. M. (1974). *The psychology of animal learning*. New York: Academic Press.

Marler, P. R., & Peters, S. (1982). Subsong and plastic song: Their role in vocal learning process. In D. E. Kroodsma & E. H. Miller (Eds.), *Acoustic communication in birds: Vol. 2. Song learning and its consequences* (pp. 25–50). New York: Academic Press.

Mayr, E. (1974). Behavior programs and evolutionary strategies. *American Scientist*, *62*, 650–659.

Moore, B. R., & Stuttard, S. (1979). Dr. Guthrie and *Felis domesticus* or: Tripping over the cat. *Science*, *205*, 1031–1033.

Morgan, C. L. (1896). *Habit and instinct*. London: Arnold.

Muenzinger, K. F. (1928). Plasticity and mechanization of the problem box habit in Guinea pigs. *Journal of Comparative Psychology*, *8*, 436–459.

Nottebohm, F. (1972). The origins of vocal learning. *The American Naturalist*, *106*, 116–140.

Ost, J. W. P., & Lauer, D. W. (1965). Some investigations of classical salivary conditioning in the dog. In W. F. Prokasy (Ed.), *Classical conditioning: A symposium* (pp. 192–207). New York: Appleton-Century-Crofts.

Premack, D. (1965). Reinforcement theory. In D. Levine (Ed.), *Nebraska symposium on motivation* (pp. 123–180). Lincoln: University of Nebraska Press.

Pryor, K. W., Haag, R., & O'Reilly, J. (1969). The creative porpoise: Training for novel behavior. *Journal of the Experimental Analysis of Behavior*, *12*, 653–661.

Reberg, D., Innis, N. K., Mann, B., & Eizenga, C. (1978). "Superstitious" behavior resulting from periodic response-independent presentations of food or water. *Animal Behaviour*, *26*, 507–519.

Rescorla, R. A. (1967). Pavlovian conditioning and its proper control procedures. *Psychological Review*, *74*, 71–80.

Rozin, P., & Kalat, J. W. (1971). Specific hungers and poison avoidance as adaptive specializations of learning. *Psychological Review*, *78*, 459–486.

Rozin, P., & Schull, J. (1987). The adaptive-evolutionary point of view in experimental psychology.

In R. C. Atkinson, R. J. Herrnstein, G. Lindzey, & R. D. Luce (Eds.), *Handbook of experimental psychology*. New York: Wiley-Interscience.

Schwartz, B. (1978). *Psychology of learning and behavior*. New York: Norton.

Scott, J. P. (1958). *Animal behavior*. Chicago: University of Chicago Press.

Seligman, M. E. P. (1970). On the generality of the laws of learning. *Psychological Review, 77*, 406–418.

Sevenster, P. (1973). Incompatibility of response and reward. In R. A. Hinde & J. Stevenson-Hinde (Eds.), *Constraints on learning: Limitations and predispositions* (pp. 265–283). New York: Academic Press.

Shettleworth, S. J. (1972). Constraints on learning. In D. S. Lehrman, R. A. Hinde, & E. Shaw (Eds.), *Advances in the study of behavior* (Vol. 4). New York: Academic Press.

Shettleworth, S. J. (1984). Learning and behavioural ecology. In J. R. Krebs & N. B. Davies (Eds.) *Behavioural ecology: An evolutionary approach* (pp. 170–194). Sunderland, MA: Sinauer Associates.

Shiffrin, R. M., & Schneider, W. (1977). Controlled and automatic human information processing: II. Perceptual learning, automatic attending, and a general theory. *Psychological Review, 84*, 127–190.

Skinner, B. F. (1948). "Superstition" in the pigeon. *Journal of Experimental Psychology, 38*, 168–172.

Skinner, B. F. (1953). *Science and human behavior*. New York: Macmillan.

Skinner, B. F. (1956). A case history in scientific method. *American Psychologist, 11*, 221–233.

Small, W. S. (1900). An experimental study of the mental processes of the rat. *American Journal of Psychology, 11*, 131–165.

Staddon, J. E. R. (1975). Learning as adaptation. In W. K. Estes (Ed.), *Handbook of learning and cognitive processes, Vol. 2, Conditioning and behavior therapy* (pp. 37–98). Hillsdale, NJ: Lawrence Erlbaum Associates.

Staddon, J. E. R. (1983). *Adaptive behavior and learning*. Cambridge, England: Cambridge University Press.

Staddon, J. E. R., & Simmelhag, V. L. (1971). The "superstition" experiment: A reexamination of its implications for the principles of adaptive behavior. *Psychological Review, 78*, 3–43.

Steiniger, F. von. (1950). Beitrage zur soziopolgie und sonstigen biologie der wanderratte. *Zeitschrift fur Tierpsychologie, 7*, 97–129.

Telle, H. J. (1966). Beitrage zur kenntnis der verhaltsenweise von ratten, vergleichend dargestellt bei, Rattus norvegicus und Rattus rattus. *Zeitschrift fur Angewandte Zoologie, 48*, 97–129.

Thompson, R. F. (1986). The neurobiology of learning and memory. *Science, 233*, 941–947.

Thorndike, E. L. (1911). *Animal Intelligence*. New York: Macmillan.

Tierney, A. J. (1986). The evolution of learned and innate behavior: Contributions from genetics and neurobiology to a theory of behavioral evolution. *Animal Learning and Behavior, 14*, 339–348.

Timberlake, W. (1980). A molar equilibrium theory of learned performance. In G. H. Bower (Ed.), *The psychology of learning and motivation* (Vol. 14, pp. 1–58). New York: Academic Press.

Timberlake, W. (1983a). Appetitive structure and straight alley running. In R. L. Mellgren (Ed.), *Animal cognition and behavior* (pp. 165–222). Amsterdam: North Holland Press.

Timberlake, W. (1983b). The functional organization of appetitive behavior: Behavior systems and learning. In M. D. Zeiler & P. Harzem (Eds.), *Advances in analysis of behavior: Vol. 3. Biological factors in learning* (pp. 177–221). Chichester, England: Wiley.

Timberlake, W. (1983c). Rat's responses to a moving object related to food or water: A behavior-systems analysis. *Animal Learning & Behavior, 11*, 309–320.

Timberlake, W. (1984). A temporal limit on the effect of future food on current performance in an analogue of foraging and welfare. *Journal of the Experimental Analysis of Behavior, 41*, 117–124.

Timberlake, W. (1986). Effect of unpredicted food on rats' subsequent reaction to a conditioned stimulus: "Context blocking" versus conditioned alternative behavior. *Animal Learning & Behavior, 14*, 276–286.

Timberlake, W., & Grant, D. L. (1975). Autoshaping in rats to the presentation of another rat predicting food. *Science, 190*, 690–692.

Timberlake, W., & Lucas, G. A. (1985). The basis of superstitious behavior: Chance contingency, stimulus substitution, or appetitive behavior? *Journal of the Experimental Analysis of Behavior, 44,* 279–299.

Timberlake, W., Wahl, G., & King, D. (1982). Stimulus and response contingencies in the misbehavior of rats. *Journal of Experimental Psychology: Animal Behavior Processes, 8,* 62–85.

Tinbergen, N. (1951). *The study of instinct.* Oxford: Clarendon Press.

Tinbergen, N., & Perdeck, A. C. (1950). On the stimulus situation releasing the begging response in the newly hatched Herring Gull chick (Larus argentatus argentatus Pont). *Behaviour, 3,* 1–39.

Tolman, E. C. (1932). *Purposive behavior in animals and men.* New York: Academic Press.

Tolman, E. C., & Honzig, C. H. (1930). Introduction and removal of reward, and maze performance in rats. *University of California Publications in Psychology, 4,* 257–275.

Tomie, A., Brooks, W., & Zito, B. (1989). Sign tracking: The search for reward. In S. B. Klein & R. R. Mowrer (Eds.), *Contemporary learning theories: Pavlovian conditioning and the status of traditional learning theory.* Hillsdale, NJ: Lawrence Erlbaum Associates.

Wasserman, E. A. (1973). Pavlovian conditioning with heat reinforcement produces stimulus-directed pecking in chicks. *Science, 181,* 875–877.

Watson, J. B. (1914). *Behavior: An introduction to comparative psychology.* New York: Holt.

Whishaw, I. Q., & Tomie, J. (1987). Food wrestling and dodging: Strategies used by rats (Rattus norvegicus) for obtaining and protecting food from conspecifics. *Journal of Comparative Psychology, 101,* 202–209.

Williams, D. R. (1981). Biconditional behavior: Conditioning without constraint. In C. M. Locurto, H. S. Terrace, & J. Gibbon (Eds.), *Autoshaping and conditioning theory* (pp. 55–59). New York: Academic Press.

Williams, D. R., & Williams, H. (1969). Auto-maintenance in the pigeon: Sustained pecking despite contingent non-reinforcement. *Journal of the Experimental Analysis of Behavior, 12,* 511–520.

Woodruff, G., & Williams, D. R. (1976). The associative relation underlying autoshaping in the pigeon. *Journal of the Experimental Analysis of Behavior, 26,* 1–13.

Zweers, G. A. (1982). Pecking of the pigeon (*Columba livia L.*). *Behaviour, 81,* 173–230.

Author Index

Subject Index